MILES BARNE'S DIARY

To the Memory of Miles Barne

Captain Miles Barne before leaving for France in July 1915.
(Courtesy of Miles Barne)

MILES BARNE'S DIARY

A Suffolk Countryman at War 1915-1917

Randall Nicol

Helion & Company Limited

Helion & Company Limited
Unit 8 Amherst Business Centre
Budbrooke Road
Warwick
CV34 5WE
England
Tel. 01926 499 619
Fax 0121 711 4075
Email: info@helion.co.uk
Website: www.helion.co.uk
Twitter: @helionbooks
Visit our blog http://blog.helion.co.uk/

Published by Helion & Company 2018
Designed and typeset by Mach 3 Solutions Ltd (www.mach3solutions.co.uk)
Cover designed by Paul Hewitt, Battlefield Design (www.battlefield-design.co.uk)
Printed by Short Run Press Ltd, Exeter, Devon

Diary text © Miles Barne
Supporting text © Randall Nicol 2018
Illustrations © as individually credited
Maps drawn by George Anderson © Helion & Company Limited 2018

ISBN 978-1-912390-07-6

British Library Cataloguing-in-Publication Data.
A catalogue record for this book is available from the British Library.

For details of other military history titles published by Helion & Company Limited contact the above address, or visit our website: http://www.helion.co.uk.

We always welcome receiving book proposals from prospective authors.

Contents

List of Illustrations

In plate section

List of Maps

List of Abbreviations

a-a	anti-aircraft
A.A. & Q.M.G.	Assistant Adjutant & Quartermaster General
Ad	Advanced
A.D.C.	Aide de Camp
Adjt.	Adjutant
A.D.M.S.	Assistant Director of Medical Services
Ambce and Ambulce	Ambulance
Ammn (and variants)	Ammunition
A. of C.	Archbishop of Canterbury
Arty.	Artillery
A.H.Q.	Army Headquarters
A.S.C.	Army Service Corps
Bde.	Brigade
Bdr	Brigadier (unofficial)
B.G.G.S.	Brigadier General General Staff
Bn. and Battn.	Battalion
Bp	Bishop
Brig.	Brigadier
C.C.S.	Casualty Clearing Station
Cmdg. and comdg.	Commanding
C.O.	Commanding Officer
C.of E.	Church of England
Cold. (and variants)	Coldstream Guards (unofficial)
Coldm. Gds.	Coldstream Guards
Comn	Communication
Corpl., Cpl. and Corp.	Corporal
Coy.	Company
C.P.R.	Canadian Pacific Railway
C.R.A.	Commander Royal Artillery
C.R.E.	Commander Royal Engineers
D.A.Q.M.G.	Deputy Assistant Quartermaster General
D.C.M.	Distinguished Conduct Medal
D.D.T.	Deputy Director of Transport
Div.	Division

Divl.	Divisional
F.G.C.M.	Field General Court Martial
Fusr.	Fusilier
G.C.M.	General Court Martial
G.H.Q.	General Headquarters
G.O.C.	General Officer Commanding
G.G., GG, Grenrs and Grens	Grenadier Guards – unofficial
Gren. Gds.	Grenadier Guards
G.S.O.	General Staff Officer (in three grades of seniority, I, II and III)
Gnr/Gnrs	Gunner/Gunners
H.C.	Holy Communion
Hpl	Hospital
H.Q.	Headquarters
H.V.	Happy Valley
How	Howitzer
Hu	Hussars
I.G.	Irish Guards
K.C.	King's Counsel
K.R.R.C.	King's Royal Rifle Corps
L.F.	Left Flank
L.G.	Lewis Gun
Lieut.	Lieutenant
L.S.	London Scottish – unofficial
M.G.	Machine Gun
M.O.	Medical Officer
Northd	Northumberland
Obj.	Objective
O.C.	Officer Commanding
O.R.	Other Rank
Pltn	Platoon
POP	Poperinghe
Q.M.	Quartermaster
Qmr	Quartermaster
Qmr Sgt	Company Quartermaster Sergeant (usually), but could be Regimental Quartermaster Sergeant
R.A.	Royal Artillery
R.A.M.C.	Royal Army Medical Corps
R.E.	Royal Engineers
Rgtl/Regtl	Regimental
R.F.A.	Royal Field Artillery
R.G.A.	Royal Garrison Artillery
R.H.A.	Royal Horse Artillery
Rly	Railway
R.T.O.	Rail Transport Officer

S.A.A.	Small Arms Ammunition
Sergt. and Sgt.	Sergeant
Tempy	temporary
T.F.	Territorial Force
T.M.	Town Major
T.M.	Trench Mortar
W.O.	War Office
Yeo and Yeoy	Yeomanry

Belgian and French Place Names mentioned by Miles Barne
(*with other spellings used by Miles Barne in brackets*)

A. Armentières – Neuve Chapelle – Loos – Béthune

Annequin
Armentières (*Armentieres*)
Aubers
Barts and Barts Alley, a communication
    trench
Béthune (*Bethune*)
Bout-Delville (*Bout Deville*)
Brickstacks, Cuinchy
Busnes
Calonne
Cambrin
Chalk Pit
Chalk Pit Wood
Chocques
Cuinchy
Duck's Bill
Duck's Neck
The Dump
Ebenezer Farm
Estaires (*Estaire*)
Fauquissart
Festubert
Fosse 8
Fouquerailles
Fouquières
Givenchy-lez-La Bassée
Hill 70
Hohenzollern Redoubt
Hulluch
La Bassée (*La Bassee*)

Labeuvrière
La Gorgue
Laventie
Le Marais, near La Gorgue
Le Rutoire
Le Sart
Lens
Lestrem
Loos
Merville
Neuf Berquin (*Neuve Berquin*)
Neuve Chapelle
Noeux-les-Mines
Noyelles
Philosophe
Puits 14 Bis
Railway Triangle, Cuinchy
Riez-Bailleul
Robecq
The Quarries
Sailly-Labourse (*Saillie-Labourse*)
Sussex Trench, a reserve trench west of the
    Hohenzollern Redoubt
Vaudricourt
Vermelles
Verquigneul
Verquin
Z 2, a trench section south of Cuinchy

B. Ypres and Belgium

Bandaghem

Bleuet Farm (*Bluet Farm*)
Boesinghe
Brandhoek
Burgomaster Farm, near Vlamertinghe
Canada Farm
Captains Farm
Cardoen Farm
Congreve Walk, a communication trench
De Wippe Cabaret (*Wippe Cabaret*)
Duke Street, a communication trench
Elverdinghe
Emile Farm
Fargate, a communication trench
Forest Area
Grande Barrière House (*Grande Barriere House*)
The Gully, front line position east of Potizje
Hasler House
Houtkerque (*Houtkirque*)
International Corner
Kaie Salient (*Kaaie Salient*)
Krombeke (*Crombek*)
Krupp Farm
Château de Lovie (*Logie*)
Maple Copse
Mendinghem
Menin Gate
Messines Ridge
Michel Farm
Mont Rouge
Pilckem (*Pilcken*)
Poelcapelle
Poperinghe
Potijze
Proven
Purbrook Camp, near Proven
Railway Wood
Reninghelst
Sanctuary Wood
St Eloi
St Jean
Steenbeck (*Steenbek*), a stream
Vlamertinghe
Watou
Westoutre

Westvleteren
Woesten
Wytschaete
Yper Lea, a stream
Ypres
Ypres-Yser Canal
Zeebrugge
Zillebeke

C. Training, Rest, Rear and Base Areas

Abbeville
Affringues
Airaines
Aire
Amplier
Audruiq (*Ardiques*)
Arquèves
Arques
Arnèke (*Arneke*)
Beauval
Belloy
Bergues
Bollezeele
Boulogne
Bourecq
Calais
Campagne
Canaples
Cassel
Dromesnil (*Drosmesnil*)
Doullens (*Dollens*)
Dunkirk/Dunkerque
Esquelbecq
Esquerdes (*Esquedos*)
Étaples (*Etaples*)
Flixecourt
Forêt de Nieppe
Godewaersvelde
Gravelines
Hallines
Halloy
Ham

Hazebrouck (*Haazbruck/Haazbrouck/ Haazebrouck*)
Herbelles (*Herbelle*)
Herzeele (*Heerzeele/Heerzeel*)
Heucourt
Hornoy
Houtkerque
Kemmel
Laleu
Le Havre (*Havre – then its usual name*)
Le Quesnoy
Le Touquet
Le Tréport (*Treport*)
Ligny-lez-Aire (*Ligny les Aire*)
Lillers
Liomer
Lucheux
Lumbres
Malo
Merkeghem
Millan
Molinghem (*Dolinghem or Dollinghem*)
Mont des Cats
Mont Noir
Mont Rouge
Naours
Ouve-Wirquin
Paris Plage
Petit-Houvin
Poix
Pont-Remy
Rexpoëde
Rouen
St Hilaire
St Omer
St Pol
Setques
Steenvoorde
Tatinghem (*Tattinghem*)
Thérouanne (*Therouanne*)
Upen-D'Aval
Vaux-en-Amiènois (*Vaux-en-Amienois*)
Vergies
Vieux Rouen
Volckerinckhove (*Volkeringshove*)

Wardrecques
Warfusée
Wargnies
Warlus
Wavrans
Winnezeele (*Winnezeel*)
Wismes
Wisques
Wittes
Wizernes (*Wizerne*)
Wormhout
Zudansques (*Zudausques*)

D. Somme – in British and French hands at 15 September 1916

Acheux
Albert
Amiens
Arrow Head Copse
Auchonvillers
Authie (*Athie*)
Bazincourt
Beaussart
Bécordel (*Becordel*)
Bernafay Wood
Bertrancourt
Billon Farm
Bronfay Farm (*Bromfay Farm/Bomfray Camp*)
Bray
Buire-sur-Ancre (*Buires*)
Bus-lez-Artois (*Bus en Artois/Bus les Artois*)
Carnoy
Citadel – at northern end of Happy Valley, near Fricourt
Cléry (*Clery*)
Coigneux (*Goigneux*)
Colincamps
Corbie
Delville Wood
Dernancourt
Edgehill, railway siding at Buire-sur-Ancre
Étinehem (*Etinehem*)
Fricourt

Ginchy (*Gincy*)
Grovetown
Guillemont
Halles (*Halle*)
Happy Valley
Hardecourt
Hébuterne (*Hebuterne*)
Heilly
Château Hénencourt
La Boisselle (*Boisseville*)
Leuze Wood
Mailly-Maillet (*Mailly-Mallet*)
Maltzhorn Farm
Mametz
Mametz Wood
Mansel Camp, south of Mametz
Maricourt
Maurepas
Méaulte (*Riault/Meaulte*)
Méricourt-L'Abbé (*Mericort*)
Méricourt-sur-Somme (*Mericourt*)
Montauban
Morlancourt
Plateau, railway siding near Fricourt
Pont-Noyelles (*Pont Noyelle*)
Pozières (*Pozieres*)
Château de Querrieu
Sailly-au-Bois
Sailly-Le Sec
Suzanne
Treux
Trones Wood
Varennes
Ville-sur-Ancre (*Ville*)
Warnimont
White City

E. Somme and Further East – in German hands at 15 September 1916

Aizecourt
Allaines (*Halaine*)
Bapaume
Barastre

Beaumont-Hamel
Beauregard Dovecote
Bouchavesnes
Bouleaux Wood (*Bouleau Wood*)
Bus
Bussu
Cambrai
Cartigny
Combles
Courcelette (*Courcelles*)
Curlu
Douage Wood
Équancourt
Étricourt (*Etricourt*)
Fins
Flers
Frégicourt (*Fregicourt*)
Gommecourt
Gouvernement Farm (*Gouvernment Farm*)
Gueudecourt
Haie Wood
Havrincourt Wood
Hermies
High Wood
Hindenburg Line
Irles
Le Mesnil-en-Arronaise (*Le Mesnil*)
Le Priez Farm (*Priez*)
Lesboeufs (*Les Boeufs*)
Le Transloy
Manancourt
Martinpuich
Miraumont
Moislains
Mont St Quentin
Morval
Mouquet Farm
Needle Trench, north west of Lesboeufs
Nurlu
Péronne (*Peronne*)
Puisieux
Quadrilateral
Rancourt
Rocquigny
Royaulcourt (*Ruyaulcourt*)

St Pierre Vaast Wood
Saillisel
Sailly-Saillisel (*Sailly-Sallisel*)
Serre
Thiepval
Vaux Wood
Velu
Warlencourt
Ytres

F. Lens – Arras

Ablain-St Nazaire
Arras
Aubigny
Bullecourt
Carency
Héninel (*Heninel*)
Hindenburg Line
The Labyrinth
Lens

Neuville-St Vaast
Nôtre Dame de Lorette (*Notre Dame de Lorette*)
Souchez (*Souchy*)
Vimy Ridge

G. French Operations South of Somme

Aisne
Champagne
La Fère
Noyon
Rheims
St Quentin
Verdun

H. Elsewhere in France

Laon
Mons
Paris

Foreword

For whom do the keepers of diaries write? By 1915, when he had already passed his 40th birthday and was a husband and father, it might be assumed that Miles Barne kept his for his family, or to prod his memories in later life as he told his grandchildren what he had done in the Great War. But his references to his wife and children are fleeting, and instead the people who populate his account are his fellow officers, his men, and old friends from school and army whom he encountered on the Western Front. It is as though the regularity of his entries were a way of recreating his social life in a professional context, and in doing so of providing continuity and order in a world where both were liable to be violently disrupted by war.

Miles Barne seems too modest and self-effacing to have imagined that his words would ever be published. Although regularly in acting command of his battalion, he never expresses frustration at being passed over for the job on a full-time basis, and he was amazed when he was awarded the DSO. However, the decision to publish this full account of a career that embraced Loos, the Somme and Third Ypres is to be warmly welcomed. Miles Barne has been extraordinarily fortunate in his editor. Randall Nicol is as proud of the Scots Guards as he was, and has brought to the editing of the text a thoroughness, concern for accuracy and eye for detail which are exemplary.

Hew Strachan
Professor of International Relations,
University of St Andrews
Broughton, May 2018

Acknowledgements

I owe a great debt of gratitude to Jane Arbuthnott who first told me about her Grandfather when I was researching *Till The Trumpet Sounds Again*. What she said and showed me put me onto the trail to Sotterley and to the great generosity, interest, help and hospitality I have received there from Miles and Tessa Barne. Not only did Miles give me every assistance with the Diary itself and his generous permission to produce this edition of it, but he also looked out other family documents and papers, which have contributed so much to the atmosphere and background of his Grandfather's home, family and friends.

Others in the Barne Family who have helped me are Patricia Barne, Charles Barne, Willie Barne, Judy Russell and Milly Skene.

I am very grateful to all of them, to Miles Barne also for permission to use some images and sketches and to the Showers Family for permission to reproduce two family photographs in their possession.

I am also very grateful to Captain David Archibald, formerly Scots Guards, Lieutenant Colonel Peter Garbutt, Home Headquarters, The King's Royal Hussars, Dom Kearney, Headquarters Irish Guards, David Blake, Museum of Army Chaplaincy, Lance Sergeant Leighton Platt, Headquarters Scots Guards, Lieutenant Colonel Harry Scott, Headquarters Household Cavalry, Pete Storer, Household Cavalry Museum Archive, Major Philip Wright, formerly Grenadier Guards, the Staff of the Commonwealth War Graves Commission, the Staff of The National Archives and the Staff of The National Library of Scotland.

I am especially grateful to Brigadier Harry Nickerson, Regimental Lieutenant Colonel and Chairman of the Regimental Trustees Scots Guards, for permission to use material held in the Scots Guards Archives.

Hew Strachan has very kindly written the foreword and I thank him warmly for that and for his continuing encouragement and interest.

None of this would have happened without Duncan Rogers and the others at Helion who have been involved in this and I thank them very much for all that they have done, as I also thank George Anderson very much for his patience and skill in preparing the maps.

My grateful thanks too to Filly, my wife.

1

Family and Military Background

Miles Barne, "Mily" or Miley" in his immediate family circle and a little wider, was born on 15 March 1874, the eldest son of Lieutenant Colonel St John Barne and Lady Constance Barne, a daughter of the Fifth Marquess of Hertford. He had an elder sister, Mary, born in 1873, a younger brother, Michael, born in 1877, a younger sister, Winifred, born in 1881, and his youngest brother, Seymour, born in 1886. Both brothers would appear in his Diary, but neither sister. By 1914 Lieutenant Commander Michael Barne had been in the Royal Navy for over twenty years and had played an important part in Captain Robert Falcon Scott's Antarctic Expedition of 1901-04, though he did not go there again, while Lieutenant Seymour Barne, a very fine horseman, was in The 20th Hussars.

Miles Barne was educated at Rottingdean School, later called St Aubyns, and Eton College, before going to The Royal Military College, Sandhurst. He was commissioned into the Scots Guards on 16 August 1893, served in the Boer War both with the 2nd Battalion and also later as Signals Officer at Headquarters 16th Brigade and retired as a Captain on 23 September 1904. It was recorded that he was leaving to serve in what was then still called collectively The Imperial Yeomanry and specifically in The Duke of York's Own Loyal Suffolk Hussars. Both his maternal grandfather and his father were Scots Guardsmen. The Barne family had owned Sotterley Estate, Suffolk, since 1744 and also Dunwich Estate on the coast. Miles Barne settled at Sotterley Hall and managed both.

He married Violet Orr Ewing, whose home was at Ballikinrain Castle, Stirlingshire, on 12 July 1904 in London and they had four children, Michael in 1905, Nigel in 1906, Anthony in 1909 and Elizabeth in 1911. Violet's two brothers, both Scots Guardsmen, would feature in the Diary. Major Norman Orr Ewing, later a Brigadier General, was first mentioned as Second in Command of the 1st Battalion Scots Guards when Miles Barne arrived in France in July 1915 and Lieutenant Ernest "Tim" Orr Ewing when about to be lent from the 2nd Battalion to the 1st Battalion on 2 October 1915 because of casualties during Loos. Another relation was Lieutenant Colonel Gerald Carew Sladen, The Rifle Brigade, later also a Brigadier General, whose wife Mabel was Violet Barne's sister. His and Miles Barne's first meeting in France was on the Somme in August 1916.

Five first cousins on his mother's side are identifiable. Lieutenant Colonel Lord Henry "Copper" Seymour, later a Brigadier General too, appeared first in October 1915 when Miles Barne met him in command of the 4th Battalion Grenadier Guards in the trench system in front of the Hohenzollern Redoubt. A second, who also appeared early on, was Lieutenant

Conway "Con" Seymour, in the 2nd Scots Guards when Miles Barne joined the 1st Battalion. He was another borrowed during Loos. The third was Captain Sir Robert Henry Seymour Dashwood, Bt, The Oxfordshire and Buckinghamshire Light Infantry, whom Miles met when he first arrived at Poperinghe in March 1916. The fourth was Lieutenant Wilfred James Dashwood, 1st Grenadier Guards, who appeared where Miles Barne was in a camp at Happy Valley on the Somme in September 1916. The fifth was Major Arthur Edward Erskine, Royal Horse Artillery, whom Miles Barne chanced upon at Headquarters 20th Division near Fricourt on the same day.

On 21 December 1906 Miles Barne was promoted Major in The Suffolk Yeomanry (The Duke of York's Own Loyal Suffolk Hussars) and continued as a Territorial cavalryman until June 1915. Then the Scots Guards requested his release back to them.

Regimental Headquarters Scots Guards were in London at Buckingham Gate, commanded by a full Colonel holding the appointment of Lieutenant Colonel Commanding Scots Guards, with a substantial staff of whom the principal one was the Regimental Adjutant. There were the two Battalions on active service and the 3rd (Reserve) Battalion at Wellington Barracks. The 1st Battalion were in the British Expeditionary Force from the start in August 1914, though neither involved in the Battle of Mons nor directly in anything serious themselves as they marched back during the Retreat. They had fierce fighting during the Battle of the Aisne, without such serious casualties as many others, but were then almost completely wiped out over three weeks at the First Battle of Ypres. Rebuilt after that, they next went into the line just before Christmas 1914 at Givenchy-lez-La Bassée, immediately to the north of the Aire-La Bassée Canal and a little west of La Bassée itself. Just to the south of the Canal they suffered heavy losses on New Year's Day 1915 in a counterattack on the Railway Triangle, east of Cuinchy, in pitch darkness over ground they had not seen before. 25 January was, as also for the 1st Coldstream Guards, one of their most grievous days of the whole war, on the receiving end of a well executed local German attack by overwhelming numbers towards the Cuinchy Brickstacks. Thereafter they had been generally fortunate in 1915. They had not been drawn into the Battle of Neuve Chapelle in March, though they might have been, either if it had gone on any longer or been more successful. Narrowly, but largely, though there were some casualties from shelling of the reserve positions where they were waiting, they avoided the Battle of Aubers early in May and there was never any possibility of their joining in the Battle of Festubert a week later. So, from early February onwards, other than when resting further back, it had been a reasonably stable period of trench tours, but not without their unpleasant risks, surprises and consequences. The 2nd Battalion landed in Belgium shortly before First Ypres, in which they suffered very severely, though not as badly as the 1st Battalion, and then went into the line at Rouges Bancs, south of Armentières, where there was a painful night attack a week before Christmas and then a very prominent part in the 1914 Christmas Truce. They had further severe losses at Neuve Chapelle in March and then far worse ones at Festubert in May. It was against that background of casualties that the Scots Guards asked for Miles Barne to return to them.

On 22 June 1915 a letter from the War Office was sent to the Officer Commanding Scots Guards at Regimental Headquarters:

Sir,

I am directed to refer to your letter of the 27th May 1915, number 270/15, on the subject of Major M. Barne, Suffolk Yeomanry, and to inform you in reply that it has been decided that this Officer's services shall be at the disposal of the Regiment under your command.

Instructions for him to report himself to you for duty have been issued accordingly.

I am,

Sir,

Your obedient servant,

[Copy stamped as signed by F. S. Robb]

Major General,

Military Secretary.

Major General Frederick Spencer Wilson Robb, Military Secretary

On 26 June Miles Barne was in London and received a telegram:

Military Secy wires your services most required with Scots Guards stop we are to report date your reporting for duty to O.C. Scots Guards stop Please telegraph what date will suit you O.C. Suffolk Yeomanry.

He noted the dates from 26 June onwards and gave himself just over two weeks. He would have to drop a rank on rejoining the Regular Army, as did others. In the event the next telegram which has survived, from the 3rd (Reserve) Battalion Scots Guards, Wellington Barracks, London, sent on 21 July and addressed to Captain Barne Scots Guards North Cove Beccles, possibly where The Suffolk Yeomanry were encamped, though D Squadron were at Woodbridge in June, read:

you will proceed to expeditionary force on friday 23rd by 2 p.m. train from Victoria acknowledge.

In the event he travelled by a later train that afternoon.

2

Introduction to the Diary

Writing with a pencil, mostly in pocket sized notebooks, which he brought from home or which Violet posted to him, Miles Barne began the Diary on 23 July 1915 as he left London for the Western Front. It records his personal recollections in the most open and straightforward way. He wrote an entry for almost every day, even if unable to do so on the day itself, sometimes making minor additions and clarifications here and there subsequently. Rarely, but, occasionally, when he later on remembered an earlier event he would add it into the text at that point. What he did not do was correct what he had written in the light of later knowledge. Only in the period after the 1915 Christmas "truce" were there any significant additions to what he had written, but these still appear to be contemporary or nearly so. He was careful not to include anything specific about future operations and limited himself generally to observations within his own immediate sphere. These included features of the countryside and agriculture, crops, flowers, woods and trees, animals and birds. Also recorded were the names of many people whom he came across. As time went on he noted more names of individual soldiers, as well as officers.

On the Western Front Miles Barne met several friends and acquaintances from Eton, but more particularly from his time in the Army up to 1904. Since then many had either stayed at Sotterley or Dunwich or else he had met them staying in other houses. Other than his brother officers in the 1st Scots Guards, wherever he mentioned a name and included a first name or a nickname (sometimes just an initial) it will be someone whom he knew well before the War. Several in his circle were from the Scots Guards, several others from East Anglia. One particular friend throughout was, by 1914, Major Charles Corkran, Grenadier Guards, later a Major General. They were exactly the same age, had been in the same house at Eton and passed well into Sandhurst with Miles Barne six places above Charles Corkran.

As far as it can be done in print Miles Barne's words here are as he wrote them, his punctuation as he used it, but it is impossible to reproduce exactly. So there has had to be some standardization. Mostly his handwriting is easily decipherable, but neither his spelling, nor his grammar, nor his punctuation were consistent. Flanders place names, on both sides of the Franco-Belgian frontier, some people's names and some items of military usage would be written down varyingly, though comprehensibly. As was common at that time, he often used dashes instead of full stops, but sometimes both, as well as using dashes between phrases. Often enough he wrote neither and frequently he began sentences without an initial capital. There are occasional errors and omissions in what he wrote and once or twice he confused "a.m." and "p.m.". Very sparingly and then only for clarity occasional paragraphs have been rearranged into correct chronological order. Otherwise, all is set out here as faithfully as it can be done and as faithfully as it can be interpreted. What may therefore look like printing errors are nothing of the sort.

If there are any mistakes, then they are mine and that extends to the explanatory text and identication of individuals and military units.

The explanations of what was going on are as brief as practicable. Most of those whom he named it has been possible to identify. Where someone is described as "untraced" it only means that I have not been able to find them. In some instances, as indicated, the identifications are only "probable" or "possible", while some of the ranks allotted can only be educated guesses at those held at the time, even though the people are definitely identified. Nicknames and diminutives are only included so far as Miles Barne used them. Unless the context is clearly different, all those named without their unit were in the 1st Scots Guards.

There can be confusion about ranks. The basic rule was that, if someone holding temporary or acting rank ceased to exercise it for any reason, such as becoming a casualty, they reverted to their substantive rank. That is, for example, why Company Sergeant Major James Oliver of the 2nd Scots Guards, shot dead early on Christmas Morning 1915, appears as a Sergeant in the records of the Commonwealth War Graves Commission. Also, when commanding a company, a substantive subaltern might be given the acting rank of Captain, but would lose it as soon as the appointment ceased. The CWGC records show the date of a soldier's death as at the latest date that he was officially reported as possibly being still alive. This was very prevalent during and after the First Ypres when many were reported as missing within what could be as long as a fortnight, if that was the period between roll calls. This led to factual, though completely understandable, inconsistencies, when there was later specific evidence.

There were three branches of the British Army Staff, the General Staff (G Branch), which handled operations, operational planning, training and intelligence, the Adjutant General's (A Branch), responsible for all personnel matters, discipline and manning, and the Quartermaster General's (Q Branch), concerned with all logistics, including medical, and transport. Many staff officers appear in the Diary, up to and including Army Headquarters level.

> At General Headquarters (the Headquarters of the British Expeditionary Force) the leading roles in each staff branch were the Chief of Staff, Adjutant General and Quartermaster General.
> At an Army Headquarters these were represented by the Major General General Staff and by the Deputy Adjutant and Quartermaster General, also a Major General, who supervised the work of the A and Q Branch staffs.
> At a Corps Headquarters there were the Brigadier General General Staff and the Assistant Adjutant and Quartermaster General, also a Brigadier General.
> At a Divisional Headquarters there were the General Staff Officer Grade I, a Lieutenant Colonel, and the Deputy Assistant Adjutant and Quartermaster General, also a Lieutenant Colonel.
> Finally, at a Brigade Headquarters there were the Brigade Major, often a Captain, and the Staff Captain.

Miles Barne underlined dates in the Diary, occasionally adding something like "Good Friday". Where he wrote a date in full that normally indicated the start of a new notebook. Military practice at the time required place and trench names to be written in capitals and that is how he usually wrote them in the Diary and how they are therefore usually reproduced here, unless he wrote them otherwise.

It is not practicable to include in the maps everywhere that Miles Barne went to or mentioned in the Diary, but the maps are as comprehensive as possible, needing also, as they must, to show locations, places and routes which he did not refer to. The normal, though not invariable, practice by contemporary map makers was to include a hyphen in a place name such as Neuville-St Vaast, which is what has been done here, though Miles Barne usually did not use them himself. The glossary lists those places that he mentioned, grouped by general area. Some of his spellings were inconsistent with the name by which places were commonly known and these are shown. In some cases the way a place name was spelled then, which is what has been used here, is not how it appears now. This applies notably in Belgium because of the transition from French to Flemish usage, but there are places in France which have altered, if for other reasons.

When he returned to the Scots Guards in 1915 Miles Barne's instinctive loyalties were to the 2nd Battalion with whom he had served before, during and after the Boer War and it was to them that he was expecting to go when he left England. He was disappointed to hear once he reached France that he was being posted instead to the 1st Battalion, but quickly settled in.

At this time, alongside the 1st Scots Guards in the 1st (Guards) Brigade were the 1st Coldstream, 1st Battalion The Black Watch, 1st Battalion The Queen's Own Cameron Highlanders and 1st Battalion The London Scottish (otherwise 1/14th Battalion The London Regiment), Territorial Force. Territorial battalions were added to Regular Army brigades to boost numbers after First Ypres. There were two more brigades in the 1st Division. One, the 2nd Brigade, comprised the 2nd Battalion and 1/5th Battalion, T.F., The Royal Sussex Regiment, 1st Battalion The Loyal North Lancashire Regiment, 1st Battalion The Northamptonshire Regiment and 2nd Battalion The King's Royal Rifle Corps, also known as The 60th Rifles. The other, the 3rd Brigade, comprised the 1st Battalion The South Wales Borderers, 1st Battalion The Gloucestershire Regiment, 2nd Battalion The Welsh Regiment, 2nd Battalion The Royal Munster Fusiliers and 1/4th Battalion, T.F., The Royal Welsh Fusiliers. Names of Regiments are given as they were known and recognised at the time. Miles Barne would mention those that he came across at reliefs or otherwise.

Though on leave quite regularly, he was in the 1st Scots Guards continuously from late July 1915 to mid September 1917, with only a single brief interruption in late July 1917, because of an accidental injury, not a wound. He was never off sick for a single day. Twice in the spring of 1917 he went on courses near Amiens.

The notebooks went home with him when he went on leave to Sotterley.

3

The Summer of 1915

Miles Barne's Diary

M.Barne
Capt Scots Guards
for private & (barely) family circulation only.

1915

<u>Friday July 23rd</u>

Left 88 Ebury Str to catch 5.40 p.m. at Victoria, where was seen off by W. Gosling in "leave" train – Ellis coming with me to join one of the Battns of Scots Guards abroad._

> Captain William Sullivan Gosling, Scots Guards, and Lady Victoria Gosling were pre-war
> friends
> Lieutenant Donald Wilson Ellis, 1st Scots Guards

Crossed Folkestone to Boulogne – roughish passage. some trouble at former place with embarkation Officer who said he had not got us down on his list – at Boulogne reported to Railway Transport Officer who told us to go to a Hotel, Louvre, where we shared a room – scrimmage – eye very sore & wore cover all the time which is a nuisance_. Met Thorpe A & S Higlanders on steamer – said he was Bde Major 5th Bde – of which Charlie Corkran was Brigadier.

> Major Gervase Thorpe, The Argyll and Sutherland Highlanders, the brother of Captain
> John Somerled Thorpe, 1st Scots Guards

<u>July 24th</u>

Reported to RTO at 10 a.m. – told us to return for orders at 4 p.m.

Wrote to V & bought picture post cards for children _ at 4 p.m. returned to RTO who said we were for 1st Battn to my surprise and somewhat annoyance, meaning I shall not probably have my own Company. I had recently seen Alby Cator who commands 2nd Bn & who had told me I shd have a Coy if with him, Col. Fludyer, cmdg Regt and Archie Douglas said I ought to go to 2nd Bn., but these matters are arranged in France.

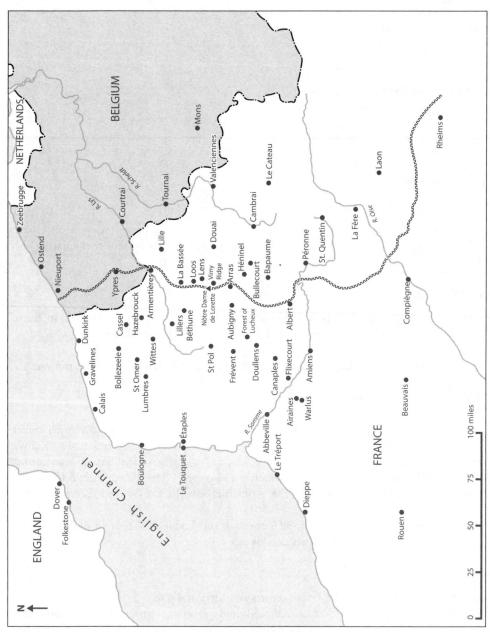

Map 1 Western Front, September 1915.

Wire to tell V. which Battn. dined at Hotel Folkestone where found Gilbert Russell, Grenadier, take seats in the "Supply Train" due to leave at 1 a.m.

> Lieutenant Colonel Albemarle Bertie Edward Cator, known as "Alby", 2nd Scots Guards, and Violet Cator were pre-war friends
> Colonel Henry Fludyer, at Regimental Headquarters holding appointment of Lieutenant Colonel Commanding Scots Guards
> Captain The Honourable Archibald Campbell Douglas, at Regimental Headquarters as Regimental Adjutant Scots Guards
> Captain Gilbert Byng Alwyne Russell, Grenadier Guards

25th

The first thing almost we see is a train full of wounded & sick – then watch the wounded being transferred out of Motor Ambulances into the train. One or two look as though they won't ever be good for much more.

Found the O.C. Train was Russell, Beds Yeoy, Gilbert's brother, he put us out at Lillers about 8 a.m., got some breakfast at a pothouse – & set off by Mail Lorry for a 14 mile drive through BETHUNE which the Germans had been shelling the few days previously, to VERQUIN where found the 1st Battn Scots Guards, 1st Brigade (Lowther), 1st Division (Haking), 4th Army Corps (Rawlinson), 1st Army (Haig)_

> Captain Claud Frederick William Russell, The Bedfordshire Yeomanry
> Brigadier General Henry Cecil Lowther, Commanding 1st (Guards) Brigade, a Scots Guardsman with whom Miles Barne served at Headquarters 16th Brigade in the Boer War
> Major General Richard Cyril Byrne Haking, Commanding 1st Division
> Lieutenant General Sir Henry Seymour Rawlinson, Commanding IV Corps
> Lieutenant General Sir Douglas Haig, Commanding 1st Army

– the Battn cmdd by Godman – Norman Orr-Ewing (my brother in law & subaltern in my Company in 1903) being 2nd in Comd, Thompson Adjt, Bartholomew Machine Gun Officer, Trafford Trench Mortar Battery Officer, Kinlay Quartermaster,

Harold Cuthbert; Mervyn Jones; Drury Lowe: R.F
John Thorpe; Hammersley: B
Poynter; A Boyd-Rochfort; Ellis (who came with me); Armstrong: C
Victor McKenzie; Neil Fergusson; Mackworth-Praed: L.F.

> Lieutenant Colonel Sherard Haughton Godman
> Major Norman Archibald Orr Ewing was wounded on New Year's Day 1915 at the Railway Triangle, Cuinchy
> Lieutenant Arnold John Thompson
> Lieutenant Claude Bartholomew †15.9.16 with 2nd Guards Brigade Machine Gun Company
> Lieutenant Cecil Edward Trafford

Quartermaster and Honorary Lieutenant David Kinlay

Captain James Harold Cuthbert †27.9.15

Lieutenant Arthur Mervyn Jones †21.11.16

Lieutenant John Alfred Edwin Drury Lowe

Captain John Somerled Thorpe †15.9.16 with 2nd Scots Guards

Lieutenant Hugh Charles Hammersley

Captain Arthur Vernon Poynter

Lieutenant George Arthur Boyd Rochfort

Lieutenant Guy Spearman Armstrong †27.9.15

Captain Sir Victor Audley Falconer Mackenzie, Bt, was wounded in October 1914 during
    First Ypres

Lieutenant Neil Muir Fergusson

Lieutenant Cyril Winthrop Mackworth Praed

The four rifle companies in the 1st Scots Guards were Right Flank or Right Flank Company, B Company, C Company and Left Flank or Left Flank Company.

Shortly before this the British agreed with the French to take over more of the line from the Béthune-La Bassée road down to Grenay, just south of the Béthune-Lens road and a little west of Loos. The 1st Scots Guards had already had experience of this neighbourhood, based on the ruins of the large farm complex at Le Rutoire, and would go back there again. Behind it to the west was a slightly rising slope which largely hid Vermelles from enemy observation. The other part of the line where they were doing tours was close to Cambrin and the Béthune-La Bassée road where the trench lines were very close together and very dangerous. This was their next destination in a section known as Z2.

Victor McKenzie is on leave so I am put in charge of LF Coy till his return, & find the Battn is due to go into trenches at CAMBRIN. this evening, so we parade at 5 p.m. & march 7 miles there – the last part along a wide road BETHUNE-LA BASSÉE, pick up some picks & shovels, dive into a communication trench & so on like so many moles, not having much idea what the ground is like above ground. L.F. is to be the Reserve Coy held in readiness to make the "counterstroke" in case anything goes wrong in the front line.

I share a very damp & smelly "dug out" with Fergusson, who sleeps like a hog. Rather an earnest time taking over from the [blank] Gloucester Rgt, making arrangements for the night in the dark – & all such new work to me – had quite a lively night – & have to "stand to" once or twice – not much sleep till after the regular dawn stand-to, 2.30–3.30 a.m., but am bound to say it is not an enjoyable time exactly.

1st Battalion The Gloucestershire Regiment, 3rd Brigade, 1st Division

26th

Had a good look round our trenches, which are very near the Germans, varying from 25 to 60 yards, but there are several mine craters between us held by the Germans, 2 or 3 of which are quite close to our parapets, the edge of crater & our parapet touching each other.

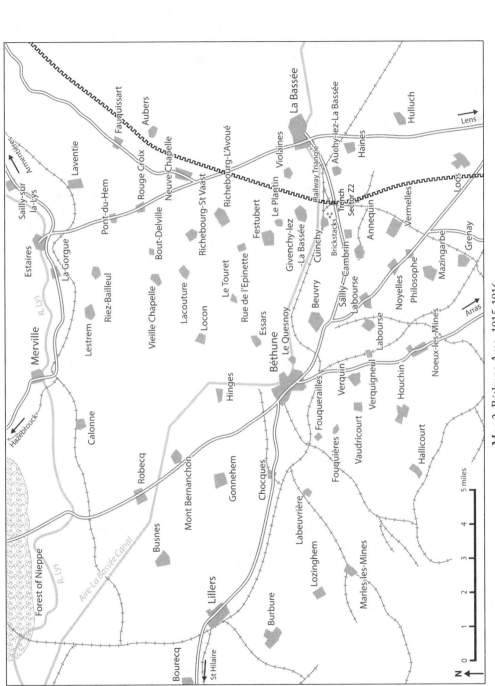

Map 2 Béthune Area, 1915-1916.

The days are fairly peaceful in the trenches, broken by very noisy & angry "Hates" locally – generally one in the morning about 9-10, then another about 4 and again about 6 to 7 which usually is continued on & off during the night_ At these periods the air gets full of projectiles of all sorts & it is extraordinary how few casualties we have.

A good many beetles & earwigs about, & the trenches are made additionally smelly by having dead Frenchmen & some Munster Fusiliers buried in the parapets – the latter inexcuseable.

> These dead were presumably from the 2nd Battalion The Royal Munster Fusiliers, 3rd Brigade, 1st Division.

27th

The only event today was a trench mortar bomb – horrible things trench mortars – going off just outside our dug-out & wounding Trafford's servant who was stirring the soup for dinner. I came in a few moments later & found all the food smothered in dust – such a mess, & the servant very unhappy – his arm badly damaged & and another cut in his leg.

28th

Our 3 nights are over & are relieved by 1st Bn Coldstream & march back about 3 miles to SAILLY-LABOURSE which we reach at 7 p.m.

Handed over to Darrell.

Very glad to get to a more peaceful spot, but can hear all the firing going on – hardly sleep a wink – & see glare of the "verylights," and the guns etc constantly passing my window – ground floor – is also very disturbing. Have quite a nice cleanish room brick floor, electric light.

> Captain Guy Marsland Darell, 1st Coldstream Guards
> Very Lights, the British version, appeared in the Diary in several forms, but were so called generically irrespective of which side was using them. These signalling and illumination flares were fired from a Very Pistol.

29th

Parade at 8.30 a.m. to march through PHILOSOPHE to VERMELLES to dig trenches_ A good deal of shelling of PHIL – while we are out & returning, so I choose to come back by another & safer route, nearly through NOYELLES.

I did not say that one night about 26th, after a deal of firing the Germans began shouting & chaffing & calling out "Turn out the Scots Guards" etc. and eventually put up hundreds of helmeted heads – all close together – our men then put up their heads (about 1 to every German's 5) – after more chaff a shot was fired when down went all the heads again._

30th

Victor McKenzie returns, again to VERMELLES parading at 1.30 p.m., back by 7 p.m.

31st

Back to relieve the 1st Bn Coldstream in the trenches at CAMBRIN again_ Take over from Hopwood: I am now put to B. Coy, with Thorpe, who are in the most unpleasant part – so we have plenty more anxiety.

Captain Edward Byng George Gregge Hopwood, 1st Coldstream Guards †20.7.17

This night Harold Cuthbert chose to go out with a Corpl, most bravely but unnecessarily, to see whether a certain crater was occupied or not – it was. The Corp was killed & had to be left out there, H.C. wounded in head but not badly.

10372 Corporal George Thomson Robertson Stewart †31.7.1915

Aug 1st

We had 1 man rather badly wounded & 2 more slightly.

During today Arthur Boyd Rochfort distinguished himself by seizing a bomb which landed on parapet by a working party & hurling it away – it exploded almost as it left his hand – a very gallant deed – several men would otherwise have been wounded, perhaps some killed. He wd have been safe had he done nothing.

Every night there is a wiring party – putting up wire entanglements in front of a trench, in this case impossible in front of front trench as too near the enemy, there

Aug 2nd

are usually some casualties _ one poor Coldstm man was killed, this the first dead man I saw, being carried down – about July 27th.

Probably 13023 Private Joseph Rindsland, 1st Coldstream Guards †26.7.15

The trenches here are mined & countermined in every direction – very jumpy work for the miners I expect – listening posts etc, and if we hear the Germans mining before they hear us, up has to go the mine (& vice versa) & begin all over again. Hence all these craters. "Vesuvius" is just outside our parapet_ Several have names.

Aug 3rd

The horrible three days & nights are over, and are again relieved by Coldsm & back to SAILLY-LABOURSE about 5 p.m.

Go for a walk with Norman to look at a new line of trenches made nearby.

Some rain. Early to bed.

4th

Slept like a log & feel much better for it_ rifle & billet inspection.

Parade 1.30 & go to dig at Vermelles again._

On return hear that Lowther the Brigadier has been asking for me, this has happened so often, & I have not seen him yet_ I must make an effort to see him soon.

Total Casualties in our 6 days in the trenches, 3 killed and 15 wounded.

> 8633 Private John Gamble †26.7.15
> 9920 Private Alexander Whyte †28.7.15
> 10372 Corporal George Thomson Robertson Stewart †31.7.1915

The Coldstream had more than this their first night when they relieved us, one bomb killing 2 platoon Sergts who were talking together – evidently making so much noise that the G's [Germans] bombed.

> Probably 2547 Sergeant Albert Edward Hatton, 1st Coldstream Guards †28.7.15
> Probably 11430 Sergeant G W Jackson, 1st Coldstream Guards †28.7.15

5th

Paraded 8.30 a.m. to dig at VERMELLES again. This place by the way is an absolute ruin hardly a roof left up – it was held by Germans last November for about 6 weeks against the French – the Chateau in particular being an objective, & defended to the last. The French mined up to it, thinking they were under it, but were short – & then stormed it, losing very heavily._ The whole place is a pitiful sight, no civilian inhabitants left now of course. A beautiful old Church is in ruins.

In afternoon rode into BETHUNE with Norman O.E. and Sherard Godman – visited the Church, which has some very fine glass windows – this town has been shelled recently, but luckily without success – except at the Railway Station.

Dined at Battn H.Q. & afterwards to L.F. & C. Mess where found everybody very cheerful – songs sung by Thompson & Armstrong.

> Depending on the circumstances behind the line, instead of there being a single officers mess there would be one for the Battalion Headquarters officers and two others, each for the officers of a couple of companies.

I don't think I mentioned above that on Aug 2nd, the Germans put up a notice on their parapet "Hier werden Kriegserklärungen angenommen" – meaning litterally, "Here will declarations of war be received." – & colloquially "Let's hear when you want to have a fight."

I was studying this with Thorpe's periscope, when – crash – & they broke the periscope to smithereens – it made me jump pretty well, & only shows what extraordinary shots their snipers are, to get it first shot –, probably 40 yards off the periscope measuring about 4 in x 3 in. They have even broken many of our smaller periscopes which the men use!

My bedroom is very comfortable – considering all things – but being on the ground floor & on the big road, very noisy & dusty – all night there is almost a constant procession of guns, ammunition & supply waggons, & vehicles of every description going both ways.

This is a flat sort of country, with coalpits every here & there (fosses), apparently fertile, by the look of the crops – mostly oats, wheat & roots – but I should think in winter must be dreary beyond description. there are clumps of trees here & there – mostly poplar, & a few walnuts._

In the distance to the South is the wooded ridge of "Notre Dame de Lorette" and Souchy with "the Labyrinth" lies beyond where desperate fighting has been taking place for many months._ At times one can hear the guns there, sometimes for an hour or more – day or night – an incessant rumble.

> The high, large, wooded ridge of Nôtre Dame de Lorette between Loos and Arras, captured by the Germans in October 1914, was thereafter subject to heavy French attacks from December that year onwards. In the course of these they gradually drove the Germans back at great cost to themselves. There was also bitter fighting for the villages of Carency and Ablain-St Nazaire and for Souchez at the southeast of the ridge. The Labyrinth was a large German defensive complex on the southwest side of Vimy Ridge to the south of Neuville-St Vaast.
> The dates of British attacks further north from December 1914 onwards coincided with the main French attacks here and the Battle of Loos would follow this pattern.

6th

Paraded 1.30 p.m. after being relieved in our Billets at SAILLY-LABOURSE by 5th Bn The Sussex Regt., and marched back to VERQUIN, where we relieved the 2nd Bn. 60th Rifles._

> 1/5th Battalion The Royal Sussex Regiment, T.F., and 2nd Battalion The King's Royal Rifle Corps, both 2nd Brigade, 1st Division

Am short of sleep & everyone will be glad of the 6 days rest. My billet is a room in a very primitive & quaint old farm house in a side street.

The farmer & his sister live there together. Two cows live in the room next to mine, a horse, a heifer, some pigs all close by in a sort of very compact court yard, with the inevitable kind of cesspool in the middle, but actually the house is pretty clean.

The men are scattered about in various outhouses & buildings.

There is quite a nice little garden at the back & a good view over Lorette, so one still sees the flares & "verylights" by night.

7th

Coy Drill in morning. In evening rode into FOUQUIÈRES with Godman to see the Brigadier – Lowther – who me a very kind & warm welcome. Stayed there about an hour – he is in a nice old Chateau, with what in peace time must have been a very pleasing garden. Dined at Battn H.Q.

> Brigade Headquarters were at Château Philomel

8th

Inspection of Rifles & emergency Rations.

About 11.30 a.m., who should I meet to my great surprise but Seymour, on a bike, who had come over about 16 miles to see me from WITTES. He lunched with us, and about 4 p.m. we walked together into BETHUNE, where I left him biking back. A very pleasant surprise.

I arrange to go & see him on Tuesday.

Lieutenant Seymour Barne, The 20th Hussars and No. 35 Squadron Royal Flying Corps
†23.4.17

9th

Boot fitting & repairing parade at FOUQUERAILLES – followed by a détour to make a route march.

A route march was an organised march for both exercise and marching fitness

In the afternoon a Doctor's feet inspection, when some men lost their names for having dirty feet – they certainly were so! There is plenty of water in these parts – all ready laid on, and, electric light in all the houses. I think the fact of living in a mining centre has a lot to do with it – there being plenty of coal (of sorts), and plant for making electricity.

When a soldier "lost his name", a phrase used generally, but not exclusively, in the case of a minor offence, such as having a dirty rifle or, in this instance, dirty feet, it meant that he would be reported and would appear in front of his Company Commander. In the event of a more serious offence, he would then be remanded for the Commanding Officer. Officers could also "lose their names", which would bring them in the first instance in front of the Adjutant, if junior to him.

After dinner I went out with the Coy Sgt Major to practice & try some new luminous sights which have been provided for us – we did not make very good practice & did not find the luminous paint very clear, or easy to see.

Some rain – but the atmosphere is very hot & heavy – a damp heat.

10th

Hotter than ever. Am on a Court Martial at 10 a.m., one of our Sergts for drunkenness at Folkeston when returning from leave, one of our Corporals, a similar offence at Sailly Labourse, and a man of the 1st Black Watch for disobedience of orders._

The Company goes a route march, under Hammersley.

Hear that two Officers of London Scottish, which Regt is also in our Brigade (the others being 1st Coldstream, 1st Black Watch, Cameron Highlanders) – have been blown up in a mine near CUINCHY.

At 12 noon I walk into BETHUNE, get a hired motor car & go off through CHOCQUES, LILLERS, and AIRE to see Seymour at WITTES. Aire is a very quaint & picturesque old town with a fine old Cathedral.

Found Seymour having lunch with his Squadron Leader Darling, most of the Officers being either on leave or up near YPRES digging trenches. The men of Regt all there digging except 1 in 4 left to look after the horses, which look very fit & well, & not too fat.

Captain John Clive Darling, The 20th Hussars

His mess is in a very nice farm & his room in another close by, surrounded by meadows & poplar trees, etc, but low down and will be very damp in winter._

He says our 2nd Bn passed through the previous day on the way to ST. OMER & Con Seymour called at the Regtl H.Q. to see him.

His first cousin, Lieutenant Conway Seymour, 2nd Scots Guards

It was quite an amusing outing, besides the pleasure of seeing Seymour "At home"._

Such a number of Motor Lorries parked by the roadside, & so much to look at everywhere_ on the way home was overtaken by Green (of the Barne Arms) now a commissioned Officer of the Army Service Corps! He stopped and had a chat – has something to do with serving Ammunition to the heavy Batteries of the 1st Army. I expect he is very useful at his job. Got back about 7 – running over a poor little dog in the last ¼ mile_

Though spread among three different brigades, each in different divisions, the eight Foot Guards Battalions currently in the BEF had hitherto in 1915 all been between the neighbourhood of Neuve Chapelle in the north and that either side of the Aire-La Bassée Canal, though those in the 1st (Guards) Brigade also now knew the area as far south as Le Rutoire. All eight were leaving their current formations and gradually moving north to St Omer to join the newly forming Guards Division, but could not do so until their replacements arrived.

Miles Barne, in addition to its usual meaning, also used "amusing" for something he found interesting or impressive, "unamusing" the reverse.

Lieutenant Charles Green, Army Service Corps, tenant of The Barne Arms, Dunwich, nowadays The Ship.

Aug 11th

My Coy all on fatigues, transporting barbed wire etc from a big R E Depot at a coalmine near here to some back trenches, loading up lorries etc.

In afternoon rode with Norman O.E. to see Genl Cuthbert ("Cupid") & have tea with him: found him looking somewhat greyer & fatter than when I last saw him, over a year ago, but very cheery and optimistic. He is living in a charming Chateau Labeuvrière, very pretty peaceful surroundings & commands 140th Bde of 47th Div.

Brigadier General Gerald James Cuthbert, nicknamed "Cupid", a Scots Guardsman, Commanding 140th Brigade, 47th (1/2nd London) Division, T.F.

Captain Harold Cuthbert in the 1st Scots Guards was his nephew.

12th

Had my hair cut by Sgt (Piper) Martin, an old soldier of 20 years service – fearful talker – but I am told an extremely gallant man. He is one of the few who have been out with the Battn all the time.

991 Sergeant Alexander Martin †9.2.16

Norman O.E. goes on leave. We parade at 6.30 p.m. to go into the trenches at LE RUTOIR, about 6 miles march. Arrive at VERMELLES at 9.30 p.m. where are met by the guides of 1st Gloucester Rgt who we are to relieve – & wander off into the dark to our places, B Coy is in reserve trenches, but very scattered – we don't get settled down till 12.15 p.m. when Hammersley & self go to our dugout & find our servants have an excellent meal of cold tongue etc ready – very welcome – stand to arms 2.55 a.m. to 3.55 a.m.

13th

Rather a short night & disturbed by rats with which the ceiling of dugout is infested, one can see their eyes gleaming through the straw, and they send down a shower bath of chips of straw onto one – personally I find the best plan is to put a newspaper over one's head.

In morning Thorpe arrives back_ I rearrange the company in trenches write letters & sleep.

These are quite peaceful trenches, but horrible going round at night, long solitary walks along deserted old German trenches, broken-in dugouts & goodness only knows how many corpses ½ buried in the various parapets.

Battn H.Q. is in a very ruined farmhouse.

14th

The only event of any consequence is a visit from Gavin Hamilton, who used to command B. Coy, now on Pulteney's Staff, cmdg 3rd A. Corps, accompanied by Bob Ward, who is a despatch carrier between "GHQ" & the War Office.

> Captain Gavin George Hamilton, Lord Hamilton of Dalzell, Scots Guards, very briefly commanding B Company earlier in 1915, now ADC to Lieutenant General Sir William Pulteney, a Scots Guardsman, Commanding III Corps
> Bob Ward – untraced

I also met some Officers on Rawlinson's Staff cmdg 4th Army Corps, in which we are, who said the 2 Battns had arrived to relieve the Coldstream & ourselves, to go & join the "Guards Division"_ There is much speculation about this Gds Divn, & opinions vary as to its desirability – of two things I am certain, (1) that it would be a formidable force for attacking the Germans, (2) that if it "takes the knock" there is no 2nd Guards Division to take its place.

15th

Very few events day or night – we do a good deal of digging & improving of trenches, especially at night.

In day time I wander round exploring the trenches, & seeing where we are to be next time.

Do some spying, with C.O. from a ruined house, of the German position_

We are relieved about 7 p.m. by 1st Bn Coldstream – one Fielding relieves B. Coy – & back to billets at VERMELLES in ruined & roofless houses,

> Captain Rowland Charles Feilding, 1st Coldstream Guards, author of War Letters to a Wife

Hammersley & 100 men have to go back to the trenches, parading at 10 p.m. to dig. Find a beautiful parcel from Violet – containing a cake & other food, cigarettes & writing paper for the men – an air-cushion – & other useful & welcome things.

16th

The unfortunate Hammersley & party get drenched through & through, return about 2 a.m.

Our billet is quite fairly comfortable – all 3 in a small room – my sleep somewhat disturbed because the mice found the contents of my pillow, & mattress consisting of unthrashed barley, very good to eat, so were scuttling about under me all night – also our peace was disturbed by a battery of howitzers about 200 yards off firing intermittently throughout the night & early morning over our heads at the Germans, who luckily never replied till on parade about 10 a.m. when a few rounds appeared & continued in a desultory way for an hour or so – some were pretty near us.

Our mess, with R.F. Coy, is about ½ mile off

Had a capital bath in another roofless house.

Most of the Coy on fatigues under R.E., & return fairly soaked through by the constant thunderstorms.

Walked round the back trenches with H. Cuthbert.

Collapse of Hammersley in his hammock!

17th

An eventless, but not noiseless night – for our guns all round us began at cockcrow & continued throughout the morning – no reply from Germans of any consequence.

Went to examine the "Chateau" & the 2 huge French Mine Craters there, about 25 ft diam. at the top and 18 ft deep. Such a pity not under the Chateau, which wd have saved so many French lives.

Poynter has gone sick, fever & sleeplessness. expect he will be back in a day or two.

In afternoon – our men all on fatigue back in trenches again – walked with Hammersley & Mackworth-Praed, two young Officers of the Battalion, to Vermelles Station & back by Philosophe to Vermelles, on entering which a gunner, Major Popham, met us and invited us to look round his guns & emplacements, the 18pr.q.f. field guns, & gave us a lecture on the subject of Arty, & fired off a gun for us while we were in an emplacement, which will make me deaf for a week.

> Major Gilbert Popham, Royal Field Artillery, and battery of 18 pounder quick firing field guns

A good deal of firing at night, our guns & enemy snipers_ great efforts to keep mice out of my bed – quite unsuccessful.

Find our mails have gone to ST. OMER!

18th

A German shell hit a house, the bag was one horse & 7 rats.

In evening back to the trenches, relieving 1st Bn Coldstream, B. Coy is right front company this time._

A fairly quiet night without incident.

19th

Have a good look round, can see the Germans occasionally looking over their parapets about 600x to 700x away.

A certain amount of shelling on both sides_ a Corp and 3 men of C. Coy are hit by shrapnell – the Corp in 15 places, but not killed.

Can hear every night a tremendous racket going on in Z2, where we were a fortnight ago; there is perpetual "hate" there.

Heard we have had 2 poor men blown up or blown in & buried in a mine – they were attached to the R.E. for mining work. One of them belonged to B Coy.

11083 Private Patrick McCrae †11.8.15
10692 Private Wilson McLean †11.8.15

We have a platoon of 8th R. Berks Regt attached to us for instruction – for 1 night, each of our Coys have 1 platoon. Lieut. Keeble is with us._

10th (Service) Battalion The Gloucestershire Regiment and 8th (Service) Battalion The Royal Berkshire Regiment replaced the 1st Coldstream Guards and 1st Scots Guards in the renamed 1st Brigade, 1st Division
Lieutenant Thomas C Keble, 8th Royal Berkshire Regiment

20th

While inspecting rifles this morning a German shell burst just over the front of our parapet where I was, covering us all, & the clean rifles, with dirt and dust – about the nearest shave I have had so far, as had it come another yard would have been in the middle of us, in the trench.

Norman O.E. returns from leave.

21st

A good deal of shelling – killing a Sergt (Blair) & 1 man of L.F. Coy & wounding 2 others, also 2 men of 10th Gloucester Regt who are attached to us "for instruction." The platoon attached to B Coy is under Lieut. Robinson – the Battn being commanded by Col. Pritchard.

In the evening we are relieved by the 1st Bn Black Watch, under Col [blank], our Coy by Capt Cook, one of whose subalterns was Lamb, formerly a Sergt in our 2nd Battn._

10268 Lance Sergeant James McLay Blair †21.8.15
11018 Private Frank Hodkinson †21.8.15
Probably Lieutenant Geoffrey Wathen Robinson, 10th Gloucestershire Regiment
†25.9.15
Lieutenant Colonel Henry Edward Pritchard, Commanding 10th Gloucestershire
Regiment

Major John George Henry Hamilton, Commanding 1st Black Watch
Probably Captain Denys Cooke, 1st Black Watch †18.4.18
2nd Lieutenant Charles Lamb, 1st Black Watch

We march back to billets at NOYELLES, Hammersley & self share a room, or rather garrett, over an estaminet – all the Officers mess together, for first time since I have been out, which is very nice. I sit next Norman & hear some home news, tho' not very much.

22nd

Relieved in our billets by 7th Berks Regt., & march to BETHUNE, the men remarkably cheerful & songful. My Coy is billeted in a Maltings – which we reach by 9.30 p.m. & are off early next morning

> The Battalion War Diary records their being relieved by the 8th Royal Berkshire Regiment

23rd

to DOLINGHEM.
   We hear the cross Channel boats are stopped; we leave Poynter in Bethune sick, I think a sort of nervous influenza.
   On leaving BETHUNE we march past Sir Henry Rawlinson in whose (IVth) Army Corps we have been hitherto to the tune of Auld Lang Syne.
   Pass through LILLERS & have an outspan of 2 hrs for dinners._
   A beautiful view all round the country from our village
   (Dollinghem)_ have a moonlight walk with Godman after dinner.
   A beautiful cake, some grapes and cigarettes arrive from home.

> They had halted for the night at Molinghem, just south of Ligny-lez-Aire

24th

An early start for a very hot march to CAMPAGNE.
   Quite by chance we put in at Seymour's Squadron for an hour's halt, found him looking very well & just going out for a ride with Little, so probably very soon we should have missed him altogether.
   During the afternoon had a visit from Cavan who commands our Divn & gave us a certain amount of news.
   Rumours of a German Naval defeat in the Baltic.
   In evening walk with N. O.-E. & watched my Coy bathing in the Canal.

> Captain Arthur C Little, The 20th Hussars
> Major General The Earl of Cavan, Commanding Guards Division
> Rumours of a German naval defeat were rumours

25th

Another very hot though luckily not very long march through ST. OMER to TATTINGHEM – a long straggly village.

ST. OMER is a very nice old fashioned Flemish town & fortress: some weird names of streets "Les Cuisiniers", and "Les Écusseries"._ The G.H.Q. of the English forces is here, with its numerous Departmental H.Q. & Officials with their Offices._

Greeted on arrival at TATINGHEM by Genl Heyworth, who commands one of the 3 Brigades in the Divn (that which contains our 2nd Bn) with R. Tempest his Brigade Major.

In afternoon I ride over with Norman to see our 2nd Battn at WIZERNES, don't see much of them, only Mills & Arkwright, 2 Officers recently joined from W Kent Yeoy.

Brigadier General Frederick James Heyworth, nicknamed "Pa", a Scots Guardsman,
    Commanding 3rd Guards Brigade †9.5.16
Major Roger Stephen Tempest, Scots Guards, a pre-war friend

The two officers transferred from the West Kent Yeomanry were:
Lieutenant The Honourable Charles Thomas Mills MP, 2nd Scots Guards †6.10.15
Lieutenant Esmé Francis Wigsell Arkwright, 2nd Scots Guards, with previous service in
    The 5th Lancers, whom Miles Barne knew socially

26th

Parade 9.30 a.m. and do some drill and a short route-march to WISQUES, where is a fine old chateau & Convent, the latter now used as a Machine Gun school.

Here we see some wonderful defense works, done by the French, and who should ride up but Col. Corry, cmdg 3rd Bn Gren. and George Montgomerie, riding the black mare "Annie", or "Geraldine" which he lent us for so long.

In the afternoon, a visit from Alby Cator who commands our 2nd Bn, and Ross the Qmr.

We hear that John Ponsonby is to be our new Brigadier in place of Lowther who has gone to be Military Secretary to Sir John French.

A Company concert in the evening, without a piano; quite a success nevertheless.

Lieutenant Colonel Noel Armar Lowry Corry, Commanding 3rd Grenadier Guards
Major George Frederick Molyneux Montgomerie, 3rd Grenadier Guards †22.10.15
Quartermaster and Honorary Lieutenant Thomas Ross, 2nd Scots Guards
Brigadier General John Ponsonby, hitherto Commanding 1st Coldstream Guards,
    Commanding 2nd Guards Brigade

To complete the Guards Division five Foot Guards Battalions, the 3rd and 4th
Grenadier Guards, 4th Coldstream Guards (Pioneers), 2nd Irish Guards and 1st Welsh
Guards arrived from England. The 1st Guards Brigade, the erstwhile 4th (Guards)
Brigade, commanded by Brigadier General Geoffrey Feilding, Coldstream Guards,
consisting of the 2nd Grenadier Guards, 2nd and 3rd Coldstream Guards and 1st
Irish Guards, only required a name change. The 2nd Guards Brigade, commanded by
Brigadier General John Ponsonby, formed consisting of the 3rd Grenadier Guards, 1st

Coldstream Guards, 1st Scots Guards and 2nd Irish Guards. The 3rd Guards Brigade, commanded by Brigadier General Frederick Heyworth, formed consisting of the 1st and 4th Grenadier Guards, 2nd Scots Guards and 1st Welsh Guards.

27th

Kit inspection, etc.

In evening a "3rd Guards Dinner" at the Convent at WISQUES. 38 Officers sat down to dinner, amongst them being Pulteney, cmdg 3rd Army Corps, Heyworth, Godman, Ruthven, Cator, Alston, Tempest, Bagot-Chester, Hamilton (of Dalzell), Thorpe, Cuthbert, N. Orr-Ewing, V McKenzie, Hill, Ballantyne-Dykes, A. Boyd-Rochford, Mills, Arkwright, Brand, Broadwood, C. Wynne-Finch (Adjt 2nd Bn.), Ward, Warde, Hammersley, Drury-Lowe, Mervyn Jones, Bury (who organized the dinner), Ross & Kinlay, (the two Quartermasters), MacDonald, Mackworth-Praed, Armstrong, Warner.

> The Third Guards Club is the Officers Dining Club of the Scots Guards.
> Lieutenant Colonel The Honourable Walter Patrick Hore Ruthven, The Master of
>   Ruthven, nicknamed "Jerry", General Staff Officer Grade 1, Guards Division
> Major Francis George Alston nicknamed "Cook", Deputy Assistant Adjutant &
>   Quartermaster General, Guards Division
> From the 1st Scots Guards and not mentioned previously,
> Lieutenant David Halyburton Brand †29.3.18
> From the 2nd Scots Guards and not mentioned previously,
> Major Greville John Massey Bagot Chester †28.11.17
> Captain William James Montague Hill
> Captain Frecheville Hubert Ballantyne Dykes
> Lieutenant Stewart Henry Tschudi Broadwood
> Captain William Heneage Wynne Finch was wounded in October 1914 during First
>   Ypres
> Lieutenant Francis Ward
> Lieutenant Richard Edward Warde
> Lieutenant Reginald Lindsay Macdonald
> Others not mentioned previously,
> Captain Walter Egerton George Lucian Keppel, Viscount Bury, Machine Gun Officer,
>   3rd Guards Brigade
> Captain Edward Courtenay Thomas Warner, Staff Captain, 3rd Guards Brigade

There were no toasts except the King. After dinner the table was cleared and a reel was danced by those who knew how, as well as by several who didn't:

28th

We marched the Company over to WIZERNE, where is the 2nd Battn. Took our "cooker", or kitchen on wheels with us, the men – or some of them – bathed, had dinners, saw their friends, the officers had lunch with different messes, and we got back to TATTINGHEM about 4.30 p.m.

I saw Con Seymour who had just returned from leave.

In evening the Battn H.Q. gave a dinner party & invited me – also there were Alby Cator, G. Trotter, Boy Brooke (our Bde Major), and Ross the 2nd Bn Qmr., who was a Sgt when I was in them.

Major Gerald Frederick Trotter, 1st Grenadier Guards
Major Bertram Norman Sergison Brooke, nicknamed "Boy", Grenadier Guards, Brigade Major, 2nd Guards Brigade

29th

Before I was up in the morning appeared Seymour who rode over early to breakfast, as he had to get back for some swimming sports in his Canal.

So he just had breakfast with us and wrote a letter in my room & then started back about 11.45 a.m.

In the afternoon I went a walk by myself, & got caught in a storm & was drenched through.

30th

Walked into St. O with Harold Cuthbert: saw the Cathedral & other churches.

31st

In evening a walk with H. Cuthbert exploring the country round_

The threshing & dressing of corn etc in these parts is done by making a horse do "treadmill" – which seems a very simple & economical, if oldfashioned method.

There is a shoeing smith just outside my billet – their methods are somewhat barbarous – the horse is placed in a small 'pen' just his own size & the foot to be shod is fixed up and lashed onto a bar – the spare horn & wall of foot underneath is pared off with a hammer & chisel, & apparently too much is taken off & pain evidently caused by the blows of hammer.

Sept 1st

Called at 3.30 a.m., parade at 5 a.m. & marched to WISMES via SETQUES LUMBRES and AFFRINGUES where the whole division we were told was to assemble, some said for inspection by Joffre, some even assured us the King was coming over!

We hid (we imagined from Aeroplanes) under fences round an orchard for an hour, then proceeded, being given a sort of "Scheme" to OUVE-WIRQUIN where we halted for 2 hours & had dinners, passing en route our divl commander Cavan also Billy Lambton, who has recently been given a division, and Franky Lloyd also turned up accompanied by Jack Arbuthnot on a visit to the country, but no Gen Joffre or King tho' we looked behind every bush for them.

It rained during the halt & on way home which was by WAVRANS and ESQUEDOS where the 3rd Gren are, and SETQUES our Brigade (Ponsonby 2nd Gds Bde) H.Q. arriving back at 6.20 p.m. having covered 26 miles, only 1 man of my Compy & 5 of the Battn did not walk in with us, which – considering the men were carrying their packs – was not bad. The boots are getting very bad and a new supply must arrive before we move far.

We never saw the rest of the Divn, only our own Brigade, though we know they were also out. Quite pretty country, hilly & in places woods and high fences._

Brigadier General The Honourable William Lambton, handing over as Military Secretary
   at General Headquarters to Brigadier General Lowther and about to be promoted
   to command the 4th Division
Major General Francis Lloyd, Major General Commanding The Brigade of Guards and
   General Officer Commanding London District
Major John Bernard Arbuthnot, Scots Guards, on his Staff

2nd

Rode over with NOE to 2nd Bn's Sports and "Horse Show." To my surprise found Seymour there competing, & with great success too, because he rode 2 horses in his Rgtl jumping team, and he also won the V.C. Race – out of 24 or 28 starters – the 1st in each of the 6 (or 7) heats starting in the final.

Our Battn won the Tug of War_ There was an excellent tea.

The Regtl Jumping Teams – of 4 horses – Competition was won by 5th Cav. Bde – Gen Wormald – in which S's Regt is – the 20th Hussars were 2nd, and 2nd Battn Scots Guards 3rd._ They beat the Greys & 12th Lancers, the 3rd Gds Bde Staff (Heyworth Tempest Bury and [blank]) and some other Infantry Battalions.

Hear with infinite pleasure that A. Boyd-Rochford has been awarded the V.C.

Brigadier General Frank Wormald †3.10.15

3rd

Rained Cats and Dogs all day.

4th

[blank]

5th

Walked over to lunch with Con. Seymour at WIZERNE_ met Seymour there, after luncheon we walked together to HALLINES where I looked up R. Tempest, & on to the Convent at WISQUES, where S. found a friend McGillycuddy of the 4th D.G.'s, an instructor at the Machine Gun School.

Captain Ron Kinloch McGillycuddy of the Reeks, The 4th Dragoon Guards

6th

Cricket with Newspaper Correspondents.

7th

Some Battn Boxing, against 2nd Battn also. Also a football match against 2nd Battn, which they won.

In evening N & I dined with G. Paynter at GHQ where met Lowther and J. Dawnay. Afterwards was shown some very interesting maps, marked with little flags in every direction.

Thorpe goes on leave so I have the Coy to myself.

> Lieutenant Colonel George Camborne Beauclerk Paynter, Scots Guards, was wounded in March during the Battle of Neuve Chapelle
> Possibly Major General Guy Pagan Dawnay

8th

Brigade Field Day – rather an interesting day ending up with taking a village at the point of the bayonet.

The Prince of Wales who is attached to the Divl (Cavan) Staff was out, riding about on a bicycle. He looked very young and rather unhappy, and am told is very shy indeed.

9th

Company Drill when I learned at [a] good lot. Had not done any for 11 years.

In afternoon ride over, through some rather pretty country, to LUMBRES to see some boxing between Coldm & Irish Guards. also a match between our Cpl. Finch ("The Tiger") and an Irish Guardsman Harris, who knocked out "the Tiger" in the 1st Round. Our Tug of War Team also pulled the 2nd Irish, who won entirely owing to the unfair ground. We have challenged them again.

> 9159 Lance Corporal Charles Edward Finch †2.10.16
> 6135 Private Thomas Harris, 2nd Irish Guards

10th

More Coy and extd Order drill, when I think the men are rather astonished by some of my movements, which are original to say nothing else about them.

A Presbyterian parson – Capt Gillison – has arrived & is to be attached to us.

> The Reverend William Phin Gillieson, C.F.

Rode out by myself in the evening

Norman tells me he proposes applying for leave for me next week.

11th

My application for leave goes in to Brigade Office.

Kit inspection.

Godman, who has returned off leave, Norman & I ride out to see the Lakes, but did not start in time as there is a longish walk at the end having to leave the ponies at a farm_

We visit a huge farm, the remains of the old Abbey of St Bernard – an old woman told us her house was 900 years old – she looked about the same age_ we rode round the farm buildings where we found about 40 young women on top of a straw stack, very much hindering the work apparently of the farm men – and much surprised – some amused & some scared – at our sudden appearance.

On returning to TATTINGHEM find my (& Ellis') leave is granted, and after much ado settle to start by 9.40 a.m.

12th

From WIZERNES to catch 4.30 p.m. boat at BOULOGNE, as we are unable to get a motor-car.

The only point which is very distressing is that Seymour was coming over to luncheon today – so will find me flown.

Miles Barne was meant to travel back from leave in England on 20 September.

Sept. 20th (Mon)

Tried to catch 5.40 p.m. train from Victoria but, as all traffic was suspended owing to submarines in Channel, could not go till same time

21st

when travelled with Esmé Arkwright and Baden-Powell, now 2nd in command 10th W. Yorks. A calm crossing but having to go zigzag took 2½ hours over arriving Boulogne 12–midnight

Major Baden Fletcher Smyth Baden Powell, Scots Guards, Second in Command 10th (Service) Battalion The West Yorkshire Regiment, 50th Brigade, 17th (Northern) Division, New Army

22nd

leaving 4.22 a.m. arriving at WIZERNE 7.30 a.m. and walking out to TATINGHEM with Ellis & Armstrong – on arrival there find we move at 6 p.m. and make a pleasant moonlight march to HERBELLE, a pretty little village – we don't get there till 11 p.m., so I am pretty glad to go to bed – sharing a room in a farm house with Thorpe._

His return coincided with the start of the Guards Division's move towards the Loos battlefield, by marches after dark to avoid enemy aerial reconnaissance. They lay up by day.

4

Loos

While Miles Barne was on leave there were general briefings on what was coming next, but not where or when. Lieutenant General Haking had been promoted to command XI Corps, with whom the Guards Division now were. Their role in the battle, along with the 21st and 24th Divisions, New Army, very newly arrived and inexperienced, was, as the operational reserve, to exploit the gaps in the German defences which the opening attack was expected to make. Six divisions went into action early on 25 September, with gas some help in some places and a complete hindrance in others. Success was mixed, but where it was greatest the Germans counterattacked and, other than on the southern flank, exhausted, disorganised and weakened British brigades began to give ground.

The 21st and 24th Divisions, followed by the Guards Division, were on exactly the same routes in the later stages of their approach to the battlefield. There were congestion and discomfort in very wet weather, with resultant delays which made it impossible to deliver any of XI Corps into the fighting on 25 September. All that was in addition to the absence of a defined arrangement for the transfer of command of this reserve from Sir John French as Commander-in-Chief to Sir Douglas Haig as Commander of the First Army fighting the battle.

Meanwhile, on 23 September, before moving on southeast after dark, the 1st Scots Guards waited at Herbelles.

23rd

Rode over to 3/Grenadiers in morning to deliver a letter from his wife to Geo Montgomerie, but found him out_ They are in a beautiful chateau, at UPEN D'AVAL – the men sleeping under a fine old lime avenue – such a glorious view._

Rode with Poynter to luncheon with Brinton (2/Life Gds, late) who is Camp Comdt to Genl Fanshawe comdg the Cav. Corps – found him in THEROUANNE also Laurie of the Greys, Capel of Intelligence Deptnt, who is just off to be our Laiason Officer with the French Cav. Corps, also the French Liaison Officer with our Cav Corps whose name I did not catch. They of course had a good deal of interesting news as to our immediate future – which I must not put down here.

Major George Frederick Molyneux Montgomerie and Sybil Molyneux Montgomerie
were pre-war friends
Major John Chaytor Brinton, The 2nd Life Guards, was wounded in the charge of The
21st Lancers at Omdurman on 2 September 1898
Lieutenant General Hew Dalrymple Fanshawe, Commanding Cavalry Corps
Captain Percy Robert Laurie, The Royal Scots Greys
Captain Arthur Edward Capel, Intelligence Corps

Marched about 6 – a long slow wet march (in pouring rain most of the way) to LIGNY LES
AIRE, where I turn in naked into quite a comfortable bed in a room (in a farm house) only just
big enough to hold the bed – window opening onto the bed – during the night a rat entered by
the window & woke me up by sitting on & playing with my feet – he soon disappeared out of
the window.

Rained all night but cleared on

24th Sept 1915

about 9 a.m. To get to my room I have to go through the room occupied by Grandpère &
Grandmère. They look so comical tucked up together in bed, with only their funny old weather
beaten noses shewing.

Heard that my brother Seymour is appointed Staff Captain to Genl Pitman – 4th Cav.
Brigade – am very glad as he richly deserves something of the sort, and one hopes it means he
is slightly safer in the event of any big move.

Brigadier General Thomas Tait Pitman, Commanding 4th Cavalry Brigade

In p.m. received interesting instructions from CO as to scheme for a general "push" commencing
tomorrow – & arrange to march 12 midnight so to bed 4–7.30 p.m. & again at 9.30, making
every preparation for long marches with no food etc, then orders come to march 6 a.m., &
about 11 p.m. an orderly brings me a note saying I am detailed to be a Liaison Officer with XI
Army Corps and a motor car will pick me up at LIGNY LES AIRE at 4.45. I therefore have to
arrange to be called at 3.20 a.m.

The six hour delay in starting to march on was because of the congestion on the roads,
while the distance from Ligny to Vermelles by the most direct route available was still
over twenty miles. The message telling Miles Barne about his liaison duties added that
he should expect to be away for several days.

25th

Get a large mug of coffee from my landlady and walk off to LIGNY LES AIRE with my "little-
all" on my back – feeling very sore at leaving the Coy and the Battn – some breakfast with the
CO and Norman O.E. who are good enough to express their surprise and regret at my going
– then a car arrives, & am confronted by no less a person than H.R.H. Pr of Wales which sets
me wondering what I am in for – 2 other Offrs with him.

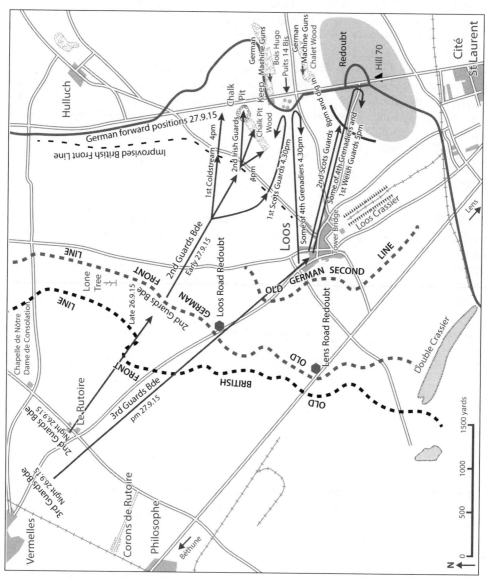

Map 3 Battle of Loos, Attack on Puits 14 Bis, 27 September 1915.

We reach NOEUX LES MINES about 6 a.m., the Headquarters of the XI Corps, where I find Gen. Haking & his Staff – bid Adieu to HRH, who is very shy and was terrified of going into Hakings Room, & am sent off to the IV Corps, (under Rawlinson) at VAUDRICOURT where I report to the Genl Staff Officer (1) Genl Montgomery – it is rather alarming, nothing but Generals – including one Buckland who is quite original & amusing – also a Major Doyle Major Hughes, Northants Regt., Capt. Parker, Welsh Fusiliers, a quaint card, Major Walker R.E., an agressive giant, Col Lee, who was a military attaché during the Spanish-American War.

IV Corps were responsible for the southern half of the battle. The right hand boundary was some distance south of the Béthune-Lens road, which ran past the village of Loos. The principal features were the twin slag heaps known as the Double Crassiers, the huge pit gantry known to the British as Tower Bridge and, beyond Loos, the ridge carrying the Lens-La Bassée road with Hill 70 at its highest point. The left hand corps boundary ran along the Vermelles-Hulluch road.

Brigadier General Archibald Armar Montgomery, Brigadier General General Staff, IV
    Corps
Brigadier General Reginald Ulick Henry Buckland, Chief Engineer, IV Corps
Major Doyle – untraced
Probably Major Edmond Locock Hughes, The Northamptonshire Regiment
Captain Parker, The Royal Welsh Fusiliers – untraced
Major Walker, Royal Engineers – untraced
Colonel Arthur Hamilton Lee, Royal Artillery

My job is practically nil, only to see that information & reports are sent on to the XI Corps. The working of the Staff is very interesting but it is no place for me, and I long to be back with the Battalion._

The details of the day are better taken out of the Papers & Official Reports – a day let us hope which will mark the turning point in the war.

I walk down to see a big batch of German prisoners, some look very young, all very tired & hungry & dirty

My companion in chains is Col. Jules Pereira, late Gren Gds, who has to stand by waiting for a Brigade, & we neither of us have much to do_ I find myself in everybody's way, & all the reports are sent on by telephone or telegraph to XI Corps as it is; it is interesting hearing the news first hand, & all sorts of interesting people appear, including Sir Douglas Haig, cmdg 1st Army.

The 3rd Cav Div. goes through when I see some friends and during the night, which is a very wet one, more turn up, the 9th Bde, consisting of 15th Hu 19th Hu and Bedfordshire Yeo bivouac close by, and make free use of Sir H Rawlinson's Huts & Tents and any food or drink they can lay hands on.

Lieutenant Colonel George Edward Pereira, nicknamed "Jules", Grenadier Guards

It is a dreadful night for those fighting and the Divn which is digging itself into "Hill 70" must be suffering many discomforts. So far the Guards Divn is still in "general reserve" under Sir J. French._ This is the one point which gave me comforting thoughts.

I sleep in the Chateau, sharing a room with Hughes

By darkness on 25 September the IV Corps situation was that over to the right the 47th Division, the only one fully successful on 25 September, had stormed the Double Crassiers and held their ground, completely securing that flank. In the middle the 15th (Scottish) Division, New Army, despite suffering severely, had captured the German front line along the Grenay Ridge, advanced through and past the village of Loos, captured Hill 70 uphill to the east and, by this time disorientated and losing cohesion, gone on instead of consolidating. A strong German counterattack drove the survivors back and off Hill 70 and off the line of the Lens-La Bassée road. The 1st Division, on the left, with great difficulty and weak in numbers, reached close to the Lens-La Bassée road to the south of Hulluch. This set the scene for what happened to most of XI Corps next, though some of the 24th Division were drawn into the I Corps operations north of the Vermelles-Hulluch road.

During the morning of 26 September parts of the 21st and 24th Divisions attacked the northern slopes of Hill 70 on the right and through the 1st Division on the left, their objectives what was now the German front line. Apart from on the northern slopes of Hill 70 most of this, hitherto a reserve position, was set well back from the Lens-La Bassée road, looking out across a wide stretch of flat ground. The Germans had had time not only to bring up reinforcements but also to strengthen their defences. In a very disordered situation, over ground pitted and littered by the consequences of the day before and about which they, including their senior officers, knew little or nothing, these New Army battalions failed. Crossing and becoming established east of the Lens-La Bassée road was impossible. They suffered severely, their losses comparable to those of most of the attacking divisions the day before.

26th

Up betimes, but not before Pereira, who is getting very restless, & I resolve to make an effort to rejoin the Battn, in this I am confirmed when "the New Army" not being as successful as one hoped in the attack, I hear the Gds Divn is to be brought up, so I beg Gen Montgomery to get me sent back, & he does so, & at 1.30 p.m. off I go in a motor car, & am lucky in hitting off the Battn not far off – we march through our old friend SAILLIE-LABOURSE & VERMELLES and occupy about 10 p.m. the trenches held by Germans which we had for so long sat opposite.

Once they reached the edge of the battlefield the 2nd Guards Brigade waited for some hours around Le Rutoire, not moving up to the old German front line trenches on the Grenay Ridge, which they then rearranged, until long after dark.

Dig and adapt them to face the other way, & at 3 a.m.

27th

Early on the 27th they moved further southeast and occupied former German trenches near the Loos-Hulluch road, the 1st Scots Guards on the right and the 2nd Irish Guards on the left being the two forward battalions in this improvised front line.

after much trouble about men's tea, rum & water, we advance to the attack. over the ground on which others had failed – passing & finding many gruesome if natural & typical battlefield sights.

Are in support of 1st Gds Bde who advance & we sit in another trench (in support) getting pretty well shelled, though, as a Gunner Col remarked "the German Gunners are losing their nerve" & making very poor practice" – we bury several dead – & at 4.30 [pm] the attack proper begins, over a horribly open and bare space onto "Hill 70" LOOS, which Sir Douglas Haig says is of such immense importance. It is a redoubt heavily entrenched and surrounded by masses of barbed wire. A tremendous Canonade precedes the attack, an awful din_ The Battn is in support & my Coy a nominal sort of Reserve, anyhow luckily for us we go in last, getting heavily shelled as we go – all appears to go well at first – practically the whole Guards Division is launched – but the leading portions come suddenly under tremendous machine gun fire at close range, the Officers in our Brigade begin to disappear, the men, finding themselves without leaders, are at a loss what to do and turn – my Coy meet them & do what we can to bring them round. The Irish Guards have some Offrs left & recover, also many of our Battn, & some Grenadrs (I know not about Coldstream) we then under Col. Butler advance to a certain wood to entrench – which we do after dark – Irish Gds just beyond the wood, Scots Gds – consisting principally of our Coy – a few of R. Flank – a fewer of L.Flank and 1 or 2 of C. Coy – remainder I know not where_ Thorpe takes charge of the Battn. It is all too ghastly to write about, about 12 or 13 Officers, including CO & 2nd in Com (Godman and N. Orr Ewing) H. Cuthbert V. McKenzie & Poynter all being casualties. We spend a horrible night entrenching where we are, looking for & bringing in wounded & trying to re-organize. Nobody seems to be able to say anything of anybody, the men dead beat, hungry & thirsty & sleepless. The night a soaking wet one. The only Officers left are Thorpe, Thompson, (the Adjt), Hammersley, Grainger, Trafford & myself. Luckily Boyd Rochfort was away sick just at that time.

The Guards Division were distinctly ordered not to go beyond the Lens-La Bassée road, it being intended to secure up to the line of it. The 1st Guards Brigade, on the left, had a relatively easy time, compared with the others, moving forward towards the road and taking over what was then the British front line short of it. The 3rd Guards Brigade, coming from near Vermelles direct towards and through Loos, entered the battlefield after the other two. For still unexplained reasons they were not to attack Hill 70 itself until satisfied that the 2nd Guards Brigade had taken the pit buildings at Puits 14 Bis [Pit 14A] slightly lower downhill and northwards towards Hulluch and La Bassée, the objective of the failed attack by the 1st Scots Guards, though some managed to get into them. When he saw British troops around the Puits Brigadier General Heyworth concluded that they had been successful, but not so. By the time he knew otherwise it was too late to stop his Brigade's attack on Hill 70 and it too failed. The lie of the land was such that it was physically possible to approach the line of the road uphill without enemy rifle and machine gun fire, but once closer to the top there was no cover.

The direction of approach of the 2nd Guards Brigade had been nearly from the northwest. Their attack began at 4 p.m. when the 2nd Irish Guards, supported by the 1st Coldstream, were to capture first the Chalk Pit and then the Chalk Pit Wood, the wood that Miles Barne mentioned. They achieved this under heavy fire from the vicinity of the Puits, though it would appear that the Germans were not occupying the Chalk Pit and its Wood other than with outposts.

The 1st Scots Guards, moving past the right of the 2nd Irish Guards, then attacked the Puits, supported by the 3rd Grenadiers, Miles Barne's time of 4.30 p.m. probably being right. When they, also abetted by some 4th Grenadiers, who had become detached from their own Battalion in the 3rd Guards Brigade, came into full view of the defenders of the Puits, of the machine guns in the Bois Hugo just beyond the road, in other positions nearby and, probably, the fortifications around the top of Hill 70, there was only one outcome. A few of the attackers did manage to get into the pit complex, but not to return. Afterwards, the only option was to dig in back down the slope. The 1st Coldstream, digging in later on across to the left, nearest to the 1st Guards Brigade, had great difficulty in establishing contact with their neighbours after dark.

Miles Barne referred to their objective as Hill 70. What they were attacking at the Puits was part of it, on its lower northern slope, although to history the name has become solely associated with the highest point.

Lieutenant Colonel The Honourable Lesley James Probyn Butler, Commanding 2nd Irish Guards

28th

A very busy time, have made a capital start at the trench in the night, the men's rations & water were obtained, the RE supplied a few more entrenching tools, & we collected a few more men, I think bringing the Battn up to 400. (250?).

The stretcher parties were conspicuous by their absence, & on all hands were they wanted, the wounded were lying in heaps untended, cold & miserable: we sent in what we could in mackintosh sheets, but a long way to the dressing station & there they seemed unable to deal with them, quickly enough_ all so different to what one had been lead to believe by the newspapers.

In the afternoon we are badly shelled, with some losses, & the Coldstream on left of our line have to give way, things get very uncomfortable, but by night fall the shelling stops and all is well. To my horror about 4 p.m. I hear Thorpe is hit & gone to dressing station so I take over the Battn, but luckily for all concerned he returns about 6 with his hand bandaged up. Grainger, one of my subalterns, had a bullet in & out of his leg, but very pluckily took no notice (I think only through fat) & so we are still intact as a Coy.

Brigadier General Ponsonby was ordered to mount another attack on the Puits on the afternoon of 28 September. Communications with Headquarters Guards Division were so poor that he could not put to Lord Cavan his idea that a night attack might have a better chance of succees. The 1st Coldstream Guards attacked in daylight, failed and lost some 250 officers and men. This is what Miles Barne was referring to that afternoon.

Lieutenant Henry Herbert Liddell Grainger

What is so horrible is knowing that there must be many wounded between us & Germans, & being unable to get them, though we do bring in several and get shot at for our pains for doing so. On these occasion one always go up to a body (I fear hundreds are lying about between us and the Germans) & sees if alive or not – such ghastly sights does one see sometimes – for instance one poor creature whom Hammersley & 2 men & self brought in raving, was lying shot through the head & his teeth lying alongside almost intact.

Found the body of Lt Col E.T. Logan, the Cheshire Regt amongst others. Had a man hit through the knee bringing in one wounded man.

> Lieutenant Colonel Edward Townshend Logan, The Cheshire Regiment, Commanding 15th (Service) Battalion The Durham Light Infantry †26.9.15. They were in the 64th Brigade, 21st Division, in the failed attack on 26 September.

29th

The 29th passes full of incident, though nothing very definite occurring – were heavily shelled in trenches, at which we work busily – the Coldstream very much worse shelled, & poor Arthur Egerton is blown sky-high out of his dugout: I suppose it was him we saw – about 150 yards off – as I dont think many were blown right up_ Towards evening Thorpe & HQ & the remains of the other 3 Companies are relieved out of their trenches, & my Coy takes over a new piece of trench. We are reinforced by about 70 Household Cavalry Cyclists, under Montgomery, and at nightfall are warned that the Germans are massing for an attack, so make every preparation, but nothing much unusual occurs during the night._

> Lieutenant Colonel Arthur George Edward Egerton, Commanding 1st Coldstream Guards †29.9.15
> Probably Captain Victor Robert Montgomerie, The 2nd Life Guards

Delighted to hear Ellis was found wounded, now only H. Cuthbert & Armstrong are missing. I forgot to say that early on 27th the former was by way of leading B. Coy to a certain place, but owing to various causes, things went wrong and we nearly got lost in the dark Harold had been out since 24 hours previously without any sleep & was pretty well done up – even he admitted. I saw a lot of him that morning and wondered if he had forebodings! He seemed rather different to usual, however he may yet be found all right.

> There was no news of Captain Cuthbert until the spring of 1917 when a report was received from the German authorities, forwarded by the Netherlands Legation, that he had died on 27 September "on or near Trench 14." Nothing more was ever heard of Lieutenant Armstrong.

30th

First thing when only just light it is reported to me that more wounded are seen in front, so we make another expedition to rescue & 3 are obtained, 2 of them drew fire but no casualty.

One is a Corp in C. Coy: one a private soldier of the Suffolk Regt_. one of the D.L.I., who had been lying there 6 days, and tried to cut his throat, but failed. Nothing can picture the appalling situation of these poor creatures, lying out in wind & rain (the former cold the latter copious) no food or water & a broken leg or something & occasionally being heavily shelled by the German Guns or shot at by those in the trenches getting a scare & blazing off their ammunition into the dark.

There is always at same time their anguish of mind at feeling they have to die of exposure or hunger.

One gallant man, who had been out for 5 or 6 days, when I asked him how he felt, said "Very well, Sir, but should be better if I had been found sooner". When able they are always so grateful to their rescuers.

During the morning the OC 7th Bn Norfolk Regt comes up to see our trench, which his Bn is to take over. He is accompanied by his Adjt, Hammond.

> The wounded private was probably from the 9th (Service) Battalion The Suffolk Regiment, 71st Brigade, 24th Division, the Durham Light Infantryman from either their 14th or 15th Battalions, both 64th Brigade, 21st Division.

> The 7th (Service) Battalion The Norfolk Regiment, 35th Brigade, 12th (Eastern) Division, New Army, were new to the Loos battlefield
> Major John Clayton Atkinson, Temporarily Commanding 7th Norfolk Regiment
> Probably Captain John Hammond, 7th Norfolk Regiment

We receive pleasant news that the French have taken 35000 prisoners and 100 guns.

There is much shelling of our trench during the day & 6 men get buried but are got out alive. It is an anxious time for all concerned.

The relief is supposed to be at 7 p.m. but, partly owing to a limber catching fire & lighting up the whole country it was delayed & my Coy did not get away till past midnight – very tired & hungry – the men having no water or food or anything till arriving back on

Oct 1st

at VERQUIGNEUL about 6 a.m. after a long weary muddy wet march over the back part of the battlefield – seeing many more ghastly sights. They are bundled into billets, Hammersley and self together in a room & we sleep on till noon – I never saw such a sleepy crowd – we had been out & about with hardly any sleep for 5 days & nights – a ration of rum was given out before the men turned in.

2nd

Thorpe & Grainger are sent home which again puts me in command of the Battn, so I spend a busy day – first a C.O.'s conference, when Genl Haking came and thanked the Division for their assault & digging on 27th_ Gen Sir John French also came round & addressed the men quite unceremoniously in the street – I was very sorry to miss seeing him.

Then in the afternoon I went with Alby Cator who commands the 2nd Battn to arrange as to dividing up Officers & we get Jack Stirling, Con Seymour, Tim O.E., Lechmere, Purvis, and Ward, so ought to get on pretty well. There is also the question of NCO's to settle.

Hear that Esmé Gordon Lennox is to come out to command this Battn, which is lucky for it.

Captain John Alexander Stirling, known as "Jack"

Lieutenant Ernest Pellew Orr Ewing, known as "Tim", †15.9.16, Miles Barne's brother in law

Lieutenant Nicholas George Berwick Lechmere †17.10.15

Lieutenant Arthur Frederick Purvis

Lieutenant Francis Ward

In the event Lieutenant Lechmere did not come. While the others returned to the 2nd Scots Guards later, Lieutenants Orr Ewing and Ward stayed for good.

Lieutenant Colonel Lord Charles Esmé Gordon Lennox had been with Miles Barne at Headquarters 16th Brigade in the Boer War. Serving with the 2nd Scots Guards at the start of the War, he was wounded in October 1914 during First Ypres.

Sunday Oct 3rd

The Battalion now under my command moves at short notice from VERQUIGNEUL to our old friend VERMELLES – where we go into billets as reserve Battalion of the Reserve Bde of the Division.

Spend day re-organizing, making NCO.'s etc – continuing equipping

Five Officers join us from 2nd Bn., viz Jack Stirling, Conway Seymour, Tim O.E., F. Ward & Purvis. This latter sees his brother's death in newspaper during evening. A very noisy night – our own guns chiefly doing most of it – many of them are close to us.

Lieutenant John Ralph Purvis, 9th (Service) Battalion The Rifle Brigade †25.9.15

4th

Wrote several letters otherwise rather an idle day, in afternoon go out with 4 Coy Commanders to arrange about wiring tonight in front of a certain trench – but owing to lack of picket pegs, only 1 Coy (B.) is able to go and do the work.

With Miles Barne's papers is a document copied out by someone who sent it to Violet Barne several weeks later, the handwriting on the envelope being the same. A few of the initials and ranks may not have been correctly transcribed and no regimental numbers were included.

Copy of a letter
From the N.C.O & men of B. Coy 1st Batt. Scots Gds.
To the Officer Commanding B. Coy 1st Batt. Scots Gds.

In the Field
2nd Oct. 1915.

Sir

We the undersigned on behalf of the N.C.O.s & men of B. Coy. respectfully beg to submit that this our application be submitted to the Brigadier 2nd Gds Brigade.

That the conduct of Captain Miles Barne on the 27th of September 1915 and subsequent days be brought to notice, he having by his coolness, ability and example kept his Company together at a most critical time, & also having repeatedly gone out in front of our trenches to rescue wounded men whilst under fire from the enemy, and that the conduct of Lieutenant H.C. Hammersley during the same period be also brought to notice his cheerfulness and example being of the greatest value and he also having several times gone out in front to rescue wounded.

We are

Sir

Your obedient servants

C.G. Clarke Sergt.
G.W. Moore Sergt.
J. Shannon Sergt.
F. Bennett A.Sergt.
J.N. McPhail
J. Fellows Pte.
W.H.Crowe S/Cpl
W. Matthews Pte
L. Bird Pte
P.J. Carter Pte
J. Matthews
A. Thomson Corpl.
E. Rogers Sgt.
J Peddie Pte.
C. Hughes Cpl

3289 Sergeant Cecil George CLARKE, Acting Company Sergeant Major †24.4.16
5919 Sergeant George William MOORE †15.9.16
5324 Sergeant Jeremiah SHANNON, later 2nd Lieutenant 7/8th Battalion The King's
    Own Scottish Borderers †1.8.18
8785 Acting Sergeant Frederick Claude BENNETT
10749 Private John Neil McPHAIL †13.9.16
9645 Private John FELLOWS
9247 Sergeant William Harvey CROWE †28.2.18
Possibly 9886 Private William J MATTHEWS, later Royal Flying Corps
12011 Private Lance BIRD †30.3.16
11900 Private Percy John CARTER, later 2nd Lieutenant The Middlesex Regiment
10755 Lance Corporal Joseph MATTHEWS †1.5.16

9516 Lance Corporal Alexander THOMSON †25.4.16
Possibly 9193 Sergeant Edward Joseph RODGERS, later 2nd Lieutenant 10th Battalion
    The Cameronians †24.4.17
11621 Private John PEDDIE
Possibly 11005 Lance Corporal Reginald HUGHES, later Labour Corps

Nothing significant came of this, though Lieutenant Hammersley was mentioned in dispatches not long afterwards. However, Captain Thorpe was awarded the MC.

On 3 October Captain Conway Seymour wrote to his mother who copied out part of the letter and sent it to Violet with a covering note.

Miles is at present commanding the Batt. I have got left flank Co with Tim Orr-Ewing as my Subaltern. I hear that Miles did most awfully well as my Colour Sergt told me he saved absolutely his Company by good judgement & pluck, he also crawled over the parapet in broard daylight, & in full view of the enemy to get in some wounded, a most gallant act as of course they were fired on all the time. I hope he will get due recognition. Tell Violet this as Miles won't.

Until 1913 infantry battalions were organized into eight companies, the senior NCO in each being their Colour Sergeant. Subsequently, with the introduction of the four company battalion, the appointment of Company Sergeant Major came into being. To begin with these were often still referred to as Colour Sergeants.

Between 27 and 30 September the 1st Scots Guards lost twelve officers wounded and two missing. Of those mentioned by Miles Barne earlier and still with the Battalion on 27 September there were wounded:- Lieutenant Colonel Godman, who would return, Major Orr Ewing, who recovered but went to the 2nd Battalion, his first wound having been on New Year's Day 1915 at the Railway Triangle, Sir Victor Mackenzie who would return in the autumn of 1917, his first wound having been in October 1914 during First Ypres, Captain Poynter who recovered sufficiently to become an ADC to Lieutenant General Sir William Pulteney, and Captain Thorpe, Lieutenant Ellis, Lieutenant Liddell Grainger and Lieutenant Mervyn Jones who would all return. Lieutenant Fergusson, hit in the knee, was the only one permanently disabled. After they came out of the line it was reported that twenty seven men were killed, three hundred and twenty four wounded and ninety three missing. If reported missing that could mean known to be dead, but unburied.

Miles Barne wrote to Lieutenant Colonel Godman once they were at Vermelles to ask how he was and tell him such news as he had. The reply did not come till 29 October and contained information about the wounded officers in so far as Lieutenant Colonel Godman had any. He went on to say how he had heard how well Miles Barne had done and hoped that he would receive due recognition. Miles Barne sent the letter to Violet Barne after writing quickly at the bottom of it,

I only send this as you say you like seeing me praised! Keep it to yourself please.

5

The Hohenzollern Redoubt

To the immediate north of the Vermelles-Hulluch road the 7th Division, Regular Army, had attacked on 25 September due east over very open ground, capturing The Quarries, short of the junction with the Lens-La Bassée road. To their left the 9th (Scottish) Division, New Army, attacked from in front of the Hohenzollern Redoubt. This, protruding out of the main German front line, was on slightly higher ground than that around it, shown on modern maps as Le Mont d'Auchy, and gave good observation over the British trenches. The Germans had begun to link it into their trench system and fortify it thoroughly. The 9th Division captured it, captured The Dump, a large slag heap behind it, and were well on towards capturing the workings and buildings of Fosse 8, the mine north of The Dump. However, the casualties had been such that, without reinforcements, which could not materialise in time, neither of these exhausted Divisions could hold on. Both began to be pushed back and those who took over from them could not hold on either. Although the 2nd Guards Brigade were then back in reserve, by dawn on 2 October the other two Guards Brigades were already manning the line in the neighbourhood of the Vermelles-Hulluch road. Then on 4 October the Germans drove the 28th Division, Regular Army, almost completely out of the Hohenzollern Redoubt and fortified it further. This led to the rapid redeployment of the Guards Division more to the left of where they had been.

5th

Orders for a move arrive early, I & 4 Coy Officers have to go and meet Brigadier in Trenches which we take over from 83rd Bde, Gen. Ravenshaw, pouring rain_ the Battn parades at 5 p.m. being heavily shelled at VERMELLES just before we start, one shell (heavy) falling almost on doorstep of Officers' mess – only 1 man wounded – we go through the most dreadfully slow relief and are not eventually fixed up and taken over till 4 a.m. on

> Brigadier General Hurdis Secundus Lalande Ravenshaw, Commanding 83rd Brigade, 28th Division

6th

We are told to work very hard and be very busy for the next few days – are in some very muddy & neglected trenches – full of equipment, old "gas" plant – evidently used on Sept. 25th – dead bodies, etc etc. We are just opposite Hohenzollern Redoubt most of which is held by the Germans, about 200x away_ we get thoroughly shelled and are having several men wounded, personally have had one or two narrow escapes, but I suppose this occurs every day.

Meet Geo. Montgomery & his Battn Doctor wandering about the trenches having had nothing to eat for 24 hours, their Battn HQ servants having lost their way – luckily we are able to help them.

Our ration party goes down at 6 p.m. but gets lost on the return journey and does not eventually turn up until about 2 a.m. Quite a lively night with incessant firing – I feel a little anxious at being weakened by the ration party's long absence.

7th

A long walk round with the Brigadier who shewed me the work required to be done. He (Gen John Ponsonby) is certainly a very pleasant man to deal with._

Delighted to hear that a draft of 2 Offrs and 268 men is on its way to us and should arrive this evening.

8th

The draft arrives early_ we spend a very strenuous morning arranging as to installing the gas plant – making recesses etc, and about 2 p.m. a severe shelling contest on both sides begins. We have 3 men killed and some wounded including 2 officers very slightly – Trafford and Ward. Ian Colquhoun brings the draft – a very useful and dependable officer.

> Installing gas dischargers was a preliminary for a forthcoming attack on the Hohenzollern Redoubt currently being prepared. It did not involve the Guards Division.
>
> Captain Sir Iain Colquhoun of Luss, Bt, was wounded in November 1914 during First Ypres
>
> Three of the four men who died that day had just arrived in the draft, having left London on 3 October.
> 6988 Private John Edwin Leigh Wright was wounded slightly during First Ypres and then sent home sick earlier in 1915 †8.10.15
> 12815 Private Robert Wilson †8.10.15
> 12963 Private Robert McDonald †8.10.15
> The fourth was 9867 Private James Cockshott †8.10.15

About 3.30 p.m. an attack is made on the 3rd Bn Gren Guards who are advanced to our right front. They repel the infantry attack but suffer severely by being taken in reverse by a heavy bomb attack out of an old German Trench. We send off B. and L.F. Coys under Hammersley and Con Seymour respectively, who spend an exciting & unpleasant evening and night. There is

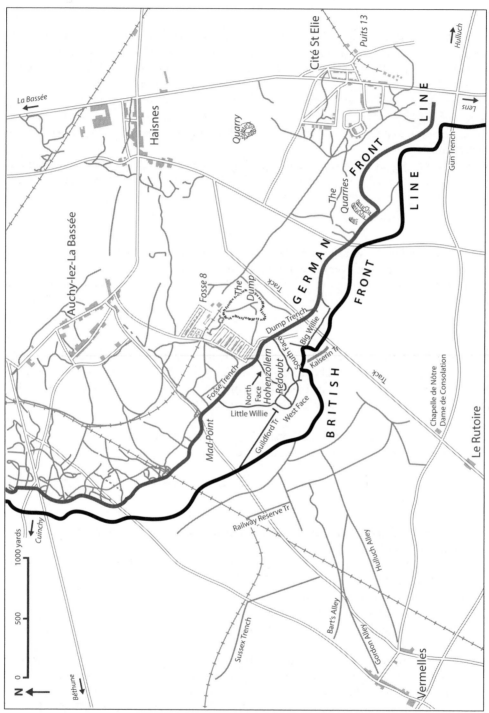

Map 4 Battle of Loos, Hohenzollern Redoubt, October 1915.

more bombing during the night, but the Grenadiers retake a portion of trench which they lost, and by morning all is quiet.

> The bombing attack on the 3rd Grenadier Guards caused serious damage. When they took over in the line on the night of 4 October the layout was uncertain, they were in some places very close to the Germans and their left led in a finger directly towards the Hohenzollern, as Miles Barne found out later. In the attack on 8 October the Germans rushed them on the left and bombed along the front line. The Grenadiers had to give way into the communication trenches while they reorganized, having suffered very heavy casualties. Nearby were the 3rd Coldstream Guards from whom 6738 Lance Sergeant Oliver Brooks, on his own initiative, led an entirely successful counterattack and restored the situation. He was awarded the VC.

It was a most disturbed & in some ways anxious night for me, or rather for the 2 Coys out, and am sent 2 Coys of the 2nd Battn under Hill and Orr.

> Captain William James Montague Hill
> Captain Arthur Roxburgh Orr was wounded in October 1914 during First Ypres
>   †17.10.15

9th

All the morning taken up with going round the Grenadier Trenches & learning the lie of the land – a terrible sight – the trench being scattered with mangled corpses, and many more on the parapets.

Am getting perfectly filthy not having had a bath or shaved or even washed my hands since we came into the trenches on 5th. Goodness only knows when we shall get out._ Our mode of living has been very primitive and our diet and cooking of the simplest. Nights are disturbed by (amongst other things) rats scratching & dropping bits of straw earth etc on our faces. Am sharing a dug-out with the Adjutant Thompson, and the Doctor – Stuart – appears for meals.

> Captain James Smith Stewart, Royal Army Medical Corps, became Regimental Medical Officer just before the 1st Scots Guards were withdrawn from First Ypres.

In afternoon we carry out relief of 3rd Bn Gren Guards in the forward trenches, with one trench practically ending in Hohenzollern Redoubt. Am relieved by Morrison who commands the 4th Bn Gren Gds which Battn relieves us, and the double relief goes off quite smoothly, barring a bit of a fracas between Col. Corry and Con Seymour. A bombing attack is made on the 1st Guards Bde on our right, but ends in smoke. A peaceful night after about 7 p.m., very close quarters in a tiny dugout – the Adjutant, a signaller, an Artillery Observation Officer and myself. The Adjt sleeps on the floor, and I in a niche just above him. The night is rather a worrying one as we are at work all the time and have a difficulty keeping up the supply of sandbags.

> Captain James Archibald Morrison, Temporarily Commanding 4th Grenadier Guards

10th. Sunday

Quiet morning, but a lot of shelling in the afternoon – can hear a terrific bombardment by the French away to the South.

In the evening the 2nd Bn Gren (on our right) organize a bomb attack rather in front of us, and ask us to cooperate, which I decline not having many bombers & of them 8 are borrowed & inexperienced Grenadiers – we having lost so many on Sept 27th._ However we undertake to help in a passive sort of way for mutual protection – the result is a terrific bombing contest which lasts most of the night, and our B. Coy under Hammersley do a great deal of firing to help. The Grenadiers find the job a harder one than they anticipated and do not make as much headway as they hoped. However, in spite of counter attacks, they hold what they get.

During the day some very polite & complimentary messages arrive from the Divisional and Corps and Army commanders about the action on 8th, mentioning our two companies which went up to support the Grenadiers.

11th

The French at it again away on our right._

We are getting a good many casualties in the Battalion – several caused by shelling – in one case 6 men were killed & buried all in a lump together, and some are being shot by snipers through the head._

    6841 Private James Rennie †10.10.15
    8996 Private Robert Charles Walker †10.10.15
    9829 Private William Muir †10.10.15
    9847 Private Richard Thomas Stoddart †10.10.15
    9872 Private James Whittet †10.10.15
    10373 Private Robert Davie †10.10.15

There are a few funny episodes which should be recorded – for instance in the Battn a certain Captain D. of 3/Gren is a standing joke – in the trench we dug & held near Loos Sept 27th et seq, he was next to us & kept sending down anxious messages "Are the Coldstream still holding the Chalk Pits?" "If the Coldm leave the Chalk Pits let me know at once." "What are the Scots Guards doing?" The answer sent back to this is said to be "Feeling very cold & trying to keep warm."_ Colquhoun's wrath was excited against this same Officer by receiving this message, "Please let me know before the Scots Guards retire"!

Some wounded in Hospital told our padre Gillison that one of his messages was "The enemy going to attack, stand to arms" and I am said to have sent back the answer, "We are ready for them! Go away!"

After being told we are to be relieved today, again deferred till

12th

The relief, a most complicated business, is ordered to begin at 4.45 p.m. & by the orders should be over by 11 p.m., but owing to the enormous number of troops in the communication trenches, everything got delayed & the whole Battalion was not clear of the trenches till 6 a.m. & did not reach our billets at VAUDRICOURT till 9 a.m., the men very weary and exhausted, about an 8 mi march.

For me it was a very anxious night, and I found the only thing to do was to get out of the trenches altogether and down to VERMELLES on the top of the ground. The last 2 Coys to get away were L.F. and C, & this was a race against the daylight, it was just touch & go, as it was we were only spotted at the last minute, tho' I never know why not sooner, & fired on, but no casualties.

We dived into the first empty trench we came to which was not for some time & were then safe.

During the night while relieving some heavy shell fire was turned onto us & we had some casualties including one poor signaller buried. One shell lit on parapet a few feet from where the Adjt & myself were, it ½ stunned me & buried the Adjt all but his face; when I recovered I realized he was under a heap of earth & began scraping with the handle of my stick (it was too dark to see his face) & heard a squeal, & found I hooked his eye! We were not long getting him out. When his head was sticking out he remarked "I'm all right" & all through has been of the utmost value & shown great pluck. I have recommended him for a D.S.O., & much hope he will get it. Have also sent in several other recommendations – one who carried Victor McKenzie out of action – Corp. in L.F. has already obtained the D.C.M.

5550 Private James Gammack, signaller, †13.10.15
10437 Lance Corporal James Aitken was awarded the DCM

The large number of troops in the communication trenches, which caused the prolonged relief, was ahead of the attack by the 46th (North Midland) Division, T.F., on the Hohenzollern Redoubt and the German line immediately north of it early the following morning, a failure with heavy casualties. Some did get well into the Hohenzollern, only to be eliminated or driven out. The report in the evening was completely inaccurate.

[Although in the Diary as on 12 October this next paragraph refers to events on 13 October]

In afternoon received a visit from Alby Cator, cmdg our 2nd Battn who wants back some of the Officers he lent us, but we found we were level so I cd not let any go. He is splendid and is just as keen about our efficiency as his own. In the evening we hear Hohenzollern is captured & also the DUMP and we are digging in on the LENS LA BASSÉE road.

13th Oct. 1915

Arrived in billets 9 a.m. after our arduous & anxious night – had breakfast & then straight to bed till 1 p.m., when tubbed & shaved off my long grey beard, & got things a bit square. de Teissier rejoined the Bn.

Captain Geoffrey Fitzherbert de Teissier was wounded in October 1914 during First Ypres

14th

Powell joined the Battn. In afternoon had to go to Bde H.Q. to hear instructions to C.O.s on many points._

Lieutenant Ronald Vanneck Powell

15th

Spent a whole long morning practising the whole Battalion at bombing – which is now the most up to date form of warfare.

At 2 p.m. had to scurry off to see the Bdr at BARTS near VERMELLES, the Bde following on at 3 p.m. – the Battn occupying some safe trenches well back._

He was presumably meeting Brigadier General Ponsonby at the point where Barts Alley, a communication trench, began east of Vermelles.

16th

A day of fatigue parties, cleaning up and repairing many communication trenches. Frogs & mice.

In the evening the 3/GG do a bomb attack.

17th

A bomb attack by 1/Coldm & 3rd Gds Bde combined, mostly our 2nd Battn. They found they could not make much progress owing to the Germans having filled up some trenches, so that our men came under heavy machine gun fire from the DUMP.

We spent the night carrying up bombs & ammunition, and the men are very weary.

Hear the 2nd Battn has lost Orr & Shelley killed, Lechmere. Warde and Clarke wounded. also a good number of other ranks.

At nightfall we relieve the 3rd Grenadiers in the forward trenches, the relief not being over till 2 a.m., owing to the guides not turning up.

Unlike the attack by the 46th Division, carried out in the open, now seen to be flawed, that by the Guards Division was by working up trenches throwing grenades. Loos was the first time operationally that the BEF had the Number 5 Grenade, better known as the Mills Bomb, used here and from now on as the standard grenade. This attack achieved a little, but at no little cost, and was thwarted as much as anything because the attackers had no (and could not have had) reliable knowledge of the layout of the enemy trenches that they were attacking. The Germans had converted some into dead ends and wherever they had placed machine guns there was no way past. The other flaw, but now being remedied, as Miles Barne described on 15 October, was that currently grenade training was still only a specialist skill so, in an attack of this type, if the trained bombers became casualties, others did not know how the grenades worked.

Captain Arthur Roxburgh Orr †17.10.15
Lieutenant Cecil William Charles Shelley †17.10.15
Lieutenant Nicholas George Berwick Lechmere †17.10.15
Lieutenant Richard Edward Warde
Lieutenant Edmund Stephenson Clarke

18th

My little Elizabeth's birthday – & I never wrote to her_
Meet Harry Seymour who now commands 4th Grens, and arrange with him about digging a new trench tonight – close to the Germans – so there may be a lively time.
Go into Hohenzollern Redoubt at least the part held by the 1st Coldstream.

Lieutenant Colonel Lord Henry Seymour, known as "Harry" and nicknamed "Copper", Commanding 4th Grenadier Guards, Miles Barne's first cousin

19th

R.F. Coy have made a good start with the new trench – it is to be the new front line: I meet Davidson of our Divl Staff, a very sound sort of fellow & we have quite a business to get the right line to meet the new trench being dug from the other end – put up 2 scarlet petrol tins as marks which the Germans amuse themselves by sniping at.
It is pitiful to see the huge number of British dead, lying round the Hohenzollern, many had got right bang up to the barbed wire and were forcing their way through, which of course many must have done as the redoubt was taken_
About 4 p.m. a tremendous fusillade was started, which turned out to be a German attack on a piece of trench which they recently lost – but while it lasted, such a din as is not often heard. It died away about 8 p.m. result not known, but very disquieting while it lasted_ we had 2 killed and 7 wounded, but were very lucky, and several men buried were dug out again.

Major N R Davidson, Royal Horse Artillery, GSO 2 Guards Division

The enemy attack Miles Barne could hear over to the right was on the 12th Division, who repelled it.

9223 Corporal Wilfred Cecil Stocker †19.10.15
12387 Private Gilbert Paterson Ryan †19.10.15
12743 Lance Corporal Neville Francis Watts Clarkson †18.10.15

20th

Our new trench still making good progress.
In course of morning met Jerry Ruthven – now on divl staff – at the new trench & he was much interested.
Jack Stirling is a most useful Officer and full of enterprise, of unceasing energy._

We are now in a very deep dugout in the chalk – very safe from shells (though in one case the concussion actually blew out our candle), and our mess consists of Thompson the Adjt, Stuart the Doctor, and myself – we breakfast & lunch up in daylight and sup below.

Are relieved by 3rd Grenadiers in evening & return back to Sussex Trench near VERMELLES, well & safely away from bombs but not for long for on

21st

we go back to front trenches, relieving two Battns – the 9th H.L.I. (Glasgow Highlanders) & 2nd Worcesters – of the 5th Bde – Charlie Corkran's – found some very good & clean trenches.

We seem now to be in the only active bit of the line, judging by the English Newspapers – everything of interest happens about HULLUCH VERMELLES and LOOS, as well as the Hohenzollern Redoubt, just where we are.

> 9th Battalion The Highland Light Infantry (The Glasgow Highlanders), T.F., and the 2nd Battalion The Worcestershire Regiment, both 5th Brigade, 2nd Division, Regular Army

22nd

No special excitements till about 7.30 p.m. when a message arrives saying the GOC has reason to believe the Germans contemplate making an attack within the next 3 days etc, so we go to bed (a granite-like board covered with sandbags crawling with mice) feeling rather jumpy.

A visit from G. Trotter, who is going to take over from us on the morrow, with 1st Grenrs; he brings the very sad news that George Montgomerie of 3rd Grenrs has been killed by a sniper – shot through the eye. He had left the trench to go & help 2 wounded men.

> Lieutenant Colonel Gerald Frederick Trotter, Commanding 1st Grenadier Guards

23rd

No attack during the night, after all.

We are relieved by 1st Grenadiers, Col. G. Trotter, during the evening and go into billets at ANNEQUIN, a mining village close behind the line, frequently shelled, but we get off without.

24th

To my astonishment who should appear early in the day but Esmé Gordon Lennox to take over from me, so I am deposed. He was very badly wounded exactly a year ago today, shot through his arm & lungs, the bullet lodging right up against his heart. I am to be 2nd in command for a bit, which means nothing to do.

25th

The Doctor, Stuart, is very ill, high tem. and unable to move with us through BETHUNE, where we entrain, detraining at LILLERS, and marching on to BOURECQ and ST HILAIRE, half a Battn at each place, Battn HQ at the former in quite a clean villa – pouring with rain all the time – and we all got drenched through & through.

I don't think I told in former diary how on Sept 27th about 2 a.m. while advancing towards Loos, two Germans were found in a small dug-out where we halted – old German Line – busy telephoning back to their own H.Q., brave men. they were hauled out and shot which I thought unnecessary.

This incident appears to have occurred as the 2nd Guards Brigade moved forward from the old German front line on the Grenay Ridge.

Hear Lechmere has died of wounds.

About 18th a German Aeroplane is brought down by 4 of ours behind our lines – the pilot & observer being both taken prisoner unwounded: this occurred close to our Transport, to the great joy & amusement of our Padre and Kinlay, the Quartermaster.

Miles Barne received a letter dated 24 October 1915.

Dear Miles

As you have just handed over to Esme Lennox – I should like to tell you how very pleased I was with the way that you commanded the Battalion during the last 3 weeks at a very strenuous period for everyone – I can only tell you I was more than satisfied and felt great confidence in you as I am sure was the case with all in the Battalion under you – I have told the Major General of this and hope he will note it I can only thank you most sincerely for the excellent work you and your Battalion have done during this hard time

Yours sincerely

John Ponsonby

6

The Start of Winter 1915-16 at Neuve Chapelle

The 1st Scots Guards, having left the Loos battlefield for good, spent the next twelve days resting, reorganising and training at Bourecq and St Hilaire, well out of the line away to the west of Lillers.

26th

Stuart is better. Walk with Esmé in afternoon, ending up with tea at Brigade H.Q., where a large party assemble including Billy Darell on Divl H.Q. Staff, and Derek Keppel who is over with the King.

> Lieutenant Colonel William Henry Verelst Darell, Coldstream Guards, Assistant Adjutant & Quartermaster General, Guards Division
> Lieutenant Colonel The Honourable Derek William George Keppel, Master of the Household

27th

A longish walk with Esmé across to HAM where Skeffington-Smith and 4th Bn Coldstream is, living in the very interesting remains of an old Monastery with some beautiful old carvings & pannelling in oak. In the garden is reposing the remains of a statue of an old Knight in Armour, of 14th Century, with his shield hung on his left arm, showing he had been killed in action.

> Lieutenant Colonel Randall Charles Edward Skeffington Smyth, Commanding 4th Coldstream Guards, Pioneer Battalion Guards Division

I dine at Brigade H.Q., where the Brigadier is in great form and full of fun & talk.

28th

Intended to be of some historical interest by the King inspecting the Division. We start in a downpour, & get as far as LILLERS in a downpour when we hear the review is cancelled, and return to our billets in a downpour.

29th

The review was put off not because of the rain, but because the King fell off his horse & hurt himself_

Walk with Esmé in afternoon, meet Pembroke & others of the Household Cavalry.

Later walk by myself & find Paul Methuen sketching & take him on – a curious creature.

The Earl of Pembroke and Montgomery, The Royal Horse Guards
Lieutenant The Honourable Paul Ayshford Methuen, 1st Scots Guards

30th

Bombing practice nearly all day. Jerry Ruthven comes over in the morning and tells us we are going to "nibble" by bombing attacks all the winter – a pleasing prospect!

31st

Wet – start a walk with Esmé but are driven home by rain – meet Colquhoun & walk with him to see the Coldstream._ On arrival back at Battn H.Q. find Seymour [appears to be his brother, Lieutenant Seymour Barne], also John Thorpe returned, to take over 2nd in command from me, and I return to Company duty, this time with L.F. Coy – my subalterns being Conway Seymour, & Tim O.E., at least the former is a Captain.

I go for a walk with Seymour which does one good.

Join the Left half Battn Mess which consists of L.F. Coy & C – the latter being Colquhoun, Methuen, Ward & McKay.

Lieutenant James Ian Macdonald McKay

Nov. 1st

Kit inspection and bombing, and inspection of billets by C.O.

My new billet is in a very nice clean room in a Brewery. It looked, I thought, a dear old building, well coloured & picturesquely matured by age – however I am rather startled to find a stone in wall with date – 1873!

The brewery was a year older than he was.

Wet all day. Bombed.

2nd

Ditto. More bombing.

3rd

Route march with C. Coy. More bombing.

Football match – left half Battn against 1st Coldstream which we won 2 to 0_ Grenadier Band came to play while this was going on.

Wire entanglement practice.

From this time on one of the five Regimental Bands was almost constantly out with the Guards Division. All were based in London. Divisional Bands were a feature of the BEF's infantry divisions.

4th

Ditto and bombing.

A visit from Major Clowes of Beccles & the London Scottish who are in Lillers: also some of the 2nd Battn including Billy Wynne Finch come over, and we hear about their bombing attack when Orr, Lechmere and Shelley were killed.

Con Seymour returns from leave and announces his engagement to Miss Butler

Major George Charles Knylt Clowes, The London Scottish
Captain Conway Seymour and Kathleen Butler were married two months later.

5th

Walk into LILLERS with John Thorpe to see some 1st Divl Boxing, but such a crowd we could see nothing. Bought some candles and notebooks for my Company. C.S. returns to 2nd Bn.

Captain Seymour, on loan since the events at Puits 14 Bis, went back to the 2nd Scots Guards.

6th

The usual bombing – & walked with McKay.

7th

Rode over with John Thorpe to lunch with 2nd Bn, found Alby Cator, Lumsden, Wynne-Finch, there. Dick Coke who has recently come out, is away.

Lieutenant James Gordon Lumsden
Major The Honourable Richard Coke, known as "Dick", 2nd Scots Guards, was wounded shortly before Christmas 1914 in the trenches at Rouges Bancs

On 8 November the 1st Scots Guards moved to the reserve brigade area behind the trenches from Neuve Chapelle northwards, where the Guards Division spent most of the winter. The trench routine involved two brigades in the line and one back in reserve. Each brigade in the line had two battalions forward and two further behind, ready to intervene if needed and otherwise usually occupied on fatigues, including resupply of those in front.

8th

An early rise, march at 6.45 a.m., beautiful morning, through HAM, BUSNES, ROBECQ, CALONNE, LA GORGUE, close to ESTAIRE to billets at a dirty big farm between the latter place and MERVILLE.

Quite the dirtiest billets I have ever been in – taken over from some Indian Troops.

The march was a long one, 15 or 16 miles, and a lot of men fell out. Their feet have got soft partly, and at BOURECQ no doubt they lived very well, and had all the beer they wanted.

> The Indian Corps were leaving the Western Front, their troops destined for the Middle East, after being in this part of the line since the previous autumn.

9th

Dug a trench to practice bombing – which we did in the afternoon, when I was hit on the temple by a splinter of a bomb – quite a narrow shave for my eye – in reality rather a good thing as it will cause us all to be more careful._ Our bombing Officer is McKay, a capital fellow very keen & quiet, has been in Lovat's Scouts.

Others who have recently joined are Ward, a stout member of a London Territorial Regt, now our authority on the Lewis Gun. Methuen, the eldest son of the Colonel of the Regt, is a curious tall delicate looking creature, pleasant when not too cynical, of artistic taste: is a Professor of Pretoria Museum when in private life, & was an Officer of the Wiltshire Yeomanry.

My new subaltern in L.F. is Martindale, who has lived in Canada for 3 years studying the Law.

John Dyer, a Captain, has returned to the Battn after being invalided, & sick for some time: an exceptionally nice little man, a nephew of "Little John" McGrigor._

There are many rumours about as regards the Germans being in a bad way, one of the strangest being an Advertt in one of their papers for sawdust free from glass & acids as a substitute for the "straw-flour" hitherto in use.

> At the beginning of the War each infantry battalion had two Maxim Machine Guns, on which the later Vickers Machine Gun was based. The number was increased to four in the spring of 1915. By this time the battalion machine gun teams were brigaded into machine gun companies and directed from brigade headquarters. Instead, the Lewis Gun was coming into service as the principal infantry support weapon, lighter than the Vickers, much more maneouverable and quicker to get into action. Currently three were issued per battalion, though the number would gradually increase and by later 1918 there were two per platoon.

> Lieutenant Francis Ward, on loan since Puits 14 Bis, stayed permanently
> 2nd Lieutenant Warine Frederick Martindale †15.9.16
> Captain Sir John Swinnerton Dyer, Bt, also known as "Jack", wounded in November 1914 during First Ypres, had since been out for some months in 1915, but was invalided to England shortly before Miles Barne first arrived, †31.7.17
> Colonel William Colquhoun Grant McGrigor, Scots Guards

Nov 10th 1915

Route march C and LF in morning.

In afternoon rode over with Colquhoun to tea with Jack Stirling in 2nd Battn, billeted about 3 miles away near MERVILLE – saw Dick Coke for the first time since he came out_ Foul cold wet weather. There is an aerodrome close here which is rather amusing.

11th

In afternoon rode with Colquhoun to tea with Roger Tempest who however was still out on an expedition with many C.O.'s etc to see the trenches which we are to take over. Found Warner (S. Gds) who is Heyworth's "Staff Captain" and Bury, the machine gun Officer both at home, & gave us tea. We had to go through MERVILLE & the 3rd Gds Bde H.Q. was by a big wood, BOIS DE NIEPPE. Awful wet cold showery weather.

12th

Route march with C. Coy. Later practised putting on the new P pattern smoke helmets: which caused a good deal of merriment.

The Padre dined last night and we played Nap – at which I lost 5 fr.

We are now in a very low lying flat country, every ditch full to the brim & quite the most dismal country I have ever seen – this would probably be so in June, but now_

We are only about 3 miles behind the firing line and can hear much gun firing and see the usual old "verrilights" going all night.

The P pattern smoke helmets were the current protection against gas. Calling them hoods, as they were also known, described them more accurately. They had two glass eye pieces and were impregnated with chemicals.

13th

Pouring – cancel parade but make a loophole under cover.

Walk with Colquhoun to see the flying ground nearby, the weather being tempestuous several machines are home.

Forgot to say I met Algy FitzRoy, who commands the Divisional Cavalry, on Monday the 8th

Captain The Honourable Edward Algernon FitzRoy MP, The 1st Life Guards, and Muriel FitzRoy were pre-war friends

14th

An aeroplane came down by accident in a ploughed field near our farm – this was at 8.30 a.m. so rather interrupted our Padre's voluntary service at 9 a.m. It had to be taken away in pieces.

At 11.30 a.m. we paraded & the Battalion marched to new billets at BOUT DEVILLE, not bad billets_ a fine day.

The Suffolk Regt 4th Battn are in the neighbourhood & I converse with some, who come from Halesworth Leiston etc. I hear the Suffolk Yeo. have had some casualties including A.B. Smith, who has a brother, a Corp. in this 4th Battn.

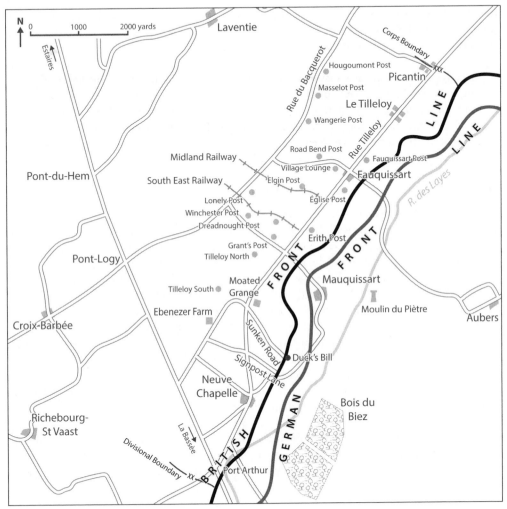

Map 5 Neuve Chapelle Area, Winter 1915-1916.

1/4th Battalion The Suffolk Regiment, T.F., had for a year been in the Jullunder Brigade
of the 3rd (Lahore) Division and, as the Indian Corps left France, were about to be
transferred to the 46th Brigade, 15th Division.
A.B. Smith, The Suffolk Yeomanry – untraced

15th

The 4 Coy Commanders go up into the trenches to reconnoitre, find them better than I expected,
quite wet & muddy, but we were able to avoid the communication trenches and keep above
ground. These would have been above our knees in places._

Because of the water table digging trenches was impossible in the part of the line that
other Guards Division battalions had already taken over. Since the beginning of January
both sides had built up systems of breastworks instead. These continued, however,
to be referred to as trenches. Miles Barne's and Left Flank's first experience of these
was around the Duck's Bill at Neuve Chapelle. This projected out from the rest of the
British front line to the east of the ruined village.

16th

We relieve the 3rd Grens in the trenches, a beautiful moonlight night, but the men are very
heavily laden and have a long walk & arrive rather weary, but have to work hard most of the night
– revetting and rebuilding. These are really not "trenches" at all, but are paths with parapets &
parados built – a wall each side – the ground is so wet & boggy, that anything you build below
ground is quickly full of water._ There is a very odd place which I have to hold in my Company,
viz "The Duck's Neck" & "Duck's Bill", a very awkward shaped place; which is sniped from all
round – however by morning we do a lot to improve it, & have no casualties there._

There are the most enormous rats, & such a number of them, in these trenches: huge brutes
which are extremely tame; Colquhoun says, if you try to hit or frighten them they turn round,
sit up & growl at you – they are very black & look like large kittens in the moonlight. Our dug
out is full of them & mice too – a perfect plague.

The Guards Divn has taken these trenches over from the Indian Corps – who seem to have
sadly neglected them, so that there is endless work to be done.

The Germans seem to be just as uncomfortable as we are, & we can see them throwing
the water over their breastworks – they also explode mines to form some place in which to
drain. There is an old mine crater just in front of the Ducks Bill which we occupy by night as a
"listening post", it is often a question as to which side gets there first, the crater being nearer the
German than our line.

17th

A big mine is exploded at 8.30 a.m. between the German & our line, I happen to be looking
in that direction at the time; those inside dugouts etc said they were shaken about for several
seconds, although the mine was ½ mile away.

One of our men, Watson, the Company "Sanitary man" is smothered to death by his (so
called) dug-out – really above ground – collapsing, the soil here is all so wet, he has been out
since the beginning of the war, & has been twice wounded.

5925 Private Hugh Shaw Watson †17.11.15

A lot of rain during the day which makes things very horrid, very cold at night, which was clear & a thick fog & white frost by sunrise on

18th

one of the prettiest I have ever seen._

"Ma" Jeffries, commanding 2nd Bn Grenadiers, Bill Beckwith, Coldstream, on XIth Corps Staff, the writer of the Daily Summary of Information, better known as the "Daily Liar" & several other outsiders, call at my Coy HQ, & I take them to see the Ducks Bill, which seems quite a famous place; it is very amusing to see their manner when going there, as they all think it dangerous & expect to be sniped at, & some are – we have no casualties, but this more by good fortune than anything else, some 100 shots were fired by snipers, one man got hit through his cap, we do a lot of building round the Ducks Neck with sandbags, & also during the night, owing to the wet soil, down comes one huge piece of our wall, but up it has to go again._ During the afternoon after much talk, we evacuate the Ducks Bill & neck, while the gunners shell a ruined house said to contain a sniper who was making himself very objectionable; this just before dusk, so I feel a little nervous till we again occupy the place.

about 7 p.m., 3 of my platoons are relieved by the same Coy of 3rd Gren from whom we took over – commd by Gordon Gilmour (a mere child), R Stanhope, owner of Revesby, being in the same Coy. The 4th platoon has to wait to be relieved & do not return to our billets at BOUT DEVILLE till past midnight, the remainder of us reaching there about 9 p.m. after a very weary 5 or 6 mile march, the men wet & tired, carrying amongst other things their long thigh rubber boots, now served out to them.

> Lieutenant Colonel George Darell Jeffreys, nicknamed "Ma", Commanding 2nd Grenadier Guards
> Captain William Malebisse Beckwith, Coldstream Guards
> Major Robert Gordon Gilmour, 3rd Grenadier Guards. The reference to him, born in 1857, as "a mere child" was a private joke.
> Captain The Honourable Richard Philip Stanhope, 3rd Grenadier Guards †16.9.16

When I return I am handed, to my delight, my warrant for returning home on leave.

19th

I shave & dress overnight & am called at 2.45 a.m. & walk into LA GORGUE to catch the 4 a.m. train, which does not start till 6.30 a.m.

Rather a long wait, which is made amusing in a small degree by the men marking time to keep their feet warm, & whistling or singing various popular songs – such an odd effect at a Rly Station. Am very sleepy, not having had much sleep the previous 2 nights, but have to walk or run up & down or dance to keep warm, bright frosty night with keen N.E. wind.

Some amusement is caused by the difficulty in finding a Officer to command the train; someone says he has seen a "pot-bellied major" on the platform, so the word goes all down the train for the said p-b-m; there is no competition! Arrive London about 5 p.m.

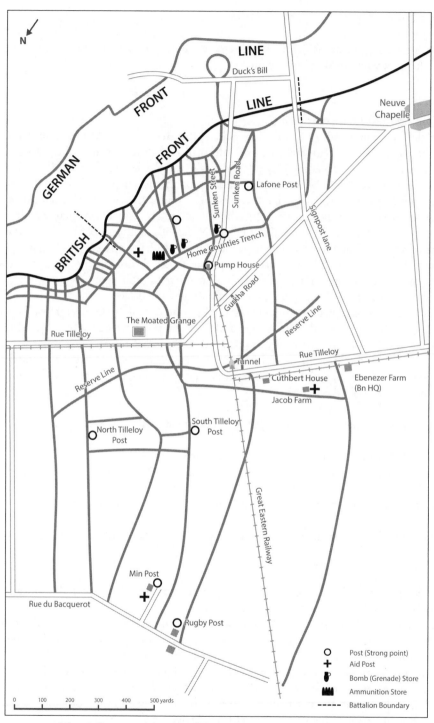

N

LINE

Duck's Bill

FRONT

LINE

FRONT

Neuve
Chapelle

GERMAN

Sunken Street

Sunken Road

Lafone Post

Signpost lane

BRITISH

Home Counties Trench

Pump House

Gurkha Road

Reserve Line

The Moated Grange

Rue Tilleloy

Rue Tilleloy

Tunnel

Reserve Line

Cuthbert House

Ebenezer Farm
(Bn HQ)

Jacob Farm

North Tilleloy
Post

South Tilleloy
Post

Great Eastern Railway

Min Post

Rue du Bacquerot

Rugby Post

○   Post (Strong point)
+   Aid Post
P   Bomb (Grenade) Store
♦♦♦   Ammunition Store
-----   Battalion Boundary

0   100   200   300   400   500 yards

Map 6 Breastworks north of Neuve Chapelle, Winter 1915-1916.

Lady Constance Barne †30.11.15

After my leave being extended in consequence of my very dear Mother's death and funeral, I leave London at 1.15 p.m. on Saturday

Dec. 4th

rough passage – seasick – via Boulogne, which reach 7.30 p.m. Go to Hotel de Paris & catch 4 a.m. train on Sunday

5th

for LA GORGUE, travelling with Colquhoun, C. Boyd-Rochford and Lionel Norman.

> Lieutenant Charles Cecil Boyd Rochfort, 1st Scots Guards, youngest brother of
>   Lieutenant George Arthur Boyd Rochfort
> Lieutenant Lionel Norman, 1st Scots Guards †15.9.16

Colquhoun & I walked out – a tedious business, calling en route & lunching with Baden, Divisional Bombing Officer, who was much like himself & full of inventions & ideas – mostly apparently coming to nought – also called on Alby Cator, Con Seymour, Jack Stirling and finally at our Battalion H.Q., where we had tea, then went on into the front trenches to join our respective Companies.

Found Tim OE looking very well – having quite a peaceful time – they have been busy draining all day.

Not a bad dug-out, but a popular rendez-vous for rats and mice. Everytime anybody woke up & turned over in the night one saw a rat dash out of the window._ The previous morning the servant opened the food box & found 5 mice inside, having the time of their lives.

The trenches are very wet and unpleasant, but might be worse._

6th

A quiet night on the whole, some sniping on both sides, and a good deal of gunning to the South._

By the way yesterday, just as Colquhoun & I were arriving at Battn H.Q. some shelling was going on at a neighbouring Batty, 2 shells bursting unpleasantly near our road – a warm welcome back after being on leave!

The C.O., accompanied by 2 Brigadiers, Ponsonby and Fielding, came round during the morning. The Germans are doing a lot of pumping, and as the fall is slightly from them to us, we get the full benefit of their water as well as ours.

> Brigadier General Geoffrey Percy Thynne Feilding, Commanding 1st Guards Brigade

7th

A good deal of rain in afternoon – walk round the village of LAVENTIE where we came into billets last night – does not seem to be nearly so much knocked about as many villages so near the firing line – we are in reserve here at 20 min notice.

Had tea with Geo. Lane, 4th Coldm, where found as an ensign one Dickinson, whom I remember at Eton, considerably senior to me – has never soldiered previously at all.

> Major George A O Lane, 4th Coldstream Guards
> Lieutenant Alan Henry Dickinson, 4th Coldstream Guards

Lionel Norman has come into L.F. Coy as my 2nd in command. He was out for six mo. previously and a very useful Officer.

A gale at night – a good deal of shelling – both sides, especially by our guns – during the day and night._

8th

Marched back to some billets about 1 mile S. of MERVILLE – rather scattered but my own room quite a clean one in a farm house. Battn H.Q. in the town.

9th

C.O. goes round billets. Kit Inspection. Wet all day.

10th

Another wet morning. Pay. & Inspectn of Rifles & Billets. In afternoon some bombing, and meet Col. McRae, R.F.A., who was with our Brigade a great deal in S. Africa. He seemed quite pleased to see me, and we knocked up some old reminiscences between us. I might have reminded him of one or two funny incidents about himself, as he rather lent himself to ridicule at times.

> Possibly Major Kenneth Matheson MacRae, Royal Field Artillery

11th

Woke up in the night at 3 a.m. to hear a tearing torrent just outside my window, I thought it was coming in – sheets of floods everywhere – & rising.

Attempted to march out with C Coy, but cd not get far – the men have no change.

More bombing practice, then rode with Colquhoun: were rather amused watching 2 6 inch guns being brought through the town and over one of the many canal bridges: it was too wide for the bridge in the ordinary way, so the roadway of the bridge had to be raised by building up with great baulks: thus allowing the guns to go between, or rather above the railings at the sides.

There was a man in C. Coy drowned last night, he seems just to have walked into a canal in the dark._

Repeatedly training had to be curtailed because the men did not have any change of clothing issued to them and often there was no means of drying wet clothes anyway.

> 13397 Private William Sharp †10.12.15

Squalls & gale all day – floods rising all day. Ride with Colquhoun.

The guns were being hauled along by motor engines with "caterpillar" wheels – the first I have ever seen.

12th

Floods still rising._

13th

Attended lecture by the Brigade Signalling Officer, in LA GORGUE._ all of us going thither in 2 motor bussis, one of which refused to go after a bit.

A clear fine cold day with N. wind.

Good deal of firing last night.

More bombing practice.

A visit from Geo. Paynter in the afternoon, accompanied by his brother-in-law Lockett.

> Lieutenant Colonel George Camborne Beauclerk Paynter, Scots Guards
> Major William Jeffrey Lockett, The 11th Hussars

Dec. 14th 1915

Met Winston Churchill in the street yesterday, a terrible looking person – never saw anything so unlike a soldier – such a low flabby face – more like an "unemployable" from the E. End.

> The Right Honourable Winston Leonard Spencer Churchill MP resigned as First Lord
> of the Admiralty following the failures in the Dardanelles and joined the Army. He was
> currently a Major under instruction with the 2nd Grenadiers. He had ridden as a war
> correspondent in the charge of the 21st Lancers at Omdurman.

Marched at 1 p.m. to billets at RIEZ BAILLEUL – a fearful spot of desolation – billets in real squalor – my own room in a cottage where there is a woman & 7 children, cant imagine where they all live, eldest 11, as there are 3 Officers, & the kitchen is permanently full of soldiers buying coffee. We have a company of 13th Welsh Fusiliers attached to the Battn, one platoon to each Company, for instruction. They do not begin to arrive from the trenches – 2 miles off – till 8 p.m. & go on straggling in up till midnight. 7 officers, all wanting to be fed!

> 13th (Service) Battalion The Royal Welsh Fusiliers, 113th Brigade, 38th (Welsh) Division,
> New Army, recently arrived on the Western Front

15th

Inspect billets & rifles & a "double" up the road, being a cold morning – dry E. wind.

The redeeming point about the place is that Baden-Powell is here with his Divisional Bombing School. Several of us went to tea there and read his papers etc. He has a 2nd in command called Thynne.

The 4th Grens, who were here before us, made an attack, or rather raid, 3 nights ago into the German trenches, which were barely occupied – they had 1 Officer & 3 men (Ponsonby the officer) hit – at least some say Ponsonby only fell into a hole & broke his leg.

> Lieutenant Richard Granville Thynne, The 1st Life Guards, later Scots Guards
> 2nd Lieutenant George Arthur Ponsonby, 4th Grenadier Guards

Again last night a raid was made and hardly any Germans were found – 1 was brought back as a Prisoner.

I hear Baden did his best to blow up the Prince of Wales yesterday by handing him a detonated bomb to play with, and letting him pull out the pin – by extraordinary good luck the fuse was a bad one, so it did not explode – really a dispensation of Providence. Baden dined with us in the evening.

> The Number 5 Grenades or Mills Bombs were inert when issued. The troops then had to insert the fuses, usually timed for five seconds, and detonators and screw them into the base of the grenade. This was called detonating, so a detonated grenade was a live one. A pin, attached to a ring, held the striker in place. Before throwing the grenade a soldier, still holding the striker firmly in place with his other hand, first pulled out the pin by its ring. When he threw the grenade that released the striker which sprang up and struck the detonator. It was quite normal to remove the pin and put it back again but the striker of a detonated grenade had to be firmly held while doing so.

16th

The little Pr. of Wales biked through in the morning, the road being 3 in deep in mud: I hope & suppose he does it because he likes to._

We parade at 3.30 p.m. & relieve the 3rd Gren Gds in the trenches. The C.O., having a very bad throat is left behind & goes on sick leave._

A good deal of sniping during the night.

My Coy is "in support", and divided into 4, at separate posts, and I live in comparative comfort at Battn H.Q. : poor Tim and a R. Welsh Fusilier Officer attached has a perfectly horrible place, wet and muddy, & "draughty"._

> "Forts" or "posts", for defence behind the forward breastworks, were later known as strong points. They were either formed from what was left of existing buildings or built up using sand bags and other materials. "Draughty" meant dangerous.

17th

In the afternoon there is a heavy Artillery duel to the South, just beyond NEUVE CHAPELLE. We have 1 man killed & 2 wounded, by snipers at dawn.

> 13912 Private William Dingwall †17.12.15

The trench boots issued to the men are capital things – I have been wallowing about in them all day & kept quite dry._

I go all round my 4 posts – some way apart. I find old Tim O.E. in the most terribly uncomfortable place – mud & water and a most wretched apology for a dugout. The men are still worse off, some of them quite unable to sit down all night – much less lie down. He is, however, bearing it all like a hero, and is as cheerful as anything when we go to see him.

18th

A very quiet night with one or two exceptional moments – a big Artillery duel early, and a batch of minenwerfer about 11 p.m.

> "Minenwerfer" were German trench mortars, the name having passed into British usage.

I walk round with Lionel Norman, who has rejoined after a go of lumbago, find Tim cheerful as ever.

We had a man wounded this morning. Also a German bullet came through the magazine of one of our Lewis Guns, but did no further damage._

A story: Tim O.E. (when a bunch of bullets were falling pretty fast & near by) "It's all right, they are not likely to hit us, they dont know we are here"

Pte – "They are d—d good guessers then, that is all I can say"._

Another. Some men of C. Coy were having some conversation across to the Germans one of whom called out: "We can't hear, tell somebody with a good voice to try" – when up spoke a braw Highland Laddie, & said in stentorian tones: "Hoo's the Crown Prince?", but he rolled his r's to such an extent that all that cd be heard was a loud burring noise, to everyone's amusement.

We are relieved by 3rd G.G. in the evening, without adventure.

19th

Rifle & Billet Inspectn.

Paid visit to Baden who gave J. Thorpe & self tea.

In same billets as last time.

We have a new Coy of Welsh Fusiliers (15th Bn) attached to us.

> 15th (Service) Battalion The Royal Welsh Fusiliers, also 113th Brigade

20th

Wrote letters in morning.

Relieved 3rd G.G. in trenches in afternoon – Eaton's Coy, a nasty little ratty dugout – very cramped even without the long legged Welsh Fusilier Officer who is with us._

A great lot of machine gunning during the relief, but we had nobody hit – right flank had 2 or 3 casualties: B. Coy is in the "Duck's Bill" etc. on our right – C. Coy is in the horrid support trench where we were last time.

> Captain The Honourable Francis Ormond Henry Eaton, 3rd Grenadier Guards

21st

A quiet night, but such a beastly wet day the mud & water simply unspeakable. Mice simply swarm in our dugout, & L.N. was amused to see them running over my lap while sitting asleep last night.

A rat has his hole just behind where Tim sits at meals, so has to crawl there under Tim's arm.

We do a lot of work during the day, building up parapets, draining and pumping._ A certain amount also at night, especially by moonlight.

22nd

Fine early but wet as usual by midday.

Thorpe, our C.O. is hit by a rifle grenade, in the "Duck's Bill" about 11 a.m., so, as Esmé is away on leave, I again become C.O. of the Battalion for a few days.

We are relieved by 3rd G.G. & return to billets at RIEZ BAILLEUL again.

The C.O. of the Welsh Fusrs, Col. Bell, is with us, a very nice little man who has been some time in the Indian Cavalry, & and a great friend of Showers._

> Lieutenant Colonel Richard Carmichael Bell, Commanding 15th (Service) Battalion The Royal Welsh Fusiliers

> From before their marriages a great friend of Violet Barne's in Scotland was Christian Stirling, from Garden, Stirlingshire. Her husband was Lieutenant Colonel Herbert Lionel Showers, Indian Army. Their son Lionel married Miles and Violet Barne's daughter Elizabeth in 1944.

23rd

The Billets are nearly as muddy as the trenches. One Hopley of 3rd G.G. is sick & staying back with us: he doesn't seem very bad, & manages to eat some of the excellent plum pudding & brandy sauce which Violet has sent me.

> Lieutenant John Hopley, 3rd Grenadier Guards, and England rugby international

24th

In morning a Medical Officer from the Division arrived & came round our billets, so was able to make application for many items which would help to make the men more comfortable. Many of these we had already applied for the previous day through Alston of the Divl Staff, who came round to our mess._

> Major Francis George "Cook" Alston, Scots Guards, Deputy Assistant Adjutant & Quartermaster General, Guards Division

In afternoon we relieve the 3rd G.G. in the trenches.
A deal of shelling at night on both sides._

7

Christmas Day 1915 and the Consequences

Following the events of Christmas Day 1914 when many parts of the line saw informal truces, as Christmas approached in 1915 the British authorities were determined that there should be no repetition. That was why the British guns shelled the German front line more than usual. What occurred on Christmas morning at Neuve Chapelle would keep many occupied until 17 January, with Miles Barne and Sir Iain Colquhoun at the centre of it.

25th

Xmas Day. Guns very busy, but in our part not so the rifles._

About 8.30 a.m. a large number of Germans walked over the parapet – and an Officer came forward to ask Colquhoun for a truce till 1 p.m. He would not grant this, but granted ¾ hr to bury dead – both sides. Some of the companies on the left saw this, and also came out – & there was some handshaking and exchange of cigarettes & "souvenirs"._

By evening all was normal. I went down about 10 a.m. with the Brigadier, and we agreed that we could not have ordered our men to fire on the defenceless Germans who came over trusting us. They put up white flags & a Xmas Tree on the parapet (no candles dolls etc). In one case I hear there was a full rigged tree put up, candles & all.

However the Divisional Commander is much annoyed at the whole thing and no difference should have been made, all should have have been "as usual".

There is anxiety in higher quarters at night, and the Adjt has to go all round the trenches about midnight, so we do not get to bed till about 2.30 a.m. The most tiresome Xmas I ever spent.

At an unrecorded time later in the day a message from Headquarters 2nd Guards Brigade was sent to the 1st Scots Guards, marked <u>SECRET</u>,

The Major-General directs that you hold a full and concise enquiry immediately on what happened this morning.

He wishes to be informed on the following points:

Why the men left their parapets and on whose orders –
What actually occurred between the lines and how long the men remained between the lines – What was the strength of the party.
Proceedings of enquiry to be in this office by 9.p.m. tonight.
Acknowledge.
G. Rasch Captain.
Brigade Major.

Captain Guy Elland Carne Rasch, Grenadier Guards
This instruction was acted on but there is no surviving record of the report.

At 10.50 p.m. that night Captain Thompson, the Adjutant, sent a message to Headquarters 2nd Guards Brigade,

Have called for report from my front line and received the following aaa Begins Germans singing and shouting but none showing over parapet a large number of fires in German trenches Germans have for some time been shelling our front line also SUNKEN ROAD ends

At 11.15 p.m. Sir Iain Colquhoun sent a message from C Company to Battalion Headquarters,

I have been along coy front and the situation is entirely normal

At 11.35 p.m. Headquarters 2nd Guards Brigade circulated a fresh message,

A Court of Enquiry composed as under will assemble at WINCHESTER HOUSE at 9 a.m. to enquire into the circumstances under which a party belonging to 1st Bn Coldstream & 1st Bn Scots Gds left their parapets on 25th of Dec and held conversation with the enemy AAA Proceedings to be forwarded to this office by 11 30 a.m. 26th AAA Commanding Officers will warn all Officers & NCOs concerned to attend & will attend themselves
President Lt/Col the honble L Butler 2nd Bn Irish Guards
Members Captain M.B. Smith D.S.O. Coldstream Gds
Captain E. Vaughan 3/Grenadier Gds

Winchester House was a large strong point.
Captain Merton Beckwith Smith, Coldstream Guards, Staff Captain, 2nd Guards Brigade
Captain Eugene Napoleon Ernest Mallet Vaughan, 3rd Grenadier Guards

At 2.05 a.m. on 26 December the 1st Scots Guards sent a message to Headquarters 2nd Guards Brigade,

Adjutant has visited front line and reports as follows begins I visited each coy and found situation normal sentries on look out and no other men on fire steps no shouting or talking aaa No Germans showing above parapet and fires previously reported had gone out aaa I interviewed officers on duty in each coy and they reported that no Germans had shewn themselves during evening but that there had been large fires and much singing in German line previous to my visit aaa None of our men had been out except wiring parties aaa Several shots were fired by sentries during my visit but there was no reply by Germans aaa Company officers report shelling of our line previous to my visit and this occurred again just as I left at 1.15 a.m. ends

Later on 26 December Miles Barne received a hand written note from Brigadier General Ponsonby,

Dear Barnes

There had been yesterday afternoon and evening so many false reports going about as to what was going on in our front line that I thought it best to send you a message asking that your adjutant should go up personally as then we could have an independent witness – I know everything was all right after you were up there in the morning but it spread all over the country – Reports in from 19th Div to say we were all deserting! I write to you as you may have been very annoyed at my asking you to send Thompson up so I tell you the reason why

Yours sincerely

John Ponsonby

The 19th (Western) Division, New Army, were in the line south of the Guards Division.

Miles Barne continued diary entries:

26th

I hear a neighbouring Divn has spread the report that we were all deserting!

A Court of Inquiry in the morning on the whole business. The 1st Coldstream, & our 2nd Bn apparently were doing the same thing.

The fat is in the fire and the higher authorities are in a great state of mind about it all.

We are relieved in the evening by 1st Irish Guards.

I have to meet the Brigadier at Rouge Croix at 4.30, who tells me that Esmé is evacuated (invalided) & that Roger Tempest is taking over the Battalion.

I am evidently in disgrace & not allowed to command the Battalion any more!

27th

Roger Tempest arrives about 9 a.m., from being Brigade Major to 3rd Guards Brigade – & throws some light on the whole subject. Apparently he had seen Cavan, who was very much annoyed because I did not issue orders to shoot the Germans showing themselves. As the Brigadier (Ponsonby) was with me, and he never said anything was wrong, nor gave orders to shoot the unarmed Germans, but he stood himself on the firestep taking immense interest in everything, I concluded that nothing very wrong was being done.

No hint was ever given me that a great point was made of "no truce" in high quarters or of course I would have issued very special orders_ On 24th I issued orders all was to be "as usual".

The orders I issued on 25th were not to shooting Germans walking about unarmed, not to leave our trenches and on no account to allow the Germans into our own except to surrender. This after hearing they were out.

I issued these orders off my own bat, and not because I received any special orders.

I did not dare say I had received no orders in giving my evidence before the Court of Inquiry, as it might have carted Genl Ponsonby, who they said ought to have given orders himself on the subject.

In afternoon I walk with Tempest to see Algy FitzRoy, cmdg Divisional Cavy, at our old farm, where we were in November. Found him very busy making a good brushwood & faggot standing for his horses._

28th

Sniping Lecture in the morning by Pritchard, who is a newspaper correspondent and big game shooter – 3 Corps Generals present, Haking, Pulteney, and Cavan, who has recently got the new XIVth Corps._ Nothing very new or wonderful is told us.

> Captain Hesketh Vernon Hesketh Pritchard was an acknowledged sniping specialist and instructor, well respected and innovative.
> The announcement had been made of the Earl of Cavan's promotion and appointment to command XIV Corps, but he was still with the Guards Division for a few more days.

I hear the Court of Inquiry about Xmas Day will be forwarded to GHQ, so I may be under arrest and court martialed yet! _

In afternoon I walk with Tempest & visit LESTREM Church.

The men have their Xmas Dinners in their various billets, Roger makes a speech to each Company. Billet sing songs afterwds, & a Battalion Concert in the evening at 5.30 p.m., when the Grenadier Band gives much satisfaction.

A bombshell falls in the shape of Esmé returning! Perhaps "bombshell" is the wrong word, as most people are delighted to see him back; so few knowing Roger and mistaking his character from the little they see of him. Personally one suits me as well as the other, both being very good pals to me.

Dec. 29th 1915

The Storm is not over yet – more questions to be answered & sent to the Brigade H.Q. by 5 p.m. I go there with Esmé, in person, and do what is required. The Brigadier treats the whole matter rather lightly, makes out a statement himself which he tries to read over, but fails to read his own handwriting, then we all have to criticize it – jokes fly about, during which Guy Baring comes in with his statement, for the Coldstream were worse off, if anything, than ourselves. The point which in high places they seem to dislike is my having told the Compy Commanders not to shoot the unarmed Germans out in the open who might be confidingly coming over.

> Lieutenant Colonel The Honourable Guy Victor Baring, Commanding 1st Coldstream
> Guards †15.9.16

No further action was taken against anyone in the 1st Coldstream Guards, whose War Diary was silent on fraternization, or the 2nd Scots Guards, whose War Diary mentioned a lot of shouting from the German Trenches, but was otherwise silent too, though recording the death of 6406 Company Sergeant Major James Archibald Leslie Oliver †25.12.15, shot early on. He had been watching the Germans standing outside their trenches. It had no effect on the brief fraternization that then took place, described by Lieutenant Wilfrid Ewart in Scots Guard.

30th

A quiet day. a lecture in the morning on the Supply Services by Col Darrell – Coldstm – the DAQMG of the Divn.

> Lieutenant Colonel William Henry Verelst Darell, Coldstream Guards, Assistant Adjutant & Quartermaster General, Guards Division.

31st

A lecture in the morning by the Divisional Commander, Cavan, on tactics etc – very interesting. In the afternoon I go into Bethune with L. Norman – our Mess President – in "Michael", the motor car belonging to our 2nd Battn, which they kindly lent us, and in the evening the Battn Officers all dine together._ The C.O. & self go to bed about 11 p.m., but the remainder see in the New Year, and then go round to the Coldstream & together they go on to Divisional H.Q. and get Cavan out in his pyjamas, sing "Auld Lang Syne" etc who makes a very nice little speech, then they try to have out the Prince of Wales, who however refused to be drawn – probably thinking they were some tipsy Tommies – then they went on and roused up the Brigadier, who thought it all a huge joke & thoroughly enjoyed it.

Had some more questions to answer in the morning concerning Xmas Day!

> "Michael" had previously been in a compound on the coast after being confiscated from a Life Guards officer by the Military Police. It was a Humber, very much resembling an ambulance, which was useful, and was acquired by Lieutenant The Honourable Charles Mills just before he joined the 2nd Scots Guards the previous summer. "Michael" was retained by them from then on, entirely illicitly, until finally condemned by higher authority early in 1918.

Jan 1st 1916

Relieved the 1st Welsh Guards in trenches near FAUQUISSART. Our relief was arranged rather early, so, as many of us expected, we were spotted by the enemy & spent an unpleasant ½ hr at a corner, where we had to wait to get the gum boots etc, being shelled – luckily no casualties, tho' some came uncomfortably close particularly to C. Coy.

The Battn H.Q. has been moved to WANGERIE, (they were shelled out of ROAD BEND) a tumbledown and picturesque little farm house – several cats about & not many rats in consequence. I sleep in a sort of loft – quite comfortable. A gale blowing from S.W., & an old house close by is blown down during the night, thereby the more exposing us to view. According to

Col Murray-Threipland (W.Gds) there are a good many bullets passing by about here, and I feel rather glad of a good chimney stack at my head.

> The 2nd Guards Brigade, previously in the line in the right half of the Guards Division's area of responsibility, were now in the left half. Wangerie and Road Bend were two strong points.
>
> Lieutenant Colonel William Murray Threipland, Commanding 1st Welsh Guards

2nd

A let off of some gas now in cylinders in our lines was to have been made at 6.30 a.m., but was deferred owing to change of wind.

In the morning I go round the line with the C.O., and in the afternoon with the Doctor, who I am very keen should go into the water question; there are too many men with high temps, & we find undoubtedly men are drinking trench water – much of which even comes over from the German Lines.

3rd

Round the Line with C.O.

In afternoon a good deal of shelling, but no casualties to us – some fell uncomfortably near us at Battn H.Q. – we hear the Irish Guards had 5 casualties while relieving the Coldm on our left. We were relieved by 3rd G.G. in evening & return to Laventie about a mile back.

Last night L. Norman & Tim O.E. and 2 Corps went out scouting the German wire etc and L.N. with 1 Corpl went right on up to the wire under German Parapet – they had no adventures & got back safely with a lot of information._ One "verry light" fell close to them so they lay like dead. A sentry shot at them – they think he heard a noise, but it was such a dark night, he could see nothing.

4th

A bombshell in the shape of the C.O. walking into my bedroom at 8 a.m. and placing me under arrest in connection with the Xmas Day events. I am to be tried by General Court Martial – the summary of evidence is taken & charge made out during the morning, & the day passes in interviews with the Divl Commander (Feilding) Brigadier, Alston & others – all of whom are very sympathetic, and doing their best to get the matter dropped. The higher authorities in the shape of Haig & Co. seem much displeased.

> Sir Iain Colquhoun was also under arrest. The new commander of the Guards Division was Major General Geoffrey Feilding, till now commanding the 1st Guards Brigade. As the eventual court martial outcome and Sir Douglas Haig's reaction would both show, a number of people further up the chain of command had by this time created a situation difficult to withdraw from without loss of face. The Earl of Cavan was a very capable soldier and commander, but his anger about what to begin with, presumably reported to him from Headquarters XI Corps, sounded far worse than it was, quickly set off a course of disciplinary action whose gathering momentum was wasteful and pointless.

The Summary of Evidence in the case of Miles Barne, taken at Laventie, was dated 5 January, not the 4th, as he recorded. He was present throughout and given the opportunity of questioning each witness but declined to do so.

1st witness. Captain G. Rasch, Brigade Major 2nd Guards Brigade, states:

On the morning of December 24th, 1915, I went to the Headquarters, 1st Bn. Scots Guards at RIEZ BAILLEUL at about 10.30 a.m. I wished to see the Adjutant with reference to some posts, while I was there Captain Barne came out of the H.Q. and spoke to me. In course of conversation he asked me casually what was going to happen on Xmas Day, I replied "The Major General has said that Xmas day is to be the same as any other day, and if anything a little more so". I rode away with the Adjutant shortly after that. As far as I can remember these were the actual words I used.

2nd witness. Captain Sir John Dyer, Bt., 1st Bn. Scots Guards, states:

On December 24th, 1915, I was in command of the Reserve Company, 1st Bn. Scots Guards, after the Battalion had gone up into the trenches. My Headquarters were at "Ebenezer Farm" which is the same as Battalion Headquarters.

During the afternoon Captain Barne issued direct verbal orders to all Company Commanders, including myself, that during Xmas Day everything was to be carried on as usual and no difference was to be made, if anything greater vigilance was to be observed in case the Germans made a surprise attack. At about 9.00 a.m. on December 25th a message came from the front line that the Germans had put up white flags and that some of them had come out of their trenches unarmed and were demanding a truce to bury their dead. Captain Barne pending a reply from Brigade H.Q. as to what action he should take, and taking into account the unusual situation which had developed, issued orders to Officers in command of companies in the firing line, that no men were to leave their trenches under any pretext whatsoever, that no Germans would be allowed into our trenches except as prisoners of war, but that in order to give them a chance of surrendering unarmed Germans leaving their trenches would not be fired on. I was in the room while Captain Barne was writing these orders and although they did not really concern my company (which was in reserve) they are to the best of my belief the orders that I received.

3rd witness. Captain L. Norman, 1st Bn. Scots Guards, states:

On December 24th before going into the trenches, Captain Barne personally gave me definite orders that on holding the trenches the following day I was to carry on as usual and to make no difference owing to the fact of it being Xmas Day.

I then questioned Captain Barne as to what I should do if the Germans came out of their trenches unarmed and seemed likely to surrender. He told me not to fire at them under those conditions but to treat them as prisoners of war and on no account to let them into our trenches under any other condition. At about 8.30 a.m. on Xmas Day I was having breakfast in my dugout when I heard a lot of shouting. I ran out and looked over the parapet and saw many white flags in the German lines and Germans standing on the top of their parapets unarmed, and a few coming towards us also unarmed. Soon after a message was passed down the line that a truce for 45 minutes had been arranged for the purpose of burying the dead. I could not trace the origin of this message. Shortly after this I received a message from Captain Barne ordering me not to allow my men to leave the trenches, that no Germans were to be allowed into our trenches except as prisoners of war and that if they came in as such they were not to be fired on.

The next two witnesses were as to character.

4th witness. Brigadier-General J. Ponsonby, C.M.G., D.S.O., Commanding 2nd Guards Brigade, states:

Captain Barne took over the command of the 1st Bn. Scots Guards after the battle of Loos and was in command of the Battalion for nearly a month, during a very critical period when the Battalion was holding HOHENZOLLERN. On all occasions Captain Barne showed judgement, coolness and courage of a high degree, and when he handed over command to his successor I wrote to him and thanked him for the excellent way in which he had commanded his Battalion at a very trying period. I informed his Commanding Officer of this also.

5th witness. Lt. Colonel Lord E. Gordon Lennox, 1st Bn. Scots Guards, states:

I have known Captain Barne all my life. During the South African War he was attached as Brigade Signalling Officer to the 16th Brigade and always carried out his work in such a satisfactory manner that he was twice mentioned in despatches. In July 1915, I was in command of the 3rd (Reserve) Battalion Scots Guards when Captain Barne rejoined the Regiment from the Suffolk Yeomanry. From previous experience I had such a high opinion of Captain Barne's capabilities that I specially applied for him to be sent out to the 1st Battn. on the first available opportunity. In October I took over command of this Battalion and found that Captain Barne had commanded the Battalion for the last four weeks in a highly satisfactory manner. From that date to this Captain Barne has acted at different times as my 2nd in Command and as a Company Commander. I know nobody in whom I would place greater trust as a Company Commander, or in the event of my absence, as Commanding Officer. I have the greatest opinion of his capabilities on all occasions.

Supplementary and undated was a further document,

Lieut. G.A. Harrison, 5th S.W.B. attached 17th Fd Company R.E. will state:

About 7.30 a.m. on December 25th 1915, I was asleep in my shelter near the entrance to "Ducks Bill". I was awakened by shouting in the firing line. When I went outside I saw men standing on the top of our parapet and calling across to the German Lines. I also noticed white flags on our parapet and the Germans. I went up to the "Ducks Bill" and on arriving there found our Infantry on the parapet and some between our parapet and the wire. A number of Germans were also out in front of their lines. There were two Scots Guards Officers standing on the parapet endeavouring to stop their men from going forward.

Several Germans (all unarmed) continued to advance and presently met some of our men about 50 yards in front of our parapet. At about that time Captain Colquhoun arrived on the scene and asked the two Subalterns what was going on. I was at that moment close to the nearer crater. I then saw a German Officer come forward and call for an English Officer, and Captain Colquhoun went forward and conversed with him for a few moments. Captain Colquhoun then walked back and ordered his men into their trenches, the German Officer doing likewise. The men at once went back into the Trenches in the "Ducks Bill", but I could still see groups of them out on the left and right. I then went back into my own dug-out.

About how far is it from the "Ducks Bill" to the Company H.Q., dug-out.

About 200 yards from the parapet of the "Ducks Bill"

About how long do you think it would take to get from the parapet of the "Ducks Bill" along the communication trench to the Company H.Q., dug-out.

From five to eight minutes.

Can you make a plan of the trenches known as the "Ducks Bill".

Yes, I have already made one and will produce a tracing.

Lieutenant G A Harrison, 5th (Service) Battalion The South Wales Borderers, attached 17th Field Company, Royal Engineers

Miles Barne's diary entries continued, principally about Christmas Day:

5th

The Brigadier is very amusing on this subject and says he would like to see them "cutting German wire" and me doing the Court Martials.

I wrote Farrer last night to combine with Luss' (who is also under arrest) solicitor & employ the best counsel he can get. At same time I applied through the "proper channels" for permission to employ a Counsel. The Brigadier thinks this will choke them off a bit, & the Judge Advocate General, on seeing the evidence, said "this is no case", so the summary had to be altered, which seems a curious proceeding. The Brigadier & everyone else who is qualified to judge thinks the people at the top have got hold of the wrong end of the stick altogether. Certainly if they expect me or any other Officer to give an order to shoot down unarmed Germans in cold blood, they are very much mistaken, and as Luss says, the men would not obey, adding "if they want it done, let them do it themselves"._

I am released from arrest.

Arthur Farrer, his solicitor and frequent guest at Sotterley before the War

I forgot to say that on 3rd a bullet went through roof of dugout where Luss & C. Boyd Rochford were sitting hitting Luss on the finger, penetrating B.R's pocket & medicine case & then a small piece of his thigh, a narrow squeak.

We relieve 3 G.G. in trenches.

6th

The night a fairly quiet one but just as I was starting to go round the trenches the Germans began shelling the first one falling close to our Battn H.Q. There is much shelling on both sides all day. In the afternoon I went up with a gunner Officer, Giffard, to his Observation Post &

had a good look through my telescope at the enemy lines & the ground behind them including the famous AUBERS Ridge.

Possibly Captain Edmund Hamilton Giffard, Royal Field Artillery †10.11.18

The Brigadier came to breakfast & says he hears if I employ counsel they will too, and so he advises me not to. I want to be assured of this before deciding. He says Haig insists on a C.M., and that I had better have a "prisoner's friend", & suggests Raymond Asquith, who is in 3rd Grenadiers. Later in the day he writes that there seems no certainty of a trial, and encloses a letter from the Major General, G. Feilding, who is also doing his utmost to help me._

Lieutenant Raymond Asquith, 3rd Grenadier Guards †15.9.16, an established commercial barrister and the eldest son of Henry Asquith, the Prime Minister, and Helen Melland, his first wife. After her death Henry Asquith married Margot Tennant, whose niece Geraldine "Dinah" Tennant married Sir Iain Colquhoun early in 1915 when he was recovering from his wound during First Ypres.

7th

Went round trenches early with C.O., & while there the Germans began shelling the Observation Post where I was yesterday. Luckily at the first shot those inside fled to cover in a dugout, the 3rd shot was a direct hit, & burst in the house, however nobody was injured – a wonderful thing. Either the Germans have discovered the "O.P." by someone showing himself there, or it has been given away by a spy._ Again considerable shelling all day.

Are relieved by 3rd G.G. in the evening._

8th

Nothing particular occurs, but I write out an account of what I remember of what occurred on Xmas Day. This chiefly for the benefit of Raymond Asquith, who is on leave in England; and been sent for to be the "Prisoner's Friend". It seems likely that I am to be tried, and rumour says that two members of the Court are to be Charles Corkran and Torquil Matheson, two of my oldest & best friends, and there are not two more fair minded men in existence.

Last night the Brigadier was arrested by the Military Police, who took him for a spy. He gave a very comical description of it all._ This place LAVENTIE seems to be full of spies – I think one reason why the Germans do not shell it more.

The G.G. have shifted their Bn HQ from WANGERIE to HOUGOMONT.

Brigadier General Torquhil George Matheson, Commanding 46th Brigade, 15th Division Hougomont was another strong point.

After a brief outline of the circumstances of his becoming Commanding Officer on 22 December Miles Barne set out his recollections of the events on 24 and 25 December, this being the account he referred to above.

On the 24th. about 10.30 a.m. seeing the Brigade Major, Capt. Rasch, sitting on his horse outside Battalion Headquarters waiting till the Adjutant was ready to go round some posts with him, and having heard nothing, I ran out to enquire if there were any special orders for the following day. It was raining and blowing hard at the time and my impression of his reply was "The General wishes everything to be carried on as ususal". He did not make any great point of this and I thought he seemed in a hurry as the Adjutant was ready for him, and he rode off.

I then saw the four Company Commanders, separately in their billets, and told them that everything was to be carried on as usual on Xmas day, and extra vigilance was to be observed in case the Germans tried any tricks.

In course of conversation with one or some of them, remembering stories of what had occurred last year, and, therefore, anticipating that the Germans might come out of their trenches unarmed and display some friendliness, I said our men were on no account to leave their trenches, but not to fire upon Germans coming over unarmed and on no account to let them into our trenches except to surrrender. I had heard a story of some Germans recently coming over to surrender and being shot at, when the general opinion seemed to be "What bad luck on them, also bad policy and so stupid not to get them as prisoners." I had heard talk of the possibility of them taking the opportunity of Xmas day to surrender, and had heard that prisoners were badly wanted for purposes of information.

I might add that one Company Commander afterwards expressed the opinion that the men would not have fired at the Germans in the open (unarmed) even if they had been ordered to. In my opinion this would have been a cowardly thing to do, and there are few officers in the firing line – if any – who could be found to give such an order. It would have been little short of murder. (I gave no orders "not to fire at any Germans in or near their trenches", as when I first knew about it the situation was that the Germans were actually out of their trenches and coming over to us.)

The Battalion relieved the 3rd Batt. Grenadier Gds. that evening, Battalion headquarters again being at Ebenezer Farm. During the night of 24th-25th a message arrived from the Brigade about extra vigilance on Xmas day and this was passed on to every Company Commander.

About 9.a.m. on the 25th., Xmas day, a verbal telephone message was received from the front line saying many unarmed Germans were out between the lines and coming over towards us. There were white flags on their parapets. I immediately sent a reply addressed to all Companies saying "Our men were on no account to leave their trenches and on no account to allow any Germans into ours except to surrender, when they were to be treated as prisoners of war, but of course not to fire at unarmed Germans coming over" – again I had hopes of collecting some prisoners – besides this the idea of shooting down defenceless Germans, ½ way over to us and who were trusting us was unthinkable. The idea of some ruse on their part also crossed my mind. I then decided to go down myself and see exactly what was going on before settling what further action to take or report – and was starting, when I met the Brigadier accompanied by the Brigade Major. At the same moment came a message from Right Flank Coy. saying several Germans had come over and wanted a truce. I handed this to the Brigadier who replied saying there was to be no truce and he sent on the same message to the Division asking for instructions. (In the course of the morning the reply came back from the Division saying there was to be no truce of any kind and this was passed on to all the Companies.) I then went down to the front line with the Brigadier where everything was practically normal, although our men and the Germans were still looking at each other. There were white flags on the German parapets and I saw one on ours which I immediately had taken down.

N.B. The orders I gave on 25th would have applied to the same situation, whether on Xmas or any other day.

9th

Yet another summary of evidence has to be taken! It really seems that they are trying to "cook" the evidence to suit the charge!

In evening we relieve the G.G. again in trenches, Bn HQ at HOUGOMONT FARM – quite a good place – I have a poky little room with the Doctor & Adjutant – am rather bothered by mice at night – my bed being made of unthreshed wheat, so the mice make their habitation in it. I do not think there are any rats in the room._

Col. Corry has to return home where he is to have a Brigade – he is not allowed by Sir D. Haig to be out here – owing to the old row of the retreat from Mons. He is very sore & sick at leaving his Battn & I feel very sorry for him. He has always been very nice to me.

> Lieutenant Colonel Noel Armar Lowry Corry commanded the 2nd Grenadier Guards at the start of the War, in the 4th (Guards) Brigade, 2nd Division, I Corps. On 23 August 1914 the German First Army encountered II Corps of the BEF at Mons. After a fierce fight against overwhelming numbers II Corps had to withdraw and break away. In II Corps the 2nd Battalion The Royal Irish Rifles were on the extreme right of the 7th Brigade, 3rd Division. Under particularly intense pressure in a very awkward position, the 7th Brigade had to pull back. The 2nd Grenadier Guards, the nearest battalion on the left of I Corps, were not drawn into the battle, but when Lieutenant Colonel Lowry Corry heard from the Royal Irish Rifles that they had orders to withdraw he could see the implications. However, he had no means of communicating with Headquarters 4th (Guards) Brigade and so, after discussing the situation with Lieutenant Colonel The Honourable George Henry Morris, Commanding 1st Irish Guards †1.9.14, who was junior to him, he gave the order for both battalions to withdraw. He was relieved of his command on 9 September 1914. Next, however, he reappeared in France in command of the 3rd Grenadier Guards as the Guards Division formed around St Omer. The removal of Lieutenant Colonel Lowry Corry this time may have had more to do with what were perceived as deficiencies of his Battalion during Loos, notably when they were attacked at the Hohenzollern on 8 October.

> From the fresh Summary of Evidence came a further statement by Captain Sir John Swinnerton Dyer, Bt, arising from his answers to the previous questions. After the initial demand from Headquarters Guards Division for answers on 25 December Miles Barne did get statements from his Company Commanders, which must have been passed on. Sir John Swinnerton Dyer now had to explain that what he wrote down then was his recollection of all the orders that he had received from Miles Barne on both 24 and 25 December. This led to pressure from the investigation that more of what Miles Barne had said was to be done or not done had been in orders on Christmas Eve, not on Christmas Day. The final question to him therefore was,

Did you or did you not receive from Captain Barne any orders about not shooting unarmed Germans on December 24th?

I did not.

The prosecution line until the very last moment was to try to make out that Miles Barne had given this order on Christmas Eve.

The date is missing from a note sent about this time to Miles Barne from his brother in law, Lieutenant Orr Ewing,

I couldn't get up as I am tied near the forts – just to say how awfully sorry I am about this wretched affair & that you of all people should be made a scapegoat_ I cant believe that anything serious will really happen but fight it to the last_ It seems piteous that Generals can waste time during a War like this trying by foul means to ruin people whose boots they ought to lick – If anything was done to you or Luss I think there would be a mutiny.
    Tim

10th

The Brigadier calls early & says he is trying to get one of the Divisional Staff sent home to tell the truth of my story – as every sort of wild rumour is being concocted – that the 2nd Guards Brigade had a regular beno on Xmas Day with the Germans, I arranged it, Luss carried it out and the Brigadier sanctioned it all & so on.
    He came back to luncheon also Asquith, & we discussed the whole situation thoroughly.
    Heard from Farrer that he could get Bodkin K.C. if required, but I wrote to say not required.
    In afternoon walked round trenches with the Adjutant.

Archibald Henry Bodkin K.C.
    Lieutenant Asquith was approached directly by Brigadier General Ponsonby while in his billet having a wash, just returned from leave. He would develop great respect for Sir Iain Colquhoun, who was calm, resolute and unperturbed, but found it harder to help Miles Barne because he was so depressed about the case. Though it does not come across directly in the diary Miles Barne was very upset by how he was being treated and by the unfair tactics being employed against him to get a conviction.

11th

The 1st Coldstream made a raid during the night. A wire cutting party began at 11 p.m., the raiding party going over at 3 a.m., & – found the German trenches empty – they went for 400 yds laterally & 150 yds up communication trenches, never seeing a soul! They brought back some bombs & machine gun cartridge belts.
    At dawn the Brigade on our right (Welsh?) let off gas; 2 of our companies reported seeing it go. There was no attack.
    At 2 p.m. yet another summary of evidence has to be taken – or rather the old amended, & this (4th) time by the Depy Judge Advocate General, Col. Mellor, who is quite civil & reasonable. Darrell is there & does not think there is any case against me. We shall see if he is right or not. On 9th, by the way, the Brigadier told me the authorities were not going to employ counsel, but would not give the fact in writing.

Round trenches with C.O. in morning.

Colonel James Gilbert Small Mellor, Deputy Judge Advocate General

Jan. 12th 1916

As I think I have previously said, the Coldstm raided the German front line trenches & found them empty. The Germans appear to have thought that they had come there & remained so organized an attack on them with bombers, from each side, in the same trench – as the moment arrived when they thought they would be approaching the English, one lot heard the other talking, and, imagining the talking was the English, began bombing, with the result that they had a bomb battle royal with eachother!

Then last night the Irish Gds who relieved the Coldstream arranged a raid, and again found the front line empty, though not the 2nd line._

A good deal of amusement has been caused by an order that at a certain hour when some Swedish Generals were to be motoring through the place, games of football should be in progress, and the men were to look cheerful!

Walk with L. Norman in morning._ Hear of the total evacuation of the Gallipoli Peninsular.

Dined with Right Half Battn Mess in the evening – on way back I look in at Left Half & there find Luss just returned from leave in England – where he had had interviews with Mr Bodkin and Arthur Farrer. He was amusing about the Xmas Day Episode and how it was regarded in England.

Dinah Colquhoun had had a difficult first pregnancy and was very worried about the birth. She begged her husband to come home to be with her. He asked Brigadier General Ponsonby for four days special [compassionate] leave, which was granted. The birth of their son went smoothly and had taken place before Sir Iain Colquhoun arrived in London.

13th

We are relieved in our billets at LAVENTIE by the 1st Welsh Guards and march to our new billets North of MERVILLE, at NEUVE BERQUIN – just vacated by our 2nd Bn, who have gone into the trenches.

We leave Asquith with his Battn at LA GORGUE, and on arrival at our new billets we hear that Luss & I are to be courtmartialed on 17th inst.

14th

Nothing of importance

Buy towel etc in MERVILLE, mine having been stolen at the last billets.

Am now in a tiny room in a tiny cottage. Carter, my poor old servant, is ill – & being looked after by Madame & Mademoiselle. Monsieur is a horseman. There is a small yellow dog here called "Milord"._

1867 Private George Carter

The Brigadier comes over to luncheon – he & the C.O. (Esmé) and in fact everybody I meet are most kind & sympathetic.

15th

R. Asquith comes over to luncheon & discusses a few points. The Prosecutor is one Hills of K.O.S.B., a well known Barrister so am glad we have got Asquith on our side.

Captain Reginald Playfair Hills, The King's Own Scottish Borderers

In morning we do a route march.

In afternoon play football against the 1st Coldm (Officers) & beat them 1 to 0._ Great fun but I get the ball full in the eye at close range which causes me not to see anything with that eye for the rest of the game.

16th

Attend Presbyterian service. Hear Pereira is to be another member of the Court tomorrow.

17th

Carter is quite well again. A motor car calls at 9.30.a.m. with Pereira – cmdg 1st Guards Brigade – on board – also another empty one & we all go off to the Divisional H.Q, LA GORGUE Esmé Luss Pereira & self in one, 2 Boyd Rochford's and L. Norman in the other – Members of the Court, accuseds, C.O., & witnesses on both sides all mixed up.

On arrival I find the Court consists of:

Genl Holland 1st Div.: President

Genl Cuthbert; Genl Pereira; Col. Daunt Irish Rifles; Col. Sandiland H.L.I.: Members

Capt Hills is Prosecutor.

There is great excitement about it all.

At 10.45 we start with much pomp.

My case comes on first, & to my – & Asquith's – great astonishment we find a new charge – instead of "Conduct to prejudice of good order and military discipline in that he at the trenches just N. of NEUVE CHAPELLE on Dec. 24th although he had been warned by the Brigade Major, Capt. Rasch, that everything was to be done as usual on Xmas Day, issued orders that unarmed Germans shewing themselves on or near their trenches were not to be shot at", which I had seen & Asquith too & had prepared to refute, the charge appeared "Conduct… Germans coming towards us were not to be shot at with a view to getting them to surrender". So that now we had to prove that this order that I practically admitted issuing, was a right and proper order to give.

This was done so successfully that the finding was, "not guilty, honourably acquitted prisoner to be released"._

The only evidence called in defence was as to character, & on this Asquith asked the Brigadier (he & Esmé, my CO were the only 2 witnesses) just a few questions, which produced his statement that he would have given the same orders himself & every other C.O. in his Brigade would have done the same._ Nor did Asquith crossexamine the witnesses for prosecution, for the simple reason that I admitted all they said.

Asquith made a very clear statement for 14 minutes – & put my case very well and very clearly – the unfortunate prosecutor made a feeble effort but had not a leg to stand on.

It is very satisfactory as a result and I am receiving congratulations from all round.

I presume G.H.Q. thought the order I gave was not a proper one, or would not have tried me on it – if so it is one in the eye for them.

Poor Luss did not fare so well, as we expected – he being tried for making a ¾ hr truce with the enemy for burying dead, and was found "guilty"- we shall hear the sentence in a few days.

My case was over by 3 p.m. when I had a scrappy lunch at Div H.Q. & walked back to billets, & attended a concert – Luss' case was not over till 9 p.m.!

Major General Arthur Edward Aveling Holland, Commanding 1st Division
Brigadier General Gerald James Cuthbert, Commanding 140th Brigade
Brigadier General Cecil Edward Pereira, Commanding 1st Guards Brigade
Lieutenant Colonel Richard Algernon Craigie Daunt, Commanding 2nd Battalion The
    Royal Irish Rifles, 74th Brigade, 25th Division, New Army
Probably Lieutenant Colonel Vincent Corbett Sandilands, Commanding 2nd Battalion
    The Cameronians (Scottish Rifles), 23rd Brigade, 8th Division. He would have been
    wearing tartan trews, as would an officer of The Highland Light Infantry.

The charge at Miles Barne's court martial was,

Conduct to the prejudice of good order and military discipline, in that he, in the Trenches North of Neuve Chapelle, on or about 24th December 1914, having been informed by Captain Rasch, Brigade Major, 2nd Guards Brigade, that the orders of the Major General Commanding the Division were that everything was to be the same on Christmas Day as on any other day, issued orders to his Company Commanders that, on Christmas Day, in order to give the enemy a chance of surrendering, unarmed Germans leaving their trenches were not to be fired upon, or orders to that effect.

8

The Rest of the Winter 1915-16 at Neuve Chapelle

The anxieties of the Court Martial behind him, though continuing to be concerned about Sir Iain Colquhoun's fate, Miles Barne returned to the routine and not so routine.

18th

Wet. Walked into MERVILLE with Padre in evening_ Brigadier & Beckwith-Smith came to dinner also several other Officers of the Battn – 12 altogether – so we had a cheery party the Brigadier being in his best form. Afterwards some played poker some nap & others in the middle bridge including myself – all at the same table!

19th

Route march in the morning – glorious day – football in afternoon, Officers v. Sergts – the former winning 3-2 goals. We were 2 all for a long time, then I had the honour of kicking the winning goal (horrid fluke) just before "time"._

20th

No excitements.

In the evening attended a Left Flank Concert, when to my surprise & in some ways pleasure, my health was drunk – or rather 3 cheers for me given – with great enthusiasm_ I dont know why particularly, but I did wonder whether they knew the result of the G.C.M.

21st

Walked into the town with Esmé.

22nd

Esmé goes on leave leaving me once more in command of the Battn._ We hear that Luss has been "reprimanded", but the C. in C. has remitted the sentence, owing to his distinguished conduct in the field. This is about the least they could do!

I have a class of Officers in the evening & do a scheme! We are also to prepare to do a raid or two if required – & so this has to be practised.

When Sir Douglas Haig received the file from Sir Iain Colquhoun's Court Martial and was able to study exactly what it was all about he directed that, while the proceedings were to stand, the sentence was to be struck out. In December 1916 he remembered again and ordered that the finding should also be quashed, that the file should be destroyed and that all mention of the case should be expunged from the record.

A class of officers was a training period, a scheme a tactical exercise.

23rd

The Divl Medical Authority tries to take our Dr Stewart – who has been with the Battn over 15 months, away. So he & I ride into see the Brigadier, & get the matter put right._

Attend the Presbyterian Service in the morning.

Night operations.

24th

Lecture on Artillery in LA GORGUE.

C.O.'s have to see the Brigadier afterwards & hear various bits of news etc nothing very exciting – Haking came in while we were there._

Bn Officers all dine together at Bn H.Q.

25th

I inspect the Transport Horses; also see L.F. doing Swedish Drill.

In afternoon the Officers again play the Sergts and defeated them 4 to 0._ I kick two of the goals._ The Doctor after all has to leave & join the 38th Div. In spite of his Agreement with the W.O. that he will only extend his service (last Aug) for 12 months on condition that he remains with this Battn._ He goes off looking very miserable and with the firm intention of behaving very insubordinately where he is going to – in spite of my begging him not to be so silly.

I write to Col. Godman & Esmé to try & get the matter adjusted from the W.O. – I dont know if such a thing is possible._

Hear that Robert Filmer has been mortally wounded by a shell, but hope an exaggeration._

Swedish Drill was physical training

Captain Sir Robert Marcus Filmer, Bt, 4th Grenadier Guards †27.1.16

26th

Hear Stewart has gone to 129th Field Ambulance.

We march at 11 to Brigade Reserve at LAVENTIE, and there relieve the 2nd Bn Scots Guards who however do not wait for us – & we find them flown.

I go & see Heyworth at Bde H.Q. who tells me Filmer has had his foot off & has his leg & arm broken – compound fractures & has 16 wounds altogether – is still alive.

A message arrives to say that tomorrow being the Kaisers birthday we have to be on extra look out – again, that large German Reinforcements are moving up to the line opposite us & towards LA BASSÉE, which almost looks like their meaning business. Time will show._

27th

No attack or unusual excitement of any sort. Some bursts of rifle & artillery fire – enemy – in early morning. The flashes of the guns I can see from my bed – at least I am half inclined to believe they are sham flashes only – so very red & rather slow.

Walk round posts with Colquhoun in morning. Arrange as to fixing up rockets & "gas gongs" (empty shell cases) in billets etc.

Go & see Brigadier in afternoon.

Bethel & Bewick join – or rather re-join as regards the former._

Hear R. Filmer has died today, for which I am very sorry._

> Captain The Honourable Richard Bethell had been out in the spring of 1915 and then been sent home after being injured, not wounded.
> Lieutenant Calverley Bewicke

Jan. 28th 1916

Some shelling during the day: we prepare to go to the trenches but the relief is put off for 24 hours – when we are to go in for 3 days instead of two._

29th

The outskirts of the village rather heavily shelled about 2 p.m.

The Brigadier calls in & says we are moving up to Ypres next week, which causes much talking & despondency! Some think it is a blind – & so on.

In the evening we relieve the 3rd Grenadiers in trenches. They are now commanded by Boy Brooke who was our Bde Major before Rasch – after this he went on Staff of 5th Corps.

> Lieutenant Colonel Bertram Norman Sergison Brooke, Commanding 3rd Grenadier Guards

30th

In morning I go round the trenches & posts, and on way back get some shells dropped unpleasantly near._ There is a thickish fog, so I amuse myself getting over the parapet and looking at our loopholes from that side – a very interesting thing to do – one sees which sort shew up and which sort are invisible etc. The Arty Observation Officer is named Dutton and has lived in Chile a good deal which he discusses well at dinner.

Wind North.

> Dutton, Royal Artillery – untraced

31st

A beautiful E wind suitable for the Germans to gas us!_

A big bombardment is to take place – the Brigadier and Major Toppin – Arty – look in while we are at breakfast – & I soon follow up to the front line, a good part of which we have to clear for the reason that the Arty might make mistakes & have accidents. At 10 a.m. I have to meet Gen Heyworth & shew him certain places in the line selected for inserting "Bangalore Torpedoes" into the German wire. These we have chosen by means of patrols etc, they have to be dragged over by night – are 15' long & are exploded by an electric fuse from our own line.

Heyworth is not in a good temper, & I do not improve it by pointing out that his Brigade had spoiled many of our loopholes. Methuen has been our Sniping Officer & is very keen & has taken a great deal of trouble, is much hurt about the matter & wrote a long report of his injuries, which I gave to our Brigadier this morning, & so we may hear more about this.

The bombardment starts at 10 a.m., & continues up to 2 p.m.; the Germans retaliate on Fort Elgin, held by a platoon of C. Coy. At the end, about 2.30 I go down there with Luss, expecting to find many casualties, instead of which we find none, only one shell having landed in the post – just showing how deceptive it is – from the front line it looked as if about 50 must have gone right into it. I then return to Bn H.Q. via Road Bend Post – after quite an eventful morning.

I only hope our guns killed some Germans.

N.B. Heyworth is commanding the Division; Fielding being now XI Corps Commander while Haking is on leave.

> Major Sidney Miles Toppin, Royal Garrison Artillery
> Bangalore Torpedoes were pipe bombs for blowing gaps in barbed wire.
>
> There were no deputy commanders at corps, division or brigade level. So, if a commander was temporarily away, as applicable the most senior divisional commander, brigade commander and battalion commander had to take their superior's place, a disruptive procedure.

Feb 1st

I go round the Trenches early, taking the Padre with me, he has never been into any front trenches before – swears he is "on duty", and is much excited.

We go round & see all there is to be seen – Methuen, the Battn Sniping Officer, has stories of having accounted for several Germans including an Officer – patrols had been out during the night and had found out more of the Torpedoe positions.

We meet Gens Feilding, Ponsonby and Anderson (Corps Staff) – all very nice and agreeable.

At 2 p.m. a bombardment is to start, so I arrange about clearing out certain parts of the line & posts etc, after which I return to Battn H.Q. – about 1.p.m. – & then the fun begins at 2 p.m. a lot of 'wire cutting' by our field guns – followed by a very heavy retaliation by enemy on Rue Tilleloy & most of our cleared part of front line & posts. I then order a short sharp & sweet reply by our "heavies", which effectually brings them to their senses, on their front line parapets – which finishes the programme about 4 p.m., luckily no casualties but 2 Grenadier Machine Gunners (all MG's are found under Brigade arrangements by Brigade MG Coy) are killed in a dugout – several dugouts – socalled but really more weather proof shelters – get blown in including the C Coy Sergt Major's.

About 6.30 p.m. the 2nd Bn relieve us – Lumsden (doing Adjt while Billy Wynne Finch is on leave) – appears first with the Doctor, also Swinton and Bethel. Alby Cator follows about 7.30, accompanied by Col Ruthven & an Admiral Sir – Colville, who is on a "holiday", visiting trenches, & wants to see a relief – what he can see in pitch dark, I dont know – the relief is not over till 8.15 p.m., when I walk back with Thompson (Adjt) & Walker – (tempy Doctor) to LA

GORGUE, starting off in an atmosphere apparently full of bullets – luckily mostly over our heads – I think the Germans must have known there was a relief going on. We get in about 10 p.m. & very glad of a good meal – the men too have soup & rum.

Bewicke who landed with the N. Zealanders in Gallipoli says the shelling there is childs' play to this._

> Brigadier General Warren Hastings Anderson, Brigadier General General Staff, XI Corps
> 18854 Private Albert Edward Corps, 3rd Grenadier Guards, attached 2nd Guards Brigade Machine Gun Company †1.2.16
> 20618 Private Joseph Egan, 3rd Grenadier Guards, attached 2nd Guards Brigade Machine Gun Company †1.2.16
> 6018 Company Sergeant Major William Pyper, C Company
> Captain Alan Swinton, 2nd Scots Guards
> Lieutenant David Jardine Bethell, 2nd Scots Guards
> Admiral Sir Stanley Colville, Royal Navy, Flag Officer Orkney
> Walker, Royal Army Medical Corps – untraced

2nd

A peaceful day, but a rather serious number of reports for "C.O.'s orders", when I have to send an unfortunate man to a Court Martial – I felt inclined to tell him I hoped he would fare as well as I did – he will probably get 5 yrs, for sleeping on his post._

The Brigadier tells me he has written a strong letter about the Doctor – Stewart – & that he hopes something may come of it.

3rd

Many rumours flying about – our going to Ypres, to Calais & every sort of place, no more leave etc.

Inspect Billets – cold strong S. Wind.

Football match v. Coldstm Officers in afternoon – when they defeated us 7:1. We sadly missed our Doctor, Lionel Norman and Hammersley.

The C.O. returns about 7 p.m. & says the Doctor is to be sent back to us – which is very good news.

4th

A gale from S.W. My old landlady comes into my bedroom early in the morning to shut my window! I think they dislike open air as much as I dislike froust!

A very idle day. Walk twice with Esmé G.L.

Attend concert, or rather cinema show in evening.

5th

Watch some bombing and sniping practice in morning. A perfect summer's day.

Trouble is brewing about the Doctor – Esmé had written to Gen Slogget, Director of Medical Services in the Army, who had ordered Stewart's return, but Gen Feilding is very angry, & says somebody has been acting behind his back, & he wont have Stewart back at any price etc etc.

I ride into MERVILLE with Esmé, Butler (Irish Gds) who is temporarily commanding the Brigade, & John Dyer – the pony Geraldine is very fit & quite a nice ride along the Canal._

In the evening another Concert – mostly Coldstream Band, who have succeeded the Grenadiers; Pr. of Wales & his sailor brother present.

> Lieutenant General Sir Arthur Thomas Sloggett, Royal Army Medical Corps, Director of Medical Services, General Headquarters. He was severely wounded at the Battle of Omdurman.
>
> Miles Barne had acquired Geraldine after the death of Major George Molyneux Montgomerie.
>
> The "sailor brother" was Prince Albert, Duke of York, later King George VI.

6th

Attend Presbyterian Church Service.

In afternoon ride into MERVILLE again with the Padre and McKay – visited Jack Stirling & Dykes in hospital.

> Captain Stirling had been back with the 2nd Scots Guards for some time, while Captain Ballantyne Dykes, previously in that Battalion, was now at Headquarters 3rd Guards Brigade, training for the Staff.

7th

In morning walk into ESTAIRES with Padre & Adjt. to try – unsuccessfully – to buy a lamp for Battn H.Q._

The C.O. tells me he has sent my name in to be a tempy Major, which is satisfactory, as it means the Court Martial is not meant to stand in my way, and that I haven't altogether made too great a muddle of things.

We march at 4.p.m. and relieve the 2nd G.G. (Glyn cmdg) at EBENEZER FARM._

> Lieutenant Colonel Arthur St Leger Glyn, Commanding 2nd Grenadier Guards

8th

A quiet but cold night, in our sepulchres, and round the line with Esmé in morning. We have an influx of "Bantams" – 1 Officer & 2 NCO's per Coy – under Instruction, who arrive about 4 p.m. – Gloucesters & Cheshires.

> In 1914 the minimum height for enlistment in the Army was 5' 3", but, following parliamentary and other pressure about this preventing shorter but otherwise fully fit men from joining up, the height limit was reduced to 5'. These shorter men had to serve in special battalions, nicknamed Bantams. The men Miles Barne came across will have

been from either the 15th or 16th (Service) Battalions The Cheshire Regiment as well as the 14th (Service) Battalion The Gloucestershire Regiment, all three in the 105th Brigade, 35th Division, New Army, recently arrived in France.

9th

Round the line with C.O. in morning.

Relieved at night by 3rd G.G. – just as H.Q. were moving off to go into billets at RIEZ BAILLEUL, Sgt Martin, Piper and Head Stretcher-bearer, was hit through the head by a stray bullet. He was a great character – had been out the whole war, never missing one day's duty: he had received a DCM. A most amusing though conceited man – many stories are told about him. When congratulated on his DCM, he replied: "It was a long time coming", & to another "If there was 1 man in the Battalion who deserved it, it was me!" He used always to cut my hair – & was going to do so tomorrow._ Nobody has a better or finer reputation for bravery – in fact he knew no fear.

991 Sergeant Alexander Martin †9.2.16

10th

Sgt Martin died during the night in No. 9 Casualty Clearing Station ESTAIRES.

Esmé's birthday. Very cold.

Baden dined with us.

11th

Went round posts in morning on Geraldine.

Pouring wet all day.

Lunched with Baden. Relieved 3rd GG in trenches. Our RE exploded mine at 7.50 p.m., which was followed by a good deal of rifle fire & machine gun fire on part of enemy.

12th

Round trenches with C.O. in morning, & saw the mine crater (through periscope). Not a very big one._

A considerable amount of Artillery Fire on both sides, but no damage done to us. The welcome news arrives that leave re-opens at once; Tim is the next to go, and is off in a day or so.

A clear frosty night._

13th

A patrol under [blank] went out and examined the mine crater during the night, & found no trace of German saps blown in, which, if the case, is rather a sell._

A light German Trench Gun in their front line has blown in one of our Loop-holes (double) which is annoying.

14th

A quiet night. Methuen, Sniping Officer, has made some very obvious dummy loopholes to draw the fire of German Trench Gun, which it did most successfully, upon which our guns were turned onto it, & are said to have knocked it out._

Meet Orford, now an officer of S.W. Borderers, late a Sgt of this Regt and City Policeman, often to be seen outside L'pool Street Station! His Battn is in the line just on the right of us.

> Captain Edgar Francis Orford, 10th (Service) Battalion The South Wales Borderers, 115th Brigade, 38th Division

Round the line in morning with the Doctor. The Bosches fire a few registering shots at the Bn H.Q. at EBENEZER FARM, so we make arrangements what to do in case they bombard.

Feb. 14th 1916. (continued.)

No bombardment took place probably as we had made all arrangements!

Were relieved by 3rd G.G. at night. I walked back to our billets at RIEZ BAILLEUL with Paul Methuen who was pretty well done up after being up 3 days & nights sniping, with practically no rest or sleep_ Luckily I was able to help him, with a drop brandy & carrying his rifle – he was very glad to get in._

I hear the Irish Guards have manufactured 2 corpses put them out in No Mans' Land with an oil drum, so arranged that on touching the corpses a bomb explodes_ It is hoped to catch out some Bosches like this! There are already so many corpses lying out that personally I doubt their sending out a special night patrol to look at them! The corpses were so realistic that some women seeing them lying by the roadside in billets crossed themselves as they passed.

15th

Went to see Mark Maitland – Grenrs – who is ill in a billet in morning.

Hugh Ross rejoins the Battn – he is senior to all other Captains. (I am now a Major & still 2nd in command).

In afternoon I go a long walk with L. Norman & see rather a picturesque old chateau – LE MARAIS – very tumble down & squalid.

> Major Mark Edward Makgill Crichton Maitland, 3rd Grenadier Guards
> Captain Hugh Cairns Edward Ross was wounded in November 1914 during First Ypres

16th

We are relieved by 9th Cheshire Rgt – & march to billets at LE SART, a mile or two west of MERVILLE._

A gale of wind from west – squalls of rain etc – which made the march, though only about 6 miles, seem like 10._

> 9th (Service) Battalion The Cheshire Regiment, 58th Brigade, 19th Division

17th

Still blowing.

Heard the Germans had taken about 600 yds of our trenches near Ypres. Bad.

Round billets of Battalion with C.O. in morning.

In afternoon walk with the Padre through a bit of the FORÊT DE NIEPPE. Find an unexploded shell (British) buried in an oak tree. There are some magnificent oaks here tall & clean._ Saw a roe deer also some cowslips – but not any great variety of flora.

18th

A wet day.

Some officers of 8th N. Staffords, who are to relieve us, came to tea. Walked with Esmé to reconnoitre our march tomorrow.

8th (Service) Battalion The North Staffordshire Regiment, 57th Brigade, 19th Division

9

The Move North Towards Ypres

19th

March, as a Brigade, to GODEWAERSVELDE, about 14 miles North. Only one man fell out & this only when pressed by the Doctor (Wilson – for Stewart seems to have gone for good).

Hugh Ross, who has only recently rejoined us after being wounded at Ypres in Nov 1914, has to be left with the Field Ambce for a few days with a high tempre.

Our billets are very scattered but in pretty country. I go round them all in the evening – find the men very squashed up, but we are only to be here 3 nights.

Good news that Russians had taken ERZERUM.

Smith-Cunningham is going on leave to-night, I am next.

> Wilson, Royal Army Medical Corps – untraced
> The Russians captured Erzerum to the south west of the Caucasus from the Turks.
> 2nd Lieutenant Robert Dick Smith Cunningham

20th

Ride over to Brigade H.Q. in morning, at STEENVOORDE, with Esmé, and in afternoon ride with him up the MONT DES CATS, which is close by. Get a fine view of the country round, including YPRES.

The Bn H.Q. is in a large farm, & I have a funny little room looking West. To get to it – ditto Esmé to his – we have to go through Madame's room. She has 6 daughters, and one son, who is serving in the French Army at SALONIKA.

> Allied operations, including the British Salonika Force, were conducted on the Macedonian front against Bulgaria from the base at Salonika. Not until the very end of the War was much undertaken or achieved there and in the meantime disease, notably malaria, caused serious casualties.

21st

Wander about this pretty country.

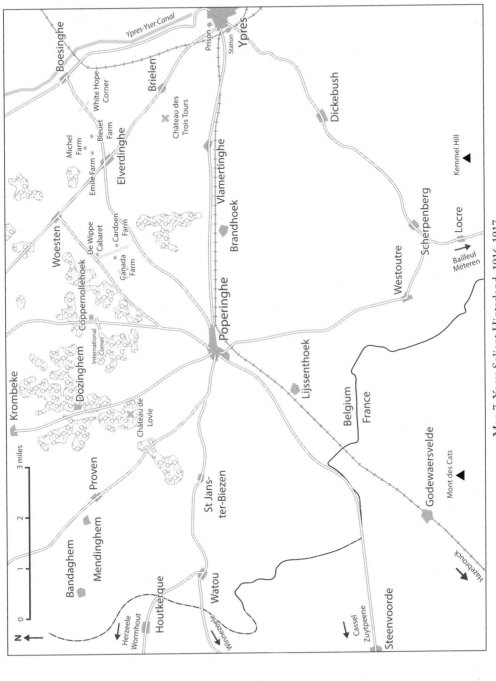

Map 7 Ypres Salient Hinterland, 1916–1917.

22nd

March to HEERZEELE in a snowstorm – very unpleasant walk – took wrong turning which made it 2 miles further and we missed our billeting party who were waiting on the proper road, thus causing a long delay – mens' billets quite fair – Officers very moderate – I am in the coldest of little rooms by myself – facing North so that the icy wind blows right in & so I have

23rd

one of the coldest nights I ever remember – & find the floor very hard.
   Go round billets with Esmé

24th

Our host has a party & so we volunteer to be out all day – Esmé & self lunch at Brigade H.Q. where I obtain my warrant for 10 days leave; hard frost deep snow – walk back with Ruthven & "the Major General" (Feilding) glorious day, no wind.
   Start on leave with the Padre 6.30.p.m., meaning to pass the night at HAAZBRUCK, but find a train just off to BOULOGNE.
   Great rumours of the French having had some very successful operations, but am not sure the Germans don't seem to have got the best of it so far.

   The major German offensive at Verdun began on 21 February, very successfully in its initial stages.

25th

Sleep at a Hotel in Boulogne – & cross at 12.15, arriving at Victoria at 4.50 p.m. where find my Violet waiting for me.

   Miles Barne was then at home until

Mar 7th

Leave Charing X in a heavy snowstorm at 9.30 a.m.
During my leave the fierce fighting round VERDUN has been taking place, and the Germans have been losing very heavily. Also the Russians have been getting on very well in Asia Minor, the last thing they have done is to take BITLIS._
   I am told off as "O.C. Troops" on board, which means I am given a deck cabin and a Staff of 2 Officers, one in Scots Fusiliers & the other in "Liverpool Scottish" to help – & virtually nothing to do, though if anything were to happen should have great responsibility, so I take good care that the orders are passed round, & that O.C. parties of troops coming on board come & report to me, etc.

   Bitlis, some way south of Erzerum
   The Royal Scots Fusiliers
   The 1st Liverpool Scottish T.F. (otherwise 1/10th Battalion The King's Regiment)

On the Channel troop transports alcohol might only be sold to commissioned officers. All ranks had to wear life jackets throughout, no lights were allowed and no smoking. Miles Barne's copy of the orders for "O.C.Troops" on the SS Invicta on this voyage contained further instructions about life jackets,

Considerable losses and damage to jackets has occurred on the Transports running from Folkestone. Officers Commanding Troops are requested to issue such orders as may be necessary to the Officers and Non-commissioned Officers with the Troops to ensure that every care is taken to prevent such loss or damage, cutting off of the tapes, etc. As soon as the Men have fallen in, prior to landing, each Man should take off his life jacket and place the same in piles of 50, and not throw them here and there on the decks, where they get trampled on, dirtied, and otherwise damaged.

Miles Barne continued,

A very good crossing – arrive at BOULOGNE about 3.30 p.m. & find a train on to CALAIS at 5.pm, where I first deliver a bed which I have brought out with care & trouble & expense & anxiety for the Brigadier, who rather sniffs as it is such a big package; then I go to a Hotel where I hear the C.O. is dining & there I find about 12 officers of the Battn & many others in the Brigade, having a very scrambly & expensive dinner. after dinner I try to find my way back to the Hotel Sauvage where I have leave to sleep, but have a great difficulty as I never remember seeing such a dark or deserted town. I am lucky to find a vacant room – the last – & turn in about 10 p.m.

The Guards Division had moved up behind the Ypres Salient ahead of taking over from the 14th (Light) Division, New Army, in XIV Corps. The Corps was responsible for the left half of the Salient from the Menin Road north to the Ypres-Yser Canal at Boesinghe. Initially, because the 14th Division had just moved into reserve, the Guards Division were not needed, apart from the inevitable fatigues, and their Brigades were sent to Calais separately for a fortnight each for a change of air. The arrangements appeared orderly to Miles Barne, but the situation that the 3rd Guards Brigade, the first to go there, found on arrival was chaotic, quite apart from the cold and storms. The 2nd Guards Brigade went to Calais on 5 March.

8th

Route march in morning. My pony is late coming for me but I start walking out to the Camp, & meet him.

The Camp is quite a good one on sand, a mile from the sea, on Dunkerque road.

The Bn has been at POPERINGHE in my absence, doing some digging of a line behind the line – have had no fighting & no casualties._ They came up here by train.

In afternoon walk with L. Norman and Abercrombie down to sea, about 2 miles off – across country – over sand dunes etc. Find tide very low, exposing wire entanglements at wide intervals. Talked to a French Coast guard sentry – & saw some very big guns by harbour mouth – also remains of a nasty accident – where apparently a waggon had been overtaken by a train – anyhow one horse was (dead) wedged under a truck which was derailed, another horse was standing with a broken leg, and the waggon was in a 1000 pieces, in all directions. Had tea at Maritime Hotel and walked back alone across country.

Lieutenant Robert Alexander Abercromby, known as "Bobbie"

9th

Coy Drill in morning after which the Brigade, along with 2 Belgian Artillery Brigades, was inspected by the C in C Sir Douglas Haig, a very simple sort of review, but the coldest wait I have had for a long time – a biting NE wind & several degrees of frost last night which was the coldest I ever remember.

In evening I walked into Calais where I tea'd at the Grand Hotel and bought some p.c.'s for children.

10th

A very interesting visit with a party of Officers of the Brigade to the Ordnance & Supply Depots – repairing shops, Bakery etc – such a wonderful sight – & makes one wonder how the Germans can manage to keep going with their enormous numbers.

The C.O. is ill, so I get the Brigadier to order him to go & sleep in the town: which he does without great difficulty, owing to our having engaged a room and a fly to take him down in.

A nasty bombing accident, whereby the Grenadiers lose 2 men killed and 21 wounded, and these unfortunately are all the best bombers.

Five members of the 3rd Grenadier Guards died at Calais on 10 and 11 March 1916.
21581 Private George A Barber †10.3.16
21429 Private Charles W T Brown †11.3.16
21036 Private Edwin Cyril Challoner †11.3.16
20343 Private Charles E Coy †11.3.16
20556 Lance Corporal Benjamin Moore †11.3.16

11th

Spend the whole morning practising bombing attack by Companies – about 11.a.m. the Brigadier comes up, and we do it a new way for his edification.

Miles Barne kept a copy of the orders for this, the idea of which was to break into the enemy line and penetrate as far as and then hold the second line. The first platoon were to double across the 150 yards of No Man's Land, for these training purposes, and occupy the enemy front line opposite. At once two bombing teams, each followed by a section, were then to head straight up the enemy communication trenches. These sections were to organise blocking parties at trench junctions as necessary. The second platoon was to reinforce the first in the enemy front line, with the third then moving quickly forward to the enemy second line once the bombers reached it. The fourth was to follow the third and also occupy the enemy second line. It was all to be done with great speed and dash, essential to success. In the event they never had to carry out this operation for real.

Yesterday was "pay day", when there were 23 men absent, so at C.O.'s order's this morning I have a big lot of criminals to settle – and all passes into the town have to be stopped.

There is to be a race meeting tomorrow, & I am to ride the C Coy grey pony, so I take him down for a gallop on the sands – he is very fast for about 3 or 4 furlongs, but I doubt his staying the 5 furlongs. I then go down to a meeting of C.O.s at Bde HQ in the town (Hotel Sauvage) to discuss Company Bombing Attacks, which evidently portends something of the sort coming off in the not very far future.

Dine at Bde H.Q., where the "Town Commandant" is being entertained. His name is *[blank]* and his staff Hugo Baring, Lowther (11th Hussars), Henderson etc._

> Captain The Honourable Hugo Baring, 11th Reserve Regiment of Cavalry
> Captain John George Lowther, The 11th Hussars
> Henderson – untraced

12th

Our engagement day – 12 years ago.

There is a Brigade Football Tournament. The G.G. have beaten the Irish, & we play the Coldm today – neither side scores in the 1½ hrs + an extra 20 min., so must play again tomorrow.

So many invalids now – Hammersley with Measles, (a horrid rumour is afloat that he has died) – Trafford, Boyd-Rochford, Thompson, the C.O., & now the Padre gone sick.

In afternoon a Brigade Race Meeting, when the Battn wins 3 out of the 6 events_ I ride the winner of the light weight race, an easy win – "The Tetrarch" must be a very fast pony. C. Bewicke wins 2 other races – also a 3rd, but is disqualified owing to the "spirit" of the conditions not being fulfilled – the conditions were badly drawn up.

The Course was a beautiful one on the sands – the judge being the Brigadier. One race was a steeplechase, i.e. over whin fences – very easy ones. Col Butler, I.G., won this easily. Tim O.E. was 4th on Kinlay's horse. 2 Officers of I.G. dressed up complete in fur collars brown billicocks & button holes were bookies, & made about £20 on the Meeting.

> The Tetrarch had been with the 1st Scots Guards since the very start of the War and was originally owned by Captain Reginald George Stracey †1.1.15, apart from Lieutenant Kinlay, the Quartermaster, the only officer in the Battalion to survive First Ypres.

March 13th 1916

Watched Coldm doing Bombing Attack practice.

Play our repetition match v. Coldm, football, defeating them 2-1., so play the final v. Grenadiers tomorrow.

The Bn Officers – I am kicked out of the team – play the Grenadiers & beat them 5-0.

In afternoon ride with Hugh Ross onto the sands & go to see an old submerged & derelict submarine.

14th

We play the final of Bde Football Competn, & win by 5:0 – beating 3/G.G. The Bdr provides & presents a bronze mounted French Cavalry soldier. Great rejoicing in the Battn.

Coy bombing assaults all the afternoon: walk with L. Norman in evening.

15th

C.O., who is very seedy still, explains the Ypres defence scheme – we dont look forward to going there.

In evening the Battn Officers play final of Brigade Officers' Football Cup (a French Infantryman supporting a wounded Englishman) v. Coldstream – a very good & level game – 2 all, & play overtime in the dark when Coldm score 3 goals & so win 5-2: very unlucky – I think part[l]y owing to their having white jerseys on, & so able to see & pass to one another.

Dined at Hotel Continental & had some extraordinary dreams about home, a band of outlaws had settled in an outhouse at Sotterley, etc. etc.

This is my 42nd birthday

16th

Leave Calais by train at 11.30.a.m. via St. Omer and nearly into Hazebrouck, to CASSEL, where we detrained and marched over the hill, not quite through the village to WINNEZEEL, where we have pretty good billets, tho' rather scattered. My own in a tiny thatched cottage, where a dove is kept. The Officers Baggage Waggon runs away, so we do not get our baggage that night, but arrives early on

17th

At last we seem to have done the cold spell. The 15th was the first clear day at Calais, such a pity just as we were leaving.

In morning ride round billets and in to Bde H.Q. with Esmé.

In afternoon ride into CASSEL, an interesting old town, & H.Q. of 2nd Army._ Have tea – with Kinlay & Thompson at an inn, with magnificent view. The place is at the western end of the ridge which also contains Mt des Cats Mt Noir & Kemmel – jutting right out of the plain.

We are in very good billets – at one is a flax dresser – a very hard worker – a slow process, & no doubt much behind the times.

There are many magpies' nests round here.

18th

Walk with Esmé in afternoon through a wood & to look at an Aerodrome.

19th

March at 8.30 a.m. to POPERINGHE: where Bn HQ & all Officers mess at a big Villa – without much glass in windows (none in my room).

The first person I meet is Bob Dashwood, who is a Bde Major of 61st Bde, 20th Divn, in our XIV's Corps. I have tea with him.

Captain Sir Robert Henry Seymour Dashwood, Bt, known as "Bob", The Oxfordshire and Buckinghamshire Light Infantry, Miles Barne's first cousin

20th

Esmé & Adjt go off early to YPRES, and get well shelled on the way back between there and VLAMERTINGHE. I go round billets which are all in houses and a convent in the town. They are in very good order, though filthy when taken over yesterday.

Jack Stirling appears from a Hospital in the Town, and I take him for a walk towards Chateau LOGIE, which the late King of the Belgians built for Madame_

> The Château de Lovie was currently the Headquarters of XIV Corps. King Leopold II of the Belgians †17.12.09 did not build it. Caroline Lacroix, his most prominent mistress, was known as Madame.

About 7 a.m. two German aeroplanes come over and drop 4 bombs quite close to Battn H.Q. Weather much warmer.

Baden appears to tea – he is looking for a suitable place for a new bombing school._

21st

A lecture on gassing & being gassed by a Medical Officer – very poor and badly delivered. Walk with Luss to get the key (from an old woman about 3 kilometres away) of a room to be Sergts Mess. She was most ungracious, in spite of our promises to pay for all damage, & would not hear of such a thing. I think the Belgians are a very 2nd rate people – a French woman would not have refused in all probability, or would have done so politely. One is always hearing stories of bad ways & manners of Belgians.

In afternoon the Band (Coldm) plays in our garden for the benefit of the men, but rather damped by rain. I later walk with Jack Stirling and Hugh Ross: In evening we all go to see "The Fancies", an excellent sort of Music Hall Show, all done by soldiers, who are struck off trench & duty, and only do fatigues by day.

Beckwith-Smith and John Dyer of Bde Staff come to dinner.

There is not yet much sign of spring here, but the woods are carpeted with periwinkles.

> The Fancies were the concert party of the 6th Division, Regular Army, from whom the Guards Division were just taking over the right half of the XIV Corps area of the Ypres Salient.

22nd

I walked with Esmé in morning – met Ross, the Quartermaster of 2nd Bn, who said his Transport had been properly shelled last night going down to YPRES – & some stampeded, several casualties to men & horses. He was looking for it at the time. The Bn had suffered in consequence. Oh! we have got our heads into a Hornet's nest here. Walked by myself exploring new Rly in afternoon.

Baden dined.

23rd

Eight months since I have been in country!

The C.O., Luss and H. Ross go off at 4 a.m. to see the Front Line Trenches – come back plastered in mud. & tell us all about them. I dont suppose they are as bad as made out_

More snow.

Long walk by myself, in afternoon in woods to North._

Tim O.E. went off to Hospital with flu 2 days ago. Some say he won't return – time will show, I expect him in 2 or 3 days or a week at latest.

24th

I draw a beautiful pair of gum boots from the Quartermaster. & a blanket. The C.O. gives us a talk about the part of the line we are going to hold. There is no doubt it is not to be all beer & skittles._

Ride with Padre behind French Lines to the North, passing through the villages of WESTVLETEREN (Westleton?) and CROMBEK. We passed the place where one of their Observation Balloons lives, and were regarded with suspicion by sentries etc., almost expected to be arrested and searched!

25th

Walked in morning with Luss who did some shopping.

In afternoon walked by myself_ The Battn Entrained at 9.0 a.m. [p.m.] for its journey into YPRES, only about 15 minutes – glided in there without a single light or sound – the engine driver seems to have made a study of this_ Schiff (Lieut Scots Guards!) who is our billeting Officer, having gone ahead as usual, was waiting for us, and on the lookout, but even then he never heard us arrive, though not 200 yds from the train.

   Lieutenant Marcus Noel Schiff †17.6.16

We made a slow & solemn march through this wretched deserted tumble down ruined town – with the ghostly remains of its once very picturesque houses & streets & public buildings watching us – to our various dug-outs – the Battn H.Q. ones being in the Canal Bank – quite good so far as comfort goes, but very far from being shellproof. The night is disturbed only by the banging of our own guns all round us – some very close – about 2 p.m. [a.m.] there is a distant intense bombardment – possibly something to do with a report we have heard that 26 trains have arrived from the E. opposite the Belgians in the North. Time will show.

   The southern end of the Ypres-Yser Canal ran into Ypres where there was a quay for barges. The eastern side of the Canal Bank was suitable to accommodate some of the troops in brigade reserve behind this part of the front line, others being in the ground floors and cellars of buildings in the town.

10

The Ypres Salient April 1916

26th

Walk round the Coys with Esmé, and to 3rd Bde H.Q., for we are under Genl Pa Heyworth for a few hours, till we have relieved his Brigade. Find him very affable._

Have a good look round the town – the Cathedral & Cloth Hall etc, or rather what is left of them, still very beautiful._

Quite a lot of gunning on both sides.

In evening walk round town with Thompson – and at 10 p.m. we parade to relieve the 2nd Battn in trenches near POTIJZE, passing through the old town defences by the MENIN Gate.

The relief is a very slow one – the trenches being awkwardly sited and arranged by our predecessors and is not over till 2 a.m. however meanwhile at Battn H.Q. we have a good chat with Dick Coke and Roger Tempest.

> The 3rd Guards Brigade were completing their first trench tour in the Salient, having taken over just north of the Menin Road from a brigade of the 6th Division, who, by all Scots Guards accounts, had lost their nerve. The conditions were more dire than they should have been even in this unforgiving environment. In the line the 2nd Scots Guards had been the left hand battalion of their Brigade, the right hand one being between them and the Menin Road.

27th

At 4.15 a.m. a huge intense bombardment begins to the S – and lasts till 8 a.m.

The Brigadier arrives about 6 a.m., accompanied by Col Heywood, Coldstream, who has succeeded Jerry Ruthven as GSO 1 of the Division: The[y] say the 3rd Divn has blown up 3 mines at ST. ELOI, which accounts for the noise, & bombardment, evidently an attack is being made at same time._ At 8 a.m. the Brigr came running breathlessly into our dugout, asking for shelter, for indeed the Bosch is shelling our neighbourhood._

We had turned in 6–8 a.m. for another nap.

> Lieutenant Colonel Cecil Percival Heywood, Coldstream Guards, General Staff Officer Grade I, Guards Division

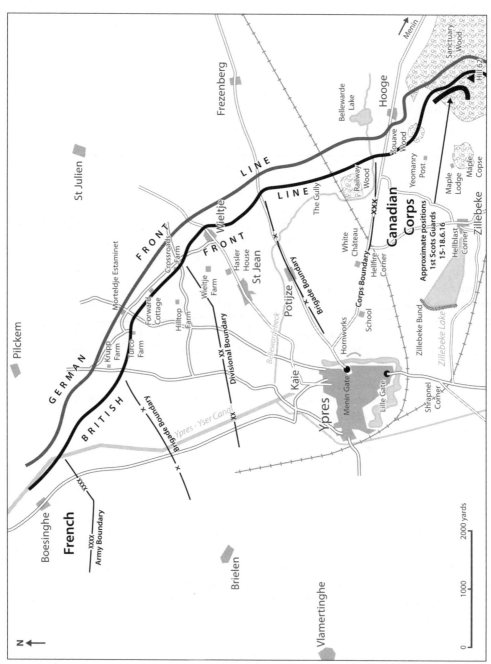

Map 8 Ypres Salient, XIV Corps sector, Spring and Summer 1916.

At 10.a.m. I went round our trenches alone; such a fearful mess, in some places hardly a "line" at all, merely heaps of mud. These trenches like those at LAVENTIE, seem to have been utterly neglected till our Divn took them over 10 days ago, and will require a lot of work on them before they are fit for anything. Hardly any dugouts, or firesteps, or drainage or traverses or parados – and we are warned that as soon as any are put up, unless well disguised, the Bosch will have them down again at once.

There are several very "draughty" corners, and I got sniped at a bit.

The Battn HQ is fairly good in sort of 2dy tube iron lining, almost in a cemetery.

> The reference to "2dy tube" is Tuppenny Tube, an early part of the London Underground.

While I am out, there is a heavy bombardment of Railway Wood on our right, held by 1/ Coldstm, the key of our position. I hear this often happens and there are good deep dugouts there. YPRES is plainly visible about 3 kilometres behind us.

Heavy gunning continues to South & over us all day. We have several casualties.

Mar 27th 1916. (contd)

Our nice Doctor Philip Smith has left us, to his disappointment, as well as ours, and we have in his place a little Yankee, Alexander, who was attached to the Canadians – rather a tiresome though perhaps clever & amusing little man.

In afternoon I go and visit R.F. Coy which I had not time to do this morning – found them very restless as their line being briskly shelled, 1 killed 3 wounded so far, & I did not loiter much in the dangerous area, which they had wisely cleared altogether, quite wisely as they are a sort of 3rd line. The Battn's total Casualties for the day 3 killed and 5 wounded, a bad start.

> Philip Smith, Royal Army Medical Corps – untraced
> Alexander, presumably Canadian Army Medical Corps – untraced
> 10455 Corporal George Ledingham McKellar †27.3.16
> 12382 Private James Wither Tully †27.3.16
> 13304 Private Henry Flavell †27.3.16

28th

Another intense bombardment practically all night on our right – don't know who, whether Canadians or what.

We heard the result of y'day's operations at St. Eloi – in places 2 lines of German trenches taken, also 1 Officer & 128 prisoners, since become 168 and now 188!

Am in a dugout with the Doctor – Alexander – a little trying at times, he tonight would read out to me a long letter from "The New Moses" whom he had once already put in a lunatic Asylum.

> The shelling and explosions of the day before and subsequently marked the start of the Battle of the St Eloi Craters, which went on for over three weeks, engaging the 3rd Division and later the Canadians.

29th

At 5 a.m. I take E. Ward and Yorke of 3rd Grenadiers round the line, the former comes all along the worst bit with me – & is uncomfortably impressed and we have to do a lot of doubling past the "draughty corners".

I remain in or near dugout for the rest of the day_ Here our men can only work by night – sleep & eat by day, but the trench conditions are as a rule very uncomfortable here, no sort of shelters, no traverses or parados in the worst places, where our trench is enfiladed by a German one at quite close range, very wet and muddy – & the last few nights have been very wet & dark, so very little work has been done – and of course all material has to be carried up a long way.

The parapets are very thin, & easily & constantly knocked down.

Captain Edward "Eddy" Simons Ward, 3rd Grenadier Guards
Lieutenant The Honourable Bernard Elliot Yorke, 3rd Grenadier Guards

Miles Barne kept a message sent that day,

To Officers in Medical Charge of Units

Please note that the report called for in this office No. 99, of 20/3/16, is not now required, except in the case of any appearance of sickness amongst the rats or in the presence of many dead ones whose deaths were not caused by violence.
FDG Howell
Captain, R.A.M.C.
for A.D.M.S., Guards Division

Captain F D G Howell, Royal Army Medical Corps

30th

Went round line early again taking a Grenadier Coy Sgt Major and Platoon Sgt. who will relieve us tonight – got sniped at badly again – the bullet seemed to go close to my ear in one place & struck a traverse about a yard off. The line has been improved during the night, but only a start made, anyhow one can now get along the trench without going on "all fours" till it is next blown in!

Such a glorious morning, even a wood pigeon cooing near our Battn H.Q., but guns and howitzers and anti-aircraft weapons etc etc going in all directions such a continuous fire as we never heard in the LAVENTIE line – but at 12.45 p.m. there commences such an intense bombardment as I have never had against me before – at 3 p.m. they knock off – we get telephone communication with Luss, C. Coy, who says in his usual drawly way "wretched shooting" & he has had no casualties, tho' all his dugouts burst in – but B Coy has 4 killed and 1 wounded – R.F. 1 wounded – L.F. we can't hear from, but the front line do not seem to have had much at them.

Col de Crespigny, 2nd Grenadiers dropped in about 12.30 p.m. to see Esmé, & had to stay with us right up till 3 p.m., as he couldn't get away. It is a marvel anybody is left, but luckily Luss was right and the shooting very poor.

At 4 p.m. the intense bombardment continues till 5.15 p.m., then breaks off, (while we have tea) till 5.45 p.m. when continues till 7 p.m. after which at intermittent periods of ½ hr or so through the night. The Relief by 3rd G.G. takes place, commencing at 8 p.m., but owing to the "straafing" is a very slow business – casualties keep happening – dead & wounded have to be found in the wrecked trenches – rifles equipment packs etc etc have to be looked for and distributed – a very dark night – the Bn H.Q. does not get away till 2.30 a.m., when by a cross country route we are able to get to our new billets in YPRES Canal dugouts safely – about 3.30 a.m. after which I go round the Coys with the Adjt – hearing dismal tales – & finally get to bed at 4.30 a.m., nearly the round of the Clock, after one of the worst, if not quite, days I ever remember – LF & RF trenches have after all been almost annihilated and flattened out – and the men much rattled and disorganized – sitting being bombarded without being able to do anything in reply is very weary and trying work – making an attack – even tho' casualties might be higher – would be preferable in many ways.

> Lieutenant Colonel Claude Raul Champion de Crespigny, Commanding 2nd Grenadier Guards

31st

Sleep till 9 a.m., tho' rather disturbed by some big shells falling unpleasantly near our dugout – 1 about 20 yards off – when the Corps Commander (Cavan) & Divl Comr (Fielding) come round – but throw no great light on yesterday's bombardment – hint at some change of our dispositions in near future !!!

I go round the Coys, and find the total casualties, in killed, wnd & missing are about 2 officers (Ward & Mann both B Coy slightly wnd) and 83 others – including about 20 to 25 killed – probably, tho' some of the missing may turn up O.K._

Later in day walk round with Esmé, we hear every sort of story about yesterday.

> Lieutenant Francis Ward, borrowed from the 2nd Scots Guards after Loos
> Lieutenant Francis Thomas Mann
> Thirty one members of the 1st Scots Guards lost their lives on 30 March. One was a signatory of the document after Loos commending Miles Barne's conduct to Brigadier General Ponsonby,
> 12011 Private Lance Bird †30.3.16
> Two more who signed it were severely injured and died of wounds,
> 9516 Lance Corporal Alexander Thomson †25.4.16
> 10755 Lance Corporal Joseph Matthews †1.5.16

Apr. 1st

At 12 midnight I am awakened by very heavy rifle and gun fire – which seems to be further S. perhaps near St. Eloi.

Later, about 4 a.m., I am awakened by the Sentry prodding me in stomach – I find he has lit my candle, & tells me there is more firing – however all is quiet on our front – I was wondering whether he was making an April fool of me or not – but the firing was being continued to the South.

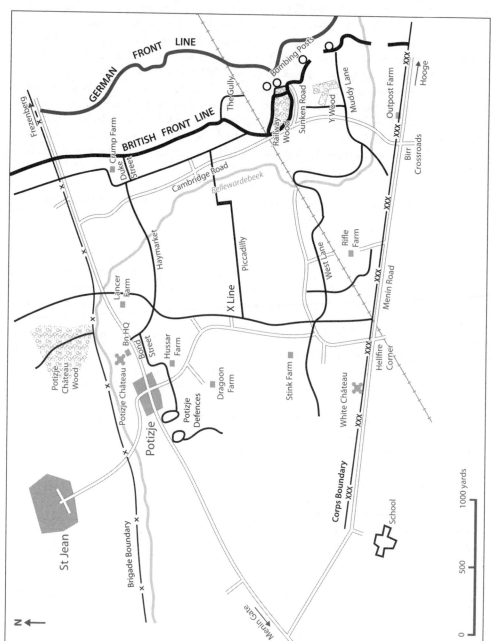

Map 9 Ypres Salient, XIV Corps right hand brigade sector north of the Menin Road, March and April 1916.

Sketch in morning, and in afternoon Tim arrives with John Dyer – the former seems quite recovered. There is much air craft activity.

R.F. Coy is billeted in the prison LF in Canal Bank not our canal however, but a tributary one. Poor old Dick Bethel seems much aged & rattled since Thursday, I hope he will be sent off for a change.

Considerable shrapnel shelling near our dugouts just where I was sitting sketching! Very nearly got Gen Pereira who happened to be walking by at the moment._

Walked round the Coys in evening with Thompson. Heard numerous stories anent Thursday's straaf – some poor creatures seem to have had a very bad time. One man was left for dead, with his forehead & most of his body buried, with 2 Grenadiers in a bombing post; both Grenadiers were killed and our man only found by almost chance, and found to be alive._

Considerable shelling in neighbourhood of Battn H.Q. All this activity is difficult to account for, those who have been here some time agree that it is more than for months past.

On 30th, the gunners estimate with curious though usual diversity of opinion, the number of enemy shells put over vary from 4000 to 100000! In any case considering the number sent over, it is extraordinary how few casualties we had in the Divn – nobody having (as at Loos) anything like ours._ Some think they meant to attack afterwards but I doubt this – unless by using gas which they never did do – the wind being wrong then, but right now_

I forget if I said that young Martindale, LF Coy was twice over buried & dug out on 30th & then this evening he was going off on a night fatigue near the front – happy as possible – I shall do all I can to get the C.O. to send his name in – as an example like that in a much shaken Coy is invaluable – and all the more creditable when the (acting) Coy Commander is in such a shaky state.

Captain The Honourable Richard Bethell was sent home and did not reappear, another who left with shell shock being Lieutenant Hammersley, also permanently.
Brigadier General Cecil Edward Pereira, Commanding 1st Guards Brigade

2nd

Several men still going away from "Shell shock" – this generally continues for another 10 days. Dick Bethel I am glad to hear is to be sent away – his nerves seem completely gone_

A very disturbed night – so much shelling of the town and close vicinity of our dug-outs. One bouquet of High Explosive Shrapnell burst all over the canal & bridge over it – I rushed out expecting to find our sentry hit, but he was quite all right.

While the 1st Bn Irish Guards Sgt Major & Drill Sgt (Kirk & Carrol) were returning off leave on their way to rejoin their Battn yesterday late – walking across the Square, they got hit by shrapnell, the former hit in stomach and not expected to live, the latter's leg had to be taken off this morning: poor unfortunate men. They had both been out since the beginning of the war._

It appears now that we are to be "in" 16 days and "out" 8, the "in" means

4 days front trenches
4 " Canal Bank & town
4 " front trenches
4 " town
the "out" means in or near POPERINGHE._

Of course the Canal Bank is very comfortable – have a good bed & dugout to myself & many advantages, but we are at very short notice and a considerable amount of shelling; and fatigues for the men, especially at night.

Both the above poor Irish Guardsmen have died._

> 108 Sergeant Major John Kirk, 1st Battalion Irish Guards †2.4.16
> 2562 Company Sergeant Major Patrick Andrew Carroll, 1st Battalion Irish Guards, lost
>   most of his left leg below the knee.

The reason the town is shelled so much at night is evidently owing to the transport which comes up, & right through as far as POTIJZE etc. The rattle on a still night can be heard for miles. Esmé has proposed that it should come up in motor lorries, but these apparently are not allowed beyond the town. It would be far less risky.

In a letter to Violet Barne on 2 April Lieutenant Orr Ewing, who had been in hospital, wrote:

I reached the Batt yesterday morning & we are in reserve till tomorrow night, but its a particularly noisy reserve – the whole place is different to any I've yet been in and hard to imagine until you are here – one hears so many stories about the place but the saying that a month of this is equal to a year anywhere else seems perfectly true_ The poor battalion had a very rough time last Thursday which I missed, it was considered to have been one of the most terrific bombardments seen and taking it all round we got off lightly considering it went on for 5 hours & they can shoot at you from 3 sides – our observation officers could see with glasses groups of German Staff officers about 6 miles back watching without doubt only too delighted_ Miley has just been round, he has the very greatest admiration and respect held of him by everyone, always he thinks of other people & never of himself_

Miles Barne continued the following night after they went back into the line:

April 3rd 1916

Relieved 3rd Gren. in trenches, starting 10.30 p.m. from the MENIN GATE (YPRES) – the relief being over by 2.30 a.m. The C.O. Adjt Dr & self waited at the MENIN GATE (which is really just a hole in the ramparts), for an hour or so to see the Coys pass, before we went off – a very unpleasant wait; there was a good deal of shelling going on in neighbourhood and one never quite knew when it would come our way – however all's well that ends well – we only had 2 men hit going in to trenches.

4th

I started up at 2.30 a.m. with an Orderly to visit the front line, which found in an appalling state after the bombardment on the 30th ult., tho' meanwhile the Grenadiers had done their best. I slipped about & stuck in mud, caught in broken trench boards etc; it was wonderful that the relief went as well as it did.

A cold grey morning, such a change from yesterday which was grilling hot.

Now comes our turn, and our "Heavies" start a huge bombardment at 10.30 a.m. which has been discussed & prepared for for days, but have to knock off about 11 a.m. owing to haze.

The Brigadier arrives about 5 a.m. to take Esmé to see some new ground, I had just returned from trenches & watched them go off into (apparently) ground swept by shellfire; however, it was really going over their heads; I was nevertheless relieved to find E. had returned safe & sound when I woke up at 8 a.m.

Our firing brought some retaliation on our trenches from the big PILKEM gun, which enfilades our trenches. Luckily no damage was done to anybody but more havoc to the trenches.

The Germans had a large calibre gun which could fire obliquely into the British forward trenches from behind Pilckem Ridge, itself providing excellent observation

A Col. Barnes – Marine with 2 junior Officers turned up to be attached to us.

Colonel Barnes, Royal Marines – untraced

At 10.30 p.m. I take the two latter up to the line where they are to be attached to Coys for instruction. I don't think they appreciate the fun! especially when they see the so-called dugout up there.

I then go on right along the line which I had not really seen since the bombardment on 30th, & Luss takes me right to the further end, when we see all the bombing posts etc, of course having to keep very quiet, as the Germans have their listening posts close by. It is impossible to get along in the trench, so part of the way we go overground, which personally I never very much care about.

The state of mud is fearful, the parties carrying up Ammunition Trench Boards and all sorts of material have a really bad time of it, shellholes every few yards etc. I get back to Battn H.Q. at 2.45 a.m., finding Esmé

5th

just about to start with the old Marine Colonel.

Yesterday's bombardment is continued at 10.30 a.m. which of course stirs up the Bosch, and they retaliate a certain amount on our front and Bn H.Q. where a dugout (close to mine!) – luckily empty – is blown in about 11.30 a.m. The bombardment – on both sides – goes on all day – our casualties being 4 killed & 18 wndd, including Coy Sgt Major Clarke of B. Coy, which is a bad loss. There were the usual many stories and narrow squeaks and altogether the Bn has been lucky considering the number of shells. B & C Coys apply to be relieved from the front line so the C.O. arranges for their relief by the 2 flank Coys tonight.

6260 Private John McKenna †5.4.16
11194 Private James Gorman †5.4.16
13704 Private James Henry White †5.4.16
13870 Private Christopher Jones †5.4.16
3289 Company Sergeant Major Cecil George Clarke, first to sign and probable prime
    mover of the B Company document after Loos, died of wounds †24.4.16

During dinner a message arrives by hand saying the Germans can hear all we say on our telephones within 1500 yds of themselves, so the orders for relief have to be altered, I am sent off to tell Ross verbally and there is a general stir up, in consequence of the hasty alteration.

Captain Ross commanded Right Flank

Our old Colonel Barnes departs at 10 p.m. taking a very tender & rather pompous farewell – he didn't much enjoy his 24 hrs in the trenches, tho' no doubt will talk a lot about it when he gets home – he came in for a lot of shelling – a very slippery muddy dark journey up to – & along a short bit of the front line, and witnessed an "air dual" with the usual undecided ending.

6th

I go up the line at 2 a.m., getting back 4.45 – the going is even worse than y'day, the night much darker; the line very thinly held – partly as owing to the bombardments there is less room for them, and partly owing to our many casualties and sick our numbers have very seriously dwindled. The men are somewhat rattled and their nerves have not yet recovered the bombardment of 30th, and till we get a new draft or a longish rest they wont appreciate the honour of being in the trenches. I found Ross & Luss both very cheerful – in fact all the Officers are – but they all say the men have temporarily deteriorated._

   Visit from the Major-Genl (Fielding) and Brigadier during morning.

   Sure enough, a prisoner had a notebook containing everything sent on the telephone by one of our Battns near St. ELOI!

   A comparatively quiet day. No shelling of front trenches, though a good bit round Battn H.Q., luckily nothing big on the dugouts – or I should not be here to write this probably.

   In evening the 4 men killed on 5th are buried just outside our dugouts – in the dark – 2 R.C.'s by Father Knapp – & 2 others by Rodgers, the C. of E. Chaplain to the Brigade – Gillieson being unable to get up here. The R.C. service usually takes 20 min on active service, but in the dark barely 5! Whether there was too much machine gun fire going on at the time, or whether the Priest had forgotten the words of the service I don't know.

   The Reverend Simon Stock Knapp, C.F., 2nd Irish Guards †1.8.17
   The Reverend Travers Guy Rogers, C.F., 2nd Guards Brigade, author of A Rebel at
      Heart

7th

The C.O. forbade me to go round the line during the night – why I cant think – which was a real disappointment, as I particularly wanted to see the L.F. Coy and Tim O-E, and the other officers who I believe really like to see a visitor up there, even though such a dull one as myself._

   The Coldstream has killed a German Sgt Major in their Barbed wire, he was evidently leading a patrol, and got discovered while inspecting our wire. They brought his body in and sent down his equipment revolver and some clothing, etc.

   Who should suddenly appear out of a hole in my dugout but a stoat, quite tame.

   I amuse myself now every evening by sawing firewood – there are heaps of broken trees and branches about – ready for sawing up.

This old Chateau and its surroundings must have been formerly very charming. A wood and shrubbery a lake & stream, bridges & so on, prettily laid out_ What will the owner think when he returns to find it all in ruins, the trees smashed about, glass houses in smitherenes, shellholes, fruit trees wripped up, dug outs everywhere, iron railings & beautiful old iron gates all broken, one little cemetery in the Kitchen garden, and another between the Chateau and the lake.

In evening there is a heavy straaf (Artillery) on the 1st Grens close by on our left – they get off very light; our Battn HQ comes in for some of this – but no casualties. About 6 p.m. I go down the line to give the orders for relief to the Companies, & get back about 8 p.m., feed and

8th

sleep till 1 a.m. when are relieved by 3rd Gren.

> Battalion Headquarters were in the grounds of Potijze Château.
> The 1st Grenadier Guards, right forward battalion of the 3rd Guards Brigade, were on the left of the 1st Scots Guards.
> The 2nd Guards Brigade were going into Divisional Reserve in camps east of Poperinghe.

I go ahead with the Doctor down to the Railway, but by 2.30 when the train has to go only 2½ Coys have arrived_ Another train goes at 3.30 a.m, without any warning, leaving about 6 officers and 40 men behind. The C.O. is dragged on by unknown hands at last moment – those left – including myself – start walking, but soon meet a train which is lucky, about 4.15 a.m. when getting light & we get into our CAMP A without further adventure. The train could not have gone any later – & had we had to walk all the way, would very likely have been shelled.

The Camp is quite a good one, just wooden huts dotted about irregularly to avoid being spotted by Aeroplanes – & surrounded by trees so unseen from German lines.

Sleep till 11.30 a.m.

Walk with Thompson in evening and see some gnrs making ready to move a 6 in gun which has been there for 3 months.

We are in the neighbourhood of the "heavies" – a big chateau at VLAMERTINGHE, close by, being the H.Q. of our Corps Heavy Artillery.

9th

We hear our 2nd Battn have been rather badly "straafed" going into the trenches, losing 3 officers & 20 men: one of the Officers is Jack Corbett, who was originally my ensign in 1903, & who had only just come out again._

> Captain John Dugdale Pelham Astley Corbett was evacuated from the Aisne in September 1914 with dysentery

Attend Presbyterian Service. Walk afterwards with L. Norman.

Saw a Zeppelin sailing over the German line at dusk last night.

Walked in evening with Tim O.E. & Luss, through VLAMERTINGHE which is in a sad state of ruin, where also we inspected the little cemetery – badly kept – amongst other graves there, was that of the gallant Francis Grenfell V.C. 9th Lancers – I think the first V.C. of the War.

Saw a good many Canadians about – a motor buses of them going up to the trenches.

> Captain Francis Octavius Grenfell, The 9th Lancers †24.5.15. His VC action on 24 August 1914 was very early in the War, but not the first.
> The Canadian Corps were in the southern half of the Ypres Salient, from the Menin Road down to the neighbourhood of St Eloi.

April 10th 1916

Glorious hot sunny day.

Walk with Esmé in morning to look at Camp C where we are to move to this evening – in a young oak wood – wooden huts of every size shape & colour – different intervals in between huts and all at different angles. Found de Crespigny & 2nd Bn Gren there.

On way back passing Camp B where are 1st Gren. I recognize an old friend in Pte Lawlor who was one of my Brigade Signallers in S. Africa. Had not seen him for 14 years.

We move into Camp C at 6.30 p.m. & are relieved in our Camp A by 2nd Coldm (J. Campbell).

Our Qmr Sgt Lemon is accosted by young Dade – a Pte in 2nd Gren. late underkeeper at Sotterley, who has been out the whole war, & kindly asks after me. I have tried to find him several times but always just miss him._

Peevor joins us from the mysterious entrenching Battalion. During dinner a bomb is dropped from an aeroplane fairly close to us.

> 19972 Private John Lawlor, 1st Grenadier Guards †27.7.17
> Lieutenant Colonel John Vaughan Campbell, Commanding 2nd Coldstream Guards
> 3024 Company Quartermaster Sergeant Henry Bertie Lemon, Left Flank 1st Scots Guards
> 16519 Private Montague G Dade, 2nd Grenadier Guards
> Lieutenant George Charles Peevor

> The 7th (Guards) Entrenching Battalion, generally called the Guards Entrenching Battalion, formed in December 1915. These battalions gave an active occupation to officers and men not yet required in infantry battalions. The Guards Entrenching Battalion were initially near Albert, working on preparations for the Battle of the Somme, gradually moved further east as it developed and were near the Cambrai battlefield when disbanded in September 1917.

11th

Such a change in weather – pouring wet.

In afternoon I ride into POPERINGHE (2¾ mi. away) with Trafford – our transport Officer – and the Padre, & visit the Divisional Canteen Stores, where I find Alston – Divl Staff.

During dinner arrives the "SOS" message, signifying that the Germans have "popped their parapet", so for a while there is preparation to move out, but after an hour or so all the excitement is over & we turn in. Apparently somebody in the 20th Div. on our left had "got the wind up" which is the popular expression for being jumpy – I hear some funny conversation amongst the signallers on the subject – when all the episode is over they said "The wind is away."

12th

Pouring wet again. Leave is suddenly stopped tonight – & the unfortunate Schiff recalled before he had left POP.

Pop was Poperinghe

13th

A fine sunny windy day_ I spend the morning going to look at the Coys drilling, and at Lewis Gun practice etc.

We now hear the Germans did make three small raids on 11th, actually in one place getting into the 20th Divn Trenches – the 3rd was an attack in 2 lines, when all the first were shot down, and the 2nd skidaddled.

They left about 25 dead lying out in the open.

14th

A visit from our (II) Army Commander, Gen Plumer. He struggled about in the mud to the place where R.F. & B. Coys were doing Extended Order Practice. He looks 70, tho' the papers call him only 59! He has the most comical old face, wears an eye glass, & is just like the typical General depicted in Punch. I hope he learned something by coming here.

General Sir Herbert Plumer, Commanding Second Army

15th

Woken up at 6.30 a.m. by sounds of apparent rapid-fire, which lasted ¾ hr. This turned out to be some Coldstream Ammn Supply on fire, about 500 x away – a great many thousand rounds must have been destroyed. Brand has returned – the last time I saw him was crawling back on all fours after being wounded at Loos.

Lieutenant David Halyburton Brand †29.3.18 was wounded in the attack on Puits 14 Bis, Loos

V. cold. Snow storms.

Walked in afternoon with L. Norman towards ELVERDINGHE inspected some of our second line trenches.

He (L.N.) has just returned from home where he had 3 or 4 days leave to receive his Military Cross.

16th

Aeroplanes very busy early – by 5 a.m., and at 6.45 a.m. there started a very persistent bombardment by a German 5.9 battery of the ground about ½ mile North of us, whether directed on to

D or E Camps, or one of our Batteries concealed up there, it is difficult to say. At any rate they continued till 10 a.m., and wounded 5 men of the 2/York & Lancaster Rgt in Camp D.

Attended C. of E. service.

Walked in afternoon with L. Norman to see his cousin, G. Bonham-Carter (19th Hussars) grave at VLAMERTINGHE.

> 2nd Battalion The York and Lancaster Regiment, 16th Brigade, 6th Division
> Captain Guy Bonham Carter, The 19th Hussars †15.5.15

Final of Coy football in afternoon, R.F. v B. Coy, a draw, neither side scoring.

Draft of 100 men arrived.

17th

Attended Battalion Snipers practice in morning.

In afternoon we had Battn Sports – quite a success – they included a Marching Order Race, smoke helmets on, and bomb throwing – also an Officers' handicap, ½ yard per year of age. I got more than anybody except Kinlay, who would not start_ Bewicke won, Powell 2nd, Esmé 3rd._

Nasty cold wet weather.

Menzies & Leach join. Chess.

> Lieutenant Victor Graham Malcolm Menzies
> 2nd Lieutenant Grey de lèche Leach †3.9.16

18th

I start at 8.45 a.m. by request of the Padre, to witness a very odd little show – namely 7 men of the Battn being admitted into the Church of Scotland & receiving the Sacrament for the first time.

After this I had to bustle off to POP to be president of a F.G.C.M._ There were two cases (1) A Grenadier who overstayed his leave, returning from England. We found him "guilty", and gave him 42 days Field Punishment No 1. (2) a Lce. Corpl. of 20th Hussars (attached to the Divn as a mounted policeman) whom we found "not guilty" of drunkenness.

In afternoon I walked alone for exercise, and found the 9th Norf. have come into camp D next to us. They are commanded by Col Stracey, brother of our Reggie Stracey who was killed on Jan 1st 1915 – the last of the Officers who originally came out with the Battn, except Kinlay the Quartermaster. After the first battle of YPRES the Battn consisted of Reggie Stracey & Kinlay and 75 other ranks.

I also had a look at where the heavy shelling was on 16th – viz at a dummy gun in a wood – dreadful havoc made amongst the trees.

Chess with Powell.

> Lieutenant Colonel Ernest Henry Denne Stracey, Commanding 9th (Service) Battalion
> The Norfolk Regiment, 71st Brigade, 6th Division
> After First Ypres there were seventy three men left in the 1st Scots Guards.

19th

The primroses from home are as fresh as anything. Attended H.C. service at 8 a.m.

Went over to camp of 9th Norfolk Regt nearby and saw Coy Sgt Major Read, son of the waiter. After that discovered some 9th Suffolk Rgt, the first man I spoke to was a Sgt Zeissel who keeps the pub at Wickham Market, Motor Cars etc, & it was he who drove me to Ipswich one night in Oct. 1903 or 1902, when I was recalled from leave to attend a Board at Wellington Bks next morning at 9 a.m. – a night I shall never forget!

I then found an Officer, who turned out to be the son of the Schoolmaster at Grundisburgh.

In afternoon walked with L. Norman to where another Suffolk Coy is to try to find Cpl A Sadler, late footman, but he had recently gone down the line sick.

> Company Sergeant Major Read, 9th Norfolk Regiment – untraced, possibly 14592
> Sergeant John Cecil Read or 16110 Sergeant Frederick James Read, both 9th Norfolk
> Regiment, both †18.10.16
> 9th (Service) Battalion The Suffolk Regiment, 71st Brigade, 6th Division
> 9938 Sergeant George L Zissell, 9th Suffolk Regiment
> Probably 15066 Lance Corporal Albert Edward Everett Sadler, 9th Suffolk Regiment,
> later 2nd Lieutenant The Suffolk Regiment

At 7 p.m. m we entrained for YPRES, but after 5 min the train pulled up, a shell having bust up the rails & we walked along the line. There was considerable shelling in the countryside from about 6 p.m. onwards, and it soon became evident that something unusual was up – we knew it when, nearing YPRES, we met a Welsh Guards Officer, who said the Germans were attacking our line, that instead of our relieving the 4th Grens, the Welsh Gds had moved up in support & we were to take their places in the Prison and neighbouring cellars. This we did and waited there hearing various rumours, including one that our 2nd Battn had been badly handled, until 12 midnight when things having quieted down a bit, we were told to proceed with our relief, which we did – relieving the 4th Grens, Harry Seymour's Bn, in the POTIZJE chateau grounds, not the same Bn H.Q. as before, but a little further E., the line being the next on the N. to where we were before._

The relief luckily went very well, tho' started so late, and was all over by 2 a.m.

A good lot of gun machine gun & rifle fire for the rest of the night.

> On 19 April the 2nd Guards Brigade were to take over from the 3rd Guards Brigade,
> with the 1st Scots Guards and 1st Coldstream Guards becoming the third and fourth
> forward battalions north of the Menin Road. The 2nd Scots Guards, whom the 1st
> Coldstream Guards were about to relieve, were very heavily shelled earlier on the
> 19th around Wieltje and then attacked in a large infantry raid. There were heavy Scots
> Guards casualties and, as it appeared, German ones too.

20th

The C.O. is seedy again & does not go round the line as he had intended at 3.30 a.m.; I go round at 10.30 a.m.–1 p.m., which means going up the Haymarket & Duke Street again. Bits of the line were badly knocked down yesterday – the 4th Gren had 5 killed and 17 wndd – our 2nd

Bn must have had considerably more. The 6th Divn on our left also suffered._ The Grenrs had a wounded prisoner – 236th Regt., the Doctor had to take off 2 of his fingers.

There were still some of our dead in the trench this morning – they will be brought down tonight for burial.

Luss returns, recalled off leave. The C.O. has to give in and "go sick" – he goes down to Divl H.Q. who promise him a bed – he confides to me that leave will shortly re-open and expects to take his & so is not likely to return for a fortnight or so – so he leaves me to carry on the Battn. Saw swallow over front line.

21st Good Friday

At 3 a.m. I go round the line, getting rather near meeting sniper's bullets on the way – my orderly – Moss, who sounds very different to what he really is (the best), and I think we may have been spotted from the German lines when against the moon, now very low down. Anyhow a bouquet of bullets splattered on the ground and buildings (we were going up "overland") all round us._ Found the Coys in front line had done quite a lot of work, clearing wreckage draining & wiring front – tho' owing to bright night they had to knock off this, having had a machine gun switched onto them.

Got back at 5 a.m. a glorious morning – woodpigeon cooing in the POTIZJE wood – one or two aeroplanes buzzing about – our "Archibald" (a species of anti-aircraft gun like an old "pom-pom") or "Coughing Kate" (there are also other names) being kept pretty busy – otherwise very quiet till 7 a.m. from when onwards there is a lot of shelling till 4 p.m.

About 5.30 p.m. a German Aeroplane came over very low down over our lines – got tremendously fired at by rifles, m.g's etc, at which he laughed heartily. It is unfortunate that in this salient our anti-aircraft guns seem unable to reach the E. end of the salient._

About 10 p.m. a lot of gunfire on our left, which continued all night developing about 2 a.m. into an intense German Bombardment – which made me wonder what was up this died away about 4.30 a.m. when I went round the line in perfect quietude (- I had intended to start about 3 a.m.). It was a most disturbed night – I didn't get more than about 2 hours sleep – as on my return at 6.30 a.m.

22nd

I had to wash and get ready to meet the Brigadier, who however is seedy & sent the acting Bde Major (Beckwith-Smith) instead to discuss various points. A pouring wet morning.

Miller has to go sick with a poisoned foot. Peevor also comes down to spend the night at Battn H.Q. with a temperature of 100, but recovers on next day.

The C.O. writes that he is better, but not returning yet.

An orderly was a message carrier or runner, of whom there was a team at Battalion Headquarters and others with the companies.
5716 Private William Moss †15.9.16
Lieutenant Ernest Miller

April 23rd, Easter Day

Went up to the line with the nice orderley, Moss, at 3 a.m. having an unpleasant but exciting journey thither – as enemy machine guns very active.

I found afterwards the reason was that the R.F. "Listening Post" had been spotted going out, & the enemy wanted to try & make sure of getting them coming in at dawn – however they got in without adventure – or casualty.

Heard the cuckoo._

A quantity of Artillery activity – very little Rifle Firing during the day.

The trees are coming out now over Battn H.Q., at least where any branches are left. There are beautiful trees – or were – larch, beech, sycamore, oak, h-chestnut, copper beech etc – some very fine specimens, clean tall stems.

The 3rd Coldm is relieved tonight by 2nd – Follet – who comes to my dugout after I have turned in & asked every sort of question about our line, which his Battn is to have next time, and made me draw a map! It was rather tiresome, the night being short as it is, and I told him I was available all the following day. He was very solemn and pompous._

> The 3rd Coldstream Guards had just been on the right of the 1st Scots Guards.
> Lieutenant Colonel Gilbert Burrell Spencer Follett, Commanding 2nd Coldstream
>   Guards †27.9.18

Miller goes sick with a poisoned foot. Powell is far from well but sticks it well. Smith-Cunningham has gone down sick having run his leg into a sharp piece of iron. Peevor arrives at Bn H.Q. very sorry for himself – spends the night there, but is better next day and takes S-Cun.'s place with the Brigade Pioneer Coy.

24th

Round the line at 4 a.m. but this morning go up the Haymarket instead of overland.

In the evening we do a very good quick relief by 3rd Grens & return to the Prison in YPRES. Esmé who is in Hospital sends us some Plovers' Eggs which have been given him – I send our thanks by Pigeon Post.

Fenner joins.

> 2nd Lieutenant Cyril Frederick Hamilton Fenner †24.9.16 with 2nd Scots Guards

We have had a wonderful 5 days – only 1 casualty, & this a man slightly wounded by shrapnel in LF Coy who were on the Canal Bank, a long way from the front line.

25th

Quite a comfortable night in my cell!

Go round billets in morning, after which to Bde H.Q. whence Col. Butler – the Brigadier is also in hospital – takes me with the Coy Commanders to the position we should occupy in case of an attack – in what is called the KAAIE salient and Canal Bank. We are evidently spotted and shrapnel is turned onto us, but we dont wait to be caught, and soon see what we want, and back to the Prison. Make the acquaintance of the "Town Major"[blank] a huge Rifleman, who also lives in the prison. We have a man, sentry on back door of prison, wounded. The T.M. complains that the shelling of the town has recently increased owing to troops' carelessness walking about and showing themselves in the streets, so I issue a long winded Battn Order on the subject.

26th

The Bn is doing endless fatigues – day & night. Weather perfect, but we are real prisoners – there are so many Aeroplanes up it is quite unwise to walk about the streets unnecessarily._

In the evening I go and visit C. Coy, where I find them amusing themselves trying to cross the canal in a tub – shooting with a small roof [rook] rifle at bottles etc – and Luss tries some fishing with my hooks, but I don't think does much good.

We now have to arrange our Lewis guns etc so as to fire at enemy aeroplanes day & night – each Coy making its own arrangements. The old "Town Major" – Capt Wigram 60th Rifles – comes to dine & raises an objection to our having one at the prison – where he also lives – he says he is more or less permanent here, & we are only visitors, & he will get the benefit, not us, of anything rash that might be done! I don't blame him.

About 7 p.m. a bombardment begins, towards St Eloi; pretty heavy & apparently by the enemy, a good many falling in this town, YPRES. About 10 p.m. till 12 midnt this is followed by one of our intensest bombardments. We dont hear what is up. I make every arrangement inwardly in case we have to move to our defence position – but nothing happens.

Each place with significant troop numbers had a Town Major, whose administrative military role was like a civilian mayor's.

Captain George Montague Wigram, The King's Royal Rifle Corps

27th

A fair amount of shells falling in our neighbourhood.

Peevor in command of the Brigade Entrenching Coy is wounded by a bomb.

In afternoon I walk over to Brigade H.Q. with the Padre, who dislikes shells as much as I do.

28th

Walk to Bde H.Q. with Luss in morning, and hear how splendidly the Shropshires retook the trenches lost by Bedfords on 20th.

Esmé is well home by now I expect – due back about 9th or 10th._ Getting rather tired of being in prison.

To their north the 6th Division had recently taken over from the 20th Division. On 19 April, coinciding with what happened to the 2nd Scots Guards around Wieltje, the Germans shelled and attacked the 8th (Service) Battalion The Bedfordshire Regiment in the same way and drove them out of several trenches just west of Morteldje Estaminet, itself in No Man's Land. After others in the 16th Brigade had failed to recover them the 1st Battalion The King's Shropshire Light Infantry did so on 21 April and held on.

29th

Walk with Brand to look at some little gardens with lilies of the valley & other spring flowers coming out apace – then poked about near Ramparts on S. side of town – very picturesque – and Rly Station.

In afternoon am sent for by Brigadier who tells me several points concerning work to be done in line during our 3 days.

In evening – about 9–10 p.m. relieve 3rd Gren in the same lot of trenches where we were last, very quiet till 1 a.m. when there begins & continues till nearly 3 a.m. the most intense bombardment ever heard away to the South. Presently a message arrives from the Brigade saying the Germans are making a gas attack at MESSINES.

The message sent at 2.35 a.m. on 30 April read:

Enemy attacking with gas by MESSINES about 5 miles south of us.

11

The Ypres Salient May 1916

30th

At 4 a.m. I go round the line Luss & L. Norman are the 2 front Coys. The enemy had the previous night made a bombing attack in a very small way – so we are doing all the wiring we can – to prevent them getting right in.

A lot of shelling in afternoon & evening – we have 1 man hit, a rib broken, in CONGREVE WALK, where Tim O.E. is, and Company Q.M. Sgt Davidson, R.F. Coy, and 2 men wounded when walking across the square in YPRES.

> 3759 Company Quartermaster Sergeant Stewart Davidson

Rumours that the Germans did no good in their gas attack last night. We are warned of another one tonight further South, where we hear another cannonade.

May 1st

I go round the line at 3 a.m, with Moss, starting overland, when we come in for a lot of bullets – the Bosch always starts this sort of thing just before dawn, so I vow tomorrow to either go up earlier or else up a Communn Trench, the worst of which however is that it takes a long time._ Aeroplanes very busy, and a lot of long distance shelling going over our heads, either into YPRES, or onto the POP road beyond I suppose. Much shelling all day, and we have a Sgt Bassett of L.F. Coy wounded, but luckily no serious damage to any of our line.

> 8297 Lance Sergeant Frederick Arthur Bassett, later 2nd Lieutenant The Essex
> Regiment

In afternoon 2 A.S.C. and 1 Medical Officer arrive having ridden all the way 28 mi. from ST. OMER, saying they wanted to see our front line! A pretty sharp straaf begins and their ardour begins to damp off – & I discourage them all I can. They say their lives are so peaceful! They stay about 1 hr in hopes things will quiet down; which they don't do, so our friends return to ST. OMER.

A notice board is put up on the German parapet saying "KUT has fallen, Rule Britannia"! this the same day on which the bad news appears in the London Papers.

About 7 to 9 p.m. there is a very fierce bombardment all apparently on a small space near RAILWAY WOOD – somebody must be getting it hot, possibly about where the 4/Grenadiers are. One seldom hears about such things.

A nasty episode occurs in L.F. Coy. A listening post – consisting of a hole not far outside our wire which is nightly occupied by us, & has been so for a long time, is approached about 9.30 by our listening patrol – on arriving there, they receive a volley – 2 of them – Cpl Miller & Wishart fall dead into the post: the 3rd runs back through the gap in our wire & falls wounded by 6 bullets into our trench – Ashton – feared by the Dr to be fatal.

> 13302 Lance Corporal Hugh Hay Miller †1.5.16
> 11770 Private George Wishart †1.5.16
> 9882 Private John Ashton †3.5.16

The Germans had evidently crept along an old bank right up to the place – the mystery is how they knew exactly where it was, and it shows how carefully they watch & study our actions, no doubt for many nights they had laid out watching the arrival of this patrol. It is easy to be wise after the event, but now one sees the folly of these fixed listening posts. It is far better to lie out anywhere in the open. Our men have no cunning about them, I have noticed it both in this war & in S.A., they shrink from doing anything which is not quite straightforward, and are quite content walking bolt upright straight ahead, rather than crouch or take any of the natural precautions. When they do take precautions it is only because made to do so by an Officer, who they invariably put down as having "the wind up".

2nd

I go up at 1 a.m. & return about 5 a.m., turn in, but my slumbers are disturbed by the Brigadier (Butler, who is just being given a Brigade of his own) about 7 a.m. to discuss various points. Another instance of our lack of cunning occurs this morning namely some new work we have recently done has been blown in by enemy's guns, which is because we have failed to disguise our new work – as a matter of fact this new work was repairing the results of bombardment on 20th Apr. Luckily only one man was slightly wounded, tho ½ buried & much "shaken".

The Welsh Guards have now been relieved by our 2nd Battn, so at last our 2 Battns are alongside eachother for the first time in trenches. Roger Tempest's H.Q. being close to ours. I look in and see Jack Stirling on the way down – the other Coy commanders are Lumsden, Kit Cator and Jamie Balfour. With Jack is young Andrew Vanneck of Leiston – which brings me nearer home! There are heavy thunderstorms during the day & much shelling from & to all directions.

> Captain Christopher Arthur Mohun Cator, known as "Kit", younger brother of
>   Brigadier General Albemarle Bertie Edward Cator, was wounded in the trenches at
>   Rouges Bancs in December 1914
> Captain Charles James Balfour, known as "Jamie", was wounded on the Aisne in
>   September 1914 and again during the Battle of Aubers in May 1915, both with the 1st
>   Scots Guards, but by this date had just been permanently evacuated with shell shock
>   after the events of 19 April

Lieutenant The Honourable Andrew Nicholas Armstrong Vanneck

Jack Stirling comes to tea – & I dine with R. Tempest, who is commanding the 2nd Battn_

Are relieved about 10 p.m. by 3rd Grens, & have a remarkably quiet relief – hardly a shot being fired – tho' 2 of our pioneers are badly wounded in VLAMERTINGHE, having got a lift in a R.E. waggon & an unlucky shell catching them, one driver being killed & one losing a leg.

The Battn returned by train – the nearest approach to an accident being when our train was going back to pick up some Norfolk Regt, without of course being able to give any warning – no lights or noise being possible – B and C Coys were walking down the line being the nearest way to their billets & only just saw the train

May 2nd 1916 (continued)

in time – which was going pretty fast – one man as it was got a pretty good blow with an open door. This time nobody got left behind at YPRES._ Luss & I were the last to get on board & this when the train was well in motion: not an easy thing, as there is such a high climb off the ground which falls away rather quickly from the rails. We get settled into Camp B about 2 a.m., the men having hot tea & rum before turning in._

Find 3 officers joining us Tennant, Ogilvie and Champion._

Lieutenant Mark Tennant †16.9.16 with 2nd Guards Brigade Machine Gun Company
Lieutenant Walter Ogilvie
Lieutenant Reginald James Champion †18.7.17 with 2nd Guards Brigade Trench Mortar
    Battery

3rd

Awaked at 6 a.m. by German shells falling but a very few 100 yds off – very unpleasant – believe they are not shelling us but some old gun emplacements not far away.

Go round the camp in the morning – the men are all in quite good huts – made a thorough inspection including washhouses, Canteen etc etc.

Later in day walked with Brand, looked at a cemetery where saw grave of Cpl Ommundsen, the well known Rifle Shot, Winner of King's Prize at Bisley etc. and also inspected some back trenches etc.

Lieutenant Harcourt Ommundson, The Honourable Artillery Company †19.9.15

The country is looking very green & prosperous: and in truth it is so in many ways – the inhabitants are making a lot of money out of us – their soil is already very fertile. One old woman remarked that she hoped the war would go on for ever – she had never had such a time.

4th

Are relieved by 3rd Coldm in evening – marching by companies to POPERINGHE where we returned to our Red Villa, the garden of which is now very nice & cool & shady, & full of blossom. Very hot stuffy day.

Hear the R.E. have exploded a long narrow mine, which 4th Grenadiers have occupied & turned into a trench, wiring & everything being done in an hour or two – by night of course, thus joining up two rather isolated bits of trench, making one of it.

5th

Went round billets in morning pretty thoroughly – a good lot of Battalion writing etc to be done.

6th

Spent practically the whole day at a Court Martial of which I was President. Two prisoners were N.C.O.'s who left their posts when acting as covering party to a digging Company – there was a scrimmage with a German patrol & some misunderstanding.

Walked in evening with Thompson, the Adjt.

Grissell dined with me.

Lieutenant Francis Grissell, Ist Coldstream Guards †I5.9.I6, son of Suffolk neighbours

7th

Visited wiring practice in morning – went to Brigade Office. Dined with Col Brooke, 3rd Grenadiers.

8th

Visited wiring practice. Walked with L. Norman in evening.

9th

Heard of Brig. Genl Heyworth's (cmdg 3rd Guards Brigade) death, having been shot by a sniper in the head, while going round the trenches._ A very popular Officer, and one whom I had known ever since I joined the Regt – he was always very kind to me though never a particular friend.

Esmé G.L. returned from leave in evening._

10th

Went to see Snipers at work in morning. A solitary walk in evening, after attending Gen. Heyworth's funeral at BRANDHOEK ½ way between here (POP) and YPRES.

Sat in a wood listening to a nightingale.

11th

A long Court Martial in morning – self President – members Eddy Ward & Fleming. we tried a Coldstreamer who had overstayed his leave in England: also two Sergts of some Line Regiment attached to the 10th Entrenching Battn – behind the 6th Division (on our left), who had gone to sleep in a dug-out, while on fatigue. Both these we had to find "not guilty" on the evidence, though in my own mind they were most certainly guilty.

Captain Edward Simons Ward, 3rd Grenadier Guards
Captain Cyril F Fleming, 2nd Irish Guards

In afternoon walked with Esmé, & then to Brigade Office. In evening entrained at 8 p.m. for YPRES, where we relieved 1st Grenadiers – & come under the orders of 3rd Guards Brigade for the moment under H. Seymour. A very amusing & somewhat abusive – on both sides – telephone argument ensues between him & Esmé, who is senior to him, & claims the command of the Brigade – of course all in chaff.

We are billeted this time in a cellar, the Companies being divided up in barracks – a Convent & the Ramparts.

Some shelling of the town POP in morning, one shell catching the 1st Coldm billets, killing 9 men & wounding 9 more, besides killing some R.E. & civilians.

10036 Private William Thomas Cockram, 1st Coldstream Guards †11.5.16
10444 Private H Wells, 1st Coldstream Guards †11.5.16
12115 Private Stanley Bridger, 1st Coldstream Guards †11.5.16
12314 Private Sydney Harold Bevan, 1st Coldstream Guards †11.5.16
13161 Private G Bratt, 1st Coldstream Guards †11.5.16
15084 Private Robert Bogle, 1st Coldstream Guards †11.5.16
15464 Private W Barker, 1st Coldstream Guards †11.5.16
15945 Lance Corporal T G Joyce, 1st Coldstream Guards †11.5.16
16074 Private H Brewster, 1st Coldstream Guards †11.5.16

12th

Quite a comfortable night in the cellar, though a bit stuffy & smelly.

Walked round some of the Billets in morning with Luss and Tim O.E. – saw where they lived, both in cellars – & quite safe ones too to all appearances except for 15 or 17 inch shells, of which plenty have been used here, in the past – presumably all now down near VERDUN. Lunched with H. Seymour who is temporarily cmdg 3rd Gds Bde, where were also Warner Bde Major, Ballantyne-Dykes, Staff Capt. etc, also Col. de Crespigny, cmdg 2nd Grenadiers. In evening we relieved our 2nd Bn, whose H.Q. are at POTIZJE – Dick Coke in command while R Tempest is on leave. Some shelling near the MENIN Gate, which we dodge, tho' Coy S.M. Pyper is wounded, hope not badly. After relief, Dick Coke & Billy Wynne Finch (Adjt) go away, & no sooner are they gone than the Bosches put an inferno of shrapnel (H.E.) onto the road – just where Coke & Co might be, to say nothing of Ration Parties & outgoing relief etc. It is quite marvellous how few casualties there are at times like this.

Captain Edward Courtenay Thomas Warner, Scots Guards
Captain Frecheville Hubert Ballantyne Dykes, Scots Guards
6018 Company Sergeant Major William Pyper

13th

Start at 12.30 a.m. with Esmé to go round the line, getting back at 2 a.m. There was continual shelling going on, mostly seemed to be onto ST. JEAN and HASLER HOUSE, but some round our Battn H.Q., where no damage was done._

At about 2 a.m. it began to rain and went on steadily until 10.30 a.m., luckily warm. The Chateau grounds are getting more & more like a wilderness & less & less like a garden etc.

We had our poor mess cart driver killed by a shell at the MENIN Gate last night, and the Officers' trench kit limber driver wounded rather badly, so Tennant's servant drove (or rode) the limber back to POP.

13529 Private Robert Fullerton †12.5.16

The POTIZJE road was badly shelled all night & during this day too – about every few minutes & bouquet landing somewhere near it – never twice running in the same spot. I went over to see Tim O.E. at the POTIZJE defences in the evening, and inspected the graveyard where many of our men killed Mar 30th are buried. It has been much knocked about & is full of shell holes.

Started to go round the line alone at 11 p.m.

14th

visited every part of it including the bombing posts between us & Coldstream – got horribly scared when going through the watery derelict trench near the Gully by a machine gun from near RAILWAY WOOD: the bullets seem to rake down the trench & hit the sides close to me, so I sat right down in the water, my dignity had to suffer, but there was nobody to see & only a born fool would have remained standing up – as it is there is a scrape on my helmet, whether from a bullet or no I cannot say – a bullet we all think it must be! Found L. Norman anything but happy, he is in an isolated bit & nobody can blame him for not enjoying it – the men all pretty damp too – raining all night – steady drizzle, but warm.

Got back to Bn H.Q. at 3.30 a.m. – slept till 9 a.m. found this had been shelled steadily all night, everybody had narrow squeaks including the Dr who was very eloquent on the subject. I had to dodge some shells when returning.

The C.O. goes into YPRES to a C.O.'s conference about 12 n.

At night our R.E. Officer who *[is]* in charge of signals etc, including an apparatus for listening to German telephones, also of the wireless installations, has to crawl out to lay a wire as near as possible to the German lines, if possible right up to their wire. He gets about ¾ of the way over, is covered by a party of C. Coy, then returns. Time will show how much German conversation we shall hear.

A C. Coy man gets sniped through the head, otherwise no casualties today.

15th

Go round part of the line with Esmé – 12.30–2.30 a.m. A good deal of sniping & machine gunning going on_ RF & LF change places, as LF has a very bad place.

During luncheon a shell bursts outside the C.O.'s dugout wounding a R.E. there, – he would have been killed had it not been for his steel helmet – breaking in the window & shattering the C.O.'s shaving soap, iron jug and mug._

I started to go round alone at about 11 p.m., went slowly all round dawdling about looking at the work in progress, also visiting the two rather isolated bombing posts between us and the Coldstream on our right.

On my way back I met Powell who said he saw somebody out in front – which was corroborated by some sentries. I asked the Corpl of a working party, where I happened to be, if the men had their rifles handy. On his saying they were 40 yards away, I told him to send the men for their rifles, this was mis-interpreted somehow into an order generally to stand to arms, for as I continued my way along, I found everybody standing to arms – & could not at first make out why. About this same time a heavy machine-gun, rifle, & bomb fire was opened away on the left – as usual it appeared much nearer than it was – Luss & I walked along to see what was up, but it seemed to get further away as we walked, so we returned. Turtle Dove *[unexplained]*.

The C.O. was up while I was but I missed him. He found a man in DUKE STR. hammering in a stake and singing at the top of his voice – between the two making a horrible noise – when asked if this was quite necessary, he replied he thought he would try & drown the noise of the hammering, so that the Germans should not hear!

16th

Got back about 2.30 a.m. a lovely morning, nearly full moon_ About 5 a.m. the Germans started shelling & kept it up till well into the afternoon._

Were relieved by 3rd Grenrs at night, getting back to our old billets scattered about YPRES about 12.30 a.m. – a very quiet and peaceful relief – a perfect night, nearly full moon, rather too bright for the R.F. Coy coming across the open, however they were not spotted._ While waiting for the relief a couple of German Aeroplanes flew over, dropping coloured lights as they crossed the line.

17th

Glorious hot day, which we spent mostly in our little back garden but I visited all the Coys in their billets. Brigadier, J Dyer, Green (bombing officer), de Crespigny, Vaughan & a few others came to see us during the day.

Aeroplanes very busy.

Heard H. Platt, 1st Coldm & Burton, 2nd Grenrs were killed night before last the former was wiring – much too bright a night for such close quarters as they were – under 100 yds from German line. He had been out the whole war.

> Lieutenant Sidney Joseph Green, nicknamed "Sniper", Scots Guards, Bombing and
>   Intelligence Officer, 2nd Guards Brigade
> Probably Captain Eugene Napoleon Ernest Mallet Vaughan, 3rd Grenadier Guards, but
>   possibly Major George Edmund Vaughan, 3rd Coldstream Guards †15.9.16
> Captain Henry Evelyn Arthur Platt, 1st Coldstream Guards †15.5.16
> 2nd Lieutenant John Stanley Burton, 2nd Grenadier Guards †16.5.16

May 18th 1916

Yesterday Schiff wanted to go down to Platt's funeral at BRANDHOEK, so phoned to the Brigade Office to ask how he could get a car. The Bde Major (Beckwith-Smith) answered, "The

Archbishop of Canterbury's", by which Schiff of course thought he was having his leg pulled – the A of C being the last person to expect to find in YPRES. However there he was, I met him in a street, in the town. long black coat, black buskins, and – a steel helmet on his head! He looked rather out of place and very hot! He had been going to lunch with the Brigadier, who was much disappointed, as he wanted to make him stand on a chair – as he always does anybody who commits any mistake at a meal.

Spent most of the day in our little back garden writing reading & gardening – in evening walked round some of the billets, and to Rly Sta. with Tim, where found some Rly tickets etc for the children.

Dined with Brigadier & with Esmé, also there besides staff – Major Young who commands a Howitzer Batty and Genl Lesley Butler, who has just been given the 60th Bde._ The Brigr was in fairly good form, but will be more so when we are completely out of the line.

Much shelling all day on both sides – several coming rather unpleasantly near our garden – I think aimed at back door of Barracks, where men will congregate together.

> Captain Merton Beckwith Smith, Coldstream Guards, Staff Captain, standing in as
> 	Brigade Major
> The Most Reverend Randall Thomas Davidson, Archbishop of Canterbury
> Brigadier General Ponsonby had a foible, in his sole judgement and on an entirely
> 	frivolous basis, that anyone in the Brigade Officers Mess who said or did anything he
> 	deemed silly, would be immediately sentenced to stand on a chair in the corner for
> 	ten minutes.
> Major Young, probably in 61st (Howitzer) Brigade, Royal Field Artillery, Guards Division
> 	– untraced

19th

Weather still perfect – rather noisy night.

Walked out with Thompson to look at the Horn Works – a sort of outwork, E. of the town – had to go through the "Sallyport" under the Ramparts & across a temporary wooden bridge over the moat or canal, & there found the most interesting subterranean vaults & passages, at which our men are constantly at work, under the R.E., improving & developing for use in case we have to hold this line at any time. These vaults etc were only discovered by somebody quite recently at the British Museum.

We are rather amused to see in the "Daily Liar" just what we had anticipated – namely that some patrol has been brilliant enough to discover – & cut – the wire which runs over to the German wire, laid with much trouble & care & risk by the R.E. Officer some nights ago – for the purpose of listening to German telephones.

I hear that the above mentioned vaults were used by British Troops when in 1720, about 17000 of them were billeted in the town. Amongst them was a General Ponsonby & Ld Stair, the latter probably in command of this Regt.

In evening walked out with Esmé when we met by chance L. Norman Colquhoun & Brand – were stopping talking a few minutes when – swish bang a big 5.9 inch German Shell crashed down about 100 yds off – this was the prelude to many others all near the Barracks & our billet – in reality it was aimed at an anti-aircraft gun – of which the crew were scattered, some wounded._

There was also one shell which landed on & broke into a cellar where we had some men quartered, luckily they were all out on fatigue, and the cellar empty.

This afternoon up in the line a Garrison Gunner was wounded out in an isolated trench, so far as I can make out, he was the sentry & by himself looking after a trench mortar. One of our men, a machine gunner, went out to help him & got killed, whereupon Stirling – of this Battn – Machine Gun Officer – went out in broad daylight, and carried both into safety – one after the other, tho' unfortunately one was past all help. Stirling himself had his haversack riddled, but was unwounded. I know him to be a very cool person, having seen him wandering up to the line overland, one morning – just after daylight, when all shooting usually stops, though of course had he been spotted he would have received a very warm welcome.

I hear he has been recommended by the Brigadier for reward._

Since writing above I find he has been awarded a Military Cross tho' in any former war he would have received a V.C.

> The War Diary of the 2nd Guards Brigade Machine Gun Company recorded that on
>   18 May a Scots Guardsman in the Company had been killed going to aid a wounded
>   R.F.A. Officer. Lieutenant Gordon Stirling, 1st Scots Guards, attached to the
>   Company †15.9.16, brought both of them in.
> 9354 Private Charles Edward Jones 1st Scots Guards attached to the Company †18.5.16

20th

An unfortunate shell landed just outside a L.F. dugout in the Ramparts, killing one man & wounding another. This was a very bad piece of luck – the shell landing between the dugout and the parados – in the trench as it were.

> 12397 Private Robert Martin †20.5.16

A very quiet day and evening, when we march down to the Asylum Siding to catch the 9 p.m. train – allowing 20 min for entraining. We had no sooner got there than the Germans began putting shrapnel very near – but this only lasted a few minutes, so we made up our minds it was intended for some Battery. All was then quiet for a while, when they began again this time just over our heads, between the Rly line & the road, but with some heavy stuff – at last the train came in at 9.30, and we were off by 9.40 p.m., there was not much time wasted in entraining; they gave us a parting shot – tho' of course I dont suppose they knew – when we were just starting entraining – we were all very glad to get away – the last shot was most uncomfortably close to the Battn crowded along the line.

We detrained at the Rly crossing on the Dunkerque road and marched to our Camp K on the WATOU road._

A beautiful night – and not half a bad looking camp.

Some of us go over to get some supper from the Coldstream (1st Bn under Guy Baring) close by in Camp L.

Violet Barne in 1904.
(Courtesy of the
Showers Family)

Officers 1st Scots Guards photographed by Captain Harold Cuthbert in late June 1915.
(Courtesy of the Regimental Trustees Scots Guards)
Seated l. to r. Lieutenant Hugh Hammersley, Lieutenant Arnold Thompson, Captain Arthur Poynter,
Captain Norman Orr Ewing, 2nd Lieutenant Claude Bartholomew
Standing l. to r. Lieutenant John Drury Lowe, 2nd Lieutenant Neil Fergusson, Captain John Thorpe,
2nd Lieutenant Cecil Trafford, Quartermaster and Honorary Lieutenant David Kinlay, Lieutenant
Lionel Norman, Captain Sir John Swinnerton Dyer, Bt, Lieutenant Arthur Mervyn Jones, Lieutenant
Colonel Sherard Godman, 2nd Lieutenant Guy Armstrong, Captain Lord Hamilton of Dalzell, 2nd
Lieutenant David Brand, Captain Sir Victor Mackenzie, Bt.

2nd Lieutenant Neil Fergusson, Lieutenant Merton Beckwith Smith and Lieutenant Colonel John Ponsonby, both 1st Coldstream Guards, Captain Arthur Poynter and Lieutenant Lionel Norman. (Courtesy of the Regimental Trustees Scots Guards)

French civilians killing rats at Sailly-Labourse, between Béthune and Loos, Summer 1915. (Courtesy of the Regimental Trustees Scots Guards)

Right Flank company cooker at Sailly-Labourse, Summer 1915.
(Courtesy of the Regimental Trustees Scots Guards)

Sniping at a German metal loophole, which later fell over, put up on a mine crater rim, at Z2 near Cuinchy, Summer 1915. (Courtesy of the Regimental Trustees Scots Guards)

Captain Harold Cuthbert outside Right Flank company headquarters dugout "Some Hut" at Le Rutoire, Summer 1915. (Courtesy of the Regimental Trustees Scots Guards)

Unnamed Coldstreamer digging a dugout entrance, Vermelles neighbourhood, Summer 1915. (Courtesy of the Regimental Trustees Scots Guards)

Officers and NCOs of Left Flank, probably at Merville, early December 1915.
Seated l. to r. Company Quartermaster Sergeant Bertie Lemon, 2nd Lieutenant Warine Martindale, Lieutenant Ernest "Tim" Orr Ewing, Captain Miles Barne, Captain Lionel Norman and Company Sergeant Major Hubert Butler. (Courtesy of Miles Barne)

The Canal Bank outside Ypres, early Spring 1916. (Courtesy of the Regimental Trustees Scots Guards)

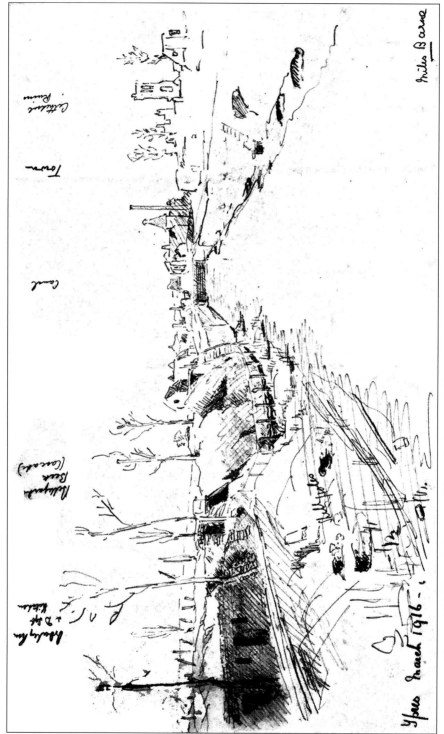

Captain Miles Barne's drawing of Ypres, looking south from the Canal Bank, 1 April 1916. (Courtesy of Miles Barne)

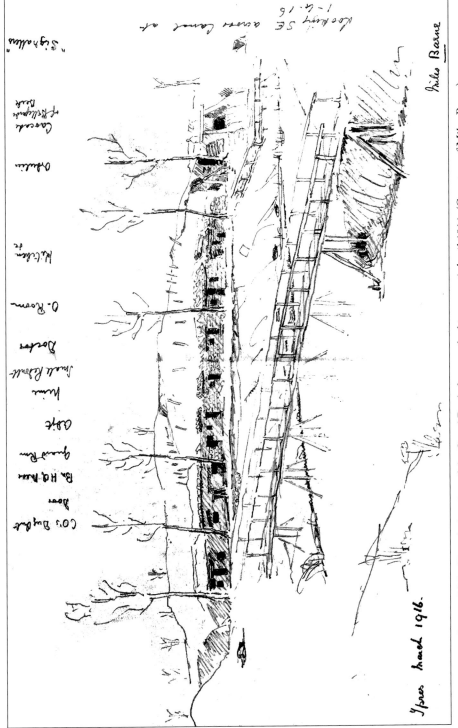

Captain Miles Barne's drawing of the Canal Bank dugouts, looking east, 1 April 1916. (Courtesy of Miles Barne)

2nd Lieutenant Grey Leach. (Courtesy of the
Regimental Trustees Scots Guards)

Lieutenant Marcus Schiff. (Courtesy of the
Regimental Trustees Scots Guards)

Lieutenant Henry Dundas. (Courtesy of the
Regimental Trustees Scots Guards)

Captain Jack Stirling, 2nd Scots Guards.
(Courtesy of the Regimental Trustees
Scots Guards)

Lieutenant Cecil Boyd Rochfort.
(Courtesy of the Regimental
Trustees Scots Guards)

Captain Sir Iain Colquhoun of
Luss, Bt, and Captain Hugh Ross.
(Courtesy of the Regimental
Trustees Scots Guards)

2nd Guards Brigade camps, Happy Valley, Somme, early September 1916.
(Courtesy of the Regimental Trustees Scots Guards)

Lieutenant John "Ivan"
Cobbold. (Courtesy of the
Regimental Trustees Scots
Guards)

Lieutenant Colonel Sherard Godman, Major Miles Barne and Lieutenant Henry Dundas in Trones Wood on 25 September 1916 during the attack and capture of Lesboeufs. (Courtesy of the Regimental Trustees Scots Guards)

Lieutenant Arthur Mervyn Jones and Lieutenant Duncan Brodie, early autumn 1916. (Courtesy of the Regimental Trustees Scots Guards)

Lieutenant Claude Mahomed, early
autumn 1916. (Courtesy of the
Regimental Trustees Scots Guards)

View towards German front line from Number 2 Post, opposite St Pierre Vaast Wood, early 1917.
(Courtesy of the Regimental Trustees Scots Guards)

Ruins of Rancourt, just west of St Pierre Vaast Wood, early 1917.
(Courtesy of the Regimental Trustees Scots Guards)

Wrecked ammunition train at The Plateau, Fricourt, after German night bombing early on 16 February 1917. (Courtesy of the Regimental Trustees Scots Guards)

Lieutenant Bobbie Abercromby.
(Courtesy of the Regimental
Trustees Scots Guards)

Captain David Brand, with three
wound stripes on his left sleeve.
(Courtesy of the Regimental Trustees
Scots Guards)

Lieutenant Frank Mann outside a dugout in the line opposite St Pierre Vaast Wood, early 1917. (Courtesy of the Regimental Trustees Scots Guards)

St Pierre Vaast Wood after the German withdrawal on 15 March 1917. (Courtesy of the Regimental Trustees Scots Guards)

Destroyed German pill box near Langemarck after the Battle of Pilckem Ridge on 31 July 1917.
(Courtesy of the Regimental Trustees Scots Guards)

With Elizabeth Barne at Sotterley during his last leave. (Courtesy of the Showers Family)

21st

Glorious weather. Go round the camp with C.O. in the morning, which he re-organizes a bit. Piping hot.

In evening rode with Luss, Bewicke, Tim & Mann round to LA...L...IE, our Corps H.Q. where is a very pretty lake, with rhododendrons, nightingales, young wild duck and beautiful trees which were very nice in this weather.

Apparently Château de Lovie

22nd

Several bombs dropped during the night, apparently on POPERINGHE, two sounded pretty close here & an aeroplane just over us.

During the morning I walked round by my myself & had a sort of variety entertainment – viz: Lewis guns, Snipers, bombers, signallers, pipers, bayonet exercise, transport etc, making myself generally objectionable & interfering.

Some rain in afternoon & evening when Tim O.E. & self rode together – a very nice ride, coming back through WATOU.

23rd

My usual variety entertainment, then some cricket, against Coldstream whom we beat – followed by rounders, when they beat us.

24th

Rode over to BURGOMASTER FARM near VLAMERTINGHE to see our fatigue party there – found 2 Coys of our 2nd Battn under Dick Coke – the Officers being Howard, Maynard, Maitland & Scott – there.

In afternoon played cricket against the men – & beat them – followed by football & beat them also at that – but of course on neither side a representative team.

The Band under Mr Woods, Bandmaster, arrived in our Camp to be attached to us. It has been brought out by Minto, whom we have seized on to do duty._

Lieutenant The Honourable Arthur Jared Palmer Howard
Lieutenant Anthony Lox Maynard
Lieutenant Richard Evelyn Fuller Maitland
Lieutenant Alexander Malcolm Scott
3596 Bandmaster Frederick William Wood
Captain Victor Gilbert Laristone Garnet Elliot, Earl of Minto

25th

Usual variety entertainment.

Visit from the Corps Commander – Cavan – accompanied by his A.D.C., Leigh.

Captain The Honourable Piers Walter Legh, Grenadier Guards

There has been a lot of gunning the past few days & nights – mostly to the S. towards ARMENTIERES.

More football.

26th

Ride in morning with Esmé to see some of our fatigue parties at work on a new strategic railway etc. Meet R. Tempest, also see 2 Coys of the 2nd Battn route marching – the 2nd Bn being in a camp N. of POP and almost behind the French lines.

In afternoon I ride by myself to get my warrant from Bde H.Q. at HOUTKIRQUE. after which I walk in to POP to get my hair cut. Dine with Right half Battn.

27th

Breakfast at 5 a.m. & at 5.30 the Field Cashier calls in his motor car & takes me, with Bewicke & Mann, off to LUMBRES at a furious rate, to see my brother Seymour, who is on the 2nd Cavalry Divl Staff there – on my way to BOULOGNE – a horse show for the Divn is being held – of which Seymour is Secretary – most successful in every way – and some of the teams and sections are magnificent spectacles – perhaps the most attractive being the guns & teams of J. Battery RHA who seem to have won most of the prizes, tho' really very little to choose amongst the various Regiments and Batteries.

I met a good many friends & am pointed out many celebreties including Genl Birdwood – also am introduced to Gens Chetwode & Pitman.

> Lieutenant General William Riddell Birdwood, Commanding I Anzac Corps
> Major General Sir Philip Walhouse Chetwode, Bt, Commanding 2nd Cavalry Division
> Brigadier General Thomas Tait Pitman, Commanding 4th Cavalry Brigade

To my surprise Cavan comes & sits down alongside me, the first friendly notice he has taken of me since the Court Martial.

At about 7.30 p.m. Seymour sends me in a motor car to BOULOGNE such a very pretty drive, where I find on arrival at 8.40 that a boat had gone about 7 p.m., after being assured that there would be none tonight at all. I get a bed at the Hotel de Paris – looking in at the H. Folkestone, where I find our Brigadier, who gives me commissions to do in London.

28th

Leave Boulogne at 9 a.m. Find Loch on board – now Bdr Genl on Staff of VIth Corps.

> Brigadier General Edward Douglas Loch, Lord Loch, Brigadier General General Staff, VI Corps

Arr Victoria 2 p.m. where V. meets me. Fine crossing. Two French Airships hover about all the way over, they are said to be very useful for spotting submarines.

12

The Ypres Salient June and July 1916

June 8th

Leave Victoria 8.15 a.m., being caught as O.C. Troops on board the train; on arrival at Folkestone I have to march the men to the rest camp, as the boat is not off till 4.40 p.m. spend the day writing & wandering about & calling on my cousin E. Carleton.

> E. Carleton – untraced

After marching the troops to the ship, I escape & travel by the mail boat – dine at the Club at BOULOGNE – arriving about 12 midnight at HAZEBROUCK where I get a bed after some difficulty – as the train on does not go till

June 9th

9.50 a.m., previous to which I walked round the rather picturesque old town. Arrived back at the Battn at BOLLEZEELE about 11 a.m., having come on a motor lorry from ARNEKE Station.

> The Guards Division were out of the line in training areas northeast of St Omer, the 1st Scots Guards being in billets at Bollezeele.

Found the Battn out training – walked out to the ground, saw some bombing practice – experiments with smoke etc, then round to Bde H.Q. at VOLKERINCKHOVE, where I delivered over my purchases to Brigadier & had tea. Heard great news about Russian Advance against Austrians.

On return found the Battn Officers playing rounders & then football, so joined in._

> At the Chantilly Conference in December 1915 the British, French, Italians and Russians undertook to attack simultaneously in six months time. The German offensive at Verdun affected this wider strategic plan but the Russian Brusilov Offensive, begun on 4 June, was initially a significant success.

10th

Practice the assault with Coldm on our right. Some trenches have been dug, an exact replica of what we are destined to attack and many details well thought out, to get us really familiar with the ground, which however is sure to be quite different when the time comes._

> The attack that they were practising was to take Pilckem Ridge and would have been put into effect if the early attacks on the Somme had gathered more momentum.

In afternoon attended some boxing competitions between the 3rd Gren & 2nd Irish Gds – some good fighting – some very moderate.

In evening motored with Esmé & Luss to a Blue Seal Dinner at WORMHOUDT, where I found myself sitting between Ch Corkran and Alby Cator, two of my oldest pals, both now Brigadiers – so enjoyed my evening very much, there were also present many others I knew well, but alas! there were a great many others absent & never again to attend – about 60 members having been killed since the war began!

> The Blue Seal Club was founded in the mid 19th Century as a drinking club for unmarried officers of the Foot Guards but developed into a dining club, with entry by election. Miles Barne probably became a member while a company commander after the Boer War, but members could be elected after they had married or after they had left the Army. The rules were changed in 1919 so that officers of the Household Cavalry were eligible.

Sunday June 11th 1916

Rode in evening with Esmé to Bde H.Q. to attend a pow-pow concerning an attack to be practised tomorrow – a lengthy affair – all C.O.s of the Bde – Artillery Commanders, Trench Mortar Battery Officers, Signalling Officers, etc etc all having & airing their own opinions on every subject brought forward.

12th

Practised the attack by day in a downpour – started at 7.15 p.m. to do it by night but before going as far as the Church, a messenger arrived to say all was cancelled – tho' fine at the time it turned very wet later & the men, who have now no blankets, would have suffered much.

Rode with Mann in afternoon & walked with Brand in evening.

To my astonishment this morning about 5 a.m. my old landlady came into my room and shut my window because she said the rain was driving in._

13th

Out to the training ground again to practise the attack.

At 3.15 p.m. I took the train – a pouring wet day – sort of tramway to BERGUES, a very picturesque old town with brick faced ramparts and a huge moat all round it, old red tiled houses and four odd shaped old towers – churches etc – gateways with drawbridges and other mediaeval objects._ Then I went by rail to DUNKERQUE, walked down to the harbour to look for my brother Mike on board his Monitor H.M.S. M *[blank]*.

Commander Michael Barne, Royal Navy, Commanding H.M. Monitor M.27

Found he was still over in England though expected back at any time. Was shewn over a sister ship HMS M *[blank]*, by her commander *[blank]*, whom I found on board the destroyer M26 playing roulette with 5 or 6 others.

Was told a number of yarns & anecdotes in a very short space of time, then caught the 7.26 train back to BOLLEZEELE, where I found my pony waiting, I rode out straight to the training ground where was just in time to see the Grens & Irish do a night attack in the rain, amidst rockets, very-lights, etc etc – our own attack was again deferred owing to the wet – then I met Esmé who gave me the astounding news that during the day orders had come for us to be at one hours notice but now we were to move at midday tomorrow, to go up to the line at YPRES to help the Canadians.

What would my feelings have been had I returned from D. to find the Battn gone!

> Between 2 and 13 June a localised battle went on along the ridge south of the Menin Road, between the Germans, who struck first, and the Canadian Corps. At the end of two weeks of ferocious fighting the Canadians had largely recaptured the most important ground that they lost initially, including Hill 62 or Tor Top, and overlooking Ypres, principally in a well planned and executed attack on 13 June, but their casualties throughout were very severe. It is known to history as the Battle of Mount Sorrel.
> In order to help them the 2nd Guards Brigade were sent up to hold part of the line temporarily, in the southern part of Sanctuary Wood, with Maple Copse behind. Neither they nor anyone else knew precisely where they were on the ground.

14th

Fresh orders arrive during the night. The C.O. goes off to YPRES with the Brigadier, leaving me to bring the Battn on by motor busses and lorries at 10 a.m. a very lengthy proceeding, eventually arriving at BRANDHOEK about 5 p.m. & going into a camp near there which the Canadians only turn out of at 7 p.m. When at last the men get their dinners about 7.30 p.m., on the arrival of the cookers, we are told to turn out and occupy Camp C less than a mile away, so off we go at 8.30 p.m., luckily a bright moon is behind the thick clouds – mud & wet every-where, and cold as March. Bn H.Q. in a filthy farm house, the kitchen of which is used as a sort of estaminet by the Canadians._ Dirt everywhere.

The C.O. & four Coy Commanders go up to the line about 8 p.m. to go round & only return

15th

about 3 a.m. having found the line in such a state that none of the Officers knew exactly where it was, as they never got beyond Bn. H.Q.

We have now had to alter our time to be like the Daylight Saving Act has made it become in England, one hour on.

Visit from Brigadier about 10 a.m.

In afternoon the C.O. sees all Officers to explain the situation – the Canadians have written most gratefully to the Brigadier for our coming to their rescue_

At 5 p.m. I attend (for Esmé) a C.O.'s conference at the 2nd Irish Gds H.Q.

At 9 p.m. we parade – I carry a pack & everything on me that am likely to want during the 3 days, even food – we entrain at BRANDHOEK at 9.45 p.m. detraining at YPRES, march to the [blank], where we find the Canadian guides, all very businesslike. After much sorting & arranging, & taking up bombs etc the Coys march off about 2 or 2½ miles across country – wet & muddy – to our trenches in front of ZILLEBEKE, near which place is the Battn H.Q. in a cellar, officers signallers orderlies and all, in the same room – not the height of comfort – no water except what we brought with us and unable to light fires day or night._ However we sleep well though the atmosphere is horrible.

Our Canadian brethren are not all relieved till about 1.30 a.m.

16th

after which I go out and round part of the line, tho' not all having to get back before it is light. The Cann Officers had been filling us up with stories of the desperate fighting June 2nd & subsequent days – a fearful time they must have had of it. Their stories cannot have been much exaggerated, for I never saw anything like the state of the ground & trenches as well as "Maple Copse" etc. A R.E. dump near the line was an amazing sight – wire sandbags mauls etc etc being chopped up & hurled in every direction – all mixed up with dead bodies, or bits of them._

This day turned out to be a very noisy one indeed and we had a good many casualties.

It is difficult to remember the exact sequence of events – there were some very intense bombardments – particularly one about 11 p.m., mostly on the Coldstream on our left – we saw some green rockets go up which we took to be "SOS" signal, so put on our equipment & got ready – with all signallers etc etc – for any emergency – a bit later a gas gong or horn was heard, so we all donned our gas helmets, and sat awaiting events. However the gas, if any, never came our way & I believe the green lights were really some German Arty signal.

Soon after this Trafford appeared with our rations, and a bit later the Brigadier accompanied by his Bde Major (Guy Rasch), R.E. Officer, Rogers the Bde C of E Chaplain, Green, Bombing Officer, Trench Bde Signalling Officer and [blank]. The only wonder was that the Vet & Interpreter were absent! He seemed in good spirits as usual, & thought it a capital joke that he had been caught in the Coldstm lines while they were being bombarded.

Trench happened to remark how glad he was he didn't live in our Bn H.Q., so the Bdr made him go & stand in the corner, as there was not head room to stand on a chair.

Just before this Mann appeared with his arm broken by a shell, reporting that Schiff had been killed – there were also several others wounded.

Lieutenant Trench, Royal Engineers, Signalling Officer, 2nd Guards Brigade – untraced

17th

At 2 a.m. I went off with the orderley Allen, to see what was happening in the front line B & C Coys, all communication being cut off. Got as far as the edge of SANCTUARY WOOD where they were, when a terrific bombardment was opened on it, a sight I shall never forget – the shells seemed to be bursting by the score at a time all round us. We 3 (I had also a guide from B Coy

Pte. Casey who had brought Mann down) squatted in a bit of old comn trench expecting every moment to be our last_

Saturday June 17th (contd).

We also thought it quite impossible that anyone should be alive in the wood where B & C Coys were: after what seemed like an hour the fire slackened so I determined to try & get back to L.F. Coy which we did successfully – about 400 yards, found no officer so took command & got ready thinking the Germans might very likely be coming over. After further search I found all the Officers together and presently Brand came in with a few others, wounded in 2 places, shoulder & back.

He could not give much information about B & C Coys, but Sgt Jacobs of L.F. appeared, apparently about the sole survivor of his post, saying he did not think the front line (C & part of B) had caught it very badly, so I settled to try again, this time taking about 6 men carrying water & rations for these two Companies – all volunteers for the job I believe.

> 8476 Private Frederick Albert Allen
> 10495 Private Patrick Casey †15.9.16
> 9604 Lance Sergeant Albert Edward Jacobs

There was a fortunate lull in the firing just when we had to go, but dawn was appearing & so I expected to have to stay the day there.

We had some difficulty in finding our way to any part of the line – all trenches blown in & shell holes about a foot apart everywhere, fallen trees, bits of wire etc etc etc, but soon came on a party – now H.Q – of B. Coy, under Lt Leach, where we dumped the water etc. I sent back the men to their Coys & told Leach to try & send the water on to C Coy & remainder of B. I then went forward cautiously to look for more men, almost expecting to meet Germans – the place for a while seemed deserted – not a sound – only dead & remains of human beings – not a sign of a trench – was on point of giving up owing to approaching daylight when suddenly came on a bit of trench – full of men of B Coy huddled together, followed this along till came on another batch, then another, & then to C. Coy where found Luss, as usual quite happy, but not knowing how many men he had left or where they were, & would not know probably till tonight. I saw a certain number of dead bodies – & pieces – including poor Schiff – but could not judge numbers as I had only seen a small part of the line.

I then came away in almost broad daylight – feeling very sorry for the poor things, and rather a brute to leave them, but thought it just as well to report what I had seen to Esmé, & he was glad to hear what I could tell him._ Some signallers & officers servants of B Coy had been killed and I expect we shall find they have suffered worst being in the middle of the wood. The whole thing appears such a jumble up in some ways, that it may be difficult to relieve the front Coys, and bring away their wounded, & hardly possible to bring out the dead.

> By the time they were back it was around dawn on the morning of 17 June. There were Canadians to their right.

At 9.30 p.m. Mark Maitland temporarily commanding 3rd Grenadiers and his 4 Coy Commanders – McKenzie, Eddie Ward, Woolridge Gordon & Dick Stanhope, all come up to us to see where to go on taking over from us tomorrow night – I take the two latter to the forward trenches and they have a good look round_ We get back without adventure about 2 a.m. Their bombing officer, Gunnis, also comes with me.

The other two and Mark go with Esme to our other trenches near MAPLE COPSE.

Captain Allan Keith Mackenzie †16.9.16, nicknamed "Sloper", younger brother of
    Sir Victor Mackenzie
Lieutenant Robert Wolrige Gordon
Captain Geoffrey George Gunnis †13.10.16

18th

Another sharp bombardment of Canadians about 10 a.m., otherwise quiet morning as far as we are concerned.

We are inclined to think the battue yesterday was caused by a little bombing-show the Canadians had on, and the Germans thought it was a general attack.

wonderfully quiet day and night: hardly a shot fired.

To hark back, on 16th-17th we seem to have come off wonderfully well in spite of the heavy fire. I expect being in a wood really helped, as the Germans plastered the whole wood not knowing exactly where our trenches were, and did not concentrate their fire on our trenches.

Our casualties seem to be about as follows – 1 Officer killed, 2 wounded, 12 other ranks killed, 25 wounded.

I dont think I said that the front trenches we took over from the Canadians were the ones where they had had so much fighting – they lost them (then support trenches) on June 2nd & retook them about 10th or 12th, both sides losing very heavily. The ground in consequence shews every sign of very severe fighting having taken place – dead everywhere, tho' we have buried many. Luss brought out a German Machine gun_ the trenches themselves could hardly be called trenches, no wire in front, and of course worse than ever since our bombardment night of 16th-18th *[17th]*.

Some guns were lost and retaken by Canadians in Sanctuary Wood – 3 field guns – our gunners were to go and get them out last night, they were fought up to the last. Close by were found the bodies of a Canadian Scottish & a German gripping eachothers throats.

The amount of equipment ammunition lying about almost rivalled Loos!

A quiet afternoon on the whole although some shelling.

At night we are relieved by 3rd Grenrs & take their place in the dam of ZILLEBEKE Lake, except half of R.F. Coy which remains in the remains of the village of ZILLEBEKE where there are a few cellars. I go ahead about 10 p.m. to take over. The Transport with rations arrived up, also bringing water, and Tim O.E. with it, who of course was full of news & rumours. The relief was not all over till about 3 a.m.

19th

A thick morning mist. A new C. of E. Chaplain, Head by name is with us for the present, usually with the Grens. A very quiet day in the dugouts by the Dam.

The Reverend Frederick Waldegrave Head, C.F., 3rd Grenadier Guards

20th

The day opened with a heavy bombardment on our left, followed by one entirely directed on a How. Battery to our right. Luckily, I was told by a Gunner Officer, this particular Battery, tho' it had made small efforts at concealment, had made great efforts at protection from shellfire, so we hope not much damage was done: the practice at it seemed to be wonderfully good.

It is a long time since I have given a list of the Officers of the Battalion. At present as follows:

Lt.Col.	Lord E. Gordon-Lennox.
	self
Adjt.	Lieut Eric McKenzie
Qmr.	Capt Kinlay.
Medl Officer	Alexander
Transport "	Lt Cecil Trafford
Bombing Officer	" Brand – just gone away wounded
Sniping Officer	" Powell
R.F. Coy	Capt Hugh Ross
	Lt. R. Abercromby
	" Shortt
	" Champion.
B.	Lt. E.P. Orr-Ewing.
	" Leach.
C.	Capt Sir Iain Colquhoun of Luss.
	Lt. Calverley Bewicke
	" Powell.
	" Menzies
D. *[L.F. Coy]*	Capt. Lionel Norman
	Lt Martindale.
	" Bradshaw.

Those not mentioned before,

Lieutenant Eric Dighton Mackenzie, youngest of the three Mackenzie brothers, wounded on the Aisne and again at Loos

Lieutenant William Edward Dudley Shortt †12.10.17

Lieutenant William Patrick Arthur Bradshaw

Lieutenant Powell was responsible for sniper training while also a company officer in C Company.

There have been a large number of Officers come & gone for various reasons since I joined in July 1915 – impossible to remember all, but amongst others, Paul Methuen, Dick Bethell, Bartholomew (now comdg Bde MG Coy), Stirling (M.G.), Tennant (M.G.), Cecil Boyd Rochford, John Thorpe, Arthur Boyd Rochford and of course several others wounded at Loos, besides Cuthbert, Armstrong, and Schiff killed, Stuart the Doctor, John Dyer now on Bde Staff, Jack Stirling, Con Seymour, Mackworth-Praed, Phillipson, Callander-Brodie, Thompson (late Adjt), Hammersley, Drury-Lowe, Tempest (for 2 days), De Teissier, Liddell-Grainger, Purvis, F. Ward, Peevor, Fenner, Dawkins.

Those not mentioned before,
Lieutenant Hilton Philipson
Lieutenant John Clark Brodie Callender Brodie
Lieutenant Guy Stacey Dawkins †25.9.16 with 2nd Scots Guards

The total casualties on night of June 16th-17th turn out to be   1 Officer killed 2 wounded.
16 other ranks killed 26 wounded

Righteous indignation of the C.O. who was called up by John Dyer on the telephone, but, on the CO replying, J.D could not remember what he wanted to say!

A lot of shelling all day – some big stuff into YPRES – & several very near our dugouts – so much so that we took refuge in a deep hole made underneath. On emerging after all was over, a ½ dead rat was found sitting on the trench boards – expect several others were killed. There seem to be more here than anywhere, with many young ones – the place seems to swarm with them at night, & stinks accordingly.

There were great jokes when the Brigadier came round, about our first having watched the Bde HQ in YPRES being shelled, and thought it quite a good joke, and then when in the afternoon we were being shelled, the Brigade Staff is supposed to have been much amused. The Brigadier orders Hugh Ross to draw a series of pictures to suit._

At night the two padres Head and Rogers, had to go up to the line and bury Canadians & Germans who were being collected by the Grenadiers all over the place. They returned just before daylight.

Captain Ross was an accomplished artist and cartoonist

21st

Quiet up till about noon, after which about 1½ hours shelling unpleasantly near us.

Hear the Grenadiers have had quite a quiet time.

During the afternoon some shelling most of the time till the Canadians arrive at dusk, by driblets. They come in no special formation, and do things quite differently to other people. Their discipline is conspicuous by its absence, or rather its uniqueness, for there must be some sort of Discipline. But they bring trouble on themselves and get many unnecessary casualties – everyone of our Battn has some story of the odd way they do things & their disregard of conventionality, which however does not pay.

At night we go out joining our Motor Buses & lorries at the Asylum thence to Camp "E", a very pleasant spot.

A bombshell arrives in the shape of an order to Esmé to report himself to the 4th Army H.Q. on 23rd, which I suppose means getting a Brigade.

June 22nd 1916

A lovely morning – summer. Several German Aeroplanes come over & also some shells – presumably at a gun somewhere near. Have my hair cut by Pte Thornton.

Private Thornton – untraced

In afternoon ride with Tim to look for brother Seymour near RENINGHELST. but hear the Cavalry are further South.

On return watch some Canadians playing Baseball, the*[n]* ourselves play rounders – after which L. Norman, Trafford and I sow some mustard & cress etc seed._

Sloper McKenzie and Eddy Ward dine with us, the C.O., Esmé's, last dinner with us as C.O., as we all expect he will get a Brigade.

23rd

11 months today since I landed in France.

Am President of a F.G.C.M. when there are 5 cases to deal with – one of which is for desertion – to whom we give 10 years penal servitude, owing to his having a pretty good character._

Ride with Tim & Bewicke in afternoon to see polo – Tim played a chukker on the B Coy pony "Lassie".

Heavy thunderstorm in evening & wet night.

Miller rejoined – Dundas & Childers joined the Battn.

> Lieutenant Ernest Miller
> Lieutenant Henry Lancaster Nevill Dundas †27.9.18
> Lieutenant William Leslie Eardley Childers

Camp was shelled early with H.E. shrapnel again.

S. McKenzie and E. Ward dined with us.

24th

To Bde H.Qrs in morning. In afternoon a visit from Alston, and then attend a C.O.'s conference at Bde H.Q. when many interesting events in the future – regarding the line etc are discussed.

After this there is a Sergts' Concert, with the aid of the band, which the Brigadier attends.

I forgot to mention y'day Esmé's departure at 2 p.m. for MERICOURT due E of AMIENS, the H.Q. of 4th Army. He goes off in the Pr. of Wales' Motor car.

> Headquarters Fourth Army, on the Somme, were at the Château de Querrieu, between Amiens and Albert, Méricourt-L'Abbé being the closer to it of the two villages called Méricourt in the vicinity, another called Maricourt being further east.

25th

I inspect the Camp in the morning.

In afternoon ride with L. Norman, looking for some men we had to send away as caretakers of some "posts" in the neighbourhood – could not find them.

In evening Rounders v. 3rd Grenadiers – drawn game.

S. Burton & H. de Trafford dined with us.

> Major Stephen John Burton, 1st Coldstream Guards †20.7.17
> Lieutenant Humphrey Edmund de Trafford, 1st Coldstream Guards

26th

Went up to the line with 4 Coy Commanders to see where we are to go tomorrow & next day. Rode as far as the "Trois Tours" Farm, a huge renovated (very hideously) old chateau surrounded by a huge moat, & walked on.

Was shewn round the line by Col. Follett – cmdg 2nd Coldm: not a very pleasant bit of line, some of it only 40 yds across to the Germans. We shall be there next to the French on the Canal Bank.

Early this morning, or late last night, we made a terrific bombardment, which was followed by a raid by the 20th Divn – said to have been very successful.

Downpour of very heavy rain tonight.

What condition will the trenches be in!

> The Guards Division were now the left hand division in the XIV Corps area in the Ypres Salient. The 1st Scots Guards were about to take over from the 2nd Coldstream Guards on the extreme left, near Boesinghe, with the French immediately next to them along the Ypres-Yser Canal.

27th

Rather a busy day preparing for taking over trenches. Move at 9.30 p.m., rather regretfully leaving our nice camp in the wood.

A conference of C.O.'s previously at Bde H.Q. to discuss the operations which we used to practise at BOLLEZEELE, & which appear now likely to come off._

A 2 hours quiet walk to the Canal Bank where we go into dugouts for one night – no hitch of any sort.

Our left is on the French, with whom Dundas goes as "liaison" Officer._

28th

Round the line in morning, and again at night starting at 1 a.m. on

29th

when I found the trenches rather complicated & wander about almost lost. Back & to bed at 4 a.m., & off again with Col Brooke, cmdg 3rd Grens at 11 a.m. to shew him round – which was a long business, as we did a lot of prospecting through periscopes. eventually getting back to lunch about 2.30 p.m.

Another conference at Bde HQ at 5 p.m.

30th

At 12.30 a.m. met Sloper McKenzie – took him round part of the line – when we got as far as the right of R.F. Coy (left of our front) a tremendous bombing was heard – we hastened on & found a little bombing show going on on the extreme left of our line by the Canal, where by the way we join the French.

I found Hugh Ross on in the bombing posts – quite exciting while it lasted – very confusing bit of trenches – wherever I went a voice warned me to "mind that corner" etc. the German

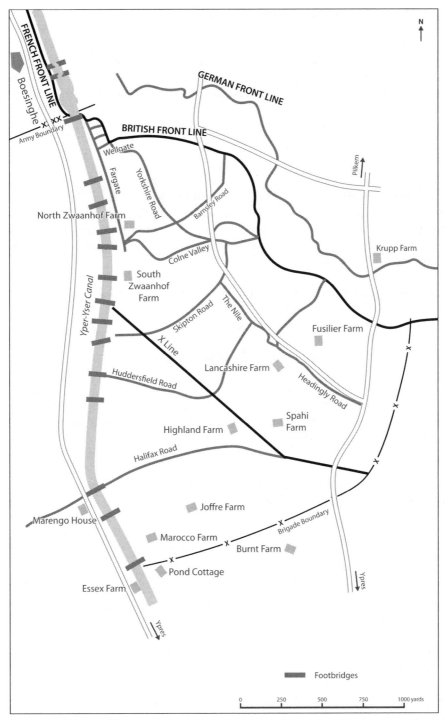

Map 10 Ypres Salient, XIV Corps left hand brigade sector south of Boesinghe, June and July 1916.

machine guns were very busy & seemed to come in every direction. There were 4 men wounded, & Ross had quite a business to get them away._ It all died off by about 2.30 a.m., & I eventually got to bed by 3.30 a.m.

Up to the line again in afternoon to make final arrangements as to our relief tonight – when the 3 G.G. take over from us & we are again in Brigade reserve on the Canal Bank – spend all night thickening our roofs as tomorrow we are to do a big bombardment, expecting retaliation from the enemy_

Trafford brings up rations and water (none is here procurable so all has to be brought up in petrol tins) not meaning to come again till night of 3rd.

July 1st

Our bombardment begins at 9 a.m., the enemy commencing his retaliation by direct hits on our dugouts or very close to them – up to lunch time we have only 2 men wounded.

During the morning we hear for the first time openly of the beginning of the great advance: namely that "the 4th Army and the French have reached their first objective everywhere." Very good news – what will the next step be I wonder.

> Miles Barne noted what they first heard about the opening of the Battle of the Somme.

We also hear the Russians have taken KOLOMEA.

> Kolomea was a Russian objective in the Brusilov Offensive.

During the day various telegrams arrive about "the push", but leave us rather hazy as to the net result. A bombardment by us began about 9 a.m. & lasted all day ending up with a raid by the Welsh Gds a few doors off to our right – the success of which was rather doubtful. They were to attack seize & consolidate a certain trench called the MORTELJE ESTAMINET.

They seem to have got there but report says they were unable to remain.

> The 1st Welsh Guards raid on Morteldje Estaminet was near where the 16th Brigade, 6th Division, lost and then retook part of their front line in April.

The retaliation of Germans was pretty severe & a good many shells came on Canal Bank & near our dugouts – only 1 man in the Battn however being wounded.

2nd

To Brigade H.Q. with Col Brooke in morning for a long confab on the defences of the Canal Bank etc.

Our spare moments are now occupied with dominoes and chess.

At night there is another heavy bombardment, followed by a raid by 2/Irish Guards on the Krupp Salient.

They bring back 1 prisoner, & inflict some losses, but receive a good many themselves. Pym, the Officer who went over was not damaged, but did not return.

Krupp Farm, just inside the German lines on the Ypres-Pilckem road, gave its name to a small German salient opposite the right hand battalion of the 2nd Guards Brigade. Lieutenant Francis Leslie Melville Pym, 2nd Irish Guards †2.7.16

3rd

Still no news of Pym. I hear he has been recommended for a V.C.; he was last seen going for a machine gun section single handed, & hanging onto a German's throat.

Chess with Bewicke & Ross. An expedition with R.E. & others to examine FARGATE a disused trench, which we are to find a big working party for repairing & draining.

Good news of "the Advance".

Some shelling during morning.

4th

An idle day in many ways._

Luss – just back from leave – & I lunch at Brigade H.Q.

More chess._

We relieve 3rd G.G. at night in front line – quiet relief. I go round at 2 a.m.

5th

No excitements._ Again (a different way) before lunch.

More chess_ Meet by chance young Barnard-Smith of Carlton Colville, one of the 6th Div. Gunner Officers – on duty in our area.

Lieutenant William Woodthorpe Barnard Barnard-Smith, Royal Field Artillery †21.10.16, son of Suffolk neighbours

6th

About 1.30 a.m. this morning the Huns opposite us suddenly "got the wind up", fired off scores of verry lights, rifles, machine guns, etc etc followed by trench mortars and shrapnel – also bombs on our left – evidently they had spotted a working party of Grenadiers in a drain, & thought we had a raid on! All was quiet by 3.15 a.m., & we only had 3 slight casualties.

Personally I never knew anything was going on and slept soundly from 12.30 a.m. till I was called at 8 a.m._ For some reason or other the sentry had neglected to call me.

I went round 10 a.m. getting back at 1 p.m., all the way round.

To the Brigade H.Q. at 5.30 p.m. to hear about a raid to be carried out by 3rd Grens tonight, when we have got to thin our line or not as I think best._

7th

The Raid comes off at 1 a.m. but not a great success, we hear. There have been too many, and the enemy is too watchful, & knows how to act.

I go round at 3 a.m. getting back rather weary at 5.30 a.m.

Play chess with Jackson R.E. Many rumours going about that our "biff" is not coming off just yet – the 6th Divn Gunners having been replaced by our own Guards Divn Gunners, who had been employed digging special emplacements.

News from the advance in the South is tailing off, but they have done well.

Some shelling of our line in afternoon – no casualties though many squeaks, a Sgt got a bullet right through his steel helmet, (head piece, not brim) & never touched him.

> Jackson, Royal Engineers – untraced
> It was becoming clear that an attack on Pilckem Ridge was no longer likely.

8th

Went round 2.30 a.m. back 5 a.m. All well. Had rather an exciting journey up FARGATE on way out, owing to activity of machine guns and snipers – got very hot._

Up part of the line in afternoon, & to reconnoitre our positions for defence in case of attack – write orders for this.

Attend conference at Bde H.Q. in evening. Chess. Bn is relieved by 3rd G.G. and goes into Bde Reserve in Canal Bank Dugouts again._

Sunday July 9th

A very quiet day as far as work goes – some shelling as usual – commencing with a "straaf" by us at 2 a.m.

A huge luncheon party in my dugout – 9 of us – all 4 Coy Commanders, to eat a most excellent pair of cold tame wild ducks from Sotterley – also asparagus, and we all enjoyed the meal much after the 4 days in trenches._ Afterwards more chess.

Cecil Boyd-Rochford and Daniel arrived to rejoin.

> Lieutenant Russell John Daniels

Great news of the big Russian Advance.

> The Brusilov Offensive again

Luss had a long letter from Esmé who had seen the whole of the French Advance, even the men popping the parapets, with the naked eye.

A visit from John Thorpe who has returned to 2nd Battn to command a Company – but is most anxious to come to this Battn. I have offered to change places with him, but I don't know what will come of it.

> Captain John Somerled Thorpe was wounded at Loos and then at the Duck's Bill just
>   before Christmas

10th

A bath: the first since we have been in the line; inspected Fargate with a view to a party working there tonight – which they did under C. Boyd-Rochford, but as there was heavy retaliation for a 20th Divnl Arty straaf they could not do much.

Hear we are to hear epoch-making news from Russia very shortly.

11th

Went twice up to Fargate again, 2nd time with Dundas who will be in charge of the party tonight – & expect he will do it well. He is very keen & was Capt of the Oppidans at Eton. Some shelling. Had 3 men hit last night, only 1 at all badly.

In afternoon spent some time with Trench, Brigade Signalling Officer, arranging communication across the Canal for our positions when we are attacked_ Battn H.Q. will have to get across or it will be separated from the Battn._

> At Boesinghe No Man's Land was the Ypres-Yser Canal, a muddy morass, but from just south of there the lines began to bend out towards the east, so that the forward British troops had the Canal behind them. There were several bridges across, all draped in hessian to conceal movement, but exposed and vulnerable to enemy machine gun fire.

News from the "push" down South, also from Russia continues very good. We hear that 1 Corps Commander (Fanshaw) 4 Divl Genls, including Stuart-Wortley and de Lisle -, and 6 Brigadiers have been sent home, so this ought to make a certainty of it for Esmé.

> Lieutenant General Hew Dalrymple Fanshawe, Commanding V Corps, was not dismissed.
> Major General The Honourable Edward James Montagu Stuart Wortley, Commanding 46th Division, was dismissed.
> Major General Henry de Beauvoir de Lisle, Commanding 29th Division, was not dismissed.
> Brigadier General Lord Esmé Gordon Lennox was appointed to command the 95th Brigade, 5th Division, with effect from 21 July after his predecessor was wounded.

12th

My wedding day.

Shelling commenced early close to Battn H.Q., and in fact all along the Battn dugouts._ I walked up to see the work done last night in FARGATE, and got shelled there by "Pip-squeaks" – a quiet middle of day but from 4 p.m. to 8.30 p.m. a lot of shelling at random, a good deal at the bridges and we had 2 men killed, 9 wounded – some heavy stuff – fearful escapes in places – 2 dugouts were blown in. The thickest of the shelling was round B. Coy, & Tim's dugouts.

Hear that Sherard Godman and not Norman O.E. is to command this Battn._ We relieve 3rd G.G. in front line trenches at night, and the relief goes very well.

> A "pip squeak" was a low trajectory German field gun shell.
> 7755 Private Charles Biggar †12.7.16

11397 Private Thomas Hislop †12.7.16

It had been widely believed that, though Lieutenant Colonel Godman was the senior, Major Orr Ewing was coming to command the 1st Scots Guards. Both were wounded at Loos.

13th

Little Michael's birthday, bless him.

I go round the line 2.30 a.m.–5.15.a.m. all quiet.

Am sent for in evening to the Brigade about a covering party for some drainers, under the R.E. Later another question arises, and again I go down to Bde H.Q. where I dine – Brigr in great form. Afterwards a message arrives to say extra vigilance is required for the next three or four days – does not say why! So I go up to the line to warn Coy Commanders, and return via FARGATE at 3 a.m. on

14th

Enemy machine guns very active on the bridges – which I do not waste time in crossing. These bridges are a permanent source of danger discomfort and anxiety to us – and one is always glad to be safely over. There have been several casualties there – if any attack took place, they wd be heavily barraged & have frequently been broken down.

We hear the covering party last night were tried to be rushed by 6 Germans, who however found us ready – & only 5 ran away leaving the 6th – by some misunderstanding between the NCO in charge and the R.E. Officer, the Hun was not picked up – I propose having this done tonight._

At 3 p.m. I go round a good bit of the line with the Artillery Liaison Officer, who has a very good periscope and inspect German wire & parapets.

While up there an urgent message came from Brigadier wanting me at a C.O.'s conference at 5 p.m., so I had to hurry off & got there by 5.30 p.m., when some interesting things about our future were discussed.

Amongst other things he wants a reconnaissance made on a certain bit of "No Mans Land", as well as a trap laid for any Germans who might come back to look for the man left behind last night, so back I went to the line and made most elaborate & detailed arrangements with Dundas who was to do the reconnaissance – & Tim O.E. who commanded the front centre Company. There were to be the patrol with Dundas, the RE working party, with its covering party of 10 men, as well as a connecting party of 10 men – so we had to reinforce the front line with an Officer & 20 men of R.F. Coy.

The Brigadier is rather fussed about the warning for extra vigilance, and thinks a raid in force possible, so we take every precaution. The Welsh Guards relieve 3rd GG. as Reserve Battn, Colonel Murray-Threipland coming in to talk over the relief tomorrow night, when they are to relieve us in front line.

15th

All went well in the night, & I hope & believe Dundas has made a really good reconnaissance.

He did not run into any Germans, and there were no casualties from machine gun or any other cause. The only unfortunate thing being that the dead (or wounded) German was not found. I expect he was only wounded, and crawled away.

Arranged to go round at 10 a.m. with Colonel M-T. and other Officers of Welsh Gds, but on hearing news that the Arty were going to cut wire at 10 a.m., we defer the pleasure till the afternoon, when we get round in perfect peace. Col. M-T goes into everything in greatest detail – & spends a long time at the bridge which worries him very badly. Eventually we get back to Bn HQ about 8 p.m., are relieved there by Dick Coke of our 2nd Bn. (Roger Tempest Wynne Finch etc having gone to Paris), the Bn is relieved in front line by Welsh Guards, then we walk back starting at 12 midnight arriving on

16th

at 1.45 a.m. at Camp D., where 3rd Gren were, when we were at Camp E., have a good meal, & to bed at 2 a.m., when I slept soundly till 9 a.m.

We hear POPERINGHE has been badly shelled in the last few days, all civilians as well as Troops, Field Ambces etc etc, having to turn out.

Walked with Tim O-E in evening. Tried to get him & Eric McKenzie promoted to Captain – successful in former but not the latter._

A representative detachment from the British Expeditionary Force took part in the Bastille Day Parade on 14th July in Paris. Lieutenant Colonel Tempest commanded it and the 2nd Scots Guards filled the other key positions.

13

To the Somme

17th

Spent the day very busily with various things to do with the Regt – going round Camp – rode to see polo in afternoon – & so on.

Montgomery, Irish Guards, who is "Camp Quartermaster" came to dine – he is married to a German whose Father commanded an Army Corps at beginning of the war, and whose 4 brothers are in the German Army. He was in 12th Lancers & is standing as a Unionist for Southampton.

Lieutenant Hugh Montgomery, 2nd Irish Guards †13.9.16

18th

Rode with Hugh Ross – Rounders with Grenadiers in evening.
Met Col Mack, 9/Suffolk Rgt who is in Camp C.

Lieutenant Colonel Arthur Paston Mack, Commanding 9th Suffolk Regiment †15.9.16

There were many attractions – the 1/Coldm were playing Cricket against 9/Suffolk – & beat them – & our Band was playing not far off.

Great excitement caused by Captains & upwards being asked to volunteer to command New Army Bns, to replace casualties on the Somme. Luss & Lionel Norman apply. I hate having to send in their names.

Even if I wanted to, I am not allowed to apply, which I suppose I ought to regard as a compliment – tho' a distinct grievance – not having any chance of promotion here.

19th

A very cold night – & very disturbed by heavy Arty fire, & Aeroplanes dropping bombs, and our "coughing Kate" firing at the aeroplanes. etc.

Rode over towards ELVERDINGHE by myself – cricket in evening v. Coldstream, when I scored 1 run, being caught out before very long.

Col Mack & Baden came to dinner.

20th

Great excitement early as Corps Commander was coming to inspect us, but he never turned up, sending a wire after all was quite ready for him._

Cricket in afternoon v. 3rd G.G. who made 185 to our 155. I made 0, being bowled out by Col Brooke first ball.

21st

Brigadier inspected our Transport, & expressed the greatest satisfaction. He is a very charming man, having his little jokes all the time, & even if he had to criticize he has the knack of doing it in a very charming way._

In afternoon Etonians beat the World at cricket.

The Battn Football team beat the Belgians 5:0.

To my surprise & delight, brother Seymour turns up from HAAZBROUCK, in a motor car – when we went a little walk. He said he might be able to take me to DUNKERQUE on Sunday, so later I ask the Brigadier and he gives me leave.

Dine with Col Mack & 9th Suffolks – find their Mess Sergt (Newson) was in Heveningham Garden for 7 years._ Some more or less Suffolk Officers were present – Hyam, Stanford, Ensor, Rowbothom etc etc._

> Possibly 15197 Sergeant William E Newson, Suffolk Regiment
> Possibly Major Higham, Suffolk Regiment
> Possibly Lieutenant John Keith Stanford, Suffolk Regiment
> Captain Lionel Ensor, 9th Suffolk Regiment
> Lieutenant Jack Catchpole Rowbotham, 9th Suffolk Regiment

Later I attend the Brigadier's Garden Party, a weird scene, Band, & Pipers, dancing, easy chairs, electric light – small tables champagne cup peaches & foie-gras sandwiches – at Bde H.Q. in the wood, not far off the inevitable circle of very-lights, & the usual chorus of machine guns rifles bombs & Artillery.

In the middle Sniper Green tried to cause consternation by letting off a very-light close by, some thinking for a moment of Hun aeroplanes & bombs!

Nobody enjoyed the entertainment more than the old Brigadier.

The little Prince of Wales was there, & I had a short chat with him, when he startled me by reminding me he took me down to LOOS last Sepbr, I never thought he knew at the time who I was – & even if he did thought he must have forgotten, but suppose he has the usual Royal memory for people & faces – even my ugly one.

22nd

Our Doctor, Alexander, has gone sick & left us.

I ride alone to look out the white-post lane to TROIS TOURS where we go Monday night. Some shelling not far off._

Watch snipers at work testing new sights.

23rd

12 months today since I left England. Seymour calls for me at 9.30 a.m. in a motor car & we go off via POPERINGHE and PROVEN to DUNKERQUE, where to our great disappointment we dont find Mike, who is over at DOVER. We have to content ourselves by walking about the harbour, watching some seaplanes,

July 23rd contd

and having lunch, after which we went off through GRAVELINES to look at the ruins of an Ammunition Store at ARDIQUES, which was wrecked a few days ago by German bombs dropped from an aeroplane. A very deplorable sight – acres and acres of shells scattered in every direction – we talked to some machine gunners etc who had been there all the time, and had wonderful escapes. Whoever designed the store must feel rather foolish, for it had been proved the greatest failure._

After this we continued via ST. OMER and CASSEL, where we had tea and admired the view, getting back to Camp D at 7 p.m., finding a mixture of things going on including Coldstream Sports, Cricket, football, Church Services, boxing tournament etc etc., but most strange of all – during my absence orders had arrived altering everything, we are not to go into the line but back to the BOLLEZEELE area.

The Brigadier, Cols. Baring & Brooke & several junior officers dined with us – the Brigadier spun many long yarns which I think he enjoyed as much as his audience.

24th

Rode to look at polo match versus 1st Bn Coldstream – which they won 5-2. Our team was Farmer, Tim O.E., Bewicke & C. Boyd-Rochford._

Hear Esmé has got the 95th Bde., so now we shall not be long getting a real C.O.

25th

The 3rd GG & 2nd Irish Gds go off early_ 1st Hampshire Rgt takes place of 3rd GG in Camp E: they are fresh from the Somme, but only very few of the Officers & men were there.

In afternoon we got badly beaten at cricket by the Coldstream.

1st Battalion The Hampshire Regiment, 11th Brigade, 4th Division

26th

We move off by Companies at 12.15 p.m., marching into POPERINGHE, where we entrain on the tramway, and go via WATOU WORMHOUT ESQUELBECQ to BOLLEZEELE in 4 train[s], with some of the Brigade Staff. Before starting the Pr of Wales came round with Leigh (Grenr) Cavan's A.D.C., and shewed great interest in the Battn; he also told us that we (the British Troops) had captured POZIÈRES.

We steamed out of the Station – or rather siding – at 2.55 p.m., wondering much whether we have seen the last of "The Salient". It seems impossible to believe that we have. Take it all round the Divn have been very lucky there, & the Regt also.

Walk in evening with L. Norman.

27th

A Battn Route March, going to look at our old Trench Ground – & home through MERKEGHEM.

In afternoon rode with Hugh Ross to Brigade H.Q. at VOLKERINGSHOVE.

Later walked with L. Norman & C. Trafford.

The late Town Major of YPRES, Wigram (60th Rifles) and Bartholomew dined with us, I thought the former would never go.

28th

Companies practise consolidating. Later ride with C. Trafford & Eric McKenzie through a very pretty wood, & on to a village MILLAN, where we found – just arrived – Charlie Corkran & 3rd Bde H.Q., Harry Seymour & his (4th Gren) Battn, also our 2nd Battn. – a pleasant surprise, as we had no idea where they were.

The 4th Gren had had an unfortunate little episode, when one night they were wiring in front of their trenches – on completion of task the Officer gave the order to return to trenches, which they did, followed by their "covering" party and – also followed by a party of Germans, who came right into their trench, killed an Officer (McLure) and a Pte soldier, wounded 7 others, and took away a Sergt & 1 other as prisoners! A very easy thing to happen, but of course quite inexcusable carelessness on part of the Sergt in charge of the covering party.

> Brigadier General Charles Edward Corkran, Commanding 3rd Guards Brigade
> 2nd Lieutenant Basil George Hope Maclear, 4th Grenadier Guards †26.7.16
> Probably 21793 Private H Hulse, 4th Grenadier Guards †26.7.16

29th

More consolidating practice._

In afternoon Luss & I go by train to DUNKERQUE to once more to look for Mike, but once more dont find him, tho' I go on board his monitor (M 27). He is out fishing. A signalman & I go onto the pier to look for him & we hail a boat which looks like his, but is not, & she only turns & puts out to sea, but says will tell him. However I have to catch my train, & so miss the last chance of seeing him. Bad luck.

Arrive back at BOLLEZEELE 9 p.m.

30th

We all have breakfast at an estaminet at 5.45 a.m. & march off at 6.45, entraining at ESQUELBECQ 5 miles and leaving there 10 a.m. travelling via LILLERS, ST. POL, to PETIT HOUVIN 2.30 p.m., when we disembarked and had one of the hottest & longest 12 mile march over rolling downs & plains, & through the prettiest villages possible. A large number of men fell out in the heat, but caught up & the march into LUCHEUX, where we were billeted, was a fine sight.

The men had fallen out for various reasons – were paid y'day (!), were rather soft after trench life, the heat (quite intense) & absence of wind, the early start, & am afraid some men were weak from hunger owing to two of the Qmr Sergts neglecting their duty.

Our 2nd Bn came through the village about 10.30 p.m. & on to HALLOY, the 2nd Bn Irish Gds arrived at the other end of the village at 11.30 p.m. We hear every Battn dropped a certain number of men en route – the 3rd Bn Grenrs particularly a good lot. I went to report at Bde H.Q. on arrival, & found the Brigadier very genial as usual, just finishing dinner, he invited me to dine, but I most regretfully had to decline, as orders had not been written.

At Tattoo only 3 men are absent and all appeared soon afterwards.

> Tattoo was last parade of the day

31st

I had a terrible number of cases to settle at "C.O's Orders" over yesterday – including several N.C.O's., and the Quartermaster had up the 4 Q.M.Sgts – as well as the Master Cook.

After this I had all the Officers & N.C.O.'s. together and gave them a piece of my mind concerning the falling out yesterday. The senior Captns tell me this will do good_ Time will show.

All the men who fell out & were passed by the Doctor as "Medicine & duty", or "duty" had to go for a route march this evening – this should certainly have a good effect._

> The Regimental Medical Officer was now Captain Hugh Wansey Bayly, Royal Army
> Medical Corps, author of Triple Challenge: Or, War, Whirligigs and Windmills

We are able to let the whole Battn bathe in the stream – which will do them good, and the Battn has a real day of rest – with the exception of foot & rifle inspectn.

In afternoon I rode with Luss & Hugh Ross – the latter saw some pig (wild-boar), so they both went home & got rifles, while I continued my ride – conversed with some foresters who offered me some cider.

Luss & Hugh returned back to billets about 10 p.m. very highly pleased with themselves, having shot a roe-buck – which was with difficulty brought down & put in the Officers' Mess cart.

There is a very picturesque old Chateau in the woods here with a fine view, now an Officers Hospital – once was lived in by the great Duke of Marlborough, on one of his Campaigns.

Orders from the Brigade were late coming so about 10.45 p.m. we sent to ask when the orders were coming in – reply was in ½ an hour, nevertheless they did not arrive till 1.30 p.m. [a.m.] for a move which meant rising at 4.15 a.m.! So did not get much sleep!

Aug 1st

A 9 mile march, starting at 7.30 a.m. extremely hot – but the Bn did it well & only 4 men fell out, 2 fainted on the way up the hill, 2 more on getting into their huts! This is quite the right spirit.

Our new camp is in a lovely beech wood on top of a hill, but no water arrangements._

In afternoon I ride down to look for bathing places, & in evening the whole Bn bathes by companies & the new Dr inspected the feet, and did it thoroughly too – we only got back to dinner 9.30 p.m. & had some of the roe venison which was very good.

We are now in WARNIMONT wood, near ATHIE, about 6 mi from "the line"._

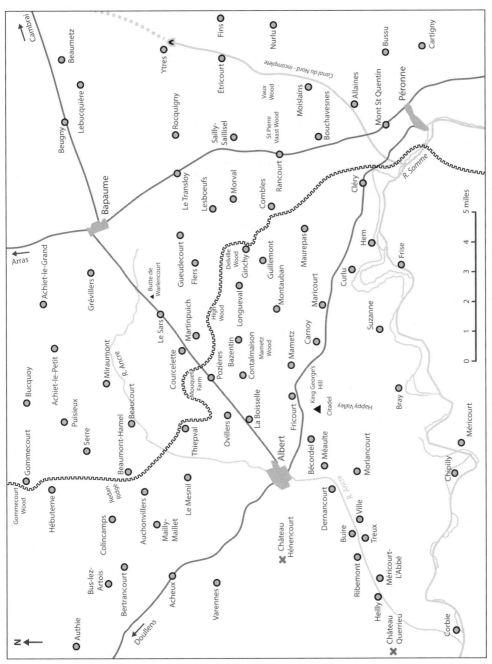

Map 11 Battle of the Somme, Line prior to 15 September 1916.

2nd

Spent the day cleaning up the camp – the men resting & bathing. I rode to the Bde H.Q. with Luss to ask various conundra. Heavy firing during night.

> The battle for the Pozières Ridge had been going on for several days and the heavy firing was probably from there.

3rd

Battn route march by Coys 5.30–8.30 a.m. Then 2 Coys bathed. I spent morning looking for Rifle Range Site & Bombing Pit Site – which were made during the afternoon, so as to give the Snipers & Lewis gunners & bombers a chance of practice.

Rode in evening with C. Trafford. Yesterday Esmé appeared, and had a lot to say about the recent fighting, when his Brigade had evidently done very well. They must be an excellent Brigade with 3 regular Bns – but all the New Army must have done splendidly – he told us a lot about the battles. Evidently the enemy has brought up a lot of extra Artillery here. From various accounts, directly we moved from "the Salient", the Germans brought down troops to oppose us here._

Excellent news from Russia.

At night, after dinner, Luss & Hugh & Eric McK. asked if they cd go off on bikes back to LUCHEUX to try & shoot a wild boar – I consented & they were to be back by 10.30 a.m.

> The 5th Division were involved in the first attacks on High Wood just after the start of which Brigadier General Lord Esmé Gordon Lennox took command of the 95th Brigade.

5th *[4th]*

Bn Route march by Companies 5.30–8.30 a.m. Not so hot.

Luss etc returned 9 a.m., but without any result, tho' they all seemed very happy – had seen nothing. The Divisional Gas Expert, Capt *[blank]* of 12th Royal Fusiliers came to lecture us in the morning. Beevor, for 15 yrs a doctor in the Regt, came to luncheon, but found nobody he knew except Kinlay & me._

> Colonel Walter Calverley Beevor, Royal Army Medical Corps

A C.O.'s. conference at Bde H.Q. in evening, when various points were discussed, tho' nothing disclosed as to our future movements._

The Brigadier says he is coming up to our camp tomorrow morning, & expects to see me with the extra stars up – viz Lt.Col.

6th *[5th]*

The usual route marching, when L. Norman decorates me & I appear at breakfast Lt.Col but "under protest" as I shall have to pull them down again when Godman arrives – if not before as it seems doubtful to me if I am entitled to the promotion.

The usual sniping and Lewis gun & Bombing practices.

In afternoon I ride out with Guy Baring to look at the way up to the line, & get a wide & very interesting view, including the country round POZIERES etc._ A certain amount of shelling is going on at some batteries on each side as we walk up, having left our horses at COLINCAMPS._

In evening Jack Dyer dines with us, & evidently there is a difficulty (as I anticipated) about my promotion, so on

6th

I take good care not to appear with stars on._

An idle day. Harold Boyd Rochford lunches, & as usual has every sort of yarn to tell us.

Captain Harold Boyd Rochfort, The 21st Lancers, the middle one of the three brothers

In evening ride over with Tim & Luss & L. Norman and Hugh Ross to see some German prisoners at ACHEUX – a fine looking lot physically – hear they are Silesians.

7th

Football match with 2nd Bn when they win 2-1: the annual cup. "Dugout" practice during afternoon.

Hear Godman has left HAVRE.

The little Prince came to see our camp – walking v. lame – sprained tendon.

When they arrived on the Somme for the first time the Guards Division came across very deep dugouts in the trench system. What the 1st Scots Guards were now practising were the procedures for coming up out of them in the event of an alarm. Miles Barne's notes for this read:

Points in connection with Dugout Drill
1.   Sentries. Outside or in passage.
2.   Number & Position of men & Lewis Guns in Trench
3.   ”   ”   ”   ”   ”   Dugout
4.   Order of Exit. Fix Bayonets
5.   Who comes out of which door
6.   Orders when one door is blocked
7.   Picks & Shivels. Ammunition & Bombs
      Rations. Water – Urine Bucket
8.   Gas, & Gasproof doors.
9.   Intelligent man or NCO near top
      Officer ½ way up.
10. Bombing party in front.
11. Man fire step immediately.

8th

Route march 5.30–8.30 a.m. when I accompanied B. Coy.

Gen Feilding comes to see the Brigade at 10–12m. when we go through various sideshows – bombing, drilling, dugout drill & so on._

Menzies leaves the Bn at last, I have been trying to get him home for some time._

> Lieutenant Menzies had been showing signs of shell shock from soon after he first arrived in the Battalion in April. He was evacuated with neurasthenia, but would return again briefly in 1917 before being slightly wounded in October at the Battle of Poelcapelle.

Ride over to tea with C. Corkran & 3rd Bde. at ARQUÈVES with Tim O.E., and on return find Col Godman has arrived, at last – 6½ weeks since Esmé left – am very glad of course to see him, but sorry to give up the Battalion. Hear the King is coming tomorrow and we move into the line.

Aug 9th 1916

Such a scramble all the morning, receiving instructions & make arrangements firstly for the King's visit, and secondly for moving into the line.

The King appeared about noon and shook hands with all the C.O.s, 2nds in Command, Adjts and Quartermasters of the Brigade. He then motored off & was cheered by the men as he went – he looked very ill & white & nervous I thought he seemed to want to say something to us each, but did not know what to say._

At 2.30 p.m. after a regular scurry, the C.O. (Godman) and I started off riding via BUS EN ARTOIS, BERTRANCOURT, BEAUSSART, MAILLY-MALLET and AUCHONVILLERS where we dismounted sending back our horses, thence by a Commn Trench to the Battn HQ of the 2nd S. Lancashire Rgt whom we are relieving. Later the Battn follows on – a very hot march, having teas on the way in M-M-. I meet them at the end of Communn Trench, and help (?) to get things sorted out.

> 2nd Battalion The South Lancashire Regiment, 75th Brigade, 25th Division (New Army)

After this I go round part of the line with the C.O. (running almost) very hungry & weary, returning to a meal at last about midnight – having had nothing since our very hurried luncheon – slept soundly till 7 a.m.

The trenches here are very good – in chalk – so far have been very quiet. It was here that on July 1st the 29th Divn failed to take BEAUMONT-HAMEL, very strongly held, although the 4th Divn on their left and 36th on their right got through, & thus rather caused a debacle. We are a good way off the Huns here, but are digging to get nearer.

> On 1st July the 29th Division were stopped in their tracks in front of Beaumont-Hamel, the 4th Division made some progress initially on their left onto Redan Ridge, though their attack was unsuccessful, while on the right the 36th (Ulster) Division, New Army,

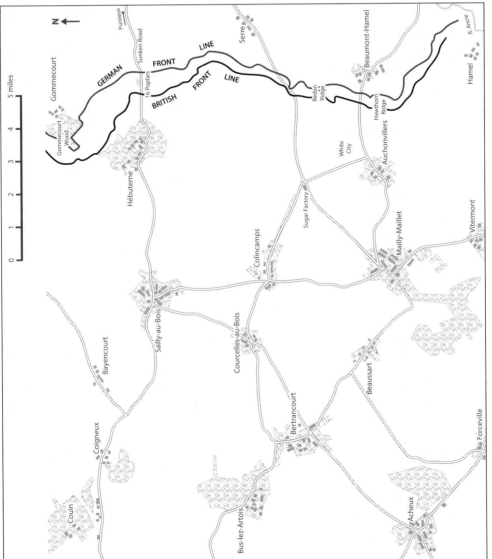

Map 12 Battle of the Somme, Line at Beaumont-Hamel and Hébuterne, August 1916.

captured the Schwaben Redoubt and could have held it had it been possible to reinforce them.

10th

Went round LF line in morning and into their new trench which is being dug nearer the Hun – later with C.O. again rather in same direction – at night went round B & RF Coys – a good deal of shelling and trench mortaring going on, we had 1 killed & 7 men wounded: on our left the Coldstream were very heavily shelled for some time – have not heard results. Their trenches are more under observn than ours.

12945 Private Thomas Riley †10.8.16

Some rain._ Good news from Italy, 15,000 prisoners, & GORIZIA taken.

The Italian offensive against the Austro-Hungarians on the River Isonzo, the Sixth Battle, during which they captured Gorizia, was their contribution to the joint Allied strategic offensive agreed at the Chantilly Conference.

11th

Nothing special occurred, some shelling – much work being done including a new Battn HQ, as our dug-out is disagreeable beyond words.
    Walked round the line with C.O., & later with the Doctor.

12th

In morning round trenches early with C.O. Later walked over with Luss to see (Col) de Crespigny, 2nd Grenrs. In afternoon round line or part of it with Tim & the Doctor, visiting the "White City", to arrange about this evening when gas is to be discharged in conjunction with the attack on our right all round THIEPVAL and MOUQUET FARM. We make elaborate arrangements for getting the men under cover during our bombardment etc, but the wind proves wrong, and no gas is let off –, however we bombard heavily, which does provoke some retaliation, but they do no serious damage to our trenches & we have no casualties._ Later – about 1 a.m. the C.O. & self wander up to see Hugh Ross in the line, and everything is normal again, tho' some shelling is going on periodically._

White City, behind them and higher up, had a bank in the chalk which fell away sharply on its southwestern side. This lent itself to an extended system of dug-outs.

13th

I go to explore a Comn Trench which we are to use next time (?) by myself_ In afternoon I wander about the front trenches alone, & in evening we are relieved by 3rd Gren Gds.
    The Division is warned that our listening aparatus has overheard 2 German Officers talking of a raid on Guards Divn tonight so special precautions are to be taken_ We return to huts at BERTRANCOURT, quite a good camp

14th

Ride over to see Gerald Sladen, who commands 5th Bn Warwickshire Regt, with Tim. We look for him in 2 or 3 villages before finally finding him at VARENNES.

Unfortunately Tim's beautiful pony, Lassie, originally brought out by Gipps who was killed, falls & breaks her knees._

The Divl H.Q. is close to us.

> Lieutenant Colonel Gerald Carew Sladen, The Rifle Brigade, Commanding I/5th
> Battalion The Royal Warwickshire Regiment, T.F., 143rd Brigade, 48th (South
> Midland) Division, T.F., was Miles Barne's brother in law.
> Lieutenant Reginald Nigel Gipps, Ist Scots Guards †7.11.14

15th

Wander round camp in morning with C.O. looking at drilling of Battn, at the steam fumigator, which is cleaning our mens' clothing, and at the Transport horses._

The Germans <u>did</u> try to raid the Welsh Gds on night of 13th, & inflicted a few casualties – but did not get into their trenches.

Never again shall we ridicule this much talked of listening apparatus!

In afternoon walked with L. Norman, to various places, having tea at Brigade H.Q., then on to see 7th Suffolk Regt, to ask after Sgt Clarke (late footman) and young Woods of Blundeston – both appear to be "missing" in the recent fighting near BOISSEVILLE.

> 12039 Sergeant James W Clarke, 7th Suffolk Regiment, was taken prisoner. Violet Barne
> wrote him letters and sent parcels to the camp where he was at Minden.
> Possibly 20562 Private S Woods, 7th Suffolk Regiment †12.8.16
> 7th Battalion The Suffolk Regiment, 35th Brigade, 12th (Eastern) Division, New Army,
> had been in the continuing battle for the Pozières Ridge, north of La Boisselle.

Dine at B.Mess, Divl H.Q. with Baden-Powell. the others in that mess consist of McLaughlin the ADMS, Howell his assistant, O.Rorke the Vet, Clanwilliam the APM., Smith his Assistant.

Weather very showery – very good news from Russia.

> Lieutenant Colonel G S McLoughlin, Royal Army Medical Corps, Assistant Director
> Medical Services, Guards Division, the senior medical officer
> Captain F D G Howell, Royal Army Medical Corps, Deputy Assistant Director Medical
> Services
> Major F C O'Rorke, Army Veterinary Corps, Assistant Director Veterinary Services
> Captain The Earl of Clanwilliam, The Royal Horse Guards, Assistant Provost Marshal, in
> command of the military police
> Smith – untraced

16th

In spite of previous orders we march at 8 a.m. to SAILLY-AU-BOIS, where we have a great deal to-do setting in order some baths and pumping arrangements taken over from 10th Bn Rifle Brigade.

> 10th (Service) Battalion The Rifle Brigade, 59th Brigade, 20th (Light) Division, New Army

In afternoon C.O., Luss, Tim, & self ride up to look at the line which we are to take over tomorrow. At 7 p.m. a motor car arrives with Gavin Hamilton, who takes C.O., Cecil Boyd Rochfort and me off to dine with Gen Pulteney, cmdg 3rd Corps, at his very big chateau at *[blank]* This was a very interesting outing as we heard a lot of what was going on, the 3rd Corps even then being hotly engaged between POZIERES and HIGH WOOD, though to look at Corps H.Q. one would have thought everything very peaceful.

From a point just outside the garden we watched the huge battle in the dim distance, – thousands of gun flashes – being able to see the whole line from THIEPVAL right round to the French's right near PERONNE. Got back by 12 midnight_

I sat between Gavin and Gen. Schreiber, whom I had not met since S.A. days when he was CRE on Colonel Barker's Column. There were also of the staff Gens Romer and *[blank]* Col. Hambro,

Gen Pulteney ("Putty") himself was looking very well though much aged.

After dinner we looked at many interesting maps & then discussed old days in the Regt Putty having been Adjt when I joined the 2nd Bn in 1893.

> Captain The Honourable Gavin Hamilton, Lord Hamilton of Dalzell, Scots Guards, ADC to General Pulteney
> Brigadier General Acton Lemuel Schreiber, Chief Engineer
> Colonel John Stewart Scott Barker
> Brigadier General Cecil Francis Romer, Brigadier General General Staff
> Brigadier General Percy O Hambro, Deputy Adjutant and Quartermaster General
> Headquarters III Corps were at Château Hénencourt, west of Albert.

17th

Relieved the 10th K.R.R.C. in trenches – Col. Blacklock. in broad daylight. Luckily there was a thickish mist, & the sausage balloons were not up._

Went round the line twice – a very puzzling bit on our left where we join the London Scottish, which is difficult to make out for certain in one or even two tours (for we went round yesterday with Col. Blacklock)

At night I go round 12–3.30 a perfect night – we hold a new bit of front line very light with isolated posts, some of which I visit – I only hope the Bosche does not realize this. Two of them approach our wire on patrol & get shot at. We send out a patrol to the "16 Poplars"._ There is some trench mortaring during the night to which our guns reply in a desultory sort of way when asked to retaliate._

The Battn H.Q. is in a farm yard in HEBUTERNE, a village quite near the line, but which has been very peaceful the whole war up to now – & even now there is not much sign of its being bombarded, but machine gun bullets at night from GOMMECOURT are a nuisance.

10th (Service) Battalion The King's Royal Rifle Corps, 59th Brigade, 20th (Light) Division
Lieutenant Colonel Cyril Aubrey Blacklock, Commanding 10th King's Royal Rifle Corps
The 1st Scots Guards, on the left of the Guards Division, now had next to them the 1st London Scottish, 168th Brigade, 56th (London) Division, T.F.
16 Poplars in No Man's Land in the direction of Puisieux was closer to the German than the British trenches.

18th

The C.O. goes off to take over the Brigade for the day leaving me in charge of the Battn.

I go round in afternoon and arrange with London Scottish on our left as to taking over a bit of their line, but this falls through, for the time being.

Some nasty trench mortaring & minenwerfers arrive near our line & that of the L.S., but not in it luckily.

The C.O. returns about 7.30 p.m., while Lindsay (cmdg, pro tem, LS) is with us, discussing the point where we join up, & after all he has to go again tomorrow.

Lieutenant Colonel James Howard Lindsay, Commanding 1st London Scottish

C.O. and self go round the line 11.30–2 a.m., seeing a L.F working party, and also another party making a sap out towards the Germans, but these get so shot at, & there are so many very-lights that much work is impossible.

19th

Grigg, Bde Major, turns up by arrangement soon after 7 a.m., and I take him round, especially to Luss, where we do much spying and crawl out in front a bit – luckily pouring with rain so we are not spotted, but get pretty wet and muddy, back to breakfast 10.30 a.m. There is much insubordinate talk & some criticism of the higher authorities over their proposals as to this sap and "post", which has to be established near the Poplars – an isolated group in no-mans-land. I said I thought the Corps Commander (whoever he may be,* we are now in 5th Corps) ought to sit in the post when made: Luss said it was a monstrous shame that men should be asked to do so – & so on. No one would mind if they could see the object of this post.

* Fanshawe.

Captain Edward William Macleay Grigg, Grenadier Guards, Brigade Major, 2nd Guards Brigade
Lieutenant General Edward Arthur Fanshawe, Commanding V Corps

About 6 p.m. Gen Kellett, cmdg 99th Bde appears, to look round – C.O. & I take him a short tour, a very old fashioned courteous but somewhat slow old man, who with his ADC, causes us all some amusement. I then go on to see Luss, where an aeroplane has just been over & dropped a bomb in the trench – killing 1 man & wounding 3. Immediately afterwards one of our aeroplanes appeared & dropped 2 bombs over GOMMECOURT – which was very clever, whether by chance or not, nobody knows.

> Brigadier General R O Kellett, Commanding 99th Brigade, 2nd Division
> 13027 Private Thomas Craig †19.8.16

I then went on to B Coy & saw the right of our line in detail.

At 10 p.m. Powell & I went down to see "Fanshawe's Folly" being started. A party of L.F. Coy was digging there under Martindale; while we were all standing about watching the men digging, suddenly a very

Aug. 19th 1916

heavy machine gun fire was opened apparently on us, though very high – down we all went – I never heard anything like the din – this was followed by pip-squeaks & trench mortars, but all over our heads.

During this straaf which lasted perhaps 15 minutes everyone lay flat, I looked up in the middle and never saw such an odd sight – the whole party stretched out like corpses – the "very lights" made the countryside as light as day – the Huns had evidently heard us, or of us, by some patrol, and had "got the wind up" properly.

The remainder of the night was quiet except for smaller bursts of m g's & trench mortars. and quite a lot of work was done. Back soon after 2 a.m.

20th

I get up at 7 a.m. to take Brigr etc round, but he & Bde Major do not appear till 9 a.m._ C.O. & self take them to inspect last night's work – the Bdr crawls right along the new sap (which was very naughty) with Grigg Luss & self, & is quite delighted with it all. We find on return to Bn H.Q. Several Staff Offrs including Teddy Seymour, lately come to Divl Staff, also the C.O. and Coy Officers of Bn which is to relieve us tomorrow._ These were all much interested & excited about this new piece of madness.

> Captain Edward Seymour, known as "Teddy", Grenadier Guards, a relation of Miles Barne

In evening I take "Sloper" McKenzie to see this trench which some of his Company is to help us to continue tonight; on the way we see one of our captive sausage balloons broken loose, floating over to the Germans – eventually they shoot at it & it comes down well behind their lines.

It turns out to have been occupied by the well known comedian, Bertram Hallam and another man. They were seen by our gunners (& by many others) to jump overboard – the latter's parachute works well and lands him safely, but Hallam's refuses to open, so he falls like a stone & is killed. Only a week or two ago he took Roger Tempest & Billy Wynne Finch up._

Captain Basil Hallam Radford, No. I Army Kite Balloon Section, Royal Flying Corps
†20.8.16, whose stage name was Basil Hallam

We work all night at our new sap & posts, and get it finished before dawn_ I get to bed by 4.30 a.m., but have to get up at 6.30, so not much sleep this night.

I had to post part of the covering party for the work, which was rather exciting in that ground, & found myself poking about revolver in hand.

During the night there were some nasty worries of trench mortars & shrapnel, and one terrific burst of m.g. fire, but all seemed "high & over" us, and no harm was done, as everybody lay flat; I dont think the Huns yet know what we are at. We had however 2 casualties during the day, one of which was a man shot in the head by a sniper, & who will probably die.

6024 Private Robert Foreman Raeburn †22.8.16

21st

Are relieved early by 22nd Royal Fusiliers, cmdd by Col Barker-Barnett. (late R. Welsh Fusiliers) but do not get away till 11.15 a.m. owing to the relief being rather a difficult one, & march to BUS LES ARTOIS, where go into huts in a wood – finding Elwes there to join us.

22nd (Service) Battalion The Royal Fusiliers, 99th Brigade, 2nd Division
Lieutenant Colonel Randle Barnett Barker, The Royal Welsh Fusiliers, Commanding
        22nd Royal Fusiliers †24.3.18
Major Henry Cecil Elwes

22nd

The Major General (Feilding) came into camp in the morning, we had everything ready for him, but he only wanted to talk about the health of the Battn, their cooking & interior economy in general.

Since they arrived on the Somme the Battalion had had a high sickness rate, associated with poor hygiene. Captain Bayly, the Medical Officer, was working on it but he needed stimulus from above as well.

Baden dined with us; he had been up with Basil Hallam the day before he was killed. There was a big explosion of ammunition and bombs at GOIGNEUX on 21st, Baden had handed this bomb store over the previous day.

14

Ginchy and Lesboeufs

23rd

Marched in brigade to AMPLIER, where we had a very nice billet for Bn H.Q., the rest of the Battn, including Officers, being in huts._

Nobody fell out – men marched splendidly, though only 7 miles.

In afternoon rode with Sherard to DOLLENS, about 3 or 4 miles, where found many of the Division having tea, and looked over the old Citadel, partly built about 1500 & partly by Vauban. Marlborough sent a raiding party against it, but found it too strong. Certainly a wonderful place – huge walls & ditches & ramparts.

24th

Marched at 7 a.m. about 12 miles to NAOURS, a pretty village, where the whole Brigade is billeted, passing through BEAUVAL, a small manufacturing town on the way.

There are rumours of our entraining during tonight, and attacking on 27th, but most miserable of all I – as 2nd in command – and some other Officers are to be left behind with 1st Line Transport to act as a Reserve, in case required: this is a perfect nightmare to me, & I cant think how one can see the Battn going off, leaving me behind – I only hope & trust there may be nothing in it all. We are not to take more than 70 per cent (or 20 in all) of the Officers into the attack.

We hear 200 per Battn of rank & file are being got ready to come out as a draft for the Division – so evidently some casualties are shortly expected.

After all orders arrive for us not to move till tomorrow afternoon, so have a very comfortable night in bed and make up for a lot of my shortness of sleep.

25th

I go in the morning to reconnoitre our march this afternoon through WARGNIES to CANAPLES, where we are to entrain at 6 p.m. in a "tactical train".

Our train which we share with 2/Irish Gds Trench Mortars 76th Coy R.E. etc etc after all does not start till 7 p.m. – tho' we left our billets at 4 p.m., and we have a long weary hungry journey – through AMIENS, eventually reaching MERICOURT a little before 1 a.m. on

Méricourt-sur-Somme, not Méricourt-L'Abbé

26th

and march about 4 miles to the filthiest of billets at MORLANCOURT, simply overrun with rats, one coming onto the sideboard while I was in the room and another in the Kitchen, goodness only knows how many in one's bedroom – which I share with Eric McKenzie – Adjt. – or in the Kitchen etc when one is not in the room_ Get to bed at 4 a.m., and breakfast at 10.

Walk in afternoon to Brigade H.Q. with Sherard, & in evening ride with Cecil Boyd-Rochford to RIAULT, where is the 1st Guards Brigade, and to DERNANCOURT, where are some German prisoners; got caught in a heavy shower & drenched to the skin.

The 1st Guards Brigade were at Méaulte

27th

Attend early service, in a shed, near Battn H.Q.

In afternoon walk up to & round the French Aerodrome where we seem to see & go what & where we like – with Sherard_ In evening I walk with the Doctor to a hill not far off & watch a big bombardment, somewhere near THIEPVAL, find Tim, Dundas, & others up there.

At night the C.O. tells us more or less what we are in for_

28th

A long morning training & practising the attack, during which time the Major General comes round & explains a few details as to what is going to be expected of us.

In afternoon I ride with Sherard round by ALBERT where we saw the curious statue of the Virgin Mary on the top of the church, nearly shot down, but hanging at more than right angles, looking as if it must come down at any minute: they say that when the statue falls the war will end! We then rode on towards FRICOURT, which before the July push was the German front line – & home across the fields. This valley of the Ancre & tributaries is very wonderful, such masses of troops of all sorts crammed together, but more curious than the troops are the horses & supply columns & Ammunition Columns and all the hundred etcetera connected therewith, such a conglomeration of bits of so many different departments: here a band playing, there a Battn doing Swedish drill, next an 8 in. Howitzer Battery shooting at THIEPVAL, then a cricket match, alongside of which is passing a Battn on its way up to take over a bit of the line, and so on indefinitely: and all the time in the not very far distance, a battle far greater than Waterloo raging.

Before starting we heard the good news of ROUMANIA coming into the "entente", & Italy declaring war against Germany.

> Roumania's decision to enter the war on the Allied side was intended mainly to acquire those areas of the Austro-Hungarian Empire with substantial numbers of ethnic Roumanians. To begin with their armies penetrated the Carpathians into Transylvania, but, under German direction, they were driven out and lost most of what then lay within their own national borders. Italy had been at war with the Austro-Hungarian Empire since May 1915.

29th

Up very early, the whole Battn digging dummy trenches 7–10 a.m. about 3 miles away, behind the French Lines. At 11 a.m. all the senior Officers of the Division, down to Company Commanders, collect at an Aerodrome, & hear a lecture and see some experiments in connection with signalling between infantry in the front line and Aeroplanes, who pass on the information to the Corps or Division.

In afternoon heavy rain, & in evening walked up hill with Sherard – took shelter from a storm in an Aerodrome; a big bombardment in French Lines – scores of French motor cars returning with Staff Officers etc to get back to AMIENS in time for dinner, so it appeared, after seeing their push starting off at 4 p.m., through field glasses.

Royds & Arthur Boyd Rochford appear from HAVRE (Commandant & Adjt) for a couple of nights.

> Lieutenant Colonel Albert Henry Royds, Scots Guards, Commandant Guards Division Base Depot at Harfleur, near Le Havre
>
> Captain George Arthur Boyd Rochfort, Adjutant, medically downgraded after being sent home sick from the 1st Scots Guards the previous autumn, at Harfleur since April 1916

30th

Battn parades for training at 9 a.m., but a real wet day so dismiss; while Sherard and self go to Brigade H.Q. and ask for lift in a motor car to AMIENS. We are lucky enough to get the Divisional car – so taking L. Norman, we go off at 11 a.m., in pouring rain, but have quite a good day, see the Cathedral which is very fine, lunch at Restt Godberts' – do some shopping and return about 5 p.m. bringing Hopwood (1/Coldm) back – he having been to try & hear news of his missing brother, who was last seen descending over CAMBRAI, his aeroplane in flames.

> Major Edward Byng George Gregge Hopwood, 1st Coldstream Guards †20.7.17
>
> Captain Robert Gerald Hopwood, The Rifle Brigade and No. 70 Squadron Royal Flying Corps †24.8.16, a cousin, not brother

We passed through QUERRIEU where is an old chateau, now 4th (Rawlinson's) Army H.Q.

Saw any number of troops both at rest – in camps etc – and on move, particularly a lot of Anzac Artillery.

31st

The C.O. goes to a G.C.M. in morning_

> Lieutenant Colonel Godman's presence as a member of a Court Martial and the visit of Lieutenant Colonel Royds and Captain Boyd Rochfort from Harfleur were probably connected. The visitors were definitely there as observers. Miles Barne did not say what it was about. The accused was Captain George Guy Bulwer Nugent, previously Adjutant at the Base Depot and before that Adjutant 3rd Grenadier Guards. The defending officer was Lieutenant Raymond Asquith, who, writing home, described much

of the circumstances, but without any names. Captain Nugent had initiated homosexual activity at Harfleur until someone else involved turned King's Evidence. Seeing no prospect of a successful defence, Lieutenant Asquith tried, by drafting a carefully worded letter, to enable Captain Nugent to resign his commission so as to resolve the situation quietly and humanely. However, there was no avoiding a Court Martial. At this, which went on at Headquarters Guards Division over two days, Captain Nugent was found Guilty of four out of five charges. On 11 September, the findings and sentence, to be cashiered and serve one year's imprisonment, having been confirmed, Captain Nugent was marched into the Orderly Room of the 3rd Grenadiers. There Lieutenant Colonel Sergison Brooke will have notified him of the promulgation of the sentence, whereupon his regimental buttons were cut from his tunic. The Military Police then removed him to the Military Prison at Rouen, en route for Winchester Prison. There was one other element which Lieutenant Asquith did not mention, namely that the one year's imprisonment was to be with hard labour. Subsequently, because the case involved an officer of the Household Brigade it had to be notified to King George V. The King's view was that the hard labour element of the sentence was excessive and should be remitted. It was.

a Battn parade in afternoon (training)_ In evening walked with Sherard onto ridge – scores of aeroplanes out – and counted 35 English or French Balloons.

A glorious day – so good for harvest.

Sept 1st

Another fine day. In morning go & watch the Grenadiers practising the attack.

In evening rode with Sherard to East – & got a new view of MAMETZ WOOD etc.

2nd

Battn attack practice in morning – long discourse by Brigadier to Officers and Sergts. Find the trenches we dug so vehemently have been filled in by French Fatigue party.

Long visit from Dick Coke.

Walk with Sherard in evening.

3rd

Long walk with Sherard in morning amongst the French. saw several interesting things including some very dirty camps.

In afternoon the Major-General inspected parties from each Battn in the Division dressed as for the attack, so as to try to get at the best rig.

A sad accident occurred this morning to our bombing officer – Leach – a bomb exploding in his hands which were completely taken off – he really showed great presence of mind & pluck – had he hurled the bomb down many others would have been wounded as well. He was also wounded in his stomach, and died on the way into the Hospital in an Ambulance.

2nd Lieutenant Leach †3.9.16 was in a building with some NCOs setting the fuses and detonators into grenades. The pin must have fallen out of one, so the striker sprang up, hit the detonater and set off the fuse. He seized the grenade, shouted in warning and ran out through the door, only to see other soldiers in the space in front of him. He turned round against the building and held the grenade against his body till it exploded. He was posthumously awarded the Albert Medal in Gold.

Sept.4th

Exciting orders came overnight for us to be at 3 hrs notice – & all leave cancelled to AMIENS or anywhere else. This no doubt owing to things having gone so well.

> Miles Barne will have heard of events further east, the final capture of Delville Wood and the securing of the southern and western approaches to Guillemont and Ginchy. The final battle for Guillemont had just begun and would end on 6 September.

Many of us attended poor Leach's funeral at CORBIE on the R.Somme, rather a pretty drive there in the 2nd Battn's Motor car, "Michael."_
On our return attended a very interesting lecture by Rev. Head on Napoleon, in the Church here at MORLANCOURT._

5th

Route march.
Luss goes to Paris on leave for 3 days.
Very good news of the French advance S. of R.Somme.
We attempt some night operations, but when beginning a message arrives saying we should return home as we may be wanted early in the morning owing to the success of the French, who have apparently taken 20 kilometres of German first line of defence – also some villages.

> French operations starting on 3 September in the valley of the Somme had gone well and included the capture of Cléry.

6th

An early rise for a Brigade Field Day and attack, which was quite amusing & instructive we had some work signalling with an aeroplane. The drums massed represented the "barrage de feu" – the big drums for the heavy Artillery, & the side drums for the Shrapnel – or "creeping barrage". At one moment much amusement was caused by the uneasiness of some drummers of one of the Battalions, who thought they were going to be called on to do this in the real show – viz. walk solemnly & slowly along in front of the attack beating their drums.
In afternoon rode with Cecil Trafford to BRAY and ETINEHEM, when we saw a number of French soldiers just out of the firing line in the latest attack – looking very worn & tired – also every sort of "detail" in connection with the French – such masses of all sorts huddled together. The weather has taken a turn for the better._
At night several of us went to "the Tivoli" – to see the "Somme Films" on the Cinematograph, which are really as a rule quite interesting – but several could well be left out – especially those of corpses. One of the best is of a company actually popping the parapet, one poor wretch getting killed even before he got to the top.

The curious thing was that to make it all more real, we had a real bombardment going on the whole time.

The official war film of "The Battle of the Somme" had been partly filmed by Geoffrey Malins on 1 July from behind the British front line as the 29th Division attacked Beaumont-Hamel.

7th

Perfect harvest weather – fresh NE breeze & hot sun.

Round the billets in morning, with C.O. and medical officer.

In afternoon the C.O., Trafford & I settled to go to AMIENS, but, not having a motor car, we decided to walk up to the main road & chance stopping a car – we had not a moment to wait when a big car came along containing a French Officer of some importance. He was not going exactly our way but volunteered to put us onto another big road, so being rather glad to see more of the country we embarked & whizzed off to WARFUSÉE, where we heard Gen Joffre had only just gone by – after waiting a few minutes there we were picked up by a French A.S.C. Officer who was conducting a convoy, and took us right into AMIENS, where we had tea, saw the citadel, a little shopping, watched the 18th Hussars and some R.H.A. go by, then started off on foot, & soon were picked up by a gunner Officer whom we persuaded to take us home via CORBIE, after quite an amusing afternoon – back just in time for dinner.

8th

Am President of a F.G.C.M. in morning on a very insubordinate Coldstreamer._

In afternoon a Brigade Field Day and attack.

Esmé, Butler and Torquil Matheson all appear to look on & criticize._ The first named came back to tea, and had a lot to say about the recent attacks on GUILLEMONT and LEUZE WOOD – all very interesting, & I expect we got several useful hints._

Walked later with the two Cecils (Trafford & Boyd Rochford) round the adjacent English Aerodrome.

The 20th Division attacked Guillemont on 3 September, eventually capturing it, with the direct support of the 16th (Irish) Division, New Army. At the same time the 5th Division, including Brigadier Lord Esmé Gordon Lennox' 95th Brigade, were on their right. They advanced successfully to the southeast of Guillemont, including capturing most of Leuze Wood.

9th

Marched at 2 p.m. about 4 miles to HAPPY VALLEY, a camp on the way up to the line, where we saw a lot of "Tanks", or sort of creeping forts on caterpillar wheels – otherwise known as "Land Dreadnoughts", or "Willies". We saw them climbing up banks and over trenches etc, we also went on board some of them – there are cocks & hens – the former have 6lb guns, the latter only machine guns. It remains to be seen what use they are, but they will anyhow astonish the Hun – they themselves say that they will revolutionize the war. I cant help thinking that just at first they will terrify the Hun until he finds out how to meet them._

Thompson, late Adjt, now GSO III of Reserve Army (Gough's) comes over & tells us a limited amount of news._

We have taken over the camp from one of Esmé's Battalions, & Gen. Ponsonby takes over Esmé's Bde H.Q. curiously enough.

Esmé tells us GINCHY is being attacked at 3.45 p.m. We hear the bombardment, which is quite terrific, and lasts till well into the night – probably us and the French putting up a barrage beyond GINCHY, as well as the German reply.

Powell has caught a fox and is trying to tame it. At present the poor little brute looks very miserable – on a chain and collar – & trying the whole time to get away.

10th

Church Service at 10 a.m. which nearly every officer attended, & heard an excellent sermon from Head. In view of the attack which we hear the Battn is in for during the week, one wonders how many of us may be attending for the last time._

On asking at the Brigade Office, we hear that GINCHY was taken last night, and the 3rd Guards Bde have gone up, & the Welsh Guards are occupying a line E. of it. Another trench has been taken further to the SE, and N of COMBLES.

This is all very good hearing._

In afternoon rode with Sherard to FRICOURT and MAMETZ to see the old lines, and also the craters & confusion caused by our attack & shell fire on July 1st – there are also some huge mine craters, though it was difficult to see whether they had really exploded under a German Trench or not – apparently not._

On our return we heard the Welsh Gds had been heavily attacked and lost about 200 – that the 4th Grenadiers were supporting them & between them some Germans, & Harry Seymour – better known as "Copper", – was sitting on his parapet with a revolver in each hand, and a knife in his teeth longing to be at them, the Division having considerable difficulty in restraining him._ Another counterattack was being hourly expected.

Very heavy firing all night._

The situation is not clear, and not very comfortable but we hope will prove to be better than rumour says.

> Between 9 and 10 September the 16th Division captured most of Ginchy, but the situation was very precarious and continued to be after the 3rd Guards Brigade took over in the village after dark on the 10th. The 1st Welsh Guards suffered very heavy casualties.

11th

The heavy firing continues till about 7 a.m., a lot of it is evidently German shells exploding & a few come our way.

At 3.30 a.m. we are mystified by hearing a Cavalry Trumpet Call – & a rumour at breakfast that the French mean to break through somewhere or other, & let their Cavalry go: we know a lot of French Cavalry is not far off.

On going over to the Brigade about 9 a.m., we hear the situation as regards the 3rd Gds Brigade is quite satisfactory, the Welsh Gds have not given up any ground – on their right are the 56th Divn, behind them in a sort of 2nd row are the 4th Gren and between them the Battalion of Huns, who really should be caught as time goes on.

Later we hear the 56th Div has given way & so these Huns are no longer surrounded.

Find Gen Jules Pereira with his 47th Irish Brigade close by, Sherard & I go over to see him, and hear a lot of very interesting points in connection with the taking of GUILLEMONT, and the attack in general.

> Brigadier General George Edward Pereira, nicknamed "Jules", Commanding 47th
> Brigade, 16th Division

In evening walk with Sherard to BRAY where we see a lot of French soldiers & transport. We see Hylton, late of the Regt, now A.S.C.

> Lieutenant Horace Anwyl Hilton, Scots Guards, retired in 1902, and now Captain
> Horace Anwyl Hilton, Army Service Corps

Many rumours afloat as to what is going on.

12th

A very dismal day for me. The Battn marched at 2.30 p.m., leaving me, Tim, Elwes, Shortt & Abercrombie to replace casualties – we (Tim Elwes & I) rode with them as far as CARNOY, where they had tea & we watched some 9.2 howitzers firing, & left them there about 6.30 p.m. They were going on at 9 p.m. to BERNAFAY WOOD, in support of the Irish Gds, who were going into the line. I never had a bigger wrench than leaving the Battn after nearly 14 months with them, and then to be left behind, while they take part in the biggest battle of the war, in a few days time.

CARNOY itself & the whole country round there is a most wonderful sight, one square mile after another simply covered with soldiers & horses & all the paraphernalia of war – quite indescribable.

On our return to HAPPY VALLEY we found the 3rd Gds Bde were coming in; D. Coke & J. Thorpe had arrived, so came to dine with us in our little camp, when we had quite a cheerful evening, Elwes waxing very eloquent concerning his experiences in Egypt & Gallipoli.

13th

Lunch with 2nd Battn, and hear a lot about their doings in GINCY from Jack Stirling.

> The 2nd Scots Guards had had a very confused and difficult time on the northern edge
> of Ginchy towards Delville Wood, with many casualties.

In afternoon went a long walk with Tim through BRAY, where we saw a lot of French Troops including some Spahi Regts with their little grey Arab horses.

14th

A wet night. How beastly for the poor people in trenches.

This day 33 years ago I first went to school at Rottingdean.

Find the Commandant of the H.V. *[Happy Valley]* Camp is one Waterfield, whose cousins we used to know years ago at Worlingham.

Possibly Major Frank Waterfield, General List

Tremendous bombardment all night. When Carter calls me he tells me that excellent Officer of B. Coy has been killed, and about 12 NCO's & men of R.F. & B also. These two Coys had to go up to GINCHY to help Irish Gds, one of whose Coys was practically wiped out – including its Captain Montgomerie killed.

This casualty – Holland – necessitates old Tim going up, which he does about 11 a.m., very cheerful and quite "all there"._

One of those killed was a signatory of the B Company letter after Loos, 10749 Private
    John McPhail †13.9.16
2nd Lieutenant Edward Holland †13.9.16
Lieutenant Hugh Montgomery 2nd Irish Guards †13.9.16

I hear a good deal of tomorrow's plans from Bewicke – 3rd Bde.

Captain Calverley Bewicke, Scots Guards, Staff Captain 3rd Guards Brigade

Saw Ch. Corkran & H. Seymour last night._

The day is very fine but a high NW Wind, bad for Aeroplanes and Balloons: I pray that tomorrow there may be less wind. & fine for the "Tanks" to get along._

Tomorrow is going to be an eventful day for many, including the Guards Division. If successful the Cavalry are going to try & get through. It is difficult to say what is likely to happen, but if all goes well the "Tanks" will terrify the Huns, and for many reasons they are likely to "get the wind up", and go._

Dundas has recovered and rejoined. so now our party consists of Elwes and self, Abercrombie, Shortt & Dundas – also Kinlay & Trafford. with about 170 O.R.

Lieutenant Dundas had been sick in hospital with stomach trouble.

By the way, yesterday, Wilfred Dashwood suddenly walked in, a Grenadier, and attached to the Entrenching Battn. He had seen Seymour recently, & thought him likely to come this way.

Lieutenant Wilfred James Dashwood, Guards Entrenching Battalion, later 1st Grenadier
    Guards †2.8.17, Miles Barne's first cousin

Tim & I also yesterday found ourselves at a "Kite Balloon Service" camp, which was interesting & where we saw several maps etc.

In afternoon walked with Elwes & saw the 2nd Cavalry Division coming into their bivouac close by here – perhaps ¾ mile off.

Had a talk to some Officers of Greys & 16th Lancers & 5th Cav Div. Staff – leaving a note for Seymour but fear he wont get over to see me. & I cannot well be away again for long – on way back found Arthur Erskine at 20th Div. H.Q., now a Bde Major of Artillery.

5th (2nd Indian) Cavalry Division
Major Arthur Edward Erskine, Royal Horse Artillery, another first cousin

Received a very nice note from Tim. There is from 6.30 p.m. onwards one continuous roar of Artillery.

We are to be ready to move at 6 a.m. though I doubt whether we shall move for ages after that.

The Battn seems to have had 50 casualties so far – has got to find 4 Offrs 200 men as "carrying party", so will actually attack 400 strong!

What an eventful day tomorrow will be, and either a glorious success or bad failure. I do not feel too hopeful tonight – especially hearing that things are in a "hectic uproar & muddle".

The Ration Train does not arrive in time which is unfortunate, and so our transport & rations cannot get off till rather late.

The battle on 15 September was given the name Flers-Courcelette, though the two villages were some way from each other and Flers, roughly in the centre of the line of advance, a long way from the 56th Division on the British right. Courcelette was just on the west of the Albert-Bapaume road.

The Guards Division were attacking from Ginchy northeast in the direction of Lesboeufs. About a thousand yards east of Ginchy, just south of the road to Morval, the Germans had formed a very substantial strong point on slightly higher ground which fell away steeply on the east side and sloped gently on the west. This, known as the Quadrilateral, had already defied several attempts to deal with it, including that by the company from the 2nd Irish Guards almost wiped out on 13 September. The 6th Division were unable to make any progress against the Quadrilateral on 15 September and were well aware of the consequences of that failure for those on either side of them. From defilade at the back of it the Bavarian infantry had been able to fire onto the right flank of the Guards Division without interruption. The 2nd Guards Brigade were on the right in the advance, the 3rd Guards Brigade being in reserve to begin with.

To the left of the Guards Division were the 14th (Light) Division), beyond them the 41st Division, both New Army, the latter advancing, with the New Zealand Division on their left, from the north side of Delville Wood towards Flers. The combined effect of where they were starting from and their angle of advance later on enabled the German support positions east and southeast of Flers to fire at the left flank of the Guards Division. The 1st Guards Brigade, on the left in the advance, had already had a very difficult start because of enemy in trenches just north of Ginchy and between there and the east side of Delville Wood.

Sept. 15th 1916

The day has at last arrived – when I find myself at HAPPY VALLEY with the Transport break-fasting at 5 a.m. instead of with the Battn popping the parapet.

Possibly Tim is right and though not with them at the beginning I may be at the end. Time will show.

We move over to CARNOY at 7.15 a.m., previous to which I ride over to look up Seymour, but fail to find him.

Well, the "push" starts at 6.20 a.m. preceded by the wonderful "tanks" and the usual barrages of Artillery fire_

Miles Barne made some brief separate notes, somewhat indistinctly, to begin with, of what he heard and when he heard it, the timings given being those of the messages,

Sept. 15th-16

Attack complete surprise

> 7.20 3rd Coldm reached 1st Objective
> 7.50 3rd G[uards] B[rigade] moving fwd
> 8.5 1/I.G.
> 2 tanks sitting on 1st O.
> 3rd on its way
> 9.7 In blue line
> Tanks over brown
> 7.40 1/I.G. 8 Offrs hit
> 2nd G[uards] B[rigade] lost direction
> 7.15 1st G[uards] B[rigade] 3rd Obj
> (blue)
> 9.15 Number of prisoners are coming in.
> 3rd Corps – Tanks doing good work
> 8.a.m. 3rd Cold digging in 3rd Objective

The first objective was the Green Line, an identified German defence line, also known as the Flers Line. Owing, however, to the undetected enemy positions in linked up shellholes in front of the Green Line its whereabouts was mistaken in the battle, many who reached it wrongly thinking they were on the Blue Line, well downhill towards Lesboeufs. The Brown Line, in between the Green and Blue Lines, did not affect the 2nd Guards Brigade because not within their boundaries, but the 1st Guards Brigade did manage to get that far and hold it, a precarious bubble, because the 14th Division were no further on than the Green Line. It was to reinforce those of the 1st Guards Brigade, mainly from the 2nd and 3rd Coldstream, at the Brown Line that the 2nd Scots Guards were ordered forward in the late afternoon.

We sitting anxiously behind hear throughout the day a perfect stream of rumours of all sorts – as to the advance, which is on an 11 mile front in conjunction with the French on our right: at first everything seems to go swimmingly: later not so well, the 6th Div on the right of Guards Division not getting on at all, being held up by the same people who held up Pereira's 47th Bde (?) a week ago. Had it not been for this, the whole operation would have been an unquali- fied success._ The New Zealanders seem to have got on well, also the 3rd Corps, and by the evening the villages of MARTINPUICH COURCELLES FLERS have been taken; some say

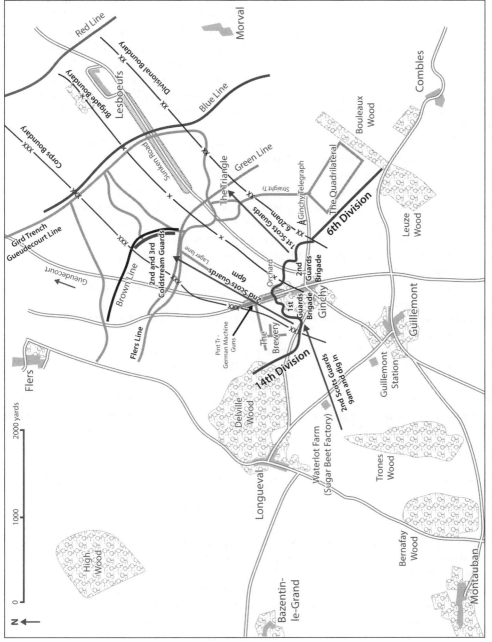

Map 13 Battle of the Somme, Attack from Ginchy towards Lesboeufs, 15 September 1916.

GUEUDECOURT also but I don't think so. The Guards Div are opposite LES BOEUFS but unable to take it owing to their right and rear being left open by the failure of 6th Divn._

The Tanks on the whole are quite a success, though some get put out of action – and some are said to have gone off into the blue, nevermore to be seen. One captured German Officer said "We really did like your old Coffee Mills". When asked how he felt, he said it was the best day of the war. A certain number of prisoners were captured, but only a few hundreds – no huge haul.

The Cavalry were quite unable to get through – the 1st Divn – 9th Bde – were close to us at CARNOY all day – and I saw H. Boyd-Rochford and Priest Alexander several times during the day – also we were near the Q branch of the Gds Divn, with whom I dined – the staff present being Alston, Darrell, Herman-Hodge and G. Lane, who hears his cousin, son of the Genl, is killed.

> Captain Harold Boyd Rochfort, The 21st Lancers
> Priest Alexander – untraced
> The Q Branch, also known as the AQ Branch, was the department of the Divisional Headquarters responsible for personnel and logistics, (the G Branch being the operational one). Colonel Darell was the head of it, Major Alston his immediate subordinate and Major Hermon Hodge concerned with logistics only.
> Major Francis George Alston, Scots Guards, Deputy Assistant Adjutant & Quartermaster General
> Lieutenant Colonel William Henry Verelst Darell, Coldstream Guards, Assistant Adjutant & Quartermaster General
> Major Roland Herman Hermon Hodge, Grenadier Guards, Deputy Assistant Quartermaster General
> Captain George A O Lane, Coldstream Guards, Camp Commandant
> Captain George Ronald Lane, 2nd Coldstream Guards †15.9.16

There are a good number of casualties amongst those we hear killed are Col. Guy Baring, one of my oldest friends & contemporaries, & John Thorpe; the follg out of 2nd Gds Bde M.Gun Company Bartholomew, Higginson, & Purcell killed, Walters Vernon Fisher & Stirling wounded, leaving only Mark Tennant & Jones to carry on.

> Lieutenant Colonel The Honourable Guy Victor Baring, Commanding 1st Coldstream Guards †15.9.16
> Captain John Somerled Thorpe, 2nd Scots Guards †15.9.16
>
> There were nine officers attached to the 2nd Guards Brigade Machine Gun Company,
> Captain Claude Bartholomew, 1st Scots Guards †15.9.16
> Lieutenant Thomas Cecil Higginson, 3rd Grenadier Guards †15.9.16
> Lieutenant Charles Francis Purcell, 2nd Irish Guards †15.9.16
> Lieutenant Graham Yuille Laundy Walters, 2nd Irish Guards †15.9.16
> Lieutenant Herbert Douglas Vernon, 3rd Grenadier Guards †15.9.16
> 2nd Lieutenant Frederick Fisher, 1st Coldstream Guards
> Lieutenant Gordon Stirling, 1st Scots Guards †15.9.16
> Captain Mark Tennant, 1st Scots Guards †16.9.16

2nd Lieutenant Arthur Guy Salisbury Jones, 1st Coldstream Guards, wounded on
16.9.16

Martindale in L.F. is killed also Chapman of our 2nd Bn., also Sloper McKenzie of 3rd Grenadiers, and many others.

Maitland 2nd Bn Scots Gds is missing. Vaughan & Lascelles, 2nd in commands of 2nd Cold. & Gren respectively tho' we cant make out why "up", are also hit – former killed – & many others.

Lieutenant Warine Francis Martindale †15.9.16
Lieutenant David Archibald James Chapman, 2nd Scots Guards †15.9.16
Captain Allan Keith Mackenzie, 3rd Grenadier Guards †15.9.16
Lieutenant Richard Evelyn Fuller Maitland, 2nd Scots Guards, was very severely
wounded
Major George Edmund Vaughan, 3rd Coldstream Guards †15.9.16
Major The Viscount Lascelles, 3rd Grenadier Guards

Of our own lot besides Martindale, who is a great loss, Childers is very badly wounded in stomach, old Tim is seen being carried off wounded, on a stretcher, but I cannot get this confirmed, Champion is slightly wounded & inoculated for tetanus but returned to duty.

Hugh Ross has gone down sick, they have had 2 or 3 baddish days & nights, and his constitution would not take it, which does not surprise me.

Lieutenant William Leslie Eardley Childers
Captain Ernest Pellew Orr Ewing, known as "Tim", †15.9.16
He omitted to mention that Captain Bayly RAMC had been hit, not seriously, in the
knee, but had to be evacuated

Col Tempest, Wynne-Finch, Murdoch, Woodhouse and Dawkins are all wounded (2nd Bn) the latter badly.

Lieutenant Colonel Roger Stephen Tempest would return
Captain William Heneage Wynne Finch would return
2nd Lieutenant Louis Forde Campbell Murdoch †19.9.16
Lieutenant Ernest Armine Wodehouse
2nd Lieutenant Guy Stracey Dawkins †25.9.16, wounded at Loos with 1st Scots Guards

Col Brooke, of 3rd Grens is hit through both thighs.

Lieutenant Colonel Bertram Norman Sergison Brooke, Commanding 3rd Grenadier
Guards, would return

The poor old Guards Division is having a baddish time, and there may be worse to come, but they have done all possible, as was to be expected, in the fighting way, & had the 6th Div got on, would have covered themselves with an extra coating of glory.

We hear the 1st Bn lost about 250 men, the 2nd Bn 200.

16th

Trafford returned from taking the rations & water up, but owing to trenches & broken ground he could not get them beyond GINCHY, where the Bn it is hoped would send for them. I much hope they did, the water especially would they require._

In morning an attack is said to be being made at 9.30 a.m., but I dont know by whom. I go to the Division with Elwes in morning and hear something of the situation which is most obscure. We go at Alston's request to wake up the Machine Gun Coy HQ of the 2nd Gds Bde, & tell them to send up more belts and ammunition_ 7 of their officers have been killed or wounded out of the 9. The other two are killed later in the day, Mark Tennant being the last – 15 out of their 16 guns get put out of action._

In afternoon the little Prince arrives and discusses the situation._

Later we hear to our delight that the Division is to be relieved by 20th Division, & we make every arrangement for sending up their rations & teas & rhum etc to BERNAFAY WOOD at 12 midnight. I see all off at 7 p.m., and then go off to look up Seymour whom I find on the road near BRAY, returning at 8.30 p.m. to CARNOY, to find all plans have been altered by Brigade arrangements, & the Battn is due at CARNOY at 10 p.m. & to be camped at the CITADEL.

Guides are arranged, roads picketed etc, but no Battalion arrives at 10 p.m. I wander up to BERNAFAY WOOD, to find confusion reigning, & orders given – by some officious person – to bivouac up there (- all a mistake – as I hear from the advanced Division office), the Battn eventually arrives at 1 a.m. there, where waterbottles are filled & we proceed to march down to the CITADEL, which reach at 3 a.m., hearing of the doings of the Battn from Luss & Sherard en route. Have dinner – my last meal was at 1 p.m. – & turn in at 4.30 a.m.

They have had a most exciting time of it, & killed many Germans & taken many prisoners: but of course at some sacrifice. Their stories are too many & exciting to narrate here.

No news of Tim, what is the reason?

Evidently Powell & Luss have done very well.

Hugh Ross was very bad with ague, & sort of shock, was chipped by a bullet & squashed by 7 killed or wounded men falling on top of him – had to go down sick.

I feel a dreadful outsider & worm to be out of all this, & trust it will never recur.

Am distressed to hear poor old Lionel Norman is killed, a real blow to us all.

The C.O. found a German Officers meal laid out ready – cold preserved meat, soda water etc, & all very clean – also cigars.

> Captain Hugh Cairns Edward Ross was very badly shell shocked and, apart from being slightly wounded, later told Captain Bayly RAMC that a small metal particle had to be removed from his eye. He would return.

17th

On further enquiries I fear poor old Tim has been killed. C. Boyd-Rochfort, Cpl. Hughes & Pte Hunter, one of his orderlies, all give the same account of what happened, and it seems beyond any doubt. He must have been shot dead through the heart, & died instantaneously.

A sad gap in the mess and Battalion – I dont think any one would be more missed by all ranks – an excellent Coy Commander – of our 4 we now only have Luss left.

> Corporal Hughes, B Company 1st Scots Guards – possibly 11005 Lance Corporal
> Reginald Hughes, later Labour Corps, and possibly a signatory of the B Company
> letter after Loos.
> Pte Hunter, B Company 1st Scots Guards – untraced

The morning we are fully employed straightening up. In afternoon I walk over with Luss & Elwes to see some of the old German trenches, on arrival back find Seymour who has tea with us.

The Brigadier makes a short speech to each Battn of the Brigade, & is cheered lustily by them all in turn – a most popular Brigadier indeed.

I go back to dinner with S. & have a very good evening – his Genl (Chetwode) making himself most agreeable – others present being Charles Seymour, Seymour GSO 3, Tommy *[blank]* the ADC Col. Davidson GSO 1, and Muirhead Ind Cavy, G.SO. 2._

> Major General Sir Philip Walhouse Chetwode, Commanding 2nd Cavalry Division
> Probably Lieutenant Colonel Charles Derick Seymour, The Norfolk Yeomanry
> Captain Seymour Barne, The 20th Hussars
> Tommy [blank] – untraced
> Lieutenant Colonel N R Davidson, Royal Horse Artillery
> Major John Arthur Muirhead, 1st Duke of York's Own Lancers (Skinner's Horse), Indian
> Army

18th

Am to look after B. Coy for the present which is very nice, after doing nothing for so long._ Spend the morning fixing up more accommodation for the Battn, which has no roofage – raining hard all day.

Hear we are to attack again on 21st, & I am not to be left behind but Luss is, so whatever happens to all of us there will anyhow be one capable officer of experience left to re-organize._

At 3 p.m. many of us attend Guy Baring's funeral._

In evening Baden appears; Sherard & I walk him back part of the way taking 2nd Cavy Division en route – finding the General & others at home, including Seymour.

We look at his mare which he thinks of exchanging with one of ours for Sherard to ride.

19th

Pouring wet night. A draft arrives 190 men, & we are busy making preparations for our next move.

Seymour comes over during the morning to the CITADEL, bringing his laminitis mare, which he swaps with one of our old hairies_ Sherard is now to ride his mare, so that an eye can be kept on her & returned to 20th Hussars after the war.

In late afternoon I ride over to see Jack Stirling and the 2nd Battn. The weather being very bad the next attack (LES BOEUFS) has been put off from 21st to 22nd._

Wind goes round to E., but still heavy showers all night & the country in a dreadful state – motor lorries etc stuck in every direction._

20th

Cold & showery.

Rifle & billet parade in morning & I also caution the Company as to certain points in connection with the next attack – loss of equipment, saving of water, and retaining hold of the rifles when bombarded._

Gen John Vaughan with Kit Cator came to luncheon with us – also young *[blank]* Cator (Jack's boy) of "the Greys". Cold & showery.

> Major General John Vaughan, Commanding 3rd Cavalry Division
> Captain Christopher Arthur Mohun Cator, known as "Kit", 2nd Scots Guards
> 2nd Lieutenant John Henry Cator, The Royal Scots Greys, whose father John Cator,
>   known as "Jack", was the eldest of the Cator brothers.

In afternoon I walked over to see Seymour, but he was out_ I also went to Kite Balloon place to hear news – Huns had been counterattacking French, but unsuccessfully.

On return had early meal 6.30 p.m., when Seymour suddenly walked in & waited till we paraded at 7.30 p.m., & saw us march off. He had looked in on his way down from the line.

We had a very muddy and tedious walk to CARNOY, where we were billeted in dugouts & bivouacs – in a sea of mud.

21st

Great preparations during morning – seeing that everything was complete.

Walked in afternoon with Sherard to see our Transport & several other things including the Brigade Office where there was such a crowd – amongst others the little Prince whom Sherard never saw & cut dead, which probably pleased the Prince, as I believe he hates being cow-towed to & saluted. Personally I always make a point of saluting the Heir Apparent, & believe everybody else, nearly, does too.

Hear the German counterattack S. of Combles was a very big affair, & the French say they never had such an opportunity since the war began, & took it. They let fly their 75's most successfully. No shelling all day.

22nd

Glorious sunny day, with keen E. Wind which will dry things up well._ Rifle & parade in morning.

My subalterns are Dundas Holmes & Brodie, but Dundas is to be taken away as bombing Officer & Adjt, as Eric McKenzie is not coming in this time.

> Lieutenant Reginald Eden Holmes †4.6.18
> Lieutenant Duncan Reynett Brodie

The re-opening of the battle seems to be put off till 23rd now. An order arrives saying 2nds in command are again to be left out – too cruel for words, much talk with C.O. as to how this is to be got round.

Walk with him in evening towards MONTAUBAN – also to Brigade Office as to washing facilities for the men.

Meet the Major General with Teddy Seymour, who does not give me much hope as to my being allowed to go in. Luss kindly offers to exchange if the worst comes to the worst, & stay out himself. This would be a great sacrifice on his part, as he dearly loves scrapping.

> Captain Edward Seymour, Grenadier Guards, General Staff Officer Grade II, Guards
>   Division

23rd

14 months today since I landed._

Route march in morning over to see Seymour – quite by chance finding ourselves at his camp at the exact time for halting. He was so surprised to see me.

Walk in evening with Sherard behind French towards MARICOURT watched multitude of aeroplanes including one or two Germans. By chance come on Esmé's Brigade Transport, and hear he is not far off – out of the line again for a bit, on our right at his old place LEUZE WOOD.

Glorious hot still weather light Easterly breeze.

Paid the Company.

24th

The C.O. tells me I am to go in this time, & he is leaving Luss out – so all is well in that respect.

Attend H.C. service.

Make preparations for our move tomorrow – reconnoitre the way up with Sherard, riding up through MONTAUBAN, sending our ponies home, & walking across ourselves.

25th

The much talked of day has arrived – the Battn marches at 6 a.m. leaving Luss & Eric behind this time; I am commanding B Coy. – through MONTAUBAN, past BERNAFAY WOOD to TRONES WOOD, where we dump ourselves down, with practically no cover for anyone; one deep dugout, & a few shallow ones. We dig some trenches for our companies.

The 1st & 3rd Gds Brigades are this time attacking – 12.35 p.m. is the "Zero" hour: when a roar

Sept. 25th 1916 (contd)

of Artillery announces the "creeping barrage" has begun.

The "Objectives" are three. Two trenches first and then a third line behind & including the villages of LES BOEUFS and MORVAL. The 21st Divn is on our left, the 5th Divn is on our right. 2nd Gds Bde (we) is in Reserve.

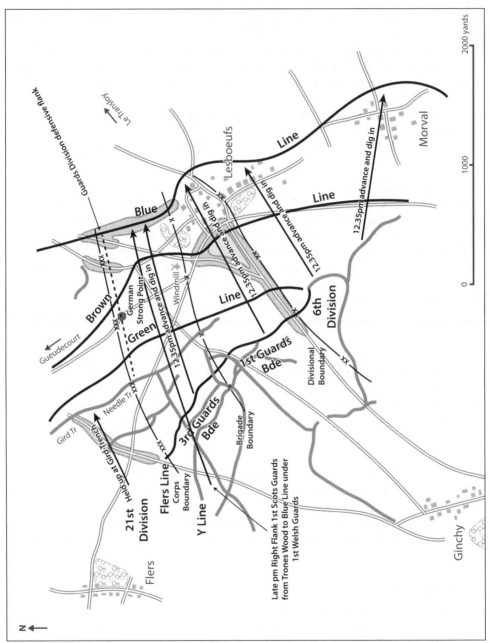

Map 14 Battle of the Somme, Capture of Lesboeufs, 25 September 1916.

At 3 p.m. word arrives that everything has gone satisfactorily except a "strong point" on left is holding up the 21st Divn which has not progressed.

The Bn is first for any requirements of the 3rd Gds Bde (left) Ch. Corkran sends down for 2 Coys; RF & B are prepared to go off under me_ We quite think we are off to take the "strong point" – but after all a further message comes to say only that I am wanted at Bde H.Q. so off I go, & have quite an interesting time hearing all that goes on. At 3.45 p.m. the third or blue line is taken including LES BOEUFS, and the Guards Division has as usual done its bit well. Not so however the 21st Divn, which cannot get on, so, as as [on] 15th, our flank is exposed, and a "defensive flank" has to be made, facing North towards GUEUDECOURT, only a part of which has been taken.

To help consolidate, our R.F. Coy, under Bobby Abercrombie, is sent off, and is placed under orders of O.C. Welsh Gds, who puts him in front line N. of LES BOEUFS, where they do some very good work.

The night is a very cold one, I return to the Battn at TRONES WOOD, where about 6 of us sleep in a heap to keep warm – the day has been a most successful one. The casualties have been heavy, but not unreasonably so – many prisoners were taken, and the line well advanced.

The Cavalry were all ready to go through, but were not allowed. It was a case of 'now or never', and Ch. Corkran urged that they should be let loose, while the Huns were disorganized, and before they had time to dig in, in their new ½ made line at LE TRANSLOY, but this was not allowed. They were given a whole night to settle down, when it was too late – wire & machine guns wont do._

This was the Battle of Morval, the village of Morval being captured by the 6th Division that day.

26th

During the morning I had to go up with B. Coy to carry up bombs for 1st Grenadiers – we had quite an interesting if somewhat arduous time – just when returning were spotted by Huns, & shelled like anything – I dont know how the Company escaped, some shells seemed to drop right amongst them. Just as we were leaving TRONES WOOD, the Huns put 17 very big crumps into it – one seemed almost in Battn H.Q., another fell on the very spot where I was crossing a few seconds previously and within 40 yds of my Coy parading – there were some casualties including Sgt Coombes our "Sick Sergt" killed.

The senior medically trained NCO assisting the Medical Officer, 7146 Lance Sergeant John Combe †26.9.16

While up near front I saw Mark Maitland commanding 1st Grenrs, also Jack Stirling pro tem commanding our 2nd Bn. The latter did splendid work yesterday – in one case 8 of our men got amongst and killed 50 Germans with bayonet.

Lieutenant Colonel Mark Edward Makgill Crichton Maitland, Commanding 1st Grenadier Guards

If only 21st Div could have got on the whole day would have been grand, & far fewer casualties.

Jack shews me where our R.F. Coy is, & assures me they are very happy.

We met many prisoners coming down, and frequently carrying our own wounded, without any escort even!

In afternoon the 21st Div make another effort, and do a little straightening up of line.

TRONES WOOD gets badly shelled again – an odious place. Peake in Coldm has his leg broken._ (I believe died a few days later).

Lieutenant Raymond Peake, 1st Coldstream Guards †30.9.16

About 6 p.m. the KDG's appear near by rather to our horror, as we felt sure they would draw Arty Fire, but luckily did not – they waited ready to go through but the call – luckily for them I think – never came.

The 1st King's Dragoon Guards, 8th (Lucknow) Cavalry Brigade, 4th (1st Indian) Cavalry Division

The Battn parades at 8 p.m. and proceeds on a long weary walk to relieve the 4th Grenrs & Welsh Gds. C. Coy is on right in LES BOEUFS, then R.F. remains where it was before, then LF and B Coys forming the defensive flank facing N. We had some difficulty finding our way – and made the most fruitless efforts to find the C.O. by orderly, also much difficulty over water & rations.

My Coy HQ was the Welsh Gds Bn HQ, where I found a Major Deane, lately imported – quite a capable person, in an old Hun Dugout: in most unpleasant surroundings – with numbers of German dead all over the place – one deep dugout near by had evidently been a sort of Dressing Station, & as patients died, they were laid out in a row – about 12 were there, I walked over them by mistake in the dark, a most unpleasant episode, as some were more than ½ decomposed; the stench round our HQ was horrible.

Major Humphrey Dene, 1st Welsh Guards

We had to try and get in touch with the 21st Divn, not too easy, as we did not know where they were, however after a bit found the 10th Durham LI, and some Northd Fusiliers._

The 1st Scots Guards, on the left of the Guards Division, were on both a divisional and a corps boundary. Their neighbours appear to have been the 62nd Brigade, 21st Division, where were the 15th and 16th Battalions The Northumberland Fusiliers. The 14th Battalion The Durham Light Infantry were in the 64th Brigade, but the 10th Durham Light Infantry in another division altogether.

The night was a quiet one so far as we were concerned & thanks to Brodie & Holmes we were all quite cheerful though had nothing to eat or drink except what we brought with us.

27th

Found a wounded Hun in a dugout – his arm almost blown off – gave him some morphia & sent him down on a stretcher.

Kept everyone quiet all day having dug well by night, for fear of attracting shell fire – did not get much very near, but a great lot over LES BOEUFS & neighbourhood. My Coy only had 2 men hit – not bad – the other Coys all had several casualties, including a poor Cpl. of LF who eventually died, he had most of his back shot away, & was in great pain._

13608 Lance Corporal John Duncan Bremner †27.9.16
14315 Lance Corporal James Horrocks †27.9.16
The heavyweight boxer nicknamed "The Tiger", 9159 Sergeant Charles Edward Finch
    was mortally wounded †2.10.16

Still we cannot quite make out where 21st Div has got to, they shew themselves all over the place, & draw fire.

We can see alas! the Huns busy digging themselves in – report it & our guns do some good practice at them.

This is not a comfortable place at all, plague of flies – stink of corpses – very cramped trenches & dugout (none for men) much shelling, if not on us, it is pretty near, & the men are terribly thirsty.

In the evening the Brigade Staff make a regular muddle as to our Ration Parties, causing much unnecessary work & walking, next to no sleep.

There were however many amusing incidents – such as an innocent looking RFA Corpl who was looking for the Officer, asking for a "very muddy trench" not knowing a bit where, nor where he had come from etc.

Then appeared a wretched RE man gone quite "gaga", whom some of our men had made prisoner & sat over him with a fixed bayonet – tho' I dont know what they thought he could possibly do.

Later one of our C.O.'s Orderlies appears with a little tired Northd Fusr, asking the way to our Bn H.Q.; he wont listen however & goes off with a ration party to the Windmill LES BFS, returning crestfallen after an hour – carrying everything for the Northd Fusr, and nearly carrying him! This time he listened & went straight off to the right place.

The next extraordinary thing was two men of the Coy managing to get drunk in the trenches at "stand to", 5.30 a.m. I hear they had been given rhum by a ration party of another Coy! Luckily there was an issue of rhum both nights.

28th

We had excellent cocoa for breakfast, cooked in a German Mess Tin. There were relics of every sort to be found – a signaller found a splendid pair of field glasses, much literature – smoke helmets rifles etc etc.

A Machine Gun Officer called Benyon turned up, quite done up – & utterly helpless.

Lieutenant Joseph William Andrew Benyon, Grenadier Guards

Much shelling all day, & at night too: one big gun in particular about every 10 min, not more than 100 yds away.

Weather perfect.

21st Div. seem to make a bit more advance, & dig a new trench which gets well shelled, mostly because they will walk about on top.

Watched a lot of aeroplane work, both ours & Huns.

We are absolutely filthy & uncivilized here, but thanks to great care on everybody's part as to keeping quiet no fires etc we have very little shelling & are quite enjoying ourselves.

In evening – or rather about midnight, we are relieved by 3rd Grenrs, a pitch black night, & we return into reserve in the old German Line (the "FLERS" line) which the Battn helped to take on 15th._

I sleep in a stinking old dug out, but being very sleepy I hardly notice the stink till next day. I think a dead Hun must have been in there for some days.

> The Flers Line was the first main German line of defence on 15 September, attacked and captured by the Guards Division, the Green Line of the attack orders.

29th

A quiet day. During morning I go out with Murray, stretcher-bearer, and Brodie to look for Tim's body or grave, & luckily find the latter about ½ mile away, and have a good look at the ground which the Battn attacked over on 15th. Find Tim's helmet on the grave with a bullet hole through it, so his death was doubtless quite instantaneous._ We collected a lot of shell cases & made a cross, also Tim's initials, & those of Pte A. Blucher his orderly buried with him, & a big circle of shell cases all round. His other orderley Casey was buried just a few yards away.

We also found the grave of that gallant Officer of the Battn Gordon-Stirling, attached to 2nd Gds Bde M. Gun Coy, but nothing to be seen of Lionel Norman's grave or body – however there were so many that one might easily have overlooked them.

I had a cross made by our Pioneers for Tim & his 2 Orderlies.

> Private Murray, stretcher bearer, – untraced
> Lieutenant Duncan Reynett Brodie
> Captain Ernest Pellew Orr Ewing †15.9.16
> 7843 Private Alfred Blucher †15.9.16
> 10495 Private Patrick Casey †15.9.16
> Lieutenant Gordon Stirling †15.9.16
> Captain Lionel Norman †15.9.16

At night my Coy has 1 Offr & 50 others on fatigue to carry R.E. Material up to front line – the Coldm is to make a dash for a German isolated trench – however this fails, & the fatigue party does not have to go. The Coldm have several casualties.

Tonight I cant face the smelly dugout so sleep on top of a sort of firestep, which Carter covers with a kind of verandah made of an oil sheet.

30th

Very noisy night – heavy shelling both sides, none bursting near us – but a Battery in action only 100 yds behind our trench.

Took out the cross to Tim's grave – then Dundas photographed it – some shelling nearby while doing this – a Battery in action close by, I only hope these graves wont get blown about by shells.

At 6 p.m. the Huns put about 15 shells amongst the Battery just behind us – big shells – it was a sickening sight – the gunners fled into our trench & in all directions._ One expected to hear of much slaughter of men & of guns being put out of action, but only 2 officers & 2 men were wounded!

About 7 p.m. the Battn was relieved by 8th Middlesex, who are to do an attack next day and establish themselves on a ridge a bit further on, where Ch. Corkran asked that the Division might go to._

> 1/8th Battalion The Middlesex Regiment, T.F., 167th Brigade, 56th Division
> This was the start of the Battle of the Transloy Ridges, carried out in the worst weather and physical conditions and achieving little at great cost. To the south the French achieved rather more, but nothing significant beyond capturing and holding Sailly-Saillisel and ground up to the west side of St Pierre Vaast Wood, along the line of the Arras-Bapaume-Péronne road. This hampered German observation behind the Allied lines.

We return to a nice camp near MAMETZ, just where on July 1st there was some very heavy fighting.

Dundas the Adjt pro tem (as Luss & Eric McK have gone on billeting) – tells us some very good Scotch stories – including the one about the bushy-tail_

Mervyn Jones & Plowden join – the latter comes to B Coy_ Holmes I am sorry to say returns to his own Coy – L.F.

> Lieutenant Arthur Mervyn Jones †21.11.16, was wounded at Loos
> Lieutenant Jasper Chichele Plowden

The Battn Officers for past week have been thus:

C.O. Col. Godman
Adjt. Dundas (Eric left out)
R.F. Abercrombie, Champion, Shortt
B. M.B. (Dundas) Holmes Brodie
C. (Luss left out) C Boyd-Rochfort Powell, Robertson.
L.F. Elwes Ellis Cobbold

> Not mentioned before:
> 2nd Lieutenant Robert James Robertson
> Lieutenant John Murray Cobbold, known as "Ivan"

The casualties in Officers of the Divn Sept 12th – 30th

	K	W	M	Total
Gren.	27	45	4	76
Cold.	23	34	3	60
Scots	14	17	–	31
Irish	8	18	5	31
Welsh	5	11	–	16
	77	125	214	

and *[blank]* other ranks; the proportion in Bns being wonderfully level.

The official casualty figures for the Guards Division in this period, including all attached officers and men, were 77 officers killed, 142 wounded and 13 missing and 926 other ranks killed, 4365 wounded and 1781 missing. Though the officer casualties were fairly evenly spread per battalion among the Scots, Irish and Welsh Guards, they were heavier per battalion in the Grenadiers and Coldstream. The 1st Guards Brigade lost 800 more all ranks and the 3rd Guards Brigade 400 more than the 2nd Guards Brigade. The 2nd Grenadier Guards lost 775 all ranks, the highest figure, the 1st Scots Guards 378 all ranks, the lowest. In addition to the missing officers of the Foot Guards there was one from the RAMC.

15

Rest and the Early Winter Weeks 1916

Oct 1st 1916

Walk with Sherard through MAMETZ. Write letters. There have been several Hun Balloons dropping bombs lately round these camps – one is said to have maimed 120 horses, most of which had to be destroyed.

> The aircraft bombing when a large number of horses were killed and injured was on the night of 27 September near Carnoy.

2nd

March 12.30 p.m. in rain to entrain at EDGEHILL, which we left at 5.30 p.m., a cold dismal journey arriving at AIRAINES, 20 miles W. of AMIENS at 1.30 a.m., thence marched to WARLUS, arriving at 3.30 a.m. – found supper ready and rhum for the men_
We are all delighted to hear Luss has a D.S.O., and Powell a M.C., as result of 15th, when both did uncommonly good work._

> Edgehill Siding was at Buire-sur-Ancre. The Guards Division moved to a training and rest area well out west of Amiens.

3rd

Settling down in billets, walked to Brigade Office with Sherard – a very pretty old Chateau.

4th

Attended conference at Brigade with other C.O.s and 2nds in command.
Rode in afternoon with Sherard – very nice country. Hear I am to get Paris leave.

5th

Rode over to lunch with Norman & 2nd Bn at VERGIES.
Doubt about Paris leave, also might get English leave!

I never mentioned that my dear old servant Carter got accidentally wounded by a German Bomb on 29th or 30th ult. It was buried – he only saw the stick which he pulled at for fuel – heard a hissing noise & ran for his life, when off it went – I hope he is not too bad.

Meanwhile one Hunter is doing servant for me.

> 1867 Private George Carter was badly wounded in the thigh and evacuated home, permanently.
> Private Hunter – untraced

6th

Battalion Parade in morning for presentation of DCM's and military medals to Pte Allen *[and others, names blank]* by Genl Fielding.

> 8476 Private Frederick Albert Allen, Distinguished Conduct Medal

Later the 2nd Battn came over to dinners with us. We gave every man a pint of beer, and all the Officers were photographed together – after luncheon._

Later I rode with Elwes through a big wood full of wild boar judging by spoor etc, but saw none_

Company Concert later – a very painful affair.

7th

Bombing Practice, Company Drill & Kit Inspection.

Sherard goes off to take the place of Brigadier who has gone on leave so I am again commanding. At 12 noon Luss, Mervyn-Jones, & I ride over to luncheon with Norman, after which we all, including Dick Warde (of 2nd Bn), motor off in "Michael" to the sea at TREPORT, a curious little town with a harbour & high chalk cliffs. Norman Luss & I go up to some Hospital where he calls on a Fenwick friend who is nursing – Luss then has a bath, while I walk another way by myself.

Dine at the Hotel de la Plage. & back to WARLUS by 11 p.m.

8th

Lunch at Norman's again, for a boar hunt, supposed to have been organized by a Frenchman, but when the time arrived only one hound turned up, so there was not much hunting done! We found a fox however!

9th-10th

Nothing of any importance occurred.

11th

Walked over with Sherard to LE QUESNOY to see Col. Skeffington Smith, but found he had gone back to TRONES WOOD with his Pioneers – a lovely old Chateau – surrounded by a high wall, which we had some difficulty in crossing!

Lieutenant Colonel Randall Charles Edward Skeffington Smith, Commanding 4th
    Coldstream Guards (Pioneers)

By the way on 9th there was a dinner at the 1st Guards Bde H.Q. – a fine chateau at
DROSMESNIL – for those who had been out since the Gds Divn was formed or previously – a
terrible squash – and on 10th I had to spend practically the whole of the lovely day at the 3rd
Grenrs H.Q. doing a Court Martial – HEUCOURT – very pretty little place – 2 of the 3 very
tiresome cases.

12th

Rode with Elwes in morning, to choose a place for practising the attack.
    Later had tea at the Brigade H.Q.

13th

Watched Bombing Practice in morning, being carried on by the new Brigade Bombing Officer
young Greer of the Irish Guards.

    Lieutenant Francis St Leger Greer, 2nd Irish Guards †1.2.17

Rode in afternoon with Mervyn Jones through a hugh wood near BELLOY, full of tracks of
boar.

14th

Watched more bombing practice in morning. Lunch with Norman O-E, at VERGIES, afterwards watching a football match between the two Battalions, when the 2nd Battn beat the first
by 5:0.
    Regimental Dinner.

15th

Walked with Luss to the Bde H.Q. in morning.

16th-17th

Nothing unusual – riding parades eyc – the latter day, we had a Battn attack practice the former
day I walked with Sherard into AIRAINES – a very pretty little place, along a trout stream, the
head waters of which consist of a wonderfully clear blue pool, which comes bubbling up out of
the chalk, near LALEU.
    After luncheon on 17th, I went with Luss Mervyn & young Ivan Cobbold to ROUEN in a
divisional car, mostly for the purpose of seeing David Barclay who was so badly wounded Sept
15th. After some difficulty & going to the wrong hospital we found him, an absolute wreck –
one eye gone, the other at present blind, a broken arm & serious injury to his back. His father,
Hugh Barclay & his sister Mrs Malise Graham were there, & later we all dined together at the
excellent Hotel de la Poste; they were very hopeful as to his recovery including regaining the
sight of his eye, but the nurse kept assuring us that this was most unlikely. I have never seen

anything like his pluck, he hardly seemed to realize there was anything wrong with himself, and kept talking of the Battalion.

> Lieutenant David Stuart Barclay, hit while in charge of a carrying party on 15 September, †24.4.17
> Hugh Barclay, a widower, had come over with his eldest daughter Cecil, married to Captain Malise Graham, The 16th Lancers.

The journey was a long one, in parts rather pretty – about 80 miles, coming home – we left about 9 – the night wet & dark, but we got along well & were congratulating ourselves on the successful way we found our way, when suddenly our driver told us we were short of petrol, & about 1 a.m. we came to a stop at HORNOY, whence we had to get out and walk home, luckily only about 8 or 9 miles. eventually getting to bed at 4.a.m.

By the way, on 16th I went for rather an interesting "Staff Ride" with Grigg – Bde Major – also Col Follett, Byng Hopwood, & Self, Jackson R.E. and 1 or 2 others. We had a scheme based on the supposition that the Germans had retired & we were following them.

That night we invited to dine with us the son of our landlady, he is the "Préfect of the Somme" an important personage – he was quite amusing, and enjoyed his evening – playing bridge etc. He was only on leave for a few days, usually he lives at LAON.

18th

In morning rode over to Divl H.Q. to try to borrow a car to go on leave; George Lane was very affable & promised me one.

In afternoon there was a Boxing Show – when several of the 2nd Battn came over, & had some inter-battn contests, most of which they won.

Saw Dumps Coke, who has come to to be Norman's Adjt, the first time for many years.

> Lieutenant The Honourable Reginald Coke, nicknamed "Dumps", in the 2nd Scots Guards briefly in 1915 until sent home with muscle pain

Later Head gave us an excellent lecture on "The Causes of the War" which was much appreciated by the men.

19th

Got up at 5.30 a.m. & found the car ready for me at 6.45, which took me to POIX, where I was joined by Bultul of the Coldstream, to catch the 8.13 train. However, it never started till 9.30 – & got later & later eventually reaching ROUEN at 2.30 p.m. Had some very funny old French folk in our carriage_

> Probably Lieutenant Walter Gordon Bulteel, Coldstream Guards

Left ROUEN again at 7.11 p.m. in the PARIS Boat Express, reaching HAVRE about 9 p.m., which we left in the leave boat at 11.30 p.m., SOUTHAMPTON at 7.30 LONDON 10.30 BECCLES 3.30 p.m.

Miles Barne then had eleven full days at home. The Guards Division stayed on where they were.

Nov. 1st/16

After some delay in London owing to the recent raid in the Channel, I left Southampton at 8 p.m., but hardly got out of the Solent, when all the leave boats, which it was thought were carrying off the congestion of several days, were recalled._ One, the "Viper", which had no wireless, got across; others had got within 30 miles of HAVRE. Spent a weary day at Sth-hampton

2nd

reembarked on the "Arundel" in evening – thanks to a dear old Colonel, who was O.C. Troops on board and who had McDougal in our 2nd Battn as his Adjt, I had one of the few berths on board – a lovely passage reaching HAVRE at 3 a.m. on

Lieutenant Ernest Trevor Murray McDougal, nicknamed "Tommy", 2nd Scots Guards

3rd

very short of food, & only got breakfast by intense diplomacy. Not allowed to go ashore, but changed onto another boat about 9 a.m., in which we left HAVRE again at 11.30 a.m., & had the most delightful trip up the R.Seine to ROUEN, a fine sunny day, which showed up the glorious autumn foliage in the forests to the best advantage. I really enjoyed this trip. Reached ROUEN at 5.30 p.m., slept at Hotel de la Poste – in a room with McDougal, borrowing a pair of pyjamas from a Welsh Guards Officer who was originally in Grenadiers._

4th

Went to see poor David Barclay in hospital – still blind, & the nurses say always will be so – just to be moved to England.

Hired motor car with some other Officers, and eventually after many adventures reached the Battn, where I had left them over a fortnight ago, at WARLUS about 9 p.m., finding Elwes in command, who has plenty to say of what he has been doing, so I take over till Godman returns probably Sunday or Monday.

Hear Hugh Ross has received the D.S.O., and the Battn had to take part in an Inspection by the Duke of Connaught of the whole Division.

The Duke of Connaught visited on a number of occasions, the last time being just before the Battle of Cambrai in November 1917.

5th

Write letters & clear up & Norman O.E. comes over, & Sherard returns from leave, so I return to duty with B. Coy.

6th

Do an attack on a wood – put up a woodcock. Rain & wind.

Ride over to tea with 2nd Battn in afternoon with Eric McKenzie – saw Norman

7th

Tried to route march but stopped by wet.

Walked with Elwes later.

Hear we are to move to our old country, LES BOEUFS etc. very soon: universal grief! Dumps Coke only assured me yesterday we were here till after Xmas. Personally I am all for getting our winter trench work share over before Xmas, & have most of January & February for "resting" – often bad months.

8th

Presided at Court Martial all morning, 4 cases, all "drunks".

In afternoon took part in rather a dull Staff Ride with C.O.s, & Adjts._

Sherards name has been sent in to do a Course next week, so I shall be taking the Battn up, which is rather pleasing to me in one way, namely that I am apparently thought fit to command the Battn under what will be very trying circumstances._

The descriptions of mud & what we are to be at sound almost the limit. In other ways, I shall be sorry not to be commanding B. Coy in the trenches, tho' probably plenty of that later on!

9th

Practised the attack as a Battn, according to the method I arranged before going on leave – for the edification of the Brigadier, who seemed quite pleased.

Fine sunny day._

Walked with Sherard in afternoon to see the Blue Grotto at LALEU again, tea at Brigade H.Q.

10th

Route march & training of B. Coy – walked through a big wood near BELLOY with Godman after luncheon, a perfect day to end up our sojourn at WARLUS with. bright & still – heavy gunfire to be heard in the distance, which continued all night.

11th

Took over the Battn from Sherard who went to a course at FLIXECOURT of C.O.s, embussed in French troop lorries under excellent French arrangements about 8.30 – self with Dundas in a French motor-car – to MEAULTE via AMIENS, a fine windless day, so the journey was a very pleasant one. Did not get into our dirty billets till after dark. Tea at Brigade H.Q. AMIENS was bombed last night, and we saw some of the damage done, luckily the beautuful cathedral was not touched._

The Battn had to debus at TREUX and do the last 3 or 4 miles on foot._

We had a man – Aspinall – killed last night, by being run over by a motor Ambulance – the Grenadiers had a man stabbed by a jealous husband, & killed.

14909 Private Henry Aspinall †10.11.16
14620 Company Quartermaster Sergeant W J Langley, 1st Grenadier Guards †6.11.16

The inhabitants of WARLUS were quite sorry to see the last of us, and several pairs of red & tearful eyes peeped at us through doorways etc! The behaviour of the men has been quite exemplary, & hardly any trouble occurred.

12th

Marched at 1 p.m. along the muddiest & worst & crowdedest of roads almost through BECORDEL, FRICOURT & MAMETZ to "H" camp which is between CARNOY and MONTAUBAN. A new sort of hut has appeared, circular & lined with matchboarding – intended to hold 25, but we have to crowd in about 50. The Officers have 2 huts. There is a good muddle on owing to our 3 Brigades for purposes of holding the line being changed into 2 "groups".

The purpose of organising the Guards Division temporarily in two groupings, rather than the three Brigades, was to minimise the amount that battalions had to move about and enhance operational continuity. The 2nd Guards Brigade battalions were divided among the other two, the 1st Scots Guards coming under the operational command of the 3rd Guards Brigade.

Water is a great difficulty, and also our new mess cart breaks down in the entrance to camp so we are rather in a bad way.

13th

I go down to MEAULTE again to Brigade Conference, and find the Brigadier in great form – stay to lunch & ride back afterwards with John Dyer & Woolridge Gordon, who is now attached to his Staff. Got back at tea time – procured another hut or two owing to 4th Grenrs moving out and a Manchester Bn coming in, weaker than the Grenrs.

Lieutenant Robert Wolrige Gordon, Grenadier Guards
Unnamed Battalion The Manchester Regiment

14th

More movements of Comps on obtaining some more huts.

Col. Darrell came to lunch so we tried to find out & get all we could out of him for our future, which from all accounts till well on through January does not promise to be very agreeable.

The Officers spent most of the afternoon ratting. I walked previously to see the Transport with Trafford._

We hear that Beaumont-Hamel has been taken with 4000 prisoners, all in deep dugouts._

Lieutenant Colonel Darell, Coldstream Guards, moved on from Headquarters Guards
Division six weeks later.

The gunfire in the distance that they could hear from Warlus was leading up to the
attacks on either side of the River Ancre which began on 13 November. They were
partially successful, Beaumont-Hamel was the most prominent place captured and,
among their heavy casualties, the Germans lost 7000 prisoners.

15th

Go round the camp in morning – more shiftings during the day – the 1st Coldm come in, &
we have to give up some huts. We dismantle some old German Dugouts & do some repairing
to the entrance to the camp.

During last night a Hun aeroplane came right over us several times & dropped some bombs
not far off – heard, amongst others, one nearly dropped on MEAULTE.

The weather is very cold & we are all perished, but wonderfully cheerful somehow. Last night
a wonderful argument was started on religion which developed into every sort of other subject
and ended with the probable duration of the war – everybody seemed to be talking at the same
time, and no two people agreed with eachother.

We get up a fine froust in our hut, with a stove etc; we had the windows open at night but I
found this was very unpopular & almost unnecessary owing to the drafts through every chink.

16th

Fine clear sunny day but cold NE wind.

The Battn parades & plays games & enjoy themselves like schoolchildren, in capital spirits,
leap-frog etc.

We set to work to make a football ground – filling up shell-holes, clearing away barbed wire
etc, for our camp is exactly on the old German front line before July 1st.

In afternoon I walk down to Mansel Camp to see the Brigadier.

Fearful conundra are appearing about our moving into the line transport difficulties, ration
bearing details – gum boots etc etc

17th

An absolutely bitter wind.

Battn parades 1.30 and moves into "D Camp" TRONES WOOD, which proves itself quite
the height of discomfort – the men have holes to crawl into with tarpaulins over the top, so badly
arranged that they run the rain water into the holes_ I walk down with Eric McK – hard frost
& dry wind luckily – meet H. Seymour on the way, just back from receiving his D.S.O. from
the King.

Look in at the 2nd Battn at MONTAUBAN, find Norman just off with Jack Stirling to see
Tim's grave – he comes back via our camp & says the grave is still in good order.

Our H.Q. Mess hut, which we share with R.F. Coy is a little tin hut of the draughtiest
description – but we sleep in quite fairly good deep dugouts. We are very merry in spite of the
squalour & discomfort & cold. Am very thankful Sherard is being spared this period – weather
& all things being considered.

18th

Wake up to find all white, & soon a wet sleet begins, which by noon makes the most indescribable slush.

Luss, Elwes, Mervyn Jones & self all go to lunch with 2nd Battn, where we have an excellent lunch of beefsteak pudding & plum duff.

Saw Arthur Erskine, Brigade Major of 20th Div Artillery on the way down.

> Miles Barne had last seen his cousin, Major Arthur Erskine, on the morning of 15
> September.

19th

Wake up to find sun shining & a Southerly wind which completes the thaw & turns the mud into pea soup.

Y'day we had to send up 2 Coys (C & L.F.) up as carrying fatigues to Needle Trench, the H.Q. of Battns in front line, today we send the other two Coys, R.F. & B., to take over the front line with 2 Coys.

This causes endless orders to fly about – as the remainder of us have to move back to Camp H., CARNOY.

This takes place in the afternoon – before which I lunch with Arthur Erskine_ I walk back with Asprey & have the muddiest walk I ever had. Meet Norman O.E. Alston Herman Hodge etc on the way.

> Lieutenant George Kenneth Asprey, 1st Scots Guards
> Major Alston was about to be promoted and take over as Assistant Adjutant &
> Quartermaster General, Guards Division
> Captain Roland Herman Hermon Hodge, Grenadier Guards, Deputy Assistant
> Quartermaster General, Guards Division

Hear GRANDCOURT has been taken by us.

Col Godman has 'flu so suppose we shall not see him again for some days.

> Grandcourt, up the valley of the Ancre, was captured in the operations begun on 13
> November.

20th

Not quite so cold, but wind still pretty cold._

Walk with Eric McKenzie – we take over the whole camp.

Make great preparations for the return of the 2 Companies tonight from the line: drying shed – braziers – blankets – tea & rhum. The soldier always prefers tea to soup or cocoa.

No sign of the C.O., but I dont expect him now for a day or two.

Rather an anxious night owing to the non-arrival of the companies till 6 a.m. on

21st

They have had a nasty time of it – Mervyn Jones & Shortt both wounded, the former a compound fracture of his thigh – 1 Sergt & 3 others killed and about 8 or 10 wounded.

> 13620 Lance Sergeant John Cullen †19.11.16
> 13344 Private Patrick Foley †19.11.16
> 12208 Lance Sergeant Alexander Horne †20.11.16
> 4574 Private Reginald Hoffrock Sharpe †20.11.16

They arrive about 5–6.30 a.m. quite dead beat, and tumble into their huts – we have a drying hut, so their trousers & coats can be dried. The day is spent at work at the football ground.

Luss & I walk down together to FRICOURT, when he goes on to the 2nd Battn at MEAULTE, I go to the new Brigade H.Q. at CITADEL.

Our dear old Brigadier, John Ponsonby has gone home for 3 months rest, while H. Seymour is appointed in his stead: a very young Brigadier – rather hard on old Sherard, who however knows he is over 50 so cant get a Brigade, and takes it very well._

While I am waiting at Bde H.Q., who should arrive but Sherard, recovered from his flu, & Kit Cator, off leave. We all lunch there, after which S & I walk back. I get a sore instep from my new boots

Nov 21st 1916 (continued)

(Ration Field Boots) so make a present of them to the Padre, whom they seem to fit very well.

One of the killed yesterday was Pte Sharpe, until a week ago the C.O.'s very willing & steady, tho' very stupid servant – whom he returned to his duty, as he could stand him no longer – he offered to get him another post as servant, but the good old thing replied: "Oh! No Sir! There are plenty of less fit men than me for those jobs" – the particular post having been with his former master, Royds, at HAVRE. Such is fate.

I play chess frequently now in evenings – with Trafford, Eric McK – Sherard etc.

22nd

We heard yesterday that poor old Mervyn Jones' leg had to be amputated, and now today that this has been too much for him & he has died of the shock. We shall miss him much, a most cheery goodnatured individual – very hard luck to get his death wound within an hour of going into the trenches for the first time since LOOS – as he only re-joined us early in October this year just before we went out to "rest"._

We hear now that we are to go into the line Dec 1st for 24 days – the Division, that is – at SAILLY-SALLISEL, taking over from the French: ground which they have recently conquered; rather stormy there just now, I hear.

23rd

Rode up to GROVETOWN to attend Mervyn's funeral at the Hospital Cemetery there – accompanied by many other Officers: found Norman, Jack Stirling & others from 2nd Battn there – they supplied Pipes etc being nearer than we.

24th

The whole Battn on road improving fatigue under the R.E., who were delighted with our work. We worked with & under the O.C. 4th "Labour" Battn R.E., who is in normal times a Civil Engineer living in George Str., Westminster.

There is much fun over a small stove which Sherard bought in Amiens. Some despise it, but it undoubtedly warms the hut a bit, we put it on the table for meals, & warm the plates, red wine, make toast etc.

25th

Pouring all day. Did nothing but chess, had a lesson or two from Gillieson & Godman, with help of the book. Several Officers went into Amiens yesterday, amongst them Eric McKenzie, who had to stay in there with a fever.

A bath.

Walked in evening with Sherard

26th

The Battn on road improvement fatigue, but owing to drenching rain did not parade.

Rained nearly all day.

27th

Road improvement fatigue again. Walk with Sherard, & in afternoon accompany him to go & get some 9.2" Howitzer Charge canisters – hundreds of empty ones are lying about – made of tin – my idea being to make paths of them, filling them with chalk – they make fairly good paths, & wd be better still if laid on some sort of embankment.

28th

Battn on draining fatigue & making paths – all in camp._ Powell returns from leave.

In afternoon walk with Sherard on the MONTAUBAN road, are much amused watching the traffic – particularly the Anzac drivers. Their faces are a perfect study. There is an endless stream both ways, & one wonders who can be holding the line, there seem so many men behind. The variety of costumes – absence of cleanliness etc is astounding & wd hold one's gaze for hours on end if one had the time._

We then went into MONTAUBAN Churchyard – the church is gone clean – hardly a sign of it except some bits of coloured plaster saints & the old colossal copper bell. The tombs are rent open & vaults exposed. The family is all buried in one vault one on the top of the other, in brick graves. A more gruesome sight we agreed we had seldom seen.

29th

Battalion (under me as usual) on road fatigue, but I hand it over at midday & go with Sherard to lunch with H. Seymour, the new Brigadier. Hear that "Ma" Jefferies – Brigadier – has been sent home, & John Campbell has had a bust up with his C.O.'s, 2nd in c's, Adjts & Coy Commanders who did not come punctually to his "conference"._

Brigadier General George Darell Jeffreys, Commanding 57th Brigade, 19th Division,
   took command of the 1st Guards Brigade on 30 December and was not sent home.
Brigadier General John Vaughan Campbell, formerly Commanding 3rd Coldstream
   Guards, had just been promoted to command 137th Brigade, 46th Division.

Also various peace rumours, all being well except Germany & we are squabbling over Antwerp! As a matter of fact I believe this is all started by the German party in America, and there is nothing in it except a desire to be able to compulsorily end the <u>next</u> war!

30th

Cold & raw S.E. wind. Walk with Sherard in afternoon to find Barnard-Smith's grave which we do at CARNOY cemetery.

2nd Lieutenant William Woodthorpe Barnard Barnard-Smith, 38th Brigade, Royal Field
   Artillery †21.10.16

Hear the Division is going to take over from the French at SAILLY-SALLISEL._
   One of the few occupations nowadays for Officers is ratting, tho' personally I find it rather cold work.

Dec.1st

N.E. wind. Thick fog – frost – a most unpleasant day._ Walk in afternoon with Luss & Cecil Trafford.
   A good deal of chess in evenings.
   Vist from Cecil Boyd Rochfort yesterday – now a Staff Capt. at 4th Army Flying H.Q., a real soft billet.
   A shortage of fuel, but we send fatigue parties off through the fog & they bring back logs galore_ since we have been here have done a lot of draining of our camp. and making paths with chalk and 9.2 in. Howitzer Charge Canisters.

2nd

Move in afternoon to MALTZHORN FARM_ luckily a pretty hard frost, otherwise the camp – an old French tent camp – would be quite unapproachable – having no regular road to it, only a sunken muddy one, no doubt in wet weather a canal.
   We take over from our 2nd Bn, who have left Kit Cator behind with a tempre, and Andrew Vanneck as Camp Commandant. The latter dines with us. Sergt Major Cutler has gone home & today Sergt Major Wadham has taken his place – Cutler going as Sergt Major to 3rd Battn._ Wadham arrived unshaven the first time in 19 years – being gaped at by the whole Battalion – his first remark being that he thought very bad arrangements were made in this country!

Lieutenant The Honourable Andrew Nicholas Armstrong Vanneck
In a Foot Guards Battalion the Sergeant Major, always known as such, is the Regimental
   Sergeant Major.
1931 Sergeant Major Thomas Edward Cutler

1542 Sergeant Major Frederick John Wadham
3rd (Reserve) Battalion Scots Guards, Wellington Barracks, Birdcage Walk, London

3rd

We move in afternoon to LEUZE WOOD (better known as "Lousy" Wood) where the Battn is much scattered, Bn HQ being in a road cutting just over COMBLES, where also all the left half Bn Officers fed and slept – everybody in a heap, the men also being very squashed up – some tarpaulins which we had been promised not turning up._

4th

Move up into the line where we relieve our 2nd Battn, who give us dinner. We have to go through COMBLES, and wander across a mile or two of "abomination of desolation" other-wise a sea of shell holes guided by a white (?) tape, never have I seen anything worse – unless it was yesterday when going through GUILLEMONT. We are now up between MORVAL and SAILLY-SALLISEL, about 400 yds away from the Hun, and said to be a fairly quiet part of the line except for shelling – we are on the slope facing the enemy, so must be particularly careful as regards fires and showing ourselves._

Start round the line with Eric McK. about 11 p.m., back soon after 2 a.m. – some rain – trenches fair, but very soft earth which will be a lot of trouble in wet weather. There was a bit of shelling going on, some of it rather uncomfortably near us, but we only had 1 man hit in the night, & he was worse from "shell shock" than his wound.

5th

Pretty continuous shelling on both sides – & fairly clear light – from Bn H.Q. one gets a good view of LE TRANSLOY and part of SAILLY SALLISEL.

Some drizzling rain – it is foul in the trenches, & one feels really sorry for the men, with no real shelter, & unable to light fires – no hot food – if we have to be here 4 days & nights every time, I am afraid our wastage will be pretty considerable.

> The winter of 1916-17 was very harsh. In the trench lines on the Somme at this time the Germans had the logistics advantage in that the area behind them was not devastated for miles and it was therefore easier to bring up all supplies and material, as well as men. For both sides the lines were where the fighting had ended up, so not yet fully formed into trench systems. It would take the Guards Division a while to set up their systems both here and just further south opposite St Pierre Vaast Wood. The circumstances were physically as bad as anything they encountered anywhere during the War and Miles Barne's prediction about wastage was accurate, most notably when they came out after three days of it, relieved on the night of 15-16 December.

6th

The Division is now divided into 2 groups, under 2 Brigadiers, the third Brigadier commands the back area. Ch. Corkran, who commands our group, came up this morning to settle about a new support line – Sherard met him & went round with him.

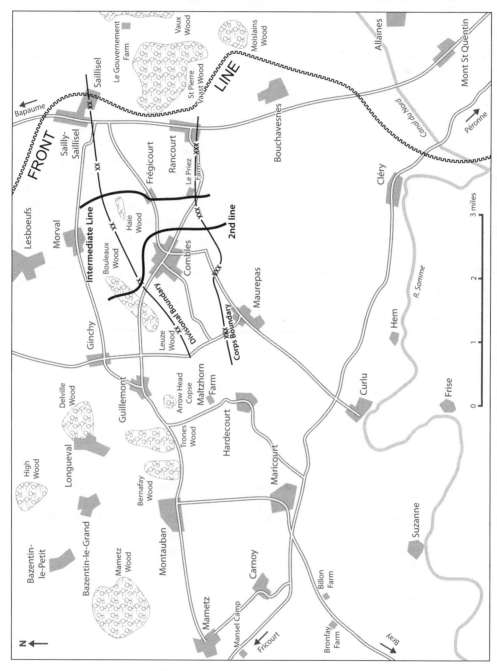

Map 15 Line at Sailly-Saillisel and St Pierre Vaast Wood, Winter 1916-1917.

Hear we are only in for 3 instead of 4 days.

Walk round the line with Sherard in afternoon._

Found a dead man whom the 2nd Battn left behind by mistake, so buried him. He had been accidentally killed, it is said.

> 13987 Private James Renwick, 2nd Scots Guards, †3.12.16 was killed by another soldier negligently firing his rifle.

A gunner liaison officer called Peto is with us tonight. The Guards Divn Artillery has relieved the French today.

Hear COMBLES gets badly shelled, & a valuable RAMC Sergt Oliver, 9th F. Ambce is killed: Our little Doctor Dark is much grieved.

> Peto – untraced
> 20007 Sergeant George Oliver, 9th Field Ambulance, Royal Army Medical Corps
> †5.12.16
> 9th Field Ambulance, attached to 2nd Guards Brigade

7th

Went round the line early with Peto – quiet time – found all well.

Visits during day from Gye RA Heath R.A., Jones (Rev)

> Probably Captain Denison Allen Gye, L Battery Royal Horse Artillery †28.2.17
> Heath R.A. – untraced
> Jones (Rev) – untraced

Relieved by Welsh Guards in evening_

Rumours of resignation of Asquith & Lloyd George – also fall of Bucharest.

> Henry Asquith resigned as Prime Minister on 5 December and was replaced by David Lloyd George. Bucharest fell the same day to combined forces under German commanders. Roumania was unable to have any further influence on the War, but did on the Peace.

A pretty quiet relief, the Bn goes to MALTZHORN FARM near GUILLEMONT again – the L.F. had one man hit by a bullet on way out and the whole Coy took a wrong turn and got lost – so were rather late getting in.

8th

We found we were shelled periodically all night – at least a spot within 200 yds of the camp was shelled, which was rather disconcerting, and we expected more peace out of the line._

Weather misty & drizzling, but not cold – this is more comfortable than bitter cold, though everything towel, socks & all clothing, boots, bread, blanket etc etc being damp does not conduce to getting rid of one's cold (everybody has one now).

Discover 2 of those shells dropped about 25 yds from where we were all sleeping.

Walked over to Divl H.Q. with Sherard, at ARROW HEAD COPSE. Heard the Divn is to be in the line till Jan 4th, which means we will have another 8 days in the line probably._ They also gave us some newspapers, & we read all the "sensational" political news.

Norman O-E appeared in the afternoon – to see his 2 Coys in this Camp, under Jack Stirling.

9th

Moved by train (15 min) to BROMFAY FARM – raining. Found a big but very incomplete camp – no water, but mud rats & filth everywhere, the camp having been recently taken over by the Divn from the French._

10th

A pouring wet night & day – very difficult to get gum boots & other clothing at all dry – especially as fuel is rather scarce._

During the night several aeroplanes came over and dropped many bombs, two of them sounded very near, but

11th

I dont know how near. We get some Lewis guns going, and eventually a couple of "Archibalds" come up.

During the day we march by road to LEUZE WOOD area, which means Battn HQ again in the Road Cutting Dugouts just above COMBLES.

Reavely joined us yesterday.

Lieutenant Archibald George Bertram Reavely

Dec. 12th 1916

Snow & sleet Wind N.W., slosh everywhere. A cheerful prospect for going into the trenches!

Walked with Sherard in morning to Brigade H.Q., past the scene of the ghastly episode of yesterday on the GUILLEMONT road at corner of LEUZE WOOD.

The first thing greeted me in the early morning when I went out to look at the weather was the 7 corpses being carried down into COMBLES.

On 11 December the leading company of the 1st Scots Guards were following about a hundred yards behind the rear company of the 2nd Coldstream Guards when shells landed on the road, killing seven Coldstreamers and wounding several more.

9569 Private Frederick William Huntsman †11.12.16
10489 Private William Charles Murrant †11.12.16
12329 Private George Cuthbert Easton †11.12.16
12500 Private Arthur Marks †11.12.16
12752 Lance Corporal Arthur James Bridgeland †11.12.16
17741 Private Sidney Egginton †11.12.16

18220 Private George Challis †11.12.16

We started off at 3.30 p.m. being relieved by 4th Grenadiers, now under Gilbert Hamilton. & we relieved our 2nd Bn in the line, which appears to be in perfectly dreadful condition, full of mud & water, and there does not seem much prospect of our being able to stick 4 days – trench boots (when on, which is easier said than done) get dragged off_ Smith Cunningham took 3 hours getting from his support trench to Coy H.Q., and then lost the sole off his boot. Many other instances of lost boots etc could be quoted, and the L.F. Orderley sent up to Battn HQ never arrived at all.

> Lieutenant Colonel Gilbert C Hamilton, Commanding 4th Grenadier Guards
> Lieutenant Robert Dick Smith Cunningham

13th

My darling wife's Birthday – we drank her health at dinner_ Many bombardments by us – no retaliation, although very heavy firing to the North. In evening I went round to see C B & LF Coys with Head, the Chaplain. Found the 2 latter Coy Cmdrs rather despondent, but Luss of course full of beans. The other 2 say they cannot possibly stay in 3 days & nights, but they have got to do so.

A fearful scare that the LF Orderley has got lost in a shell hole, but he turns up later after 24 hrs absence.

We had quite a stiff walk round, but nothing to what the poor men are doing. Found them standing stiff & cold & as a whole pretty wet & fixed in one spot.

14th

During the morning the Battn H.Q. came in for some bombardment, but bad practice was made. Ch. Corkran and Balfour paid us a visit; when they went away they had to come flying back, having been headed by some 5.9 shells.

They had to get back to entertain Frankie Lloyd & Archie Douglas to luncheon_

> Probably Captain John Balfour, Scots Guards, attached Guards Division Signal Company †21.3.18
> Major General Sir Francis Lloyd, known as "Frankie", Major General Commanding The Household Brigade and General Officer Commanding London District
> Major The Honourable Archibald Campbell Douglas, known as "Archie", Regimental Adjutant Scots Guards

The day was eventless until 7 p.m. when the enemy suddenly put up a heavy barrage on the front trenches all round, a perfectly sickening sight; our Artillery retaliated most effectively so that it did not last long. I went down about 8.45 p.m. to see how they were getting on & what had happened, rather expecting to hear of a good many casualties, but parties we met reported well, and on reaching B & LF Coy H.Q., discovered very little harm had been done_ I then went on to R.F., accompanied by the trusty orderley, Allen, (poor Moss was killed on 15th Sept.) and found Ward, who now commands it, rather upset on many points. One of his signallers had had his foot blown off (I had met him being carried back) and the state of the men's feet and tomorrow's relief rather worried him._

I then went on to L.F. again & so to C. Coy, where I found Luss quite cheerful and happy, as usual.

> 8476 Private Frederick Albert Allen was in the 1st Scots Guards throughout the war
>   unwounded.
> Captain Francis Ward

Our total casualties were only about 6 men wounded.

I got back about 12.45 a.m., very pleased to be back – and somewhat exhausted – Eric made us each a cup of hot cocoa.

15th

We did a good deal of bombardment in morning. In evening were relieved by Welsh Guards under Douglas Gordon, Murray Threipland having been sent home sick.

> Lieutenant Colonel Granville Cecil Douglas Gordon, formerly Scots Guards,
>   Commanding 1st Welsh Guards

Owing to the state of the ground the relief was a very slow one. Three Coys arrived back at MALTZHORN FARM by 1 a.m., the R.F. Coy was dribbling in all night. At about 11 a.m. on

16th

the Battn entrained at TRONES WOOD siding – and a sorry sight it was watching them filing by – we had to leave several behind with "trench feet", and many who came with us could barely walk. Many had lost great coats, rifles, equipment & other things. Our 3 days & nights proved too long under the existing trying conditions.

Before entraining Sherard & I walked over to see Gen Frankie Lloyd & Archie Campbell [Douglas]; on a visit at our divisional H.Q. Found the latter in, & he came to see us entrain.

We got to BROMFAY FM. in time for dinners – all in open trucks, sleeting all the time. The Grenadiers entertained some of us to luncheon. Spent the evening till dark draining the precincts of our Battn H.Q.

17th

A great day of drying & cleaning up and trying to make good equipment and clothing._ Read up back papers, including the "Peace Proposals", & heard of the great French advance & victory near VERDUN, 9000 prisoners & 80 guns besides going forward 5 kilometres.

Attended Church & H.C._

Walked with Elwes – had a bath and wrote letters.

> In December Germany, understanding that the longer the War went on the less likely
> they would be to win, called for peace discussions with the current military situation as
> the starting point, never likely to be considered by the Allies. So, if Britain and France

rejected discussions, then they could be shown up as being responsible for prolonging the War. Meanwhile, the United States were attempting to play peacemaker with a "No Win" settlement. President Wilson had also recently asked the warring nations to publish their war aims.

Meanwhile, in a very well planned and executed attack between 15-18 December the French concluded the Battle of Verdun by recapturing most of the important ground not recovered earlier.

18th

Trained back to MALTZHORN FARM – very cold in open trucks – found the 2nd Bn just going off to the Trenches.

19th

Bitter wind & hard frost – snow later. Explored the way across country for tomorrow via ARROW HEAD COPSE: such a forlorn way too, never saw ground so broken up by shelling. Found Raymond Asquith's grave at a little cemetery between TRONES WOOD and GUILLEMONT.

Lieutenant Raymond Asquith, 3rd Grenadier Guards †15.9.16

Heard the French had taken up to now, in the past few days near VERDUN, over 11000 prisoners 105 machine guns 115 guns etc etc.

The Germans here are said to be anxious to fraternize, and consider the war practically over! An unpleasant surprise for them that we dont think the same_ No doubt they are told they have won.

20th

Colder than ever, but better than wet. Ground sprinkled with snow.

Paraded 2.30 p.m., and relieved 2nd Battn in same old trenches.

Sherard is kindly sending in my name for a month's leave from the time we get out of the line – Jan 4th! It sounds too much to expect.

A quiet relief – had cheery dinner with 2nd Bn. I went round LF B & C trenches 9.30–12.45 a.m., found all pretty quiet, though a few pipsqueaks flying about – one unpleasantly near the path just ½ min in front of me. All very cheery & hoping the hard dry weather would continue, but this is not to be for on

21st

we go up to look round & find it has been raining again, & all slush & mud & thaw – most unlucky.

Eventless day. Chess.

About 9.30 p.m. I start to go round with Eric McK and 2 Orderlies, had only gone ½ way down to the line when some very heavy shells began landing just in front of us, apparently near LF Coy HQrs._ pieces flew past us, so discretion being the better part of valour, we retreated till all was over, and then started again. Saw Elwes, & F. Ward in R.F. Coy, which was the far side of a marsh, and most difficult of access – my gum boots were frequently half dragged off. Eric McK went to the other Companies. I found the journey a very arduous one altogether – the trench (front line) itself was in a terrible state, much worse than the other Companies. Was very glad Sherard went there last night & not this one, I really dont think he would have managed it, his old heart being none too sound.

Very quiet night.

We have with us now one Pretyman, of our 2nd Battn, who is commanding their "Sapping Platoon". Hinton has ours.

He is busy now on a bit of trench close to us at Bn H.Q., and has revealed many corpses – French he thinks – on stretchers – in fact the whole vicinity must be most unhealthy, wherever you dig almost, you find a corpse – some German.

> Lieutenant Frank Remington Pretyman, 2nd Scots Guards †4.7.17
> Lieutenant Herbert Allan Hinton

22nd

A lot of shelling on both sides, but we had no damage done.

Were relieved by Welsh Guards – under Douglas Gordon again – and got away 8.30 p.m. passing out the usual way via HAIE WOOD, COMBLES, LEUZE WOOD & GUILLEMONT to TRONES WOOD siding, where the men all had hot soup or tea, (having had some in COMBLES too) embarked on the train, leaving there at 1.15 a.m. on

23rd

arriving back at BROMFAY FARM at 2.30 a.m., where the men had more tea, and rhum, finding braziers burning in their huts – and very glad we all were to turn in. Of course the Officers all had supper galore.

One finds out here one can always eat; as Luss says the next meal is the only thing to look forward to.

The entraining in high trucks in the dark, of men very tired & footsore is not an easy or pleasant thing, and very bad for the tempers of all concerned – one man I heard bump his leg badly which brought forth the most unusually eloquent flow of unsavoury language._ Drill Sgt Piper, standing by remarked "That's enough, you are not saying your prayers now": to which a third party replied out of the darkness, "No, but he ought to be!" – and so the fun goes on – nobody ever seems to be out of temper for long at a time, and the men never grumble.

Found Shortt waiting in camp for us – wounded 4 or 5 weeks ago – quite recovered.

Bobby Abercromby returned from doing a 6 wks course.

A hurricane came on in the morning – partly unroofing several of the huts – sheets of rain, but dropping towards night.

A Bath.

Began to eat our Xmas parcels – starting with a turkey sent by Eric McK's Mother, & very good it was too.

6018 Drill Sergeant William Pyper, formerly Company Sergeant Major of C Company,
was wounded in May 1916 just outside the Menin Gate

24th

A stormy night_ Some shelling of neighbourhood during morning_ they have evidently one big longrange gun on a railway, which fires incessantly at something or other.

Paraded 12.30 p.m., went by train to TRONES WOOD, and marched to LEUZE WOOD Area – a lovely clear sunny day – too clear. However we got safely into our respective billets – C Coy going on to HAIE WOOD.

This road is becoming past a joke – shells pitch right _in_ it apparently.

25th XMAS DAY!

Opens with us making a heavy bombardment 8.30 a.m. & others later.

Peace & Goodwill! Many severe orders to the contray are published – at least against our "fraternising" with the Germans, as has been known on former Xmas days in some parts!

I walked over in morning with Ellice & Ivan Cobbold to see B. & L.F. Companies.

Lieutenant Donald Wilson Ellis, who first travelled out with Miles Barne in July 1915

I dislike this place, there is too much shelling & some most disagreeably near. We looked for a short cut when they go into the line tomorrow night avoiding COMBLES, but without avail – mud too great.

Visit from Brigadier.

Grigg returned from his course – where he met brother Seymour, & popped into our Bn H.Q. to ask where the Brigade was. So now he will resume being our Brigade Major. John Dyer and Luss both

Dec. 25th 1916. XMAS DAY (contd)

came to dinner, which consisted of Soup, Roast Turkey stuffed with chestnuts, Bread Sauce, Plum Pudding with Brandy Sauce and Cheese. The Turkeys were sent by McKenzie's Mother, and were quite deliciously tender.

During dinner rather an upset occurred in the shape of a 4.2 shell arriving and landing just across the road, not more than 10 yards from our hut luckily the side is sandbagged ½ way up & nobody damaged – even the sentry who was just outside escaped most miraculously, and then 15 min later came another, with equally harmless results, & just missing the mouth of a dugout where some of our police live.

They certainly have the range of this road to a nicety, and something will have to be done about it, as there is so much traffic, & in clear weather is under direct observation I believe.

26th

Another fine clear day. No special events, but a good deal of shelling on their side, and a very heavy bombardment 12–4 p.m. on ours.

In evening we relieved the 2nd Bn (S.Gds) in the old line, very quiet relief.

They said during the bombardment a German had come over to give himself up, saying the Bombardment was more than he could stick, and their trenches were being blown to billy-o.

I went round part of the line 2–3.45 a.m., seeing Luss who has been granted a month's leave, after being refused first and my name being sent in – however I am glad he has it. Coy Commanders have the most arduous time of anybody.

I daresay I shall get mine later tho' perhaps not in the boys' holidays, which I was so looking forward to doing.

Hear from Brother Seymour that he is going in for flying, I feel sorry as the game is a dangerous one, but I admire him, and feel for his wishing to be more active.

27th

Visit from Brigadier fairly early – yesterday was pouring until we actually got into the trenches which are in a deplorable state. Then it came out a lovely night and today is like summer, tho' a bit hazy. Aeroplanes everywhere.

Some excitement was caused by a balloon descending, which turned out to be a German one containing a bundle of French Newspapers, edited E. of the line – the only papers of course the French can get in their "occupied" territory – this apparently being their surplus stock sent over for the benefit of the French in these (?) parts – & of course the paper is really no more than what is published every day in Berlin.

During the day numerous people, of all sorts & ranks, wander down to us, to our great annoyance, all helping to give away our position & the duck-boards, so that at night the Germans will know exactly where to fire. The C.O. is fairly rude to some of these people and usually makes them – especially Staff Officers – walk back by a circular route through the mud, instead of over the duckboards.

I go round the 3 left Coys with Kinnaird, recently joined, to show him what occurs. He has been out as an ADC for 16 months but never done a day's Regimental duty. We are out 10.30–1.30 a.m. a beautiful night with a touch of frost.

Lieutenant The Honourable Arthur Middleton Kinnaird †27.11.17

28th

Grey & cold & frosty but dry, such a blessing. The men in the trenches last night really seemed quite cheerful & no special complaints.

Grigg – who has returned – came up during the afternoon, and told us that the TRONES WOOD SIDING had been heavily shelled, and broken up, so we have to march back to BOMFRAY CAMP tonight.

He also tells us that the BOULEAU WOOD Dugouts have beeen badly shelled, one direct hit killing 8 Welsh Guards and wounding 7._

168 Private C James 1st Welsh Guards †27.12.16
259 Private D Hughes 1st Welsh Guards †27.12.16
330 Sergeant Oswald Murphy 1st Welsh Guards †27.12.16
342 Private C Tinklin 1st Welsh Guards †27.12.16
637 Private Thomas Charles Williams 1st Welsh Guards †27.12.16

780 Private GD Evans 1st Welsh Guards †27.12.16
1583 Private George Edward Young 1st Welsh Guards †27.12.16
2290 Private J Jones 1st Welsh Guards †27.12.16
2402 Private WT Davies 1st Welsh Guards †27.12.16

The relief is a very bad one, a very dark & foggy night, pouring with rain, & there is a muddle about the Companies – some unforeseen confusion, so the last Coy is not relieved till 4 a.m. on

29th

Luckily with great difficulty I persuade Sherard to go on about 3.15 a.m.; we do not reach BROMFAY till 7.30, we Eric & I catch him up just before reaching there – he having walked the whole blessed way – we having ridden from HAIE WOOD through COMBLES and LEUZE WOOD to TRONES WOOD, our grooms hanging onto our stirrups.

The men all put in at MALTZHORN FARM CAMP, where they got tea and rum, before proceeding, so that the whole journey went off quite well for the whole Battalion, more tea and rum on arriving at BROMFAY. In spite of a certain amount of shelling all the way to TRONES WOOD, there were no casualties.

C. Coy did not arrive till 9.45 a.m.

The day is spent sleeping and washing – & at night the Officers all dine together, having their "Xmas" Dinner – after which Gillieson takes his departure for ÉTAPLES, being replaced by one Taylor._

The Reverend Charles William Gray Taylor, C.F.

30th

March to LEUZE WOOD area. I do it alone, the Col. having to ride, & I missed Dundas somehow; who is doing Adjt instead of Eric left behind.

Every time now we leave a few Officers out of the line – there is so little room in Coy HQ's in the line, & it gives their nerves a rest for the "rainy day".

Very little shelling, and the Battn gets in safely, but a lot of shelling after we are in, and several more quite near us during the evening – as on Xmas Day, but not so near.

31st

Walk over with Powell & Kinnaird to see C and R.F. Coys._ saw the dugout where the Welsh Gds were killed and our cookers, one of which was damaged. Quiet journey over. Some more shelling near our dugouts, but no damage done.

Jan. 1st 1917

We made a heavy bombardment as the New Year opened – to which the Germans feebly retaliated.

At 6 a.m. they put three very heavy shells very near us – one right on the top of Sergt McCulloch's (Police Sergt.) dugout, which was not by any means a deep one – another close alongside a Gunner's hut – luckily the soil is so wet and loose, that the shells go pretty deep before they burst._ Visit from the Brigadier (H. Seymour) who is a wonderful person and not a bit "the General"_ he is always on the go, up to the line and everywhere else, and never takes an Orderley with him.

We also have visits from Col. Osborne Oxford & Bucks LI., of 20th Div., who takes over our Billets, and Col. Gilbert Sherwood Foresters, who will take over our part of line tom'r'w. At 4 p.m. we move off and relieve our 2nd Bn for the last time in this part of the line – Col Gilbert accompanies us, and goes round the line. I believe our relief – tho' a <u>very</u> quick one – was spotted, as whizz-bangs were fired off intermittently up till 12 midnight on duck-boards & along trenches, some unpleasantly near us just as we were getting near Battn H.Q.

> 10208 Lance Sergeant William McCulloch
> Lieutenant Colonel John E Osborne, Commanding 6th (Service) Battalion The
>   Oxfordshire and Buckinghamshire Light Infantry, 60th Brigade, 20th (Light) Division,
>   New Army
> Lieutenant Colonel Leonard Gilbert, Commanding 10th (Service) Battalion The
>   Sherwood Foresters, 51st Brigade, 17th (Northern) Division, New Army

We had a very nice New Year present, in the shape of being told that the Battn was only going into the line for 1 night instead of 2. We dined [at] the 2nd Bn H.Q. before they went out, and everybody very cheerful.

Dundas & I – with Allen the Orderley – went round the line at 11 p.m., returning about 1.30 a.m., after 12 m. a very quiet night.

2nd

A very clear morning. Considerable enemy shelling, for which we had to retaliate, and a real heavy retaliation it was too.

Were relieved by 10th Sherwood Foresters in evening, all over by 7.35 p.m., and a real good relief too, in spite of "New Army", and bright moon – marched to TRONES WOOD by 10.30 p.m., & there had to wait till 1 a.m. before the train appeared when we embarked very quickly about 2,000 on the train! and left about 1.45 a.m. on

3rd

having a hot soup cold tongue & champagne supper! when we drank Sherards health it being his birthday, but this was turned into drinking mine & Eric's, for the latter had met us and broken the news that we had both got "D.S.O.'s", which as regards myself I could not well believe & thought they were pulling my leg, but later on I see my name in the list. Would that I felt more deserving!

> These awards were in the New Year Honours

We reached CORBIE at 11.40 a.m., where were met by Brigadier & Staff, and marched to our billets, quite good ones, and how the men do deserve a rest now !

The Battn has been wonderfully lucky altogether – since Nov 9th when we left WARLUS – except for the few when Mervyn-Jones was killed, we only had 1 other killed, or died of wounds – not so many as we had at WARLUS, when two men were accidentally killed.

13270 Lance Corporal William Dorans, killed in a Lewis Gun training accident †26.10.16
14909 Private Henry Aspinall †10.11.16

My billet is a very clean looking one in a large villa. looking over the Cemetery where poor young Leach, Sloper Mackenzie etc were buried.

Another pleasant surprise awaits me today, for permission is given for me to go on one months leave, so I shall get it after all during the boys' holidays._

The C.O. insists on our new ribbonds being sewn on, and I leave CORBIE at 1 a.m. in a truck with a diminutive Officer who was originally too small to pass his "medical" into the Army, also with Hall of Grenadiers – spend some uncomfortable hours at AMIENS, which leave at 7 a.m.

Probably Lieutenant Charles Aubrey Hall, 3rd Grenadier Guards

4th

in a comfortable train, dozing some sleep en route, lunch at La Couronne, ROUEN – leave again 7.30 via HAVRE, luckily being allowed to travel on the mail packet – reaching LONDON at 10.30 a.m.

16

St Pierre Vaast Wood and Later Spring 1917

When they came back to the Corbie neighbourhood after New Year the Guards Division understood that they would have a month out of the line. However, on 4 January they were told that they were to go very shortly to relieve the 8th Division, XV Corps, from near Sailly-Saillisel down to the west side of St Pierre Vaast Wood, all just across the main Arras-Bapaume-Péronne road. XV Corps were to move to their right to take over more of the line from the French. By the time that Miles Barne came off leave the Guards Division were out of the line again and the 1st Scots Guards were at Méricourt-L'Abbé, up the Ancre from Corbie.

Sunday Feb. 4th 1917

Left London 4 p.m. via Southampton – capital crossing, though I was unable to get a bunk, but quite a good seat on board – very cold.

Arrived HAVRE at 3 a.m.

5th

not allowed to land till 6 p.m., when we were told to go & get rooms, though there were none to be had! I went straight to F. Hervey-Bathurst, Grenadier, who is the Military Landing Officer, & he very kindly gave me a bed dinner etc – one Brodrick also dined. Snowing hard.

> Captain Sir Frederick Hervey Bathurst, Bt, Grenadier Guards
> Brodrick – untraced

6th

Bathurst lent me his motor car, so I went up to see Royds etc at the Guards Base Camp – where I was conducted round & shewn everything like a King – and then caught the nominally 1 p.m. train – "Leave Train" which started at 4 p.m., lunching previously at a very plebeian little restaurant, which was very amusing – there being some of all sorts there.

Had 5 very smoky fellow travellers, so I had to insist on the door being open partly – which I don't think they quite liked.

Lieutenant Colonel Albert Henry Royds, Scots Guards, Commandant Guards Division
Base Depot

7th

Arrived at MERICOURT *[Méricourt-L'Abbé]* at 10 a.m. & found the Battn there in billets, nearly all the Officers sick or *[on]* leave or on courses etc_ Col. Godman commanding the Brigade Eric McKenzie the Battn, so I take that over, especially as he is in bed.

Walk over to VILLE to see the Brigade, & Sherard confides to me that his name has been sent in to command some sort of farming arrangements._

8th

Very cold weather – the thermometer has been down to 6° below zero not far off.

Walk again, and attend lectures etc – lunch at the Brigade, dine with C. Boyd-Rochfort at H.Q. 4th Army Flying Corps. Sat next to a Col. Godman, Yorkshire Regt, cousin of our C.O.'s, and had quite an interesting evening.

Lieutenant Colonel Arthur Lowthian Godman, The Yorkshire Regiment

9th

Walk with C. Trafford to see Sherard, & along R. Ancre etc. Saw snipe etc.

I hear that during last month Frank Greer, Irish Guards, the Brigade Bombing Officer, had died as the result of an accident, also the Brigade Bombing Sergt.

Lieutenant Francis St Leger Greer, 2nd Irish Guards, †1.2.17
14284 Sergeant Henry W Gordon, 3rd Grenadier Guards †1.2.17

Today another accident occurred at bombing practice – wounding a Grenadier Officer & 4 men – one piece hit, but did not penetrate old Sherard, who was looking on, & just missed Guy Rasch, who is temporarily commanding 3rd Grenrs.

Incidents which occurred during my absence on leave keep cropping up_ In the part of the line where the Battn has been the two sides were very close to eachother: and we could not relieve or walk about without being seen, so for some reason, by mutual understanding, neither side fired at the other, tho' the Germans really were not half so much seen as us. Apparently the powers that be heard of this, with the result that 2 officers, Brodie and Dundas, went over with written statements "Any German showing himself after today will be shot."

The 1st Guards Bde seem to have been very scornful of the peaceful situation, & boasted "When we get into the line etc" However rumour has it that "war" in that spot is so bad for us that "peace" has again been declared!

Digging is quite out of the question.

The general practice of the French and German infantry was to leave each other alone when there was no serious fighting going on, not the policy of the British infantry or military authorities. So, when the British took over more of the line south of Morval, they inherited an informal lull, not extending to artillery. Because of the state of the front and support lines and posts at Sailly-Saillisel and St Pierre Vaast Wood and of the communication trenches, until such time as the Guards Division had put these and everything else into basic good order the lull was convenient. Once it ceased to be useful Brigadier Lord Henry Seymour considered it wrong simply to open fire on the German infantry without warning. So he detailed Lieutenant Brodie, who spoke German, to give them notice, while Lieutenant Dundas went for the fun of it.

10th

Had to go, as President of the Court of Inquiry into the Bombing Accident, to take evidence at GROVETOWN C.C.S., from Lieut Orriss & 3 other wounded Grenadiers. This took all morning; cadge luncheon off the Brigade at VILLE on way home, & walked back along the river with Sherard, saw several duck etc.

Still very cold.

Lieutenant Walter Gerald Orriss, 3rd Grenadier Guards †29.3.18

11th

Walked by myself along river – through HEILLY where there is rather a well placed chateau.

Wilfred Dashwood came to take over our billets – & fed with us.

Lieutenant Wilfred James Dashwood, 1st Grenadier Guards †2.8.17

Attended lecture on censoring of letters – learnt nothing new.

12th

Left MERICOURT at 9.45 a.m. and marched via BRAY to BILLON FARM

On the way the Battn was photographed by a French Company for Cinematograph purposes; so we shall be seen in the Paris Music Halls no doubt.

Arrived about 2 p.m., walked over with Sherard, still Brigadier, to see Grenadiers etc.

Luss & Kinlay return from leave

13th

Whole day occupied by the Court of Inquiry on the recent bombing accident.

Walked over in afternoon with Sherard to get more information at GROVETOWN C.C.S.

Bubbles – alias – Bagot-Chester – is now Camp Commandant here, & dined with us.

On our walk came upon an English Aeroplane which came down accidentally, no great damage done so far as we could see, but the officers present wd not answer any questions, which I suppose was very wise.

Visit from Lieut Butler 6th Dorset Regt., late Coy Sgt Maj of L.F. Coy.

He said that at the recent attack we made on SAILLY-SALLISEL the Huns put up no fight and simply ran back through us with their hands up, not even stopping when they met our first line.

One Cooper – an Officer – joined us, but goes sick straight away and goes to Hospital.

Major Greville John Massey Bagot Chester, nicknamed "Bubbles", Scots Guards
   †28.11.17
5327 Company Sergeant Major Hubert Butler, later Lieutenant 6th (Service) Battalion,
   The Dorsetshire Regiment, 50th Brigade, 17th Division
Lieutenant Gerald Melbourne Cooper

14th

Col Godman goes on leave. We wonder much if he will ever return to the Battn.

   Very cold weather indeed – bitter wind from N.E., but the health of the Battn is excellent.

   Walked by myself to look for suitable training ground.

   Dined at the Brigade, sat next Bubble*[s]* (Bagot Chester), who is the Camp Commandant of this Camp.

15th

The whole Battn is on a fatigue destroying & salving timber from dugouts, old French ones, in a valley near here.

   Last night Brand woke up in the middle of the night & saw the side of the hut on fire – just in time to put it out. He says he had a visit from Providence.

Captain David Halyburton Brand †29.3.18

In afternoon the Brigadier (H. Seymour) took me off for a longish walk to SUZANNE, where we went to a very hideous & gaudy château. He walks a great pace, & so I got very hot, but am all the better for it.

16th

Change in wind & quite mild after a hard frosty night.

   Woken up at 4.20 a.m. by bomb dropping & Hun Aeroplanes close by. One came & dropped 3 incendiary bombs on a huge Amtn dump at the PLATEAU which caught fire and continued all day – it was a wonderful sight when I first looked out about 5 a.m., big gun Ammtn, bombs of all sorts, SAA, verylights, red green & other coloured flares etc etc all going off together, more than one ever saw at the Crystal Palace. A terrible waste of Amtn and money. There was one huge explosion at 9.30 a.m. H. Seymour was standing 500 yds off & thought the end of the world had come: a huge sheet of flame seemed to advance directly onto him._ A good many gas shells were exploded, so we had to make sure that all ranks wore their new sort of "respirator" in the "Alert" position._

The box respirator came into general use through the autumn and winter of 1916-17 and was issued to the 1st Scots Guards just before Miles Barne came back off leave. It was accurately described as a gas mask, rather than a helmet or hood like its predecessor. It was carried in a haversack with two compartments, in the second of which was a cylinder containing the filter, connected to the mouthpiece by a tube. It was effective against all forms of gas, but, apart from where it covered the face, no protection otherwise against mustard gas. When there was a threat of gas troops were ordered to carry the haversacks in the "Alert" position, resting on their chests and slung round their necks.

A lecture was given by Capt Hely-Hutchinson of Irish Guards explaining the new war loan, and how men might help._ The shells etc going off owing to somebody's carelessness (the Amtn must have been stacked in too big heaps & too near together) were not a very good argument in favour of lending.

Captain Maurice Robert Hely Hutchinson, Irish Guards

Some rain at night._

17th

Very mild but thick fog. Practised Coy attacks 3 Coys in morning, 1 in afternoon. A lecture from a Major Campbell of the Army Gymnasium Staff on Bayonet work, and a very sound & amusing lecture it was too – and appealed to the men properly – a real bloodthirsty individual he is. The Major General (Fielding) appeared for it and we had some hide & seek for him, as he did not arrive by the expected way.

Major Ronald B Campbell, The Gordon Highlanders

We are to do a Battn attack for the Brigadier on Monday, & I have to have some detailed orders written, so spend my time at this, nowadays, very complicated matter._

18th

We practise the attack as a Battalion & it goes off quite well.
    Lunch at the Brigade, then inspect the ground for the attack tomorrow with Percy, who is acting Brigade Major_ Spend most of spare time finishing writing my Orders for the benefit of the Brigadier._

Possibly Captain William Percy, Grenadier Guards

Hear there has been a further biggish success on the Ancre with 500 prisoners taken.

From soon after New Year the British restarted operations up the valley of the Ancre. These gradually worked forward in very difficult conditions, but did contribute locally to the Germans abandoning part of their defences earlier than planned before they later withdrew to the Hindenburg Line.

19th

The mud is again getting "beyond words". After raining all night again, we do the (practice) attack before the Brigadier, and it all seems to go very fairly well, though of course not beyond criticism.

A lecture on bombing at 2.30 p.m., and on Lewis Guns to the Officers at 5.30 p.m. I have to go to be cross examined by the Brigr in afternoon about my Attack Orders.

Brand goes on Lewis Gun Course.

20th

Mann rejoins. Another L.G. Lecture to Officers by Smith-Cunningham.

> Lieutenant Francis Thomas Mann, wounded for the second time at Sanctuary Wood in June

In afternoon attend a Brigade Bayonet Exercise Competetion.

Play Chess with C. Trafford usually in the evenings._

21st

Work at Cookhouse drainage etc – mud is fearful. Luss takes an involuntary bath in a drain.

Battn Concert in evening.

Gave away "Divisional Parchments" to about 30 men & NCO's of the Bn who had won them for "continuous good service", including my groom Thomas & servant Carter. Also some cooks, drummers quartermaster sgts, tailor etc.

> As it was impossible to obtain official awards for all who merited them, particularly those whose essential roles kept them out of the fighting, the Guards Division granted special Certificates to recognise them.
> 4807 Private George Thomas
> Miles Barne's servant, Private Carter, was in hospital in England and did not return.

Feb 22nd 1917. Thursday

Nasty thick fog. Companies mostly on fatigue.

In afternoon walk with Cecil Trafford to see the remains of the Ammtn Dump which was burned. – a doleful sight – pieces of shell & huts chucked about in all directions – one bit of corrugated iron stuck up on the tip top of a poplar tree_

23rd

Again thick fog._

Marched at 9 a.m. to PRIEZ FARM, leaving B. Compy at MAUREPAS en route.

Relieved 1st Bn Coldstream there.

Most of the Battn seems to be on fatigue all day and every day._

In afternoon, in accordance with the "Defence Scheme" I go up with the Coy Commanders to look at some of the line – find de Crespigny with 2nd Bn Grenadiers there – much upset by having had 2 officers hit yesterday by one shell, one of whom, Lawson Johnson, has since died. Also by finding that the Battn on his right – of the [blank] Regt, seemed very careless of all ordinary precautions, and was chancing things terribly. He declared that the Huns had only to walk over any night, and would easily take possession of their trenches._

A heavy mutual bombardment about 9 p.m., which dies away in about ½ hour.
We are here only half a mile from the Battn H.Q. in the line.

> This was on the Guards Division's right boundary, near Rancourt.
> Lieutenant Arthur McWilliam Lawson Johnston, 2nd Grenadier Guards, †22.2.17

24th

More fog.

Visit early on from the Brigadier of 1st Guards Bde, "Ma" Jefferies – under whose orders we now are.

Walk round the dugouts of the Battn and visit some of our many fatigues – some burying telephone cable 6 ft deep, some at work on a sort of reserve line, & so on.

Luss & I go to lunch with the Brigadier, whose Staff consists of "Becky" Smith, O'Neill and Jackson. They are at Douage Wd, we go via COMBLES, and return across country in a sea of mud, where there are a lot of guns in position – these are just behind our dugouts and make an unceasing din – we are warned not to stand on top of our dugouts as their shells only miss the dugouts by 3 ft!

> Lunch was at Headquarters 1st Guards Brigade.
> Captain Merton Beckwith Smith, Coldstream Guards, Brigade Major
> O'Neill – untraced, but Captain The Honourable Henry Barnaby O'Brien, Irish Guards,
>   was Staff Captain
> Jackson – untraced

A mail arrives after having none for 5 or 6 days. One of the HAVRE boats is said to have been attacked by a submarine, so the service is off for the time. One never knows what to believe.

Some gas shells arrived close to our dugouts and a few bigger HE Shells – no casualties, but the men put on their gas masks very quickly._

25th

More fog and some frost. During the morning some very exciting news arrives to say the enemy in front of 5th Army seems to be falling back, evacuating some trenches and villages including MIRAUMONT.

> This followed on from the British operations during the previous weeks up the valley of the Ancre.

Some rather heavy shelling of our neighbourhood in the afternoon, one arriving very near our cookers.

Several gas shells so we are all at the "Alert", with our new box respirators on our chests.

Later comes a message which declares that a prisoner has given away that they are retiring gradually to a line just E. of CAMBRAI, blowing up roads wells etc as they go.

We have just heard of a man who drank some "lachrymatory gas mixture" out of a rum jar, thinking it was rum. He was taken to the "Aid post" where he was very sick, to the extent that everyone, doctors & all, had to turn out wearing their gas masks.

During the evening various official messages arrive telling us of the line to which the enemy have withdrawn, namely commencing on the South at LE TRANSLOY, which they still hold, our line goes round including WARLENCOURT IRLES, BEAUREGARD DOVECOTE, and SERRE, where it rejoins our old line: a most satisfactory chunk to have got, and by its shape we must take more ground yet – as a very pronounced German salient remains at GOMMECOURT, and back to opposite ARRAS.

26th

Luss goes to judge some 3rd Gds Bde Boxing: I am not allowed to go, in case any sudden orders arrive, and we are all ready to move at ½ hrs notice: to follow up any forward movement that there might be opposite us – in the event of the Huns retiring.

The Irish Gds had patrols out (in fact no doubt every unit had) but there was no sign of any withdrawal: though I am inclined to think their Arty is quieter than usual._ About 7 p.m. however the enemy opened what seemed quite a heavy barrage on the Brigade on our left – after which we saw S.O.S. signals & rockets going up, and so our own gun[s] replied with their barrage, & in 20 min all was quiet again. We can only suppose the enemy were very jumpy, or else were contemplating a raid, which never matured, so far as I could hear.

About 9 p.m. very much the same sort of thing happened, only a bit farther North.

27th

No further news came in till about midday, when we heard the Australians had got on a bit, and GOMMECOURT appeared to be evacuated!

Were relieved by 2nd Battn under Norman, and we marched back to huts at MAUREPAS. The Camp Adjt McTaggart Stuart in Grenrs made a muddle, & we had to shift after getting in into another part of the camp, instead of going in where 3rd Gren. under Thorne were expecting us, before they went up to the line.

> Captain Edward Orde McTaggart Stewart, Grenadier Guards
> Lieutenant Colonel Augustus Francis Andrew Nicol Thorne, Commanding 3rd
> Grenadier Guards

While all this was going on, 3 Hun Aeroplanes came over not very high up, were shot at by our own a-a guns, some of the pieces arrived into our camp, all amongst us, but hit nobody.

28th

At 5.25 a.m. we hear the bombardment and barrage for the 29th and 20th Divn Attacks to our left. The 29th Div., we hear later, are successful, but not so the 20th._

I inspect the Camp in the morning & walk in afternoon with Ivan Cobbold – looking at some old French and German trenches. near HARDECOURT.

In the evening we hear KUT has been taken by Genl Maude, & the 5th Army has got to PUISIEUX, but is unable to stay in IRLES. Doubtful about GOMMECOURT.

Wonderful rumours that the Germans have taken YPRES!

Two Officers joined us from home today – one is Prettejohn who was for a short time in the Suffolk Yeo., the other Finnis, who I discovered was at Rottingdean School with me & left me there in 1886, and I had not seen him since then, over 30 yrs ago.

> 2nd Lieutenant Richard Buckley Prettejohn
> Lieutenant Charles Roche Finnis

March 1st

Watched Coys training in the morning – lunched at the Brigade H.Q.

Had to have a parade of all the N.C.O.'s, as one of their names had been forged, and a case of whisky bought under false pretences – the Canteen Manager came to try & identify the forger, whom he failed to find, so I hope the Battn has been cleared.

In the evening we saw an Engish Kite Balloon come down in flames – to the South, so Luss Brand Cobbold, & I set out on foot to see what there was to be seen – we walked till it got dark and then had to return. We heard it was at CURLU, and was brought down by a German Airman.

The 5th Army seem to have got on very well, & have got GOMMECOURT.

2nd

Start on horseback at 6.15 a.m., with 3 Coy Commanders to go round the line – (Luss Mann and Brand) meet Col Thorne, 3rd Grenrs, at his H.Q. & he takes me round in a thick fog, which is just as well as the line is only 30 yds apart in places, & being only held in "posts" we have to walk about on the top.

Things are pretty quiet, but just a bit of shelling sniping and rifle grenading.

There is a bit of excitement on because we have been told that one (if not 2) of the Battns of the Bde has shortly to do a "raid", and all O.C.'s have to make arrangements for this – the object being to see how strongly the Huns are holding their line, & if there is any sign of their retiring._ The front we are on, namely western edge of ST. PIERRE VAAST WOOD, hardly lends itself to this, still we have got to make an effort & obey orders.

Get back to MAUREPAS about 12 noon.

In afternoon walk to Divisional H.Q. with Eric Mackenzie, and have tea there. Have a great wrangle with Cook (Col. Alston) about the method of "claims", the fault not being his but that of the system, by which we apparently play into the hands of the French population on every opportunity, & pay up whether they are entitled to it or not._

On our return to our camp, we find that Col. Godman has returned from leave so my term of commanding (23 days) has once more finished.

He & I walk together in the evening & there is a lot to be said by both parties, for many episodes have occurred in the Battalion, Officers & NCO's coming & going, and so on.

Today Bobby Abercromby goes as Adjt of the "Works" Battn._

> Very temporarily a Guards Division Works Battalion formed from within the Guards Division to work on the roads, salvage and anything else requiring manual labour.

We make all the necessary and elaborate plans for our move into the line tomorrow.

3rd

When this comes we get an order deferring this for 24 hours – there is much speculation as to what this is all about: everyone guesses something different.

Walk with Sherard in morning, & again in afternoon to the Bde H.Q., and walk back with the Brigadier.

We are apparently only postponing the relief owing to some sort of attack by the Corps (XVth) on our right near BOUCHAVESNES.

4th

This comes off at 5.15 a.m., when we can hear the intense bombardment._ During the morning we hear that the 8th Divn has made quite a successful attack and taken 100 prisoners.

> This successful, but costly, local attack by the 24th Brigade, 8th Division, captured and held two lines of German trenches on a ridge east of Bouchavesnes.

I go to Church (& H.C.) and hear Head preach – he is a topping parson – a real man – loves going round the trenches – and very popular with the men.

A very cold wind.

Relieve 3rd GG in the line in evening: a very noisy relief but no casualties. The Huns are evidently attempting counter attacks on the 8th Divn, and put a great lot of shells over that way._

I go up to the line early in night to arrange about a new Lewis Gun Emplacement. I get into an old sap, followed by Mann Cobbold & C.Sgt Major Shields, & not being sure of my whereabouts have my revolver ready which I think frightened Mann much more than any possibility of meeting Germans.

The line is very unsatisfactory being held in "posts", but not connected up. There are 3 posts right out in front to which access is only possible by courtesy of the Huns, who up to date have not interfered much, but today they shot a Grenadier. All reliefs have to be done over the top, & it is only a matter of time when there will be trouble.

Unfortunately we have had a young Transport Driver (Peyton) killed by a shell on his way up.

> 7407 Company Sergeant Major John Shields, B Company, later 2nd Lieutenant Scots
> Guards
> Two members of the 3rd Grenadier Guards died in or near the line, 21835 Private
> Bertram Morrell †4.3.17 and 24706 Private Adam Walter Scott †4.3.17
> 13537 Private Henry Paton †4.3.17

We were to have found two young Naval "Subs" in the line, but owing to the relief being put off (this turns out to be a punishment on Grenadiers for not carrying out a little raid which they said they would do) they have gone down.

Later, at 12.15 a.m. I go up & round the line again with Sherard. We go and look carefully over the L.G. post being made; and crawl about in saps etc. Sherard insists on doing the same

& going right out into No Mans Land, even beyond our "covering party". I was very glad when he had seen all he wanted & we came in. Quite a quiet night, but it snowed hard & by morning everything was white.

5th

Battn H.Q. came in for some shelling about 11 a.m. when we took to ground in our deep dugout – two burst very few yards in front of the door while I stood there, & nothing came my way: these shells are so wonderfully local in their effect.

The Brigadier comes up at 3 p.m. & I go round part of our line with him, through a bit of RANCOURT too.

We are wired off and have posts on our right in case the Division there is driven back. These we call the "Anti Bantam" Defences, as a Bantam Brigade was on our right at one time.

There are some desperate bombardments by the guns on our right – whether the Huns were attacking or what was happening we dont know.

6th

Sherard & I go round at 2 a.m. returning at 5 a.m. just as the moon was setting & early dawn appearing.

A good deal of shelling going on scattered about, and we have a Corp. killed and 3 men wounded (one is Gilmour my double) – also the B Coy Orderly hit by a sniper in the stomach (Shand) and I dont think he will recover – a capital fellow & old friend of mine._

> 15831 Lance Corporal Edward George Taylor †6.3.17
> 14695 Private David Gilmour lost his arm
> 13037 Private Charles Alexander Shand †6.3.17

Tuesday March 6th 1917 (contd)

We went round most of the right of the line, and into the 3 Advanced Posts, which are only 30 yds from the Huns – they only allow us there by courtesy, as part of way is "on top"; some day another Regt will be there, & trouble will ensue. They shouted out to C. Coy: "we will allow your reliefs but not working parties". The ground falls from us to them, so they get a good skyline, & we cant see them.

In afternoon I walk up with Luss & Eric Mackenzie to the former's Coy H.Q., and explored RANCOURT. We were highly amused watching an air fight – first of all 3 v. 3 planes, then one of the Huns had to clear off home, coming down all the time, but got over their line alright. After that the other 2 Huns kept at a safe distance, especially as our 3 were joined by a 4th._

There were 3 more "bombardments" during the night by us on the Hun front line, and it was a noisy night.

7th

I went up with Ivan Cobbold – now Battn Bombing Officer – at 2.30 a.m., and went round some of B Coy's posts – a bitter wind and got pretty wet. The posts are all isolated and the Huns below us, so they get the skyline. They have started sniping a good deal & hit one of B. Coy

Orderlies. On way back about 5 a.m. the duck board walk had been blown up by a shell since I had passed – a very good shot at it.

We were relieved in evening by 3rd G.G., a particularly quiet day & night – back to MAUREPAS. We wonder much whether the Huns are going to retire opposite us – they were seen by some men of C. Coy to be throwing away a lot of bombs over their parapet, most of which never exploded at all.

Bitter wind from N.E., hard frost at night

> After Lieutenant Leach's death Lieutenant Dundas was appointed Bombing and Intelligence Officer, but he had now gone to be Bombing and Intelligence Officer at Headquarters 2nd Guards Brigade. Lieutenant Cobbold replaced him.

8th

Very cold again & more snow.

Brodie returns from sick leave, while Adams-Acton goes, having sprained his ankle, & not long ago having fallen over a precipice & broken an arm, a leg and 5 ribs! Hilton has also gone sick – and Powell ditto while on a course at FLEXICOURT.

He has now gone home, so we must get a new Sniping Officer.

> Lieutenant Gladstone Murray Adams Acton
> Lieutenant Herbert Allan Hinton
> Lieutenant Ronald Vanneck Powell damaged a cartilage while at the Fourth Army School at Flixecourt.

Walk in afternoon with Sherard and George Lane of the Division.

We saw a big fire going on behind the German Line, which we took to be PERONNE.

> Captain George A O Lane, Coldstream Guards, Camp Commandant, Guards Division

9th

Wind still very cold, but gone to S.E.

Walked up to have a look and found PERONNE still smoking.

In evening Sherard and I dined at Divisional H.Q. and had a most wonderful dinner – I sat next the General (Feilding) who was very affable – & full of old reminiscences.

We are rapidly losing all our oldest and best N.C.O.'s who are going to what they call "take" commissions. We have to send a certain number every week – it is getting rather serious._

Snowstorms.

10th

Quite mild & muggy & thick fog. Rain later.

March up to PRIEZ FARM in evening – relieving the 1st Bn Coldm there.

11th

Walked up to Battn H.Q. in the line in morning to start snipers dugout – later we relieved 3rd G.G. in the line – quite muggy & lovely sun. Some horrid shelling close to Battn H.Q., & one very near our Mess at PRIEZ just before we moved off, which put Sherard and me underground very quickly.

Went round the line with Sherard 11 p.m.–1.30 a.m., and had quite an exciting walk – first of all we were in a trench, and were challenged by one of our own bombing posts – the challenger would not wait for the answer, but kept repeating the challenge and eventually called up his post: & we could see the bayonets gleaming & bolts being worked etc._ it was rather an isolated post, and I think they were a bit jumpy.

After this we walked among a nasty dirty wet trench, during which time there were a lot of trench mortar bombs falling about – we presently met Brand with about 8 or 10 men walking on top – and on a skyline to the enemy – we stopped & talked & presently, not to my surprise, a shower of TM Bombs arrived all in a bunch just behind us, & after this for a time, there was a lot of TM activity, but no casualties – it fairly scattered the gathering, and in the end all was well.

Battn H.Q. got shelled during the night, which is tiresome, and dangerous too, as we have to go to ground. The so-called dugout where Ivan Cobbold & I sleep wont keep out anything in the way of shells – an "elephant" dug-out.

Made ourselves some cocoa & soup always on returning to Bn H.Q., it is a long walk – our Bn Orderley (Allen usually) is always glad of some too.

> Miles Barne's use of "elephant" refers to the thick corrugated iron now in use for dugouts all along the line, inserted for structural support, not simply lining, typically after the requisite space had been excavated from a bank or slope. The effect resembled an underground Nissen hut, though much smaller. A deep dugout was much safer from shells.

12th

I go round at 11 a.m. by myself, and wallow about between the various posts in the front line – now nearly full of water – in some places right over my trench boots – had a good look at the German line and "No Mans Land", from every sort of angle. Got back to a late lunch – heard of the occupation of BAGDHAD.

> The Mesopotamia Expeditionary Force entered Baghdad on 11 March.

Battn H.Q. is again shelled at odd times during the night, beginning at 8 p.m. during dinner.

At 11 p.m. I again go up to the line with the orderley Thompson – meet Brand going round, so I join him and visit several of our left posts – going on top of ground all the time – which I do not relish, though old "Brandy" is very brave and really enjoys it – we get lost once & mixed up in some wire in "No Mans Land" – a quiet night except for some machine guns occasionally.

Back to Bn H.Q. by 2 a.m., very glad to turn in, but had hardly done so when a volley of enemy shells arrived in our bit of sunken road, so that I got up & took refuge for a time in our funk hole – when all was quiet out I came & again turned in, but exactly the same thing happened, so this time I settled to spend the remander of the night in the "dug-out", and slept solidly till 9 a.m.

Private Thompson – untraced

13th

The chief event of today is the sudden order for the battn to do a "raid". Only received this at 2 p.m. when the C.O. returned from a Brigade Conference. We had a confab of Coy Commanders and it took us all our time to prepare the thing. Brodie was selected to command the raiding party of about 25 strong, including bombers, orderlies, signallers, bayonet men, carriers,

Preparations are made for every detail including the signal of firing 2 volleys from one of our posts to return. The main order is to take prisoners, chiefly this – but subsidiarily to occupy the German line if given up, which is thought possible.

Well, to get on, at 8 p.m. a patrol goes out from our No 8 Post, consisting of 3 people, a N.C.O. & 2 men, with wire cutters etc – who discovered a gap in the German wire in a suitable place. Then at 9.15 p.m. Brodie went out with the same NCO and 2 different men, with a roll of tape – Brodie & one man came back to No 8 post (from the above mentioned gap) unwinding the tape – while the NCO & 1 man waited to watch the gap & if possible improve it.

At 10 p.m. the whole party crawled over the parapet and along the tap[e], lying down outside the gap – at 10.40 our guns put a deliberate bombardment onto the Hun line to make them keep their heads down. At 10.45 this is "lifted", & a "curtain" fire is formed beyond the point of attack. At this hour ("ZERO") also Brodie and his whole party went through the gap the left party (they were divided into Right Left & Centre parties) went off to the left, wandered along a trench which in the inky blackness they thought must be the Hun Line, but eventually it lead round back to our own line – the right party went off to the right; Brodie & his centre party went straight on – & after about 80 yds they saw a German Sentry's head in a "post" – they proceeded to stalk it, when 2 more Huns appeared & joined him, then went away.

Brodie decided to rush the sentry but when it came to the point the mud was too sticky for his party – so he told a man to throw a bomb into the post, where no doubt there were other Huns sleeping; unluckily the bomb did not explode, only awoke the men who threw two bombs back at the party – one of our men then shot the sentry & threw some more bombs – Brodie himself was wounded (in arm) also 4 men, so thinking he only had about 3 whole men left and the alarm being raised – also not knowing whether there were other German posts close by, he decided to withdraw.

This all took much longer than was anticipated, so the volley firing was not of great use.

Meanwhile the right party seem to have wandered round & almost got mixed up in Brodie's show, unknown to eachother, owing to the darkness.

All were back, including the wounded, in our line by 12.30 a.m., but with no prisoner – however they think at least three Germans were killed.

This was all reported to the Brigade, but did not meet with the Brigadier's approval, so at 2.30 a.m. we received a message, telling us to make further attempts – tho' now the moon was right up & the enemy thoroughly on the lookout – & we knew it would be without avail.

However we had to try, so I was sent up with Luss to arrange with Brand, and he went out himself with a Sergt and 4 men, down a sap from our No 10 Post, on the chance of finding a German post, and being able to rush it. This he was unable to do.

244 Miles Barne's Diary

I returned very wet at about 4 a.m.

14th

More rain.

During the day alas! poor old Sherard has to go to Hospital with Shingles – perfectly miserable, & so once more I take over the Battn, with Luss as 2nd in comd._ This turns out to be a very interesting day, as the Germans evacuate their line in front of us, and we take over their places along the western edge of the wood and have patrols out through the wood all night. I have quite a busy time writing orders and making every sort of arrangement for advancing, which seems likely to take place at any time now – a most disturbed evening & night.

15th

My birthday!

During the night our patrols went all over ST. PIERRE VAAST WOOD & reported all clear.

At 10 a.m. the show began, Luss being in command of our two front companies with the Ad Guard. while I remain ignominiously behind with really only two of our Coys in reserve under me as well as one Coy of Grenadiers. A booby trap was reported, but no particulars.

At 12 noon we heard the 1st Gds Bde and the left of our own Bde were hung up – we being on right of the whole Corps, & in touch with the 2nd Battn of W. Yorks on our right – while Luss & his two Coys were getting on fairly well, and said to be "bombing dugouts"._ They reached their "subsidiary objective" at 12.15.

2nd Battalion The West Yorkshire Regiment, 23rd Brigade, 8th Division

It is miserable for old Sherard to have to go just now of all times, even if we go no further for the present – the Doctors say it is likely to be a lengthy business, though we did not tell him this._ During the remainder of the day nothing much happened as the 1st Gds Bde got hung up at SAILLISEL

By the way yesterday the first intimation we had of the Huns going was their heavily shelling their own front line – after which Brand took a solitary walk through the woods! They are very up to time about it all, prisoners having told us they intended clearing the wood by 15th.

Ivan Cobbold has a tempre of 101.6 so we are likely to lose our Bombing and Intelligence Officer.

Visits during the day from every sort of Officer imaginable from General Gathorne-Hardy downwards – the Divn on our right is also moving forward.

Brigadier General The Honourable John Francis Gathorne Hardy, Brigadier General General Staff, XIV Corps

16th

Ivan is better. The Advance is slightly continued. In afternoon I went up & walk all about the wood – most interesting, also all over the place where the raid was – No Mans Land etc etc. a little shelling & m.g. fire, but none very near me. Every sort of souvenir to be found in the wood & in dugouts – all have to be sent in to H.Q.

Bn is relieved by 3rd G.G. in evening 2 Coys returning to PRIEZ, and two remaining in Reserve Line.

March 17th 1917

PRIEZ FARM

There have been a few green plover about lately – otherwise practically one never sees a bird – except odd magpies, rooks, hawks & starlings.

Put in Brand's name for a M.C. after his personal reconnaissance of ST. PIERRE VAAST WOOD – went over in afternoon to see the Brigadier, who made me change it to a D.S.O. – as he said if B. had not gone over we might still be sitting in our old line.

A very exciting day of News, starting with the taking of BAPAUME – then death of the Duchess of Connaught – Abdication of the Czar, & other minor matters.

> The Duchess of Connaught and Strathearn †14.3.17

We also hear that Genl John Ponsonby is coming to take over the 3rd Gds Bde, while Ch Corkran goes home for 3 months. Norman O.-E. is made a Cavalier of the order of Savoy!

18th

Walked up to ST. PIERRE VAAST WOOD with Eric Mackenzie and Brand, and had a further look round – the Grenadiers have buried a large number of the French dead – perhaps more black troops than anything else – lying about.

Unfortunately Brand's old wound (or one of his three) has begun giving him trouble, and he has to go to Hospital. We are getting so short of Officers again for various reasons that I am applying for two to be allowed to return.

The enemy continue to retire and we now are in touch with them at BUS – LE MESNIL – MOISLAINS sort of line. The French have occupied NOYON.

> Captain Brand was first wounded not long before Miles Barne arrived in the 1st Scots Guards in July 1915, again at Loos and again at Sanctuary Wood. He was awarded the MC for his enterprise in exploring the German front line.
>
> In the autumn of 1916 the French had managed to get into St Pierre Vaast Wood, but could not hold it.
>
> Though the German withdrawal was progressing, the north-south line which Miles Barne noted here was still well short of the Hindenburg Line west of Cambrai.

17

Roads, Railways, Courses and Personal Tragedy

19th

Move to COMBLES – into Divisional reserve, being relieved by 4th Grenrs under GILBERT HAMILTON, who by some Staff mistake arrive much too soon, so we have to give them lunch.

After getting into our next billets, go and see the Battn which is quite ½ mile away in tents. Then set to work to make something of our very ramshackle old house, building a place up on top as a mess, and sleeping in the cellar – quite a big job, and a very messy one._

Then I take a solitary walk and look at our old Xmas Day H.Q. between here and LEUZE WOOD, also at an old derelict tank. It is quite a different thing walking about now to then – when one used to scurry about feeling at any time one might have a shell on one's head.

Found some snowdrops, so picked a bunch.

The enemy is still retiring and very few are left at MANANCOURT etc but they are holding NURLU strongly.

A rumour is current that our airmen have seen large bodies retiring behind the HINDENBURG line, as if they were not going to hold it at all.

20th

All four Coys go off on fatigue on the BAPAUME-PERONNE road, so Luss Eric Mackenzie & I go for a long walk first to see all the Sept. 15th ground where we look for Tim's grave & cant find it, also see the scene of the Battn's attack – then go on through LESBOEUFS and LE TRANSLOY, where we eat our lunch, then onto the BAPAUME road, where we get a fine view of the country to the West. Then back to COMBLES via our bit of Decr line: all of the greatest possible interest.

On arrival home Ivan Cobbold rejoins from Hospital – & soon afterwards to everyone's surprise walks in Col. Godman! He is quite cured.

Ivens joined us yesterday. The Doctor – now one Darling a Scotchman – was much distressed about the rats, which ran all over him.

The rumour now is that the Germans are going right back to the MEUSE!

Lieutenant Francis Burdett Ivens
Possibly Lieutenant James Walker Darling, Royal Army Medical Corps

246

21st

Very cold wind from N.E., and light snow showers.

In morning walked with Sherard to the Divl H.Q., still at MAUREPAS, saw Heywood and got some news from him. The 1st Bde is coming out of the line, & then the whole Divn to be employed road making, a nice job for a "Corps d'Elite"!

They dont seem to know what the Germans are at.

Lieutenant Colonel Cecil Percival Heywood, Coldstream Guards, General Staff Officer Grade I, Guards Division

We later met Cavan, our Corps Commander, who told us some news but nothing startling. He says the Germans are probably weakening their line here to collect a big reserve (55 Divns) to attack somewhere, & this must be either to take Calais or Paris. They are sending a biggish force to mee*[t]* Maude at BAGDHAD.

In afternoon I walked first to look at the new Cookhouse being built for our camp, then again to look for – & found – Tim's grave in very good order. I looked all round the famous "Quadrilateral", and BOULEAUX WOOD, which was all very interesting._

Our horrible cellar is crawling with rats – odiously tame, they come & look at us feeding, Luss killed two in the corner today.

22nd

Rode up through FREGICOURT to SAILLISEL with Sherard, and walked on to GOVERNMENT FARM and VAUX WOOD, which was all very peaceful., except for just a few shells bursting in the distance. Saw our 2nd Bn and Welsh Guards at work on the roads, but not our own Battn who were in SAILLY-SAILLISEL – on the main BAPAUME road.

We hear Genl John Ponsonby has returned to take over the Brigade, H. Seymour going to command his own old 3rd Bde. Everyone will be delighted to see J.P. back.

Gouvernement Farm and Vaux Wood were beyond the east side of St Pierre Vaast Wood.

23rd

Presided at a Court Martial on a Coldstream Sergt who malinguered when going up into the trenches. He was a very third rate actor and liar! & made out a very poor case.

Moved to BROMFAY CAMP, riding thither with Finnis.

In afternoon walked with Sherard, & saw old Genl John Ponsonby, who is back as our Brigadier, and looking very fit – in great form.

Then walked round by SUZANNE & the SOMME, found a Frenchman ploughing, which was the first healthy sign of repatriating the conquered territory we had seen.

Eric Mackenzie at last becomes a Captain._

24th

Walked with Sherard to the Brigade HQ early, after a very cold night – a bitter NE wind blowing.

At 2 p.m. the Battn moved to CLERY, about 7 miles – quite a pretty spot up the R.SOMME. We have to pitch our camp ourselves on a perfectly bare slope of hill, facing S., with a good view of the River and the hills round PERONNE.

As soon as possible we start collecting material out of CLERY and neighbouring old gun pits & trenches, for making cookhouses mess huts latrines tailors and shoemakers shops etc etc. Luckily it is fine & dry. We are told we are likely to be here for 2 months making Railways & so on – in fact we hear the new broad guage is to be made from MARICOURT to PERONNE in a week.

Our Staff seems quite mystified by the Hun movements – some say they are stopping in the HINDENBURG line, some that they are going beyond it. Nobody seems to know: we met F. Gathorne-Hardy the "B.G.G.S." of the Corps, who knew no more than anyone else.

In evening Eric & I went to search for the R.E. who are giving us instructions about the fatigues we are to do, but failed to find him, only had a long walk across and by the river. Saw a lot of coots.

Very cold night. We are all in tents, which arrived without any pegs, so the Battn had to set to work to make about 3500 pegs before they could do anything else.

25th

Walked in morning with Sherard & Eric to look at the new Railway site – then Charlie Willoughby who commands the 120th Brigade came to look us up, & we went back to lunch with him – in some dugouts about ¾ mile away.

> Brigadier General The Honourable Charles Strathavon Heathcote Drummond Willoughby, a Scots Guardsman, Commanding 120th Brigade, 40th Division, New Army

Later walked with Sherard to look at the Coots & ducks on the river – a few widgeon & great crested grebes: when he went home I walked on alone – a glorious evening – towards PERONNE, to see where our fatigue parties were working – had a talk to a Canadian Pioneer Officer, who was a CPR Engineer in ordinary life.

> The work on the railway bed and then the track was under a Canadian Railway Construction Company.

Heard a woodpigeon & saw many ducks on the wing – just missed seeing some geese which I heard.

Crossed the river by a new pontoon bridge between HALLE and BAZINCOURT – on which I found the R.E. Officer who had made it – luckily I had admired it before I discovered this. He told me Gerald Sladen was near by._ The former village was quite untouched by shells, although Germans had evidently been living there – just behind their line.

Brigadier General Gerald Carew Sladen, Commanding 143rd Brigade, 48th (South Midland) Division, T.F.

The Camp is now getting quite shipshape, and every sort of odd place has been built. every department being quite fairly comfortably accommodated.

26th

Horrid cold NE showers with sunny intervals.

Walked alone in evening – along river & across bridges – a lot of grey crows feeding by the edge.

We heard a day or two ago of Bobby Abercromby having a nasty accident, he was as usual treasure hunting & got blown up by a bomb – he does not seem bad, but a young Pym, whose brother was lost in the Irish Gds raid last June, was seriously hurt.

Brand & Brodie & Irwin have all gone home.

Lieutenant Claude John Pym, 2nd Irish Guards †26.3.17
Lieutenant Henry Strutt Irwin

There has been an explosion in BAPAUME Town Hall, they say some sort of clockwork fuse left by the Germans_

The Germans had left a concealed delayed action mine, with a chemical fuse, in Bapaume Town Hall, which went off at night on 26 March. Most of the casualties were Australians, as were those of the second mine not far away, but there were very few as most of the Brigade Headquarters had moved on.

27th

Another similar explosion elsewhere, this time catching some Brigade Headquarters.

The C.O. had to go to see the Brigadier, I rode off alone to see Gerald Sladen, said to be in or near PERONNE which town I traversed – it must have been a picturesque old place, with its ramparts and moats & many old buildings – and heard he was in the village of BUSSU about 2 miles further east – so went there & found his Brigade Major interviewing one of the C.O.'s, who said G.S. (the Brigadier) was out fighting, attacking a wood_ The village and his H.Q. were all ruined, but the surrounding country was the most untouched I have seen for some time & quite pretty tho' a horrible day with snow showers. I came home by AIZECOURT (or near it) and MONT ST. QUENTIN, and never saw such wire entanglements as the Germans have put up in this part of the world & all round PERONNE, the trenches themselves are not anything special. I met some heavy guns on my way home, blocking the road near CLERY, and there was a fearful block of traffic, with an irate Brigadier who could not get along_ I was taken for an ASC driver I think by an old Gunner Colonel.

The Battn is getting on famously with its daily fatigue. On getting back to camp I walked down with Eric McK. and Mann to see them & got very wet in a snowstorm, later I walked alone to look at some old trenches, full of every sort of horror.

28th

Wind NW – snow showers. Walked in afternoon with Sherard to PERONNE, meeting 5th
Cav. Divn (which includes many Indians) on their way back – they cannot do much good now
– while the enemy is more or less stationary. Rumours that the French have got through the
Hindenburg Line between LA FÈRE and ST. QUENTIN

29th

Walked along river in evening with Sherard & got very wet. Cold heavy showers from S.W.
  Brand has got a Military Cross, which he richly deserves.
  My name is sent in to attend the Telescopic Sight School Course (sniping) on Apr – 1st, at
PONT NOYELLES near AMIENS.

Friday March 29th *[30th]* 1917. CLERY

Walked down twice to look at our Railway progress – it is a difficult job on marshy ground,
hundreds of shell holes have to be filled in with bricks & rubble from the battered village.
  Barton joined us (age 36 but looks like 63) with a draft including Coy Sgt Maj Penman. He
is said to be Ld Methuen's Agent.
  Cold & showery.

  Lieutenant Walter Lindsay Barton
  7884 Company Sergeant Major George Penman, later 2nd Lieutenant The King's Own
    Scottish Borderers

31st

The Railway bed is practically ready before the sleepers and rails have arrived, so the Battn gets
a day off._
  In afternoon Sherard & I walk round by HALLE and along the Canal – he is much perturbed
by hearing he is to report at Army H.Q. tomorrow, besides hearing that his name has been sent
in as Instructor in a C.O.'s School at Aldershot. Everyone admires him for having given up a
home job for the sake of getting out here last year, & nobody could ever say he had not "done his
bit", but he himself is miserable at the idea of having to go home – if he has to – and of course it
is very trying being told he is too old for a Brigadier, and seeing so many mere boys posted over
his head. Of course really he is too old in many ways to command a Battn, but still he does it
very well, and most of us like him enormously.
  I am to go to the School of Telescopic Sights for a week tom'w so ride in for the night to
BROMFAY, getting a ducking in a very heavy shower of sleet & rain on the way, dine with
Cecil Trafford, playing dominoes with him and Kinlay afterwards: our "2nd Line" and some of
"1st Line" still *[blank]*

April 1st

Sherard called for me with servant (Hunter) and luggage at 10 a.m., as he had to report at
A.H.Q., dropping Hunter & luggage at PONT NOYELLE en route. We found after some
trouble Genl Holman, the Head "Q" man on the 4th Army (Rawlinson's) Staff – who told

Sherard to go on leave and try & get a job in England, which he settled to do. Saw young Paul Methuen, ADC to Gen Rawlinson, who asked me to dinner.

> Major General Herbert Campbell Holman, Deputy Adjutant & Quartermaster General,
>   Fourth Army
> Lieutenant The Honourable Paul Ayshford Methuen, Sniping Officer 1st Scots Guards
>   the previous winter

Went on to AMIENS, lunched with S. and C. Trafford at the Godbert Restt, walked about, into Cathedral etc, and left again to report at the School where they dropped me at 5 p.m._ Major Roddick in command – a <u>very</u> Scotch old fellow.

> Major William Riddoch, The Gordon Highlanders

Dined at Army H.Q. which was decidedly alarming – others present besides the Army Commander being Generals Montgomery, Budworth, Buckland, Whigham, Holman, also Boscawen, Paget, & Paul Methuen._ I sat between the latter & Genl Budworth, and gleaned all sorts of scraps of very interesting information on various points of the war.

> Major General Archibald Armar Montgomery, Major General General Staff, whom
>   Miles Barne first came across at Headquarters IV Corps on 25 September 1915, the
>   opening day of Loos.
> Major General Charles Edward Dutton Budworth, Major General Royal Artillery
> Major General Reginald Ulick Henry Buckland, Chief Engineer, whom Miles Barne had
>   also first met on 25 September 1915
> Probably Brigadier General Robert Dundas Whigham
> Probably Captain Evelyn Hugh John Boscawen, Coldstream Guards
> Possibly Lieutenant Francis Edward Howard Paget, Grenadier Guards

I gather that the French are shortly to push in Champagne while our 1st Army does so at SOUCHY. Gen Joffre had settled to go on pushing on the Somme which was the reason for the Germans building their Hindenburg line and now Gen Nivelle has altered everything.

> General Joffre was dismissed in December 1916 and replaced by General Robert
> Nivelle, who claimed to have the perfect plan. On the strength of this he prepared
> the operations later known as the Nivelle Offensive in Champagne (there were other
> French attacks), while the British made plans for the Battle of Arras. The main stategic
> purpose was to squeeze out the German salient with Noyon at its westerly point, but
> that was negated by the German withdrawal to the Hindenburg Line. The reference to
> Souchez was the assault on Vimy Ridge, principally by the Canadians.

Haig & Rawlinson had a difference of opinion last October, the former wanted us to advance, & take the Bapaume Ridge which R. refused to do, because the roads were impassable, therefore Sutton was sent home as a scapegoat – far too much of a gentleman to object or say anything.

Paul said he was a great loss & Buckland (RE) ought to have gone instead. He (Buckland) was no hustler, had bad health & was actually in bed the first 2 days of our advance 3 weeks ago!

> Major General Hugh Clement Sutton was dismissed in November and succeeded as Deputy Adjutant & Quartermaster General by Major General Holman.

I was taken to see the Offices including the map room with several confidential maps, maps of the German "Order of Battle" showing the troops and Armies & Groups of Armies opposite to us with their Comdrs, map of the Hindenburg Line, and of all that is happening now.

I heard all the woes of the A.D.C. concerning the lack of responsibility given to the junior Staff Officers, who are sent to report on bits of the line, which they do very carefully & at end all they are asked is "if they had a good time" while their report is barely read – this sort of thing being the cause of GHQ being taken by surprise when the Germans retired. Smyth who shewed us the maps was sent to Switzerland about Xmas time to interview refugees etc, and came back assuring Rawlinson that this retirement would take place in Feb or March, to which R. replied "Oh no, they wont retire."_

Of course I was looked on as mere dirt (except by P.M.), being the only non Staff Officer present, and no doubt correctly so, but this did not worry me.

> Smyth – untraced

Was given quite a decent billet in the village of PONT NOYELLE

2nd

The work begins at 9 a.m. and goes on most of the day till 7 or 7.15 – either lectures or firing on the ranges.

The Commandant is a quaint old Scotty – Major Riddoch – fearful accent – the other instructors being Captains Gould Bates & Willey, the Adjt is 2/Lt. Criswick, an old bird who was formerly in the London Scottish, and the others above mentioned are said to be well known rifle shots._

The Officers attending the Course are not exciting to look at, but one or two seem to improve on acquaintance. The only one with any pretensions whatever to be a "gentleman" is the surliest creature I have ever struck – I sat next him at dinner – but could make nothing of him.

I am the only Officer above the rank of Lieut, and there is only one of them, Burton H.L.I.

Weather odious – samples of everything, finishing with a snowstorm which makes the whole country white again. It is not bad sort of country just round here and in this valley – plenty of woods (of sorts) and no shell holes._

> Captain Gould – untraced
> Captain Bates – untraced
> Captain Willey – untraced
> Probably 2nd Lieutenant Bernard Cecil Criswick, The London Regiment, T.F.
> Possibly 2nd Lieutenant John Lees Burton, 9th Battalion The Highland Light Infantry
>   †27.4.17

3rd

No event of importance occurred, but I dined again at Army H.Q. and heard a good deal more of interest. There is to be a big demonstration against the Hindenburg line on 7th, when I understand the French are attacking ST. QUENTIN. In places we are already right up to the Hindg Line and have taken six guns – deserted by the enemy.

Paul was quite interesting & I rather think pleased to see anyone from the Regt and not of the Staff – he was extremely affable & has asked me to dine again on Friday when Gen Smuts is to be there.

Lieutenant General Jan Christiaan Smuts

He showed me a wonderful document about Rasputin, the Russian Monk who held such influence over the Court & was murdered, a regular tool of the Germans, and a reprobate of the deepest dye. The account of him was beyond repetition – but beyond this the document gave some wonderful statements and was written by a very wellknown & good authority. Amongst other things it said or implied that most of the Rumanians were purposely captured & fighting for the Germans: also that the Russian Army was out to beat the Germans, but the Royal Dynasty was likely to get back their own. There appear to be wheels within wheels in Russia and one may be pretty sure that what is on the surface is unreal.

Miles Barne will have recorded accurately what he saw and heard, no matter how improbable.

Then he shewed me notes of information given by Sir Henry Wilson who went to see Gen Rawlinson after he (H.W.) had returned from Russia – extracts as follows: the Big Russian Retreat 1915 was a huge disaster, they lost 2000000 killed 2000000 prisoners & 4000000 casualties. & remainder returned with 1 rifle per 4 men.

In May 1915 the Germans and Austro-Hungarians attacked the Russians in Galicia in the Gorlice-Tarnow Offensive. This developed into much more, leading to the Russians being driven back and then withdrawing several hundred miles, far away from the eastern borders of Germany and the Austro-Hungarian Empire. Russian losses, though very severe, were not as high as these figures.

In the advance on KOVEL last year the Russians simply walked over with no Artillery Preparation, killed 25000 Germans or Austrians, whose line was so thin that it took a fortnight to reinforce.

This was part of the the Brusilov Offensive.

Japan has been of no use to the Allies whatsoever.

There are 194000 tons of stuff waiting at VLADIVOSTOCK to be transported to Russia. The Army is now very good but short of big guns – there are 52 Divisions of Cossacks, beautifully mounted, horses in splendid condition, with 15lbs of oats per diem.

In the Revolution in Feby the Royal Guards killed their German Officers and made their own NCO's officers & appealed to Knox to put them in order which he did.

Brigadier General Alfred William Fortescue Knox, British Military Attache, Petrograd, played no active role following the Revolution.

When the Cossacks invaded E. Prussia early in the war they committed such excesses that those caught by the Germans had the skin of their legs flayed & sewn onto their trousers to make a red stripe down their legs!

The Russians are very short of Aeroplanes, only 3 a week being turned out at MOSCOW.

To return to the former document, English prestige has dwindled to a very low ebb in Russia, our diplomacy having completely failed.

There was a variety of all sorts of weathers today – I was woken up in the night by snow on my face caused by the draft made between my open window & the door which was left open by an Ordnance Officer who has to go through my room to get at his own, next morning I explained to him the necessity of closing the door, rather strongly, whereupon he unarmed me by inviting me to dinner!

4th

More snow, but mild later with glorious sunset – am rather relieved by Major Riddoch telling me that "Majors dont do examinations!"

Lectures most of the day, only a short visit to the Ranges.

5th

Mild & springlike.

Some rather good "spotting" practice, khaki targets hidden in a wood etc, camouflaged men & so on. I find I am holding my own shooting, & was top score but one at above practice, & made a "possible" yesterday at running man.

Good Friday. April 6th 1917

PONT NOYELLE. SNIPING SCHOOL.

Walked yesterday evening alone up the river – saw some teal, coots etc., after which dined with Major Riddoch & Staff of School Instructors – & ate some of my own plum pudding which V. had sent me, too small for our big School Mess. how old R. smacked his lips over it, & the brandy butter, of which he had never even heard. He is a real old Scot – keeping his red wine bottle corked up with a wonderful sort of padlock arrangement, a most ingenious device.

Some kind of tantalus

This Friday evening I dined again at Army H.Q., sat next Genl Montgomery, who was most affable. When he came into dinner he announced that the first train would not enter PERONNE for 10 days, owing to want of ballast. this greatly enraged Rawlinson who immediately ordered his C.R.E. (Buckland) to look into the matter_

There was a good deal of chatter, & after dinner I went with Paul into the Map Room to hear the news, when some other Staff Officers saw me & pretended they did not know me to be a friend of Paul's, & began to ask Paul questions about me – he says there is so much petty business of this sort on the Staff, which sickens him of it.

General Smuts was not present.

My Ordnance Officer neighbour is one Baber of the Inner Temple.

Lieutenant Frank Herbert John Baber, Army Ordnance Corps

7th

More lectures and some final work on the range. Walked & worked out the exam problems in afternoon; tea with Major Riddoch & Co the school having closed, the mess was also empty – about 7 p.m. I was called for by a Gds Divl Motor Car, in which B. Dykes was returning from AMIENS, and eventually got back to the Battn, still at CLERY about 10.15 p.m., after various adventures, spring breaking etc – doing the last part, first in a lorry, & then in an Ambulance Car. Take over the Battn.

Captain Frecheville Hubert Ballantyne Dykes, Scots Guards, Deputy Assistant Adjutant
General, Guards Division

Easter Day Apr. 8th

Started at 7.30 a.m. with 6 other Officers & 25 Sergts to see some "Contact" Aeroplane work near MORLANCOURT: had fracas en route with a XV Corps Staff Lieut. Col. with very bad & offensive manners, who made us turn round & go the other way – there being practically no room to turn.

In evening I walked over to see C. Willoughby, where I found Jack Stirling and Douglas Gordon, who commands the Welsh Guards.

An interesting point about the visit to Aerodrome this morning was that the Officer who shewed us round was the same one who was flying over us during our Advance through ST. PIERRE VAAST WOOD on March 15th, and described our formation etc.

9th

An eventful day, tho' perhaps not for us, being the opening of the LENS-ARRAS offensive: we could of course hear the guns & knew something big was going on, though did not know what. It has all been kept very dark, and altho' we knew the 3rd and 1st Armies were going to push, had no idea it was to be so soon._

In afternoon walked with Luss to see the Battn doing its Railway Fatigue near PERONNE, and walked through the town to the Railway Station.

Dined with Norman O-E at 2nd Bn. H.Q., others present being Jack Stirling and C. Willoughby, a very pleasant party.

10th

News from North very good, the advance being on a front of 22,000ˣ to a depth of 3,500ˣ, 40 to 50 guns being taken and over 10000 prisoners._

Rode with Luss this morning and inspected Battn Transport, some of the horses getting very thin owing to shortage of oats & hay, continuous hard work, and exposure during December._

Went to Brigade H.Q., but all away except H. Dundas. Eric Greer is commanding the Brigade, J. Ponsonby the Division during Feilding's absence on leave.

Lieutenant Colonel Eric Beresford Greer, Commanding 2nd Irish Guards †31.7.17

Made some further plans for getting the camp comfortable, including washhouses, Sergts Mess & Ovens._

In evening walked over to Divl H.Q. at MAUREPAS with Luss, to ask for more tents – passed several very nasty old German trenches full of every sort of horror, which pleased Luss much. There must have been a fearful amount of fighting in the near neighbourhood of our camp last July.

11th

The news continues good, the Hindenburg Line has been broken through by the 5th Army, very many prisoners (11000) taken also 103 guns 170 machine guns and 60 trench mortars.

Walked in morning, to see our fatigue at work, with Ivan Cobbold and F. Mann.

Am to do another course: this time a Senior Officers' Course at FLIXECOURT, which is W. of AMIENS, on main line to BOULOGNE.

During day the following Officers joined us – Gordon-Ives, Duncan, Lloyd and Bradshaw.

Captain Cecil Maynard Gordon Gordon Ives was evacuated seriously ill with
    gastroenteritis from the Aisne in October 1914
Lieutenant Basil William Duncan
Lieutenant Ernest Alfred Collyer Lloyd †31.7.17
Lieutenant William Patrick Arthur Bradshaw was evacuated with conjunctivitis in June
    1916

Heavy snowstorm at night, the "advance" must be very unpleasant with the present weather conditions.

12th

Two Companies go back to BOMFRAY to get baths.

Luss and I walked over to GUILLEMONT and GINCHY to put up a cross on Mark Tennants grave. Get drenched through in the heaviest snow shower & sleet & rain I ever saw._

We seem to have been hustled back through the Hindenburg Line, the old story of trying to get on too far, no doubt. But have taken 34 more guns, making 147 in all!

Panama joins in with us & United States, & other Allies – next may come Brazil.

13th

Fine day, little wind, the first anything like spring.

Walked with Luss in morning to see the Battn on fatigue – the Railway is practically complete now, and trains running as far as PERONNE Railway Station.

In afternoon Eric McK & I rode through PERONNE to see the 2nd Battn at CARTIGNY: called on the way at a Brigade H.Q., and found it was Gerald Sladen's, so he came along with us, and we had tea with Norman & Co, who were however rather at six's & sevens, having only arrived the previous night in a snowstorm, and were in the middle of the making of their camp._

In evening the whole Battn witnessed the distressing episode of a Hun Aeroplane bringing down 2 of our Kite Balloons. These were an immense height up, and we only remarked just previously what a good chance they wd be for any enemy_ I am told they dont have Lewis Guns up with them, but can hardly believe it possible.

Heard some geese during the night flying past.

14th

Visit from Genl John Ponsonby, now temporarily commanding the Division.

Smith-Cunningham returns from Hospital, Eric and Cecil Trafford go off to Paris. & I to BOMFRAY FARM for the night on my way to my course.

Hear that LENS is being given up by the Huns – untrue_

Had a tête-à-tête dinner with Kinlay, after which played dominoes with him & beat him by very good luck. He – like so many Quartermasters – is quite a professor at the game.

15th

Was picked up in a motor car at 10 a.m. by Col de Crespigny cmdg 2nd Grenrs instead of by Col Follett as I expected, the latter being unable to attend – de C. apparently much bored by having to come.

Luncheon at the Rhin Hotel, where was joined by the Guards Divisional C.R.E., Col. Brough, also coming to FLIXECOURT, which we reached in torrents of rain about 4 p.m., the school being in a huge modern chateau, belonging to a big jute manufacturer, whose works are close by.

There are few of the C.O.s whom I have ever seen before, but was interested to find a Col. Balfour, of Wissett amongst them, now cmdg 2/5 Gloucester Regt.

The village itself is a large one, being peopled by the workers – of both sexes and all ages – at the Jute Manufactory, & now filled to overflowing by the various Officers & other ranks from the school.

My billet is an excellent clean one, though 15 min walk from the school, really rather an advantage, as one does not get much exercise otherwise.

> Lieutenant Colonel Alan Brough, Commander Royal Engineers, Guards Division
> Lieutenant Colonel Percy Balfour, The Bedfordshire Regiment, †12.12.17, Commanding
>   2/5th Battalion The Gloucestershire Regiment, 184th Brigade, 61st (2nd South
>   Midland) Division, T.F.

16th

Lecture on Physical Training early from Col White, watched the huge Officers' and N.C.O.'s class parading, then doing some engineering & physical drill.

After luncheon a lecture on sniping on the range from a very tiresome & conceited & facetious man.

To my surprise I found my old friend of PONT NOYELLE, Major Riddoch & his Adjutant at luncheon, having come over to arrange as to moving his school to this neighbourhood.

Lecture from Captain Snell of the Army Staff on Air photographs with Magic Lantern.

Also toured round in motor charabancs to see billets & messes etc in connection with the school, of which they are evidently very proud – and certainly everything appeared to be very well run.

We live in the most civilized way here, even having a string band playing during dinner.

> Col White – untraced
> Possibly Captain I.E. Snell, The Black Watch

17th

Fine morning but rain the rest of day from N.W., some snow.

First of all a lecture on R.E. work from Col. Brough the C.R.E. of Guards Division.

Then a lecture on the new attack formations by Major Wray, Chief Instructor at The School. Next a lecture on Court Martials from Col Wroughton of G.H.Q.; then a demonstration of the new attack, and lastly a very good lecture on the Battle of the Somme by Col. Luckock on Gen Rawlinson's Staff, when he gave us some startling facts & figures as regards Telephone Wire, Water pipes, Ammunition, shelling and so on: all the time he took care to rub in what a splendid General Rawlinson was (or is). He also made a great point, (rather to my surprise as he is a liner), of the attack of the Guards Divn on Sept. 15th, – in fact he dwelt so long on this that I felt almost confused though intensely proud! He looked on it apparently as the finest thing of the whole battle, even making allowances for our superior chances of training and discipline – speaking in the most eloquent & extravagant terms about it all.

After each of the lectures (except the last) criticisms and questions are invited, so a sort of "debating society" takes place.

The French seem to have started quite a good Offensive, taking 10000 prisoners near RHEIMS: we have almost got LENS, while our total is 14000 prisoners and 190 guns!

I seem to be making friends with one Major Harvey of the Gds Divl Arty, whom I knew slightly previously – & was at Eton with his brother, a Highlander, who was killed in Mesopotamia.

> Major Robert Amyatt Ray, The King's Own Royal Regiment
> Colonel John Bartholomew Wroughton, Adjutant General's Department, General
>   Headquarters
> Lieutenant Colonel Russell Mortimer Luckock, The King's Own Royal Regiment
> Major Cosmo George St Clair Harvey, Battery Commander A Battery, 74th Brigade,
>   Royal Field Artillery
> Brigadier General William James St John Harvey, Commanding Dehra Dun Brigade, 7th
>   (Meerut) Division †1.2.16

April 18th 1917. Wednesday

At FLIXECOURT 4th Army Infantry Training School.

By the way, I believe now the XIV Corps, now only consisting of Guards and 1st Divisions, is in "G.H.Q. (Genl Head Quarters) Reserve". Since last August we have been in the 4th Army under Sir Henry Rawlinson, Cavan commands the XIV Corps, & Feilding the Guards Division.

Horne commands the 1st Army, Plumer 2nd, Allenby 3rd, and Gough 5th._

> General Sir Henry Sinclair Horne
> General Sir Herbert Charles Onslow Plumer
> General Sir Edmund Henry Hynman Allenby
> General Sir Hubert de la Poer Gough

Today we started at 9.15 a.m. by motor bus to ABBEVILLE, in pouring rain.

First had a lecture from DDT, or Deputy Director of Transport, a capable looking though bored man, one of the ugliest I have ever seen, he fixed me with one eye all through his lecture, the other wandered about the room. Red hair. He explained some of the difficulties he had to contend with: 21000 lorries, 9000 motor cars, & 5000 bicycles – 36 different makes of lorries, each with 3000 "parts".

Then we were taken all round the Horse & Mule & Waggon etc yards – most of the horses are there to recover, they were worn out & half starved, but most recover in a month, they only want food & rest. Then to the Motor Transport Office & spare part Depot, which was in a big jute factory, part of which was being worked, so we had a look round that too.

We then had a hearty lunch at the Club, a very well run establishment, full of Officers beautifully turned out, goodness only knows what they were all doing there, then re-embarked in our lorry & back to the School, to hear a lecture by Gen Budworth, CRA 4th Army, whom I had met recently at QUERRIEU. He told me he had seen me riding near PERONNE, the day I went in to see 2nd Battn, so he must be a lively man, to notice & remember such small details.

He gave an excellent lecture but could not tell us much of the French Attack, except that they were rather in a muddle blocking their roads with Guns etc., not having a proper programme, he said.

After dinner, quite a good concert by one of "Miss Lena Ashwell's Concert Party".

> Lena Ashwell organised a number of concert parties in small groups to entertain the troops on the Western Front, a project she initiated in 1915.

19th "Primrose Day"_

First of all a lecture by Col. Fitzmaurice, cmdg a Brigade of Artillery, also doing this Course, on Co-operation between Artillery and Infantry.

The[n] came the Army Commander to give us a lecture on things in general, told us something of the French Attack, now they have taken 18000 prisoners. The Germans have started counter-attacking very quickly and immediately after the French have taken their trenches, Genl Rawlinson considers this a very good sign._

Next we all went out to see a new rapid wiring drill, which was nothing very new.

After luncheon we went off in our old motor buses to do a tactical scheme – the Army Commander and Genl Montgomery took 12 of us, & Genl Gathorne-Hardy the other half – I was in the latter lot. It was quite instructive. Weather much warmer.

Later a lecture by a Col. Clarke on Machine Guns, which was rather long and dreary. The weather has turned warmer if not dryer.

> Lieutenant Colonel Robert Fitzmaurice, Commanding 168th Brigade, Royal Field
>   Artillery
> Lieutenant Colonel Reginald Graham Clarke, Machine Gun Officer, XV Corps

20th

Lecture by Gen Gathorne Hardy on "Orders": when he made us all write some Battn Orders for an attack.

After lunch we joy-rode off to VAUX-EN-AMIENOIS, to see the 4th Army Trench Mortar School, run by a Col. Plummer with a wooden leg – saw some pretty work with these things – of all three sorts, "Stokes", 2 inch, and heavy (160 lbs).

> Lieutenant Colonel Edmund Walter Plummer, Royal Field Artillery

Dined afterwards with Harvey R.F.A. at Restt Des Huitres in AMIENS, where were much amused by the antics and energy of the landlady who ran the place.

Back in our lorry to FLIXECOURT by 11 p.m.

Amongst the instructors at the TM School, I found a young Fison of the Suffolk Regt.

> Lieutenant Francis Guy Clavering Fison, The Suffolk Regiment

21st

Another day out, and this time a long one, to visit a French Training camp at VIEUX ROUEN. We drove on the way right through the country where we were billeted last October – WARLUS etc.

Were conducted round by a funny old General [blank] and his English speaking Staff Officer. Had lunch at LIOMER in a café.

We first were shewn individually their 37 mm gun, mitrailleuse, rifle grenades and automatic rifle; then a regular show was performed for our benefit – an attack by two companies, which was a very good and well displayed pantomime, which I would not have missed for anything – with real bullets bombs & 37 mm shells – in fact everything except their Artillery barrage and of course no enemy!

Then we went off to see a less real show, consisting of a company doing an attack & digging in, and next a Battalion doing an attack through a wood.

All was very well "stage-managed" and much trouble taken – luckily a fine though cloudy day – home by 8.p.m.

22nd

An especially fine & sunny day, though cold wind.

Started 9.30, bussed to PONT REMY to see the 4th Army Musketry Camp, run by Col Chichester, with a wooden leg – late Worcester Regt.

He lost his leg at MONS, and was a prisoner in Germany for a year, but later was exchanged.

Lieutenant Colonel Walter Raleigh Chichester, The Worcestershire Regiment

The camp was not apparently very well run, and shewed slackness.

Entrained at 2 p.m., after a light lunch, which we had brought with us, for ETAPLES which we reached at 4 p.m. and drove to the civilized & luxurious Hotel Continental at PARIS PLAGE.

Trained back to ETAPLES for tea and walked out again to PP with Harvey and Warner, two gunners.

Warner, Royal Artillery – untraced

Weather perfect. Our hotel is close to the beach, & I have a fine view of the sea from my bed!

23rd

Drove in morning to inspect a Base Training Camp at ETAPLES, where there was nothing very wonderful to see, though the training was all pretty thorough, including day and night trench life, or the nearest they can get to it without being shot at.

After lunch went to see the Lewis Gun School on LE TOUQUET Golf Links.

Then walked with Harvey, hair cut wrote letters etc.

24th

To visit a Base Detail Camp, which was not amusing at ETAPLES, then walked out alone to PP by the river wall, another lovely day – the third running – brilliant sun, but cold North wind._ Heard the 3rd and 1st & 5th Armies began another push yesterday, taking over 2000 prisoners and a good deal of ground.

Battle of Arras: The Second Battle of the Scarpe

Entrained at 3 p.m. ETAPLES, arrived at school at 7.30 p.m., after a pretty journey up the Somme which is getting very full, the weather quite perfect – brilliant sun – on arrival at FLIXECOURT received two telegrams telling me of my dear young brother Seymour having been killed while flying, being shot down by a German Aeroplane near HENINEL, yesterday (23rd) morning – a bitter blow, but not altogether unexpected – a fine example to many others, having given up a soft job on the Staff for a particularly dangerous one – eventually losing his life.

Captain Seymour Barne, The 20th Hussars and No. 35 Squadron Royal Flying Corps
†23.4.17

25th

Heard dear old Seymour was to be buried at 10.30 a.m. at AUBIGNY, but quite impossible for me to get so far.

Quite an interesting conference attended by Staff representatives from GHQ., 4th Army & various Corps etc., and many important questions thrashed out. I brought up the subject of vegetables for the troops being grown in the devastated back areas, but could not get much satisfaction, being told that seeds would be supplied to "Units" – which is no use at all, as "Units" are constantly moving.

Came back in a XIV Corps car with 2 of their Staff – tea at their HQ where met only two generals, *[blank]*, the C.R.A., and Burnett-Hitchcock the chief "Q" man of the Corps. They sent me to find the Battn at CLERY, where I found the 2nd Bn Irish Gds, just arrived – the Battn having marched to ROCQUIGNY, where I found them after a long drive – through the wilderness, hardly meeting a soul! on a very bumpy road. This got worse and worse to the extent that I had to keep telling my driver to slow down for fear of breaking the springs: as happened on 7th, this he practically refused to do till I threatened to report him, which brought him to.

> Brigadier General Alexander Ernest Wardrop, Commander Royal Artillery, XIV Corps
> Brigadier General Basil Ferguson Burnett Hitchcock, Deputy Adjutant and
>   Quartermaster General, XIV Corps

26th

Inspected camp in the morning.

Received letters from Seymour's late General (Pitman), also one from his servant Bigden, who was evidently much upset at losing him, and from a great friend of his, Norrie, who actually saw the accident occur, not knowing who it was.

> 5574 Private A Bigden, The 20th Hussars, wrote letters both to Miles Barne and to
>   Violet Barne on 24 April 1917.
> Captain Charles Willoughby Moke Norrie, The 11th Hussars, wrote to Miles Barne on
>   24 April 1917 and described what he saw, including going over to the crash site an
>   hour later and immediately seeing the body of his friend. It was he who sent one of
>   the telegrams that Miles Barne received when he returned to Flixecourt.

> No. 35 Squadron Royal Flying Corps, working with the Cavalry Corps, were equipped
> with the two seater Armstrong Whitworth F.K.8, which, though suitable for
> reconnaissance and observation, was no match for the fast German fighter aircraft
> which dominated the skies early in 1917, distinctively in April.

Apparently he was flying in one of our slow machines, when a fast German scout appeared from behind a cloud and swooped down onto him firing – Seymour seems to have got his Lewis gun into action, but his pilot was shot through the head and knee – at first they seemed to be coming down properly, but when about 800 ft up, suddenly she nose dived, crashing to the ground, a fearful predicament to be in, & one wonders how much they realize at the time – of course when once they reach earth, death is instantaneous.

2nd Lieutenant Frederick Henry Reynell, No. 35 Squadron Royal Flying Corps †23.4.17

In afternoon walked with Luss to see Torquil Matheson now commanding 20th Division. at YTRES, about 3 miles off – we then walked to see the exit of the Canal from the tunnel – blown up by Boches, and saw some bridges they had destroyed. We are now well behind the old German line near LE TRANSLOY, in one of the many villages we used to look at from Battn Headquarters O.P. (Observation Post) in December last._

The Battn is working on the Railway Line._

Quite a serious thing has occurred, namely Luss is going off to command the 2/4th Leicesters, Territorial Battalion – a sad loss for this Battalion, though one cannot blame him for wanting to go: he deserves something better than being a Company Commander still.

Shortt & Hugh Ross both return.

2/4th Battalion, T.F., The Leicestershire Regiment, 177th Brigade, 59th (2nd North
    Midland) Division, T.F.
Captain Hugh Ross returned after wounds and shell shock in September 1916.

27th

A fine day, after a very noisy & disturbed night, a continuous Artillery barrage apparently along 5th Army front – North of us – going on all night – until 5 a.m. when most of it suddenly ceased.

Started early with Hugh Ross Eric McK & 4 Coy Commanders to attend a lecture on Coy Training by Col. Heywood at our old camp at CLERY.

It was 20 miles to ride, there & back; we went by COMBLES, returned by HALAINE, MANANCOURT and LE MESNIL, getting to our camp at ROCQUIGNY at about 3.30 p.m., ready for lunch.

Later the Officers were beaten by the servants at football, after which I walked with Barton.

Luss has to go at once to take over his Territorial Battn.

Head dined with us – a cheerful "farewell" dinner party for Luss.

A great bombardment during day and night too away to the North – can hear no news._

Saturday April 28th 1917

ROCQUIGNY. Inspected camp again in the morning and found it quite spotlessly clean & kits marvellously tidy – especially R.F. and B. Coys.

During the afternoon Luss left to take up his new job – and leaves a gap in the Battn which will be hard to fill. I rode with him previously to look at the Battn on fatigue – he was given a good send-off, the men turning out en bloc and cheered spontaneously.

Walked by myself in evening._

29th

Hugh Ross went to attend a conference on a boxing show being arranged by the Division._ I got all the Officers together and we had a talk about "training" for the open warfare which Col. Heywood promised us in 6 weeks, tho' I cant make out what he was talking about!

In afternoon I rode with Bradshaw & Smith-Cunningham the latter on my Geraldine, & I rode the old B. Coy Chestnut who blundered while jumping an old German trench, putting me down, but one leg stuck in the stirrup, nearly a nasty accident, for she stood on the ground by the trench when she got up with me dangling while my head was somewhere near the bottom of the trench, like a hare in a game larder, as F. Mann put it! Luckily I had hold of the reins, so she could not kick me even if she wanted to. I found I was able to get free by kicking the stirrup, in which my foot was stuck, with the other foot.

We went to look at both ends of the Canal tunnel, also HAVRINCOURT WOOD, and the old German Ammunition Train near YTRES which one of our gallant airmen set on fire – a complete wreck & only a few bits of twisted metal left for each truck!

Rode through RUYAULCOURT and saw several other villages including HERMIES. Saw a Cemetery nicely filled with Hun Graves near *[blank]*

Tried to attend a voluntary service in evening, but Head was so late turning up, that I did not wait.

Hugh heard that Luss' motor car broke down yesterday, & he never reached his Battalion – & lost his kit somehow! a bad start, but would not worry him at all._

The Bde HQ is moving up to LE MESNIL where the 3rd Grenrs are, the 1st Coldm & 2nd Irish Gds are moving to LES BOEUFS and LE TRANSLOY.

> The unfinished Canal du Nord went into a tunnel near Havrincourt Wood in the north and came out near Ytres at the southern end.

30th

Walked in morning with Hugh Ross and Eric McK. to see Battn fatigues – and over to LE MESNIL to see Grenadiers, found Col Thorne trying to blow up barbed wire entanglements with German bomb

In evening went over there again to hear Col Luckock lecture again on the Battle of the Somme – word for word the same as at FLIXECOURT, but glad all the same to hear it again. Very good lecture – best I've ever heard.

May 1st

Inspected our Battn Transport in morning, & also saw Rifle Bombers, Snipers, and Pipers at Musketry – which I thought a good plan. as they also servants cooks drummers etc etc are apt to get rusty.

Lecture in evening at 3rd Grenrs H.Q., LE MESNIL on Intelligence, by Col. Vivian, on 4th Army Staff – himself a Grenadier.

> Lieutenant Colonel Valentine Vivian, Grenadier Guards, General Staff (Intelligence), Fourth Army

2nd

Rode with Hugh Ross in forenoon to see our Companies on fatigue near ETRICOURT. Perfect weather.

In afternoon the Battalion beat 3rd Grens at football, and later our Officers beat the Officers of 1st Coldm, 2:1. I played outside right.

<u>3rd</u>

A very interesting little Attack & Signalling Scheme with 3rd Grens, in "skeleton", using some very useful old German trenches, near by._

After luncheon I walked over to see their C.O. (Thorne) and then walked down to see the men on fatigue – we have the whole Battalion on all day – 2 Coys at a time – the only people excused being those who are doing some "Specialist" work, such as Bombing, Sniping, Lewis Guns, Signalling etc.

About 5 p.m. suddenly Col Romilly arrived – to take over the Batt – a great surprise to us all, as we had no idea he was leaving England yet_

Walked over to the Brigade with him, where we met Jack Stirling & others from the 2nd Bn, who have now moved to NURLU to build an aerodrome.

> Lieutenant Colonel Bertram Henry Samuel Romilly, nicknamed "Romeo", was very severely wounded in the head by a shell at the Battle of Neuve Chapelle in March 1915.

Apparently there is some move on to get rid of me, as they suggest I should change places with Flossy Romer, now the Regimental Adjutant! Never heard such an idea, and I dont think I could possibly go home in these days._ I told the Brigadier I would put myself entirely in his hands & he could do what he thought best._ Romeo also was very nice about it, and wanted me to realize he didn't want me to go – nor did the Brigr and Flossy was loath to oust me, but still was anxious to come out._ The Brigr said I could have a new Army Battn for the asking.

Time will show.

> Major Malcolm Romer, nicknamed "Flossie", now Regimental Adjutant Scots Guards, was unfit because of rheumatism to come out in August 1914 and had so far been only briefly in the BEF later in 1914 before being sent home sick.

Exciting news came during dinner to say the 5th Army had taken part of the Hindenburg Line and Support Trenches, which was the heavy firing we heard early this morning._

> Battle of Arras: Third Battle of the Scarpe and Battle of Bullecourt

I apply for and obtain leave for Paris 12th – 15th, and so send a wire to Violet_

Just as we are going to bed we hear Strombos Horns going in every direction, the "Gas" Alarm. so everybody has to get hold of their Box Respirators – the only person not having them being Romeo, who however has an old "PB" helmet, which he has never learned to put on!

<u>4th</u>

We are now having daily splendid hot weather.

The new C.O. goes round Camp which is quite spotless.

A good deal more ground has been taken up North, including a bit of the Hindenburg Line.

Ride with Romeo to see the 2nd Battn which has moved to NURLU; Jack is commanding while Norman is commanding the Brigade – tho latter was there. The Major Genl & Col Heywood also popped in afterwards.

Saw our fatigue parties at work near ETRICOURT on way home.

5th

Another attack and communication scheme with Grenadiers, when quite useful work is done.

The Brigadier came to luncheon he saw the Major General about me yesterday, and it has been decided that I am to remain on as 2nd in comd for another 3 months, after which Flossy may come out, but if I like I may go to a new Army Battn now! So much may happen in 3 months that I decided to stay here – & chance having to go after 3 months! Evidently I am never to be allowed to have a Battn in the Regt – while Geoffrey Feilding commands the Divn, (not that I could reasonably expect so) but the Brigadier said he considered I "was" fit for it.

The old Brigadier was in great form – told us the famous story of how he hit Leslie Hamilton over the head with a boot in the dark – during the retreat, a report having come saying the Huns were coming.

> Major The Honourable Leslie d'Henin Hamilton, 1st Coldstream Guards †29.10.14 was Second in Command during the Retreat from Mons with Lieutenant Colonel Ponsonby as Commanding Officer.

He then told us a new story (to me) of last Oct. when the Duke of Connaught inspected the Division, & (being so soon after the Somme casualties & therefore so many new Officers with us) on asking the names of the various Officers J.P. was unable to say anything but "Dont know", till at last he recognized one whom he had only learned the previous day – on the Duke asking him, he said with a loud & confident voice "Mahomed". The Duke said "What?!!", when J.P. repeated the name. The Duke stared at J.P., & then all he said was "You dont know what you are talking about!"

> Lieutenant Claude Atkinson Etty Mahomed †31.7.17, nicknamed "The Prophet", †31.7.17

A football match v. 2nd Irish Gds in afternoon, which we won, then Hugh Ross & I walked down to ETRICOURT to see the fatigue parties, and watched a bridge over the Canal being started by some Canadian R.E., on a locomotive pile-driver.

Chess with Romeo after dinner & later a tremendous bombardment by us which turned out to be a raid (we heard next day) by some troops of 40th & 8th Divns.

6th

Romeo discussed the training with Coy Cmdrs – the 3rd G.G. coming after luncheon to have a talk about our scheme yesterday – then a cricket match v. them, when we won by 160 runs to 80._ To Church.

Romeo & I walked to see the fatigue parties, but found it further than he expected so had to return home.

So far he does not seem a bit too strong – I only hope he wont jack up at any critical moment. More chess with him.

7th

Hugh Ross lectured to Pltn Cmdrs on the new methods.

After luncheon Romeo inspected the Transport. I am now riding Seymour's mare, Ivan Cobbold has got my Geraldine pro tem.

I rode first with F. Mann to see the fatigue parties and also the bridge which is nearly finished. Later rode the grey – which is now Romeo's – with Cecil Trafford out towards VELU and back by BARASTRE, where we were much shocked to see the Germans had actually made use of a huge crucifix as an Observation Post, nailing the floor etc of it onto the Cross!

8th

A pouring wet night and morning until 1 p.m., our poor fatigue parties got drenched through.

Rode with Romeo & Eric to see fatigue parties, also to see ground of a scheme to be done tomorrow.

We have made a big bath for the men out of a tarpaulin in a shellhole – I do not think it a great success, only cold water, & the men do not care for this much.

9th

Brigade Scheme 9. am. near LE MESNIL. Lunch at Brigade H.Q. Very hot. Col Thorne has gone sick – flebitis, first time he has gone to Hospital since War began._

After lunch the Brigadier came out with us to finish off the scheme – great fun over the so-called Boche in the dugout which Hugh and I heard!

Heard the Battn is to move very shortly.

10th

Rode to see Arthur Erskine at 20th Div Arty H.Q. then on to see fatigue parties between EQUANCOURT & FINS. Did a scheme with Romeo – & the Coy Commanders – Very hot. Had to get back for a Brigade Boxing Competn at 4 p.m. in our camp, when there were some good fights – Referee Col de Crespigny. Thunderstorm.

Saw some German Aeroplanes go over – shortly afterwards loud explosions, which turned out to be Amtn Dump

Arthur Erskine dined.

11th

Battn moved back to CLERY. I left en route for Bde HQ at CURLU to get my warrant for Paris. Lunch there then Alston & Bagot Chester gave me a lift as far as EDGEHILL, where he was seeing the Gds Divl Artillery entrain, en route for ST. OMER (giving rise to many rumours) – then thanks to "Bubble", a kind-hearted doctor sent me in to AMIENS, in an Ambulance. Arrived there about 4, & met Charlie Seymour now cmdg 8th Bn 60th Rifles – with whom I went to tea – catching the 6.30 p.m. train to PARIS

Lieutenant Colonel Charles Hugh Napier Seymour, Commanding 8th (Service) Battalion
The King's Royal Rifle Corps, 41st Brigade, 14th (Light) Division, New Army, related
to Miles Barne

A lovely evening, the country looking very pretty with fruit blossom out etc

Train very slow & crowded – eventually arriving – with 2 Japs 2 English & 1 Belgian Officer at Paris at 11 p.m., and to my intense joy – hardly expecting such luck – found Violet already installed at the Hotel de Crillon.

18

Back North and the Canal Bank at Boesinghe

Tuesday May 15th 1917. PARIS

Left Violet at the Hotel Crillon at 10.30 p.m. After some difficulty getting a taxi – which I eventually shared with an Officer of the Yorkshire Dragoons – got to the Station with ½hr in hand, but even then found the train absolutely packed, barely any standing room. However by dint of being rather cunning I slipped into a seat after about an hour, when some Frenchman got out at a suburban Station – have seldom seen a train so packed – both sexes and every nationality._

> The Queen's Own Yorkshire Dragoons, T.F.

16th

Arrived AMIENS 4.30 a.m. went to look for Wright (who commands Bde Machine Gun Coy & came on from Paris earlier than I did) at Hotel Belfort – and Hotel Rhin – could not find him, tho' he had promised to give me a lift out – so went to catch the 5.50 a.m. train – which took me to BUIRES, where Col O'Keefe R.A.M.C. also appeared – sent for an Ambulance which took us up to his Field Ambulance at MARICOURT, where he gave me breakfast & sent me on to Battn again in it, at CLERY.

> Major Reginald Montague Wright, Coldstream Guards, Officer Commanding 2nd
>   Guards Brigade Machine Gun Company
> Lieutenant Colonel J J O'Keeffe, Commanding 4th Field Ambulance Royal Army Medical
>   Corps

Found everyone out training, so went out & joined them; Brigadier appeared & was much pleased about me bringing his beer.
   Much colder and rained during afternoon.

17th

Brigade marched early to BROMFAY CAMP where we arrived about 11.30 a.m., rather wet._

Walked down to BRAY with Romeo.

A most weird tale appeared in the "Daily Dump" about me and the beer, at the Hotel!

> The Daily Dump was produced every day, if possible, by Headquarters 2nd Guards
> Brigade, until the pressure of preparations for the Third Battle of Ypres forced
> its demise. Though simply typed up and then copied, it approximated to a trench
> newspaper.

18th

Marched at 9 a.m., perfect day for marching, to VILLE-SUR-ANCRE via MORLANCOURT, about 9 mi. nobody fell out.

Very busy afternoon with Romeo fixing up our training programme etc – walked with him to the river & along it: he is very conscientious and thorough, and likes to go into every detail himself.

Eric McK. went off early on leave till June 4th, a great surprise. Shortt becomes tempy Adjt._

19th

Rode early with Romeo to look for a rifle range & training ground, then busy practically all day with him & Hugh Ross making preparations for our training this next week – we hear we are likely to be here till 30th or thereabouts – after which nobody knows what – there are heaps of rumours – MESSINES RIDGE, ZEEBRUGGE, GORIZIA, & others!

Hugh lectured to Officers and Platoon Commanders.

Heard of the great Italian Offensive being started.

> The Tenth Battle of the Isonzo began with an Italian attack towards Trieste, ultimately
> stopped and reversed by the Austro-Hungarian forces.

Chess after dinner with Romeo.

20th

Brigade Church Service on the Marshes, under Poplar Trees, with sermon by the Deputy Chaplain General (Glynne late Bp. of Khartoum) – later rode with Romeo and Cecil Trafford to look at the Ranges & Training Ground for tomorrow.

> The Right Reverend Llewellyn Henry Gwynne, C.F., Deputy Chaplain General

The Town Major – Kitching R.E. dined, and stayed on very late – after the manner of Town Majors._ They usually have such lonely lives, that [they] are so glad to talk and feed with anyone else.

> Lieutenant Colonel John Everley Kitching, Royal Engineers

21st

Strenuous training in morning, but rather spoiled by rain – the Major-General came round to see what we were up to. Our training ground chiefly consists of a sort of swamp – water-meadows along the R. Ancre. We are forbidden at all costs to go onto any cultivated ground.

In afternoon rode with Romeo to see Range etc, & walked with him again in evening to the Divisional Baths – a particularly dirty old mill by the river_ Such a perfect evening – heard Cuckoo and Turtle Dove.

Our training hours are pretty long, 8 a.m.–12 noon, then 2.30 to 4.30 a.m., *[p.m.]* which in addition to cleaning up billets and preparing for following day etc is quite enough for all ranks.

Rumours that a lot of French Troops gave gone N. and we are destined to take the MESSINES RIDGE.

> French troops, having been away from there for some time, were about to move into the line along the Ypres-Yser Canal immediately north of the Ypres Salient.

Have heard nothing of Violet since she wrote from Havre on 16th – must hear tomorrow_

22nd

A pouring wet morning, Romeo attends a lecture on the Battle of Arras by Gen Maxse, and makes me give a lecture to the Officers and N.C.O.'s on patrol work – rather an ordeal but it seems to go off fairly successfully.

> Major General Frederick Ivor Maxse, Commanding 18th (Eastern) Division, New Army

In afternoon training is continued and Hugh Ross tells me my lecture has borne fruit.

Inspection of Transport by the Major General in evening. In afternoon I went out to watch B. Coy, and to see some new ground to use, & in late evening Romeo and I rode out & met the Coy Cmdrs on this ground.

Chess with Romeo after dinner.

No letter yet from Violet.

23rd

Rode out with Romeo to look at the training.

Letter at last from Violet who has arrived safely and had a capital journey but a terribly rough crossing.

Rode in evening with Romeo & 4 Coy Cmdrs to prepare tomorrow's night operations.

Adams Acton! Ellis rejoined from Havre.

24th

The Battn practised its night operations. I attended to start with, then had to go off to H.Q. of the 1st Guards Brigade to preside at a Court of Inquiry on a Motor Accident – at SAILLY LE SEC, a very pretty little village close to the River Somme,

The occupant of the car was B-Smith, Brigade Major of the Brigade. He was coming out of AMIENS with two Grenadier Officers, Buchanan and Walker. They met another car, neither driver gave way enough, the result being a collision, I have often wondered why this does not happen oftener – both drivers swore the other was wrong, but as a matter of fact it is a sort of creed amongst drivers not to give way. This Court took from 11 a.m. to 3 p.m.

> Captain Merton Beckwith Smith, Coldstream Guards
> Lieutenant John Neville Buchanan, 2nd Grenadier Guards
> Captain Cecil Francis Alex Walker, 2nd Grenadier Guards

I lunched at Bde H.Q., with Genl Jeffries & Co: sat next to Rocke, now just returned (wounded Sept 15th) to command 1st Irish Gds.

> Lieutenant Colonel Cyril Edmund Alan Spencer Rocke, Commanding 1st Irish Guards

On arrival back at VILLE just had time to help Romeo to write his Battn night Operation Orders – then a meal, and out to take part when all went fairly well, getting back about 12.30 a.m. on

25th

Rose quite late; rode up to look at last nights digging work – back for an Officers' Conference on various subjects, followed by an early lunch and out to meet the Brigadier & all C.O.'s, near HEILLY, for a Brigade Scheme – which was quite interesting and a beautiful ride & weather – very hot – but I was rather afraid about Romeo who felt the heat a good bit, & riding just after lunch – we must take care.

Back by 6 p.m., a concert where I sat between Adair (son of Flixton) and my very distant cousin Thornhill of Darrham! both in 3rd Grenrs. Dined at Bde H.Q., where found the Brigadier in very good form, quite at his best; he was full of stories of old days & old people which was amusing. Told us the story of Queen Maude and the picture.

> Captain Allan Henry Shafto Adair, 3rd Grenadier Guards, a Suffolk neighbour
> Lieutenant Noel Thornhill, 3rd Grenadier Guards

26th

"Gas" Lecture in morning.

An astounding apparition turned up in shape of Gillieson! could hardly believe one's eyes!

Brigade Sports at MERICOURT (*Méricourt-L'Abbé*) in afternoon, whither I walked along the River with Romeo & Arthur Kinnaird, just back from leave – Irish Guards won nearly everything – their C.O. (Greer) being a wonderful runner himself.

John Dyer dined.

Watched some Anzacs boxing, & hundreds of them bathing. otherwise a very pretty walk.

27th

Early Service in YMCA hut – after which one of the busiest days I have ever had, doing various schemes – and writing out things in connection with the Battn Training. In evening walked with Romeo to look at ground for tomorrow's work

28th

Early start and long morning – companies doing "Advanced Guard" and "Local Attack" one at a time.

Did "Orders" for Romeo, who had to go to Bde H.Q. After lunch had to go to do Outpost work with 3 Coys – Brigadier looking on which was rather alarming, listening to me giving out my Orders!

Grilling hot, but a nice cool rain in evening.

Romeo dined at Division.

Orders arrived for move 30th.

29th

Morning occupied by doing a "scheme" under the Brigadier with all other Cmdg Officers of the Brigade, 2nd's in command & Compy Commanders at HEILLY, which is a very pretty village with wonderful old Chateau walls.

Hugh Ross saw a Hoopoe, but could not find the nest.

On return to VILLE found Elwes waiting for us! He has come out pending getting a new Army Battalion.

Later walked with him and Romeo.

Nipper Poynter dined with us, also Cecil Boyd Rochfort. The former has come out recently to be ADC to Genl Pulteney – having been very badly wounded at LOOS, and unable to get about much yet on foot, or to ride. He was in great form & very amusing.

30th

Day rather slow work – all morning taken up by a long pow-wow of Battn Officers.

In afternoon walked alone on "the swamp" by river, feeling quite sad at leaving this part of the world. A lovely evening – saw a pair of redstarts.

Paraded at 8.15 p.m., marched to entrain at HEILLY, except R.F. who follow tomorrow.

Glorious evening – all went very well, had a wonderful meal alongside the train, ham and salad, hard-boiled eggs and wine. Felt very greedy, but the men also had their tea, and I think they realize they are looked after as well as possible.

Started at 10.55 went via AMIENS, ABBEVILLE, ETAPLES,

31st

BOULOGNE CALAIS and ST. OMER to detrain at ARQUES at 9 a.m. Chess with Romeo in the train – he did not feel very grand, said all his teeth had got loose again, as they were after he was wounded.

In morning he seemed very tired and would not eat any breakfast hardly – ours was exceptionally good same as supper except cocoa instead of wine.

Passed through much familiar country en route.
Reached our new billets at WARDRECQUES about 11 a.m.
Walked in evening with Romeo to look for bathing place on Canal.
Perfect weather.

June 1st

Round the billets with Romeo in morning – rode in afternoon to prepare scheme for tomorrow – then to look for our 2nd Battn at CAMPAGNE where we were billeted one night in Aug /15. but failed to find them.

The Brigadier came round after dinner, and was most amusing, in tremendous form with wonderful long stories – how he had to "stellenbosch" his C.O.'s etc.

> From the Boer War, to "stellenbosch" subordinates was to sack them.

2nd

A long morning doing "fire control", when I take charge of the "enemy", who have to have the right amount of visibility.

Bramwell Jackson of Suffolk Yeoy, now ADC to Genl Godley commanding the 2nd Anzacs turned up to luncheon, which was rather amusing, and he was full of the coming "push", and much surprised that we did not know all about it._

He said we have 40% more Artillery than ever before, and masses of Infantry._

> Captain Cyril Bramwell Armitage Jackson, The Suffolk Yeomanry
> Lieutenant General Alexander John Godley, Commanding II Anzac Corps

Sunday June 3rd 1917

WARDRECQUES. By arrangement with Jackson, who sent a motor car for me, I went over to luncheon at H.Q. of 2nd Anzac Corps (Gen Godley) sat between him and Edward Greene, who is Staff Captain to his Corps Heavy Artillery, and who was kindly invited for my benefit. Heard quite a lot about the coming push by the IX (Gordon) X (Hunter Weston) and 2nd Anzac Corps, with our XIV Corps in reserve.

> Probably Captain Charles Albert Edward Green, Royal Garrison Artillery
> Lieutenant General Alexander Hamilton Gordon, Commanding IX Corps
> Lieutenant General Aylmer Gould Hunter Weston, Commanding X Corps
> The Battle of Messines was imminent.

Afterwards they arranged a meeting with Walter Guinness for me, so I went off and found him just E of BAILLEUL. He is Brigade Major of 74th Bde and was busy preparing for his Brigade's part. He was most interesting telling me what they were going to do and how, but did not know exactly when, He said he had flown all over the line & part they were to take. A "biff" by us was obvious from the air, for one thing all our newly made Railways in those parts stood out like white lines, being ballasted with sand.

Major Walter Edward Guinness, The Suffolk Yeomanry, Brigade Major, 74th Brigade,
25th Division, New Army

On return to WAR *[DRECQUE]S* rode with Romeo, Elwes, & Kinnaird to prepare a practice attack tomorrow.

4th

Carried out the practice attack in morning.

In afternoon walked in St Omer with Romeo – we started riding, but R. got nervous about slipping up on the "pavé", in case he should damage his head – he was not too well.

The "pavé" was the cobbled road surface.

Later into ST. OMER again in a motor charabanc to attend the "4th June" (Corps) dinner, which was attended by about 250 Officers! Various songs were sung, the Carmen, Boating Song, and "Vale", etc. It is not often that An Army Commander (Gough), Corps Cmdr (Cavan), and about 8 Generals are seen standing together on a table shouting Latin!

Returned in a motor car with the Brigadier, as the motor car *[charabanc]* did not look like starting for some time.

The dinner was a merry one & several amusing speeches (nothing serious) and episodes, but I recognized but few contemporaries.

The Eton College Chronicle of 14 June 1917 recorded the names of two hundred and six Etonians who attended this "Fourth of June" Dinner. The Earl of Cavan was in the chair and as the words of the songs, six verses of each of the first two, were all printed out, everyone sang lustily, accompanied by the Coldstream Guards Band.

5th

Various parades etc.

Lunched with 2nd Battn with Romeo.

Brigade "Cooker" Water Cart etc show in evening. The Major General has "Competitions" on the brain. The best Cooker Water Cart Limber in the Brigade is to compete in the divisional show – the Grenadiers won everything in our Brigade. They have a very good Transport Officer & horse master in Ducenoy, better known as "Joburg"._

Lieutenant Max Duquenoy, nicknamed "Joburg", 3rd Grenadier Guards

6th

With Kinlay to ST. OMER to buy prizes for our swimming sports. Bought a newspaper and found Kinlay had got a M.C.

Some heavy thunderstorms & rain in evening.

Had the Brigade Bayonet Fighting Competition, which we won, so now our team is to compete in the Divisional Show – this is far more satisfactory than the Cooker Show! for which latter we hear the Corps Cmdr has curled Geoffrey Feilding's hair, as a waste of time & energy.

Went to a so-called Pantomime of the 3rd Bn Coldm in evening – otherwise rather a good concert.

7th

The great day has come for the attack & capture of the MESSINES-WYTSCHAETE ridge, and by evening we hear 5000 prisoners have been taken and the ridge carried.

The Battalion went up to the training ground to be gassed & smoked for practice, and I thought it quite a good arrangement.

Smyth returned from Hospital.

2nd Lieutenant John Field Fairfax Smyth †22.7.17

We held our Water Sports in afternoon in the Canal, and spent quite a good 3 or 4 hours. The 2nd Battn joined with us, though we ran the show; they beat us at the Water Polo, Tug of War (both on land & in water) but on "points" I think we had slightly the best of it.

> The Water Sports were held in the Canal de Neuf-Fosse, southeast of Wardreques Station, at 2 p.m., with the Coldstream Guards Band in attendance. Prizes included pocket books, lamps, cigarettes, razors in leather cases, cigarette cases, tobacco pouches, pipes and as third prize in the diving competition a pair of vases of St Omer. The Daily Dump's coverage of the water sports included mention of the second half of the water polo match as being "chiefly remarkable for the continuous whistling of the referee who it is said exacted all the penalties he could, in order to save the life of his Company Officer, Captain Mann, who was having rather a thin time of it in goal." There were intermittent interruptions to the competitions caused by the passage of Inland Water Transport barges. The Daily Dump concluded, "In spite of the Mayor's protest that the Quartermaster-General's Branch had apparently overlooked the necessity of providing bathing drawers for our army, several ladies graced the proceedings with their presence and applauded with that enthusiasm that is so characteristic of the French female sex."

8th

Paraded 7 a.m. marched through the old familiar places (WIZERNES etc) to ZUDAUSQUES having a long 5 hour halt at HALLINES, where the men bathed, fed and slept.

The Battn billets rather scattered about in three small hamlets, Battn H.Q. is in a huge farm house & buildings. Much stock kept. Walked about with Romeo making preparations for our Musketry tomorrow._

9th

Rose early, and rode down to the Ranges 3 miles away by 6 a.m.: found Teddy Seymour there running the whole show, we and the Grenadiers (who by the way marched over there 14 miles in the heat of the day and looked very exhausted) fired simultaneously.

I waited till about 11 a.m. when Elwes turned up to relieve me – Romeo came with him. I returned to Billets with Romeo – had a very hearty & welcome luncheon – my breakfast at

4.45 had been very scanty – then sat down to help Romeo write orders for tomorrow – rather a complicated sort of day, as we are to go back to WARDRECQUES direct from the Ranges._

Visit from Alston, O. Lyttleton and Herman-Hodge, who motored Romeo & me back to the Ranges – where they left us to walk home._

> Captain Edward Seymour, Grenadier Guards, General Staff Officer Grade II, Guards
>   Division
> Lieutenant Colonel Francis George Alston, Scots Guards, Assistant Adjutant and
>   Quartermaster General, Guards Division
> Captain Oliver Lyttleton, Grenadier Guards, Staff Captain, 2nd Guards Brigade
> Major Roland Herman Hermon Hodge, Grenadier Guards, Deputy Assistant
>   Quartermaster General, Guards Division

10th

Elwes went early to the Ranges, but fog prevented any shooting till 9 a.m.

I walked up about 12 noon & remained till we finished about 4.30 – marched back to WARDRECQUES without episode, having teas on the way, so that the march became a very successful one and nobody fell out. Arrived about 10 p.m.

11th

Got up quite late, but had to preside at a FGCM on 2 Grenadier Corporals who had got drunk in AMIENS, and an insubordinate Coldstreamer.

In afternoon attended Divisional Cooker etc Competitions, and Bayonet Fighting. This latter meant a representative team from each of the 3 Brigades – our team had been chosen for our Brigade, but unfortunately was last – the 3rd Brigade was 1st, the 1st Brigade 2nd. Our 2nd Battn won the Cooker Competition._

Romeo is far from well.

12th

Romeo commands the Brigade while J.P. is on 3 days leave in England, so I have the Battn again.

March at 6.15 a.m. to WORMHOUT as a Brigade, arrive there, 15 miles, about 2.30 p.m., a very hot and trying march, teas en route from 10–11 a.m., a few men fell out, but nothing very serious._ WORMHOUT is rather a nice old town, it is where we had the Blue Seal Dinner last June, and also where we were at HEERZEEL.

The Battn H.Q. is in a Butcher's Shop – only the butcher is not there, is a cripple, having been wounded in Belgium early in the war.

Romeo went off to see the line, & returned about 4 p.m. after which Elwes & I walked to the Brigade H.Q. with Romeo & Loyd, the same chateau which I had lunch at when J. Ponsonby was there in Feb 1916, the day I left to go on leave.

Very hot day & evening.

> Captain Henry Charles Loyd, nicknamed "Budget", Coldstream Guards, Brigade Major,
>   2nd Guards Brigade

13th

Battn marched 7 a.m. to M Camp – in Brigade. a stifling march, and a lot of men dropped out but rejoined before the end.

Personally I went up with Col Hopwood Wright (Machine Gun) and Anson (Trench Mortars) to see the line & was taken round & given lunch by Col Taylor, 17th R.W. Fusiliers. Rejoined the party at ELVERDINGHE Chateau & motored back to "M" Camp, near POPERINGHE.

> Lieutenant Colonel Edward Byng George Gregge Hopwood, Commanding 1st
>   Coldstream Guards †20.7.17
> Major Reginald Montague Wright, Coldstream Guards, Officer Commanding 2nd
>   Guards Brigade Machine Gun Company
> Probably Lieutenant Frederic Anson, Grenadier Guards, 2nd Guards Brigade Trench
>   Mortar Battery
> Lieutenant Colonel Henry Jeffrys Taylor, Commanding 17th (Service) Battalion The
>   Royal Welsh Fusiliers, 115th Brigade, 38th Division

Started off to ride into the town to see Romeo (Bde HQ) but met him coming out.

The line is one taken over from the French in Sept last, & now next to the Belgians. It is the next sector on the left of where we were in July 1916 on Canal Bank._

Our Bn H.Q. is in a very comfortable and luxurious abode, & so far has not been seriously shelled.

14th

Marched at 4.30 p.m. having teas en route, during a 2 hr halt, to the line, where we have only 1 Coy in a reserve line, and 3 Coys in buildings near Battn H.Q.

Very hot march, but luckily it got cooler after the halt, the relief was over by 12.30 p.m.

15th

I went round at 2.45 a.m., up to front line and a long round. Thick fog. Returned about 6 a.m.

A Belgian Officer sent an Orderley over to ask for a bottle of whiskey. I replied by ignoring this and asking him to luncheon. He arrived punctually & with much ceremony & speech making & apologies – talked the whole time 16 to the dozen, found mutual acquaintances with Duncan, both he & Duncan having lived in the Congo._ The Belge told us several rather interesting things about the French & Belgians, pressed his visiting cards on us, drank a good deal of port and finally departed jabbering volumes of pretty speeches & apologizing for his inability to return our invitation, and vowing eternal friendship.

> Lieutenant Basil William Duncan

In late afternoon I went round the line with Duncan to the left of the new line, along Canal Bank and back through BOESINGHE Chateau grounds – or what is left of them – for this part is much shelled._ Luckily all was quiet, so I was able to see practically the whole line in the day, and hardly had a shell near me.

We had large working parties out at night, so I went round with Eric McK., a third time in 24 hrs, at 12 midnight, getting in about 2 a.m.

16th

Slept late.

Went round the line, front and everywhere, at 2.30 p.m. with Guy Rasch, cmdg 3rd G.G. who relieve us tomorrow, & never got so hot in my life._

Many visitors, including the Brigadier and Romeo, who will not be returning to us till tomorrow. Brigadier arrived in his shirt sleeves, very hot.

Many new Batteries are now getting into position in these parts: this always means increased enemy shelling.

17th

Went out with Hugh Ross at 1 a.m. to visit our line and working parties. Found "Right Flank" working deepening a trench in the wrong place – I shewed the Officer in charge, Cooper, personally previously by day, but by night, he mistook one sort of trees for another.

Some shelling and a man (Quigley) in L.F. was killed. The first casualty since March 17th.

    Lieutenant Gerald Melbourne Cooper
    14335 Private Hugh Quigley †17.6.17

Got in at 3 a.m., and was called again at 4.30 a.m. to accompany the Brigadier all round the line, in connection with a raid which we are to do.

Went over the whole front from N. to S., eventually getting back at 8 30 a.m. rather hot & very glad of breakfast & a wash, only having had 2 hrs lie down all night.

Do a bit of sleep during the day.

Romeo came up to luncheon and took over. Cols Heywood and Brough both came in to luncheon so we were a large party._

    Lieutenant Colonel Cecil Percival Heywood, Coldstream Guards, General Staff Officer
        Grade I, Guards Division
    Lieutenant Colonel Alan Brough, Commander Royal Engineers, Guards Division

We were relieved at night by 3rd G.G. under Guy Rasch. Col Thorne he hears has gone home, with varicose vein trouble._

Had a very quiet relief_ C. Coy had to go up to do some work in a forward Commn Trench. Turned in about 1 a.m., slept soundly in spite of Aeroplanes coming over and troubling us.

18th

Quite a lot of shelling round ELVERDINGHE Village and Chateau. We have 1½ Coys there and I dont think they are having at all a nice time of it. In evening Romeo Eric & I went down there to see them – all quite cheerful but have not much cover. Hugh Ross is the "Assistant-Commandant" of the Defences, according to the scheme. He went to report himself & his orders to the

June 18th 1917 ELVERDINGHE

Brigadier, whose only remark was "Oh! Are you! I'm the Commandant! – Let's give a ball", after which he took no more interest in the matter, which only shewed his great confidence in Hugh Ross, as well as his sense of humour.

Guns keep arriving, all night one hears the "caterpillars", so when the time does come._

19th

We had quite a lively night. Shelling of the back of chateau etc – all night, and at 3 a.m. an enemy aeroplane came over; we had all our 8 Lewis Guns ready: & they all loosed off without delay, but did not bring it down – it was also "archied" & many other people shot at it, so had a pretty rotten time.

R.F. & B Coys were heavily shelled all day at least their neighbourhood, & had 1 man killed and 1 wounded.

14393 Private Hugh Irving †19.6.17

I walked up there with Elwes during the morning & in afternoon rode over with him, past Corps & Divl H.Q. to see old Sherard who is not far off commanding the 32nd "Labour Group"._

He was very glad to see us but very unhappy in his solitary surroundings.

A quiet night._

Lieutenant Colonel Sherard Haughton Godman, Commanding 32nd Labour Group

20th

Watched a rehearsal of our raid, which is to be done by Mahomet and 30 men of C. Coy. We have found a piece of ground which represents in many ways the Canal & its banks.

All our thoughts are now concentrated on the raid, which is developing well – we tried the mats which are to be used for crossing the Canal. quite a simple affair: and everything promises well.

I went to see Hugh Ross by myself – he had had no more casualties, but there was a good deal of very unpleasant shelling going on in his part of the world: mostly aimed at some batteries.

Lieutenant Claude Atkinson Etty Mahomed †31.7.17

The mats, three feet wide and seventy feet long, were of wire mesh covered with canvas, fixed firmly to wooden slats. These, reasonably easy to carry and simple enough to unroll across the thick mud of which the Canal currently consisted, would enable men to cross without sinking in.

All the rehearsals and training were ahead of the opening of the Third Battle of Ypres. As far as the Guards Division were concerned the outline plan currently meant that the 3rd Guards Brigade would not be involved until the very start of the battle.

21st

Visit from Norman and Douglas Gordon, who had been up to look at the line, into which they will not be going until just before the attack.

A good deal of shelling again some very near our farm, but nothing very near.

Cecil Trafford came up and said the Transport Lines were being shelled; alas! My dear little Geraldine, recently ridden by Ivan Cobbold, was killed, being hit on the head with a piece of shell. What is really worse is that my poor Groom's brother (Thomas) was killed while the two brothers were talking to each other. They had not met for 3 years, till this occasion when they found themselves near together._

> 80325 Driver James Thomas, 254th Tunnelling Company Royal Engineers †19.6.17, not
> on the same day that the 1st Scots Guards Transport Lines were shelled.

Not far off a tentful of 10 men playing cards were all killed – and other horrors.

22nd

Various visitors as usual, including Gen Feilding, Major Bagot-Chester etc, all much interested in our raid – also Col Rocke and 5 other Officers of 1st Bn Irish Gds, whom I took up part of the way to get a sketchy view of the line.

We have a new Presbyterian Minister attached to us – by name Somerville – Gillieson has gone. Also a new C. of E. parson, Phillimore, who takes Head's place, Head having gone to the Division, to take McCormack's place, McC. having gone to the Corps.

> The Reverend James Alexander Somerville, C.F.
> The Reverend Stephen Harry Phillimore, C.F.
> The Reverend William Patrick Glyn McCormick, C.F.

Marched off at 10.15 p.m. to relieve the 2nd Bn Irish Gds in the front line. A very noisy and dangerous relief – we were lucky to have only 2 men wounded, the Irish Gds had 2 killed that we knew of, besides 5 wounded: possibly others afterwards.

We had the usual very narrow escapes, one shell pitched very close to Romeo & me, he found it shook him a good bit & was very tired – even said "This little trip is going to do me in"._ Personally I was very frightened, but not shaken.

> 9128 Private George Gallagher, 2nd Irish Guards †22.6.17
> 9898 Private T Gannon, 2nd Irish Guards †22.6.17
> 11121 Private J O'Hogan, 2nd Irish Guards †22.6.17

23rd

The usual stream of visitors which gives everything away, including our Battn H.Q. This place is warming up and getting very lively. It is very difficult to make the private soldier realize that individuals showing themselves to the enemy or aeroplanes simply give away lines of communication etc. Here some gunners like going on the Chateau lake in a boat, other folk push a trolly in broad daylight, working parties, orderlies & every sort of person. These individuals always think one is in a blue funk oneself, & they are quite allright, quite forgetting that their care-lessnes makes it dangerous for other folk.

A very early rise, and at 2 p.m. *[probably am]* Romeo and I go round the line not getting back till 7 p.m. *[probably am]*. He is marvellously deliberate & thorough, never satisfied with anything but the very best – whether writing orders or buying claret.

The line, which runs along the Canal-bank, besides some very intricate support and Communication Trenches, requires much time and work spent on it. The Division whom we succeeded can have done nothing, the trenches etc get regularly shelled and so ordinary repairs alone mean a lot of work.

Late to bed. Romeo is getting very tired and worried with various small things, tho' has a marvellous power of pulling himself together.

Much shelling during the night all round our Hd Qrs, also there was a barrage on LF Company's front, killing 1 and wounding 5 others.

> 14059 Private Joseph James Thompson †24.6.17
> 14606 Private William Leitch †24.6.17

24th

Brigadier arrived at 6 a.m. and took me round the line. We had hardly started 200 yds, when I found an arm lying in the trench, and other odds & ends. I heard afterwards that 4 poor engineers had been caught by a shell, 1 had lost an arm, 2 were killed, and 2 were mortally wounded, so the Medical Officer said, tho' it is difficult to hear further particulars of these things._

> The 55th, 75th and 76th Field Companies were in the Guards Division.
> 65768 Sapper Richard Duck, 76th Field Company Royal Engineers †25.6.17
> 81099 Sapper Thomas Armour Scott, 76th Field Company Royal Engineers †25.6.17

Back to breakfast at 8 a.m., and spent a busy day, going round line again, with Romeo, during morning, choosing sites for new fire and "assembly" trenches – and later on preparing for the Raid, which Romeo has asked to be postponed 24 hrs owing to its having been published far and wide, in Brigade Orders etc, a copy being sent over to the Belgians, who are never to be trusted one inch.

In afternoon the steady flow of visitors of all sorts went on, so that poor Romeo all but jacked up & got quite alarmed with himself. I am urging him to get a week or 10 days leave & go to see his Doctor, both for his own sake and the Battalion's, a bad breakdown at a critical period in the near future might be very bad for him._ We have a very serious talk over it all together, but he cannot get any sleep – partly owing to the multitude of visitors, partly the preparations & orders for the raid, and partly the lateness of rations water etc, he has to sit up to see Trafford & make further arrangements. He sees that a C.O. has such huge responsibility & that it may be too great a strain for him.

A very noisy night, partly because some of our carrying parties drank some rhum they were carrying for other Companies & got drunk, and later owing to the heavy shelling – there were several casualties including our Smith-Cunningham commanding the Brigade Sapping Company, wounded.

25th

Early start at the final arrangements for the raid, everything being done by 9.20 a.m. when 'Budget' Loyd – Brigade Major – appeared for breakfast, followed by crowds of other Officers, Staff of various sorts, Grenadiers coming round to take over before relief tomorrow night, gunners, R.E. Trench Mortars etc etc. I went round with Guy Rasch – now Lt. 'Col'. Rasch – hoping Romeo might get some rest, but when I got back, he had had no chance.

Found Mahomed & Bradshaw had completed preparations for the raid, during the night, clearing the wire from our parapet, for the party to get out carrying their long rolled up canvas mats with them for crossing the Canal, 3 parties of about 12 each, 50 yds apart, led by Mahomed in the centre.

Two more of our Kite Balloons were brought down by an enemy aeroplane yesterday, & the occupants burned to death: Romeo & I saw the culprit dashing back a small very fast machine, we were shooting at it, making poor practice. However two enemy aeroplanes were brought down near here.

In evening, after sleeping all the afternoon, Romeo came down the line with me, to see C. Coy and have a talk to the Raiders. They were all very cheerful and in splendid form, as ugly a looking lot as anyone would ever hate to have up against them_ for the raid their faces were blacked – which did not help matters at all in the way of making them more beautiful – every detail was ready.

The raid went off quite successfully the first two main objects being attained namely testing crossing on the mats and reconnoitring the YPER LEA: the third object – namely obtaining a prisoner or two for identication purposes was not successful, simply because there were no Germans in their trench between our parties – tho' there were some further along. Everything went very smoothly with one exception & all got safely back, with no casualties, about 2 a.m.

Mahomed came up, wet through, to Bn H.Q. directly afterwards, looking (as the Brigr put it) more like the Sultan of Turkey than ever, and we took down full particulars for reporting._

Eventually to bed at 4 a.m.

The Yper Lea was a stream which here ran into the Canal from the north east.

26th

Breakfast about 10 a.m. during which Col. Heywood arrived, then later the Brigadier, with whom I went up to the line. He afterwards lunched with us.

In evening Romeo & I walked along the Support Line & explored a bit.

At night we were relieved by 3rd G.G. – the relief being over at 1.30 a.m.: had a very quiet walk back to ELVERDINGHE, when crumps began to arrive and went on until daylight & more – we got into our new camp at CARDOEN FARM about 3 a.m. when found Elwes with supper ready, including some champagne he had bought in POPERINGHE, which went down well.

Romeo very tired, but he is applying for leave, the Brigr also talked about him to me this morning.

27th

Rose pretty late; the Major General arrived while Romeo was doing "orders", and asked me if I thought he could stand the strain of a several days "advance". I hardly knew what to say, as nobody knows.

Strolled with Romeo in afternoon – he is very anxious about himself which is a bad sign – the Maj General told me Romeo was going on leave & I would have to take over, but said nothing to R about it, which we thought very strange.

In evening an order came to dig some narrow slit trenches to get into in case of shelling – we did so – the men worked splendidly, and the job was done by 11 p.m. During the night there was some very heavy shelling but only one into camp – luckily did no harm. Some Companies manned their slits, where they slept soundly & fairly safely.

Word came during the evening that Romeo was to go on leave so we asked for a motor car to take him to BOULOGNE, never expecting he would get it. However he did, & started off at 12.30 a.m.

28th

More shelling of the neighbourhood throughout the day. A very noisy Aeroplane fight in early morning, when a German one was brought down, tho' I cant say I saw it._

Last evening a German aeroplane brought down one of our balloons – on fire – the 3rd we have seen in a week, the 2 occupants however jumped out & descended safely in their parachutes._

I had to preside at a FGCM during morning._

In evening walked over to see Brigadier on one or two topics – partly as to the recommendations in connection with the raid. Found the poor old thing having a horrid time being shelled – especially at night, & our guns making his room (upstairs in the Chateau at ELVERDINGHE) perfectly horrible._ Why they have never actually got the Chateau nobody knows, except that it is said to belong to an Austrian. Ivens came with me, and hated our own guns worse than the enemy's. Hear we are to be inspected by the King on 7th._

Lieutenant Francis Burdett Ivens

Romeo is being put in for a Brigade at home, much the best thing for him in reality._

June 29th 1917

CARDOEN FARM, ELVERDINGHE

Another noisy night, but no shells actually arrived in camp.

Edwards joined us.

Lieutenant John Keith Edwards

In evening move about ½ mi down the road into a camp at WIPPE CABARET Cross Road – several Belgians are here in cottages, so the Camp does not get shelled.

Shelling however of near neighbourhood begins at 9 p.m and continues all night, so that some of us find sleep rather difficult.

Reynolds, Tim's servant, is now cook for the Battn H.Q. Mess, and in many respects is excellent, makes delicious salads & knows how to "serve things up" – far better than our ordinary cook Cockerton who is on leave.

    9556 Private Arthur Reynolds
    5453 Private Jesse Cockerton

30th

A pouring wet day, luckily no fatigues etc till night – as some of the men are in bivouacs, we are rather lucky to find an empty hut not far off, so that all can be under a proper roof. Our huts are very good in this part of the world, having been made originally by Belgians or French, who take a lot of trouble over this sort of thing.

There are many Belgian Civilians all round us here, we all think they have some understanding with the Germans, who do not seem to shell exactly where the Belgians live – when the Belgians pack up and go, as they do from time to time, they are said to light a bonfire, after which the Huns immediately start shelling. It is notorious that no sooner do we place a gun in position than it gets shelled the following morning. Pigeons are brought by fishing boats from ZEEBRUGGE to DUNKERQUE and released in our neighbourhood. We look on every Belgian as a Spy. They have lost everything nearly so all they want is peace, & to be able to go on with their work – which they are able to do under the Germans as well as formerly by themselves.

In evening I had to attend a Brigade Conference about the coming push, & heard many interesting details.

Some shelling at night very near our hut, on which pieces of shell & mud fell.

We had some huge fatigue parties out – 600 men – burying cable. A heavy barrage by us between 1 and 2 a.m.

19

The Battle of Pilckem Ridge and After

Although already well advanced, in July the preparations intensified for the Battle of Pilckem Ridge, the opening of the Third Battle of Ypres.

July 1st 1917

Rode over to Divl H.Q. to see some model (miniature) trenches etc of the country we are to attack. Took all Coy Cmdrs with me & a few other Officers. Met Brigadier there in good form, full of his description of being invested the previous day in some Belgian Order, by a Belgian General – was most amusing about it. Went on to see old Sherard, whom we met walking in the road – rather pathetic, very lonely – but looking well.

In afternoon Norman O.E., Jack Stirling and Tommy McDougal came over, they are in a camp nearby, I walked back with Norman afterwards to tea with them. He was full of his coming "push"._

2nd

Marched (after a rather quieter night, tho' about 10 shells landed quite close to us) at 9 a.m. to HERZEELE._ A panic seized me on the way that we ought to be in platoons instead of in Companies, so we split up, especially as several Germans were up overhead – also as the Major General passed us! However on looking up the regulations, we were quite right in companies. Had dinners & a long halt en route, good deal of trouble about water.

Arrived in at 6 p.m. – after which I ran round all the billets, which are very scattered, at various farms – late dinner.

3rd

Found Col Gordon Gilmour who used to command the Grenadiers, out here as an "Area Commandant" – he gave me a most effusive greeting.

Colonel Robert Gordon Gilmour, Grenadier Guards

Rode out to see where our digging of facsimile trenches was to be, in morning, with Hugh Ross & Elwes.

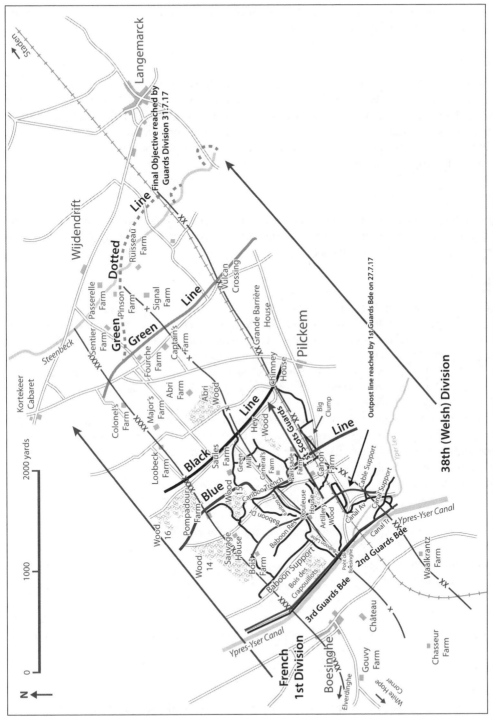

Map 16   Third Battle of Ypres, Battle of Pilckem Ridge, 31 July 1917.

In afternoon whole Battn, except 100 men being inoculated, went out to dig, 3.30 to 7.30 – home soon after 8 p.m. Very hot. Our digging in all amongst the standing crops etc seems quite criminal – such beautiful crops! as a rule.

4th

Rose at 4 a.m. for the Battn to start digging at 6 – and finished our task by 9.30 a.m._

Orders begin to roll in in connection with the King's visit on 6th, a "got up show" is being arranged – at same time we have to study the real show, so I get all the Officers together in the afternoon & go through the whole thing – so far as I could – both shows.

News arrived of the new Russian advance and capture of 10000 prisoners._

Walked by myself in evening.

5th

Spent a long day out. In morning we practised the real show, "popping the Canal" etc, on the trenches we had dug – then dinners, and afterwards we practised the "put-up show" – with the rest of the Brigade_ Back in billets by 6 p.m.

6th

A lovely day – paraded 9.15 a.m., and did our "put-up show" before the King and swarms of big wigs – Generals & Staffs of every degree. The King was put into a meadow, and shown it all, & no doubt was told it was exactly what we were going to do on "the" day, though it differed in many respects, for the sake of making a good show for him.

Very few of the troops even saw the King – & most of those who saw him, saw him only in the distance, as I did and from our point of view it was a total failure, & might have been otherwise – I hope he enjoyed what he saw!

No doubt he was anxious not to interfere with our training, but as a matter of fact what we did has all got to be forgotten, (not easy) and a good ceremonial parade would have done discipline good and the men would have liked to see the King, and cheered him.

Seldom have the authorities made worse blunders.

Dined at the Brigade – sat between Ridley, Grenadier, and Col Gordon Gilmour, late cmdg Grenadiers, & now come out as an old dug out to be an "Area Commnadant"._

Probably Captain Edward David Ridley, Grenadier Guards

Russian news continues good.

Romeo returned from leave.

7th

Did a Battalion Attack, against the Dummy Trenches._ Many new orders and instructions._

8th

Rain in morning.

In afternoon did the Battn attack again. The thing is gradually shaping itself._

In evening a dinner party – our guests being Cols. Gilmour & Godman, and Gen Cuthbert – sat next to him and heard a good lot of news – he commands the 39th Div. and has grown very fat. He says the coming push is likely to be a huge success and the war will end this autumn.

We are evidently going to have a tremendous quantity of guns, as well as 500 French guns on our front.

> Major General Gerald James Cuthbert, nicknamed "Cupid", Commanding 39th Division, New Army

9th

Battalion Attack again in morning._

In afternoon helped Romeo at some writing preparations, for his orders. He goes into every detail most thoroughly, & thrashes out all the pros & cons before he decides upon any point, and always asks one's opinion, which is very flattering of him – sometimes he is quite annoyed if I don't help him on some trivial point – on one occasion he said quite peevishly "You wont give me your advice" – in reality he knows quite well, but likes to hear what others think._

Attended a Brigade Confce with him in evening, and saw "models" from all 4 Battns & Machine Gunners, Riflemen, Bombers, Rifle Bombers, Lewis Gunners, Runners etc. dressed up as for the Attack.

I foresee I am again going to be left out when the time comes.

10th

A Brigade Attack. We are to be the right front Battn, with Irish Gds on our left, Grenrs behind us, and Coldm behind Irish Gds.

All went very smoothly.

Afterwards the Brigadier assembled all Officers & Platoon Commanders, and addressed them on the subject of the coming show.

Worked out more details for Romeo in afternoon – he usually has a nap which helps to keep him going.

11th

Another Brigade attack in morning practised, but I had to preside at a FGCM on two men who were absent over leave from England.

Walked with Romeo in evening.

12th

The third and last Brigade Attack Practice, when all details are finally worked out._

In evening another Brigade Conference, which annoys Romeo, as so much irrelevant matter is discussed.

After this Romeo & I went to dine with Left Half Mess – on return from which we found some papers etc and did not get to bed till 1 a.m., he is very difficult on these occasions and will not go to bed, but vows every sort of hate against the perpetrators of the papers, how badly worded etc, and will not get to business – of course there are always interruptions too, which he finds very disturbing._

13th

Rode with Romeo in morning to see Companies wiring._

In evening walked with him & Elwes & Duncan to both half Battn Messes, concerning some alterations in the work & programme.

The news of two Battns getting knocked out in North, near the sea is unpleasant, but of no very serious consequence. The Germans are clever at seizing their opportunity: this must have been done during a gale at sea, & in hopes of obstructing our coming Offensive.

I forget if I have put in what a nuisance we all consider the Belgians – for whom to a great extent we are fighting – they almost admit they only want to be left alone & wd be quite happy as German Subjects, & hate fighting. This country is full of spies and are no doubt often Belgians in German pay.

They send pigeons over. Never does a gun get put into position without being shelled the following morning! WOESTEN was not shelled for a year until the Canadians went there one night.

Directly a farm is evacuated by its (Belgian) people then it gets shelled, probably catching some British soldiery. The whole of this area (- E of POP) is now being cleared out before the big show, & bombardment, begin.

The C.O.'s sister has a parrot called Dudley. I have daily reports of how Dudley is, what he says & does.

14th

March at 7.30 a.m. back to the "FOREST AREA" near POPERINGHE – resting at a farm en route for dinners. A very hot march & 14 men fell out – 1 or 2 pretty bad. Norman O.E. came to see us march in, and I think thought the Battalion looking rather jaded._ I dont ever remember a more hot & stuffy hour than one part of our march.

The camp is nothing wonderful having been pitched a wet night by Grenadiers, so there is much to be done in the way of camp improvements, & camouflaging.

When the King had lunch at LOVIE CHATEAU with Gough our (5th) Army Commander, he was shelled, so Haig ordered Gough to clear out and he is now at WATOU, through which we marched. I met Hargreaves who is attached to the Staff temporarily. He told me we had got back most of the lost "Dunes" – but the 2nd Bn of 60th, & some Northamptons were really exterminated, except an Officer & 32 men who swam the Canal! The Germans there are having a very poor time.

Captain Caryl Liddell Hargreaves, Scots Guards

On 10 July a German local attack on the east side of the Ypres-Yser Canal at the coast near Nieuport overwhelmed the 1st Northamptonshire Regiment and 2nd King's Royal Rifle Corps, 2nd Brigade, 1st Division.

The Irish Guards have had a raid, also 2nd & 3rd Coldm.

July 15th 1917

"FOREST AREA" near POPERINGHE – ELVERDINGHE

One night recently the Germans made a raid into a Battn of Irish Guards' Trenches: they left several dead, but unfortunately seem to have taken away an Officer, Eyre, as prisoner. His revolver – all 6 rounds fired off – was found near some dead Huns!

> Lieutenant Harry Joseph Bagshawe Eyre, 1st Irish Guards †14.7.17

The raid made a fortnight ago by 2nd G.G., was not a great success – they lost 2 Officers – Basil Blackwood & Gunnis – & did not kill or capture any Huns.

> Lieutenant Lord Ian Basil Gawaine Temple Hamilton Temple Blackwood, 2nd Grenadier
>   Guards †4.7.17
> 2nd Lieutenant Ian Fitzgerald Stuart Gunnis, 2nd Grenadier Guards †4.7.17

Spent today cleaning up & improving camp – attended a long "voluntary" service – dismal in the extreme – in afternoon, during which Norman O-E walked over – then came Alston.

The Bombardment today was put off – for some reason – but strange reports are flying about as to German Guns, and certainly they are doing very little firing._ Have most of them been taken back or what?

Walked with Romeo and Norman.

16th

A very quiet night – very mysterious – was told our guns were firing merrily yesterday, but received practically no reply.

In afternoon rode with Romeo to Divl H.Q. to see the sand & cement model of the German trenches which the Divn is going to attack – very completely made now.

In evening we both dined with 2nd Battn.

The bombardment has begun – the storm is brewing. We are getting some reply, and a big Ammtn Dump was blown up during luncheon, not very far away._

We have huge fatigue parties carrying at night, & everything is very active & busy. Last night we had 2 men wounded.

17th

No very exciting event, but the bombardment is going strong. We hear the French are not ready.

Rode over by myself in afternoon to see Ned Milner, at WESTOUTRE where he is a Area Stores Commandant. He was of course delighted to be looked up, and had a lot to say. He is in quite a pretty little place, close under MONT ROUGE – I went a little evening walk with him._

> Major Edward Milner, formerly Scots Guards

18th

Romeo is getting very worried now about the Battle, & it is very difficult to help him & save him worry – usually it only makes more.

We had 18 men gassed during the night on fatigue, some very lightly, others rather badly.

A visit from Cupid in afternoon, also from Jack Stirling & Billy Wynne-Finch – the former is just back from leave & brought me a letter from Violet.

Some shelling during the night of neighbourhood of our camp.

Walked with Romeo in evening and then Norman & Kit dined with us – during dinner some shells went over our heads & landed not far off_ This went on periodically through the night.

Captain Christopher Arthur Mohun Cator, known as "Kit", 2nd Scots Guards

19th

Walked with Romeo in morning._

Secker (Revd) & Duquesnoy ("Joburg") dined with us.

The Reverend Walter Herbert Noel Secker, C.F.
Lieutenant Max Duquenoy, 3rd Grenadier Guards

Champion, an officer of the Battn – attached to the Brigade Stokes Battery was killed by a sniper._ He was firing his Mortar, and apparently looking over the parapet at each shot to see where they were going.

Lieutenant Reginald James Champion †18.7.17

20th

Walked with Romeo to see LF practising for another Raid we may have to do_ in the sham Canal here, near our Camp.

Irish Gds & 4th Bn G.G. did a joint raid last night, the former found considerable difficulty in crossing Canal, & this where we shall have to cross on the day.

A deplorable episode has occurred namely Byng Hopwood and Stephen Burton have been blown up (C.O. & 2nd in Cd of 1st Bn Coldm Gds in this Brigade) & killed today – the former was one of the best C.O.'s in the Division, & been out the whole war.

Lieutenant Colonel Edward Byng George Gregge Hopwood, Commanding 1st
    Coldstream Guards †20.7.17
Major Stephen John Burton, 1st Coldstream Guards †20.7.17

The 2/Irish Gds seem to have had a very bad day too, & lost many men & several officers recently.

A tremendous bombardment at night – we have several fatigue parties out.

Jack Stirling & Billy Wynne-Finch dined.

Romeo much harassed by his Operation Orders and alterations in Brigade Orders etc A disturbed night in every way arranging as to the fatigue parties etc., orders for them arrive in so late._

Redmond Buxton turns up by mere chance.

Major Abbot Redmond Buxton, The Norfolk Yeomanry, a pre-war friend

21st

Busy morning spent helping Romeo to prepare orders for Raid and coming operations.

Attended funeral of Byng Hopwood & Stephen Burton.

Walked over to 2nd Bn with C. Trafford, saw Norman etc.

Moved at 9.30 p.m. to a farm where had a horrible night shells crashing all round us (at least they sounded like it though in reality not very near) and our own guns simply awful, such a racket – a gas alarm about 1 a.m., when we had to put on our masks; I was woken up – had hardly gone to sleep – by the Strombos Horn – put on my mask & went to see if Romeo was doing the same, but found him still asleep. It was a false alarm and nothing happened. Several dumps were set off in neighbourhood & blazed all night – aeroplanes overhead dropped bombs – & altogether very unpleasant_

22nd

Smyth was killed by a shell when on fatigue this morning up near the line – in broad daylight – a very useful Officer_ I am told he stayed to see his men out of the particular area being shelled when he was caught by a shell.

2nd Lieutenant John Field Fairfax Smyth †22.7.17

A quiet day comparatively; our guns however did some execution, and claim to have had 32 direct hits on German Gun Emplacements.

At night our search lights very prominent, & some Aeroplane Activity._

23rd

Two years today since I landed in France! How lucky I have been up to date!

Presided at a FGCM in morning on two insubordinate Irish Guardsmen._

Col Perowne & his son came in yesterday; last night when the 2nd Bn went into the line the son was gassed.

Lieutenant Colonel John Thomas Woolrych Perowne, Royal Field Artillery
2nd Lieutenant John Victor Thomas Woolrych Perowne, 2nd Scots Guards

There were very severe casualties from gas, including for the first time mustard gas, in the 2nd Scots Guards.

We had some fatigue parties out, some of them were slightly gassed. All had to don their masks, & could do little work.

Much shelling during the Day – several more of our dumps set on fire – we had several casualties. This is getting a serious question in the Division. all Battns are getting pretty short of men now.

Last night appeared an Officer of 16th R.W.F. on our right, as Liaison on the day. When our Mahomed discovered he was from the Argentine he came over, & they quacked in Spanish for the rest of the night.

1 German Officer and 18 Pte Soldiers have today given themselves up to the French on our left._

Spend much time trying to help Romeo with Battn Operatn Orders, but it is difficult for 2 people to do this & results in much waste of my time._

A noisy night: I daresay much of it is our own bombardment which is pretty heavy & the enemy must know exactly by now where we are coming over!

We have got to do a Raid, entering the enemy line in 4 places. This is being done by LF – Lloyd being the Officer.

They practice constantly, but the fatigues are so heavy, so much has to be carried up to the line – so there are few men left to play with.

Lieutenant Ernest Alfred Collyer Lloyd †31.7.17

This second raid, mainly to recheck the viability of the mats, following the difficulties the Irish Guards had had a few days before, was because the consistency of the mud was now more liquid. The mats would not work for men crawling across unless it was fairly thick.

24th

Bombardment (ours) is terrific – throughout the day it warms up – & towards evening the Bosch sends over a good lot of stuff too, some unpleasantly near the camp, but not so many casualties as yesterday.

Am afraid the 2nd Battn has had a very bad time of it, what with gas & shells, and so has every Battn in the line – really very serious and Battns will be very weak by the time the show starts. It is a great pity we could not have gone in just before "Zero Day" – as the French do – with fresh troops – now not only are we short in numbers but the men have been so shelled etc that their nerves must be a bit affected.

Romeo is getting very depressed & says he is going off his head. He is very difficult when like this & has to be humoured by us all. I fear I dont soothe him at all, & it is difficult to know what to do or say, so say as little as possible, for fear of putting my foot into it.

25th

Four Officers of the 2nd Battn have been gassed.

Everything now was pretty well settled & ready to going into the line & popping at the appointed hour, when a message suddenly came saying the relief is postponed whether owing to the French not being ready, or to the Russian Débacle or whether only the weather, we dont know_ Every sort of guess is being made of course.

Romeo had to go to Bde H.Q. to see the Corps Commander (Cavan) who of course was full of confidence in the result, and had messages of every sort of encouragement: how much stronger we are than the Germans, both in men & guns etc etc.

In evening I walked with Romeo slipped backwards in a ditch fell on a stump of a tree and broke a rib – which is very painful at times – especially lying down – and extremely tiresome. If Romeo gets knocked out, & I have to go up to take his place I shall find a great difficulty for a week or 10 days from now.

26th

The Dr wants to have me X rayed tomorrow.

Such a commotion all our elaborate plans & orders being off. and the whole show deferred for some days.

In afternoon I had to go to CANADA FM., No. 3 Field Ambulce, to be examined, where another Dr pronounced a "fractured rib", & that I must go "down the line".

Imagine my feelings. After being 2 years out here without going into a Hospital at all to be sent off like this from a foutling little accident just before the biggest battle of the war – too maddening for words, & I shall never be able to face the Bn again. I feel as if I ought to be shot.

Was sent off in an Ambce with 3 poor wounded men of our 2nd Bn to No. 63 CCS near PROVEN, where I spent the night – a bed next to one Pinto, of Coldm, wounded all round me, feeling a real skrimshanker.

> Lieutenant Richard J Pinto, Coldstream Guards, 1st Guards Brigade Trench Mortar
> Battery

July 27th 1917

Left No. 63 CCS PROVEN in a Hospital Train at 9.30 a.m., having a long & tedious journey down to BOULOGNE where eventually arrived about 9 p.m. & was sent to No. 7. Stationary Hospital. To my amusement I was called a "lying" case, so was carried about to & from the train on a stretcher, & got well bumped about_ I did not worry particularly about myself as I am not bad, but this long journey seems rather hard on bad cases, there were many poor wrteches in the train – Officers & men – who were evidently in great pain all the time._ The journey might have been done in ½ the time.

On arrival had a hot bath and a comfortable bed, the room looking out over the Harbour_ My 2 room Companions are Pinto Coldm and Somerby, Bde Major of 115th Inf Bde – who however was shortly removed to another ward.

> Somerby – untraced, 115th Brigade, 38th Division

28th

About 10.45 a.m. the Drs deign to come round, & ask in the briefest way what one is there for – taking evidently very little interest in one's reply.

There are numerous sisters, all seem to be ladies, & (what I have always rather dreaded about going to a Hpl) one of them explained that she is Albemarle's daughter, most tiresome having anybody that one knows (even tho' indirectly)._

Captain The Viscount Bury, Scots Guards, was her brother, she, unnamed, being one of many sisters.

I only trust I shall not be here long. Was xrayed in morning, but as these were bad developments, was done again in p.m.

29th

My rib much better and great hopes of an early return to the Battalion.

Pinto was operated on – his wound was a very odd one at back of foot, at first it healed up, then broke out and a bit of the tendon kept appearing through a hole made for the purpose (or looked like it): this had to be trimmed off. He was carried back to bed about 1 p.m., looking like a corpse, (I told him I hoped they wd remove him before night if he was one) but began to wake up by 2 p.m., when of course he was very sick – & remarked: "They never took me away did they?"

The chief anxiety of the Orderlies was as to his false teeth (imaginary).

Can see the leave boats going out & coming in from my bed.

30th

I am told I am to get away on Wedy.

Rumours that the Germans have retired opposite us, and the push indefinitely postponed.

I got up about 11 a.m. & went out but it rained steadily all day.

31st

Met Col Perowne in morning & walked with him to try & get a car to take me off to the line. No success.

In afternoon walked up to see young Perowne in hospital, having been badly gassed._ Later saw his Father who had had no luck & got no car.

More Rain.

At last – after a multitude of rumours – came the official communiqué saying the push had started & all 1st Objectives taken._ considerable number of prisoners. This was the date expected when I came away – Alas! that I should be out of it completely. The great day!

Aug 1st

After much ceremony eventually left BOULOGNE by train at 10.30 a.m. While waiting at the Station I watched a Hpl train unloading – a pitiful sight: all were from the "push" – one Officer told me he was in a Tank & the Tanks had a very poor time of it: the weather was – & is, for pouring harder than ever today – very much against us – both for Observation purposes and for moving guns etc.

Passed many Hpl trains en route & several lots of German Prisoners.

Lunch at CALAIS where found Wigram formerly Town Major of YPRES, also Norman who is RTO there, brother of Lionel.

Captain George Montague Wigram, The King's Royal Rifle Corps

Norman – untraced, Railway Transport Officer, Calais, and brother of Captain Lionel
    Norman †15.9.16

Arrived at HAAZEBROUCK 3 p.m. to find my Baggage all gone! Left there 4.30 p.m. in
Guards Van, arr POP 6 p.m. Slept at Club_

2nd

Motor car from Divn fetched me at 9 a.m. – went to Div HQ where I saw Alston also our Bde
HQ – all said they were glad to see me back – I heard some news about what splendid work
had been going on – but of course there were casualties – Romeo had to go down – not really
wounded, but a shell had bust into a dug out where he was & he had to be carried off_ Hugh
Ross had been cmdg the Battn excellently & many people – especially Bradshaw – had highly
distinguished themselves – but old Prophet (Mahomed) & Lloyd were killed – Hope Cobbold
Finnis Edwards Cooper being wounded._ Hope lost both his eyes.

Lieutenant Claude Atkinson Etty Mahomed †31.7.17
Lieutenant Ernest Alfred Collyer Lloyd †31.7.17
Lieutenant William Douglas Hope
Lieutenant John Murray Cobbold
Lieutenant Charles Roche Finnis
Lieutenant John Keith Edwards
Lieutenant Gerald Melbourne Cooper

In his Report on the battle dated 7 August Captain Ross commented on the heavy
casualties caused to the two leading companies by German artillery during the
night before the attack started, then substantially mitigated by British counter
barrages. Another key point he made was that, owing to the uneven start lines of
the 38th Division and the Guards Division, which their own barrage plan could not
accommodate, most of the trouble the 1st Scots Guards encountered when they
advanced was from enemy positions outside their flanks. These, unaffected by the
British barrage, were notably Big Clump to their right and Artillery Wood to their left.
Generally, he wrote, the German trenches and wire had been suppressed, leaving some
snipers and machine gun posts, particularly in those few concrete strong points unhit.
He also stated that two valuable factors were the arrangements and discussions which
had gone on previously with adjoining formations and the importance for all ranks of
being able to study beforehand the sand and concrete models of the battlefield.

Arrived back at the Battn at 10.30 a.m. to everyone's surprise – & took over command.

Thursday Aug. 2nd 1917 (contd)

ELVERDINGHE.
    Found the Battn just going into the line – so by Brigadier's Order I left Hugh Ross out (much
to his annoyance) and took the Battn up – we took over from 1st Irish Gds (Pollok) in support
line.

Lieutenant Colonel Robert Valentine Pollok, Commanding 1st Irish Guards

There was no "line" but a good many connected shellholes etc. Went up over the ground taken on 31st July, and heard a lot more details. Owing to the enemy retiring 2 or 3 days previously, we had had to go over the canal and take over a new bit of ground, & this was when most of our casualties occurred, before the actual Zero hour – they were pounded by Artillery for 36 hours, & then, when they advanced, they had no barrage for some little time owing to the unevenness of the front._

In front of the Guards Division the Germans partially withdrew, possibly without orders, and their abandoned positions were quickly seized and occupied. This did mean that there did not have to be an assault crossing of the line of the Canal, but moving up to the new start line for the attack was more exposed. It also disrupted the artillery barrage plan.

We made Bn H.Q. in a little German concrete house – there were quite a number of these about – but it was a fearful squash, and I do not think I ever felt so suffocated. There was considerable shelling going on all the time, and all these concrete houses were especially marked down – not at all healthy places. Ours was GRANDE BARRIERE HOUSE.

3rd

The Relief was over by 1.30 a.m. I started to go round about 3.50 a.m., and found the men standing up to their middles in mud and water looking the picture of misery. Had a few shells pretty near me, and no doubt the enemy knew our line and shelled it accordingly.

The day was fairly peaceful. 2/Irish Guards were on our left – their new C.O. is one Fergusson, Eric Greer having been killed – a terrible loss for that Battn._ also "Father Knapp", a worse loss, for he was the most charming and bravest chaplain in the Army.

Lieutenant Colonel Robert Hamilton Ferguson, Commanding 2nd Irish Guards
Lieutenant Colonel Eric Beresford Greer, Commanding 2nd Irish Guards †31.7.17
The Reverend Simon Stock Knapp, C.F. †1.8.17

In evening we had to be relieved by 3rd Grens, and then go forward and relieve 1st Irish in front line, a long & rather complicated proceeding. It was not made easier by a heavy barrage starting in the middle & by some Irish Guards guides not turning up, others being lost when trying to lead up our platoons, one never arriving at all – the whole platoon eventually spending 20 hours amongst the Grenadiers!

Following the attacks on 31 July the front line here was now just along the Steenbeck, a stream a little south of Langemarck.

The Divn on our right was very "windy", and kept putting up "S.O.S." to which our guns answered every time at once, which naturally called down the German reply, but as often on us as on the other Division.

During the day we found a wounded German in a hole he is said to have been a sniper & sniped from there, but I doubt this very much. He was in great pain when I saw him, and sent him off to the Dressing Sta.

Our total losses on 31st & 2 previous days were 261, including Officers – so now the Battn is very weak._

Our new Bn H.Q. was in another concrete house, called CAPTAINS FARM.

4th

The relief was over by 3.30 a.m., but as one could not go round in daylight I did not go round at all, I could not have got there and back in time, and a very heavy barrage would have had to be crossed twice also. It always came down between Bn HQ and the actual trenches, on a certain road, and was going on nearly all night. We had several casualties.

Spent the day, which was comparatively fine, after several days steady rain, peeping out at our own Artillery hammering the Huns, some awful shelling, which surely no nerves could stand for long.

At 3.35 that afternoon Lieutenant Reginald Henry Dalrymple, commanding B Company in the front line, sent a runner down,

Situation Report
Holding line from where RAILWAY crosses STEENBEK in touch with 38th Divn and with RF on the left about 30 yds N of road over STEENBEK.
[There followed a very rough sketch map]
Am consolidating to the best of my ability, under heavy shell fire. – almost impossible to get any depth owing to water & nature of soil._ AAA
Guides been sent down now. AAA
all necessary observations will be taken as far as possible. AAA
Under heavy snipers fire in daylight.

It was a situation both precarious and very uncomfortable.

In evening the weather became clear & fine, and out came many German Aeroplanes, gliding all over us, & only one French which of course had to clear off, and none of ours at all. I reported at once, and apparently others did the same, so later – but too late – ours began to appear.

A visit, by the way, yesterday from Genl Wardrop, who commands our Corps Artillery. He asked a lot about the Artillery work on 31st, which Mann Shortt & Duncan were able to explain, all having been there.

Brigadier General Alexander Ernest Wardrop, Commander Royal Artillery, XIV Corps

At night we were relieved by the 2nd Bn, under Jack Stirling – and all went off very smoothly. He had been a Liaison Officer with the French, and was rather interesting._ Kit Cator was very badly wounded but much better, and will probably recover_ Wilfred Dashwood alas! was dying having been hit in stomach poor thing – a terrible ending.

Lieutenant Wilfred James Dashwood, 1st Grenadier Guards †2.8.17

On relief, over by 11 p.m., we walked down, finding a lot of new trench boards, to BLUET FARM, where we had tea chocolate & cigarettes (run by Divisional Canteen) & rhum sent by Kinlay, then entrained at 1 a.m.

5th

at ELVERDINGHE, arriving at BANDAGHEM near PROVEN at 6 a.m., going into PURBROOK CAMP close by – where the men had breakfast – changed their feet & then turned in until 12.30 p.m., when they had dinners, spending the afternoon cleaning up and more sleep._

Alston came round during the day, & said Tempest & Romer were out, and I was to go to command at HERZEELE, but he would let me know.

Elwes had left HERZEELE to command the 9th Bn R. Irish Rifles – causing a vacancy. I thought my doom was sealed.

Lieutenant Colonel Roger Stephen Tempest, was wounded near Ginchy on 15 September 1916.
Major Malcolm Romer
Major Henry Cecil Elwes
9th (Service) Battalion The Royal Irish Rifles, 107th Brigade, 36th (Ulster) Division, New Army

6th

Tempest arrived, with Romer about 11 a.m., and immediately set to work to set things in order. He is a wonderful person, and full of go.

Walked with these 2 in afternoon to see the Brigr who has very splendidly ordained that as Tempest is likely shortly to get a Brigade, Romer will command the Battn, and I remain as 2nd in command. Meanwhile I am to go on leave for a time! What a topper he is.

7th

Brodie and I went into DUNKERQUE. First of all we stopped a lorry, but this did not go very far, so walked on: soon being overtaken by a very smart looking motor car, which we held up, and, to our confusion rather, we found it contained no less a person than General Montgomery – "M.G.G.S." to Rawlinson, 4th Army, now at MALO near Dunkerque._ He was very kind and took us as far as REXPOEDE, where he had to stop an hour to see the French Army Commander._

We had no difficulty in being picked up again a third time, by an Air service car, on which we found the Adjt of No. 23 Squadron RFC, Pye-Smith by name of the Surrey Yeoy, and arrived at DUNKERQUE at 4 p.m. found Mike was out but due in again at 8 p.m., so waited – but unfortunately at 7 a thick fog came down, & we heard they were anchoring for the night, so I pretty well gave up seeing Mike – I was befriended by Captain Ramsay, cmdg HMS M 25, who very kindly gave me dinner & during which meal, suddenly a man arrived saying the Monitors were just then coming into the harbour, so after all I did see Mike – telephoned to Genl

Montgomery who had offered to send me back, and eventually arrived back at BANDAGHEM, (PURBROOK CAMP) at 12 midnight. Mike brought his ship alongside quite beautifully, but not so de Crespigny, his companion in a sister Monitor – who seemed to make a fair mess of it: and some of the sailors were laughing at him.

> Captain John M Pye Smith, The Surrey Yeomanry
> Commander Bertram Ramsay, Royal Navy
> Commander Claude Philip Champion de Crespigny, Royal Navy

8th

The Army Commander (5th Army) Gen. Gough came to see us in camp, and saw a few little parcels of Officers and Sergeants, patting them on the back after their recent advance._

In afternoon Sherard took me a joy ride round to see some of his labour companies. & then in to POPERINGHE to try and find my baggage missing since Aug 1st when I returned from BOULOGNE – but no trace of it can be found – so very tiresome.

Heard of Wilfred Dashwood's death – died of wounds received on 31st, having been shot in the stomach.

9th

A huge fatigue party went up by train to work somewhere near Canal under Romer.

Ross Mann and Bradshaw all went off for the day in Sherard's motor car to BOULOGNE.

Walked with Roger & Flossy.

10th

Walked with Roger & Flossy – the former has taken over the Brigade, so Flossy is commanding the Battn.

Went to ask for my baggage at PROVEN.

Harry Seymour came over to tea.

> Brigadier General Lord Henry Seymour, Commanding 3rd Guards Brigade

11th

Walked with same two, again to ask about my baggage – which I hear arrived at International Corner, but as the Guards Divl railhead is being changed to PROVEN (only about 2 miles off) they could not send it there direct but had to send it via CALAIS.

Shortt and Holmes went to see Mike & dined with him at a Restaurant.

12th "The twelfth."

Walked with Roger up the River Yser, watched some French soldiers, and an old Belgian – fishing, but catching next to nothing.

Football Matches, Bathing, Route Marching, and Specialist training form our chief amusements & occupations.

Walked in evening again to ask after my baggage – one Haig, R.T.O., was very helpful and did his best.

Haig – untraced

Kit Cator has been uncommonly ill, but is much better now & likely to recover.

Bradshaw gone off with our party to HEERZEELE.

Was President (on 11th) of a Court of Inquiry on a certain amount of equipment & stores lost on 31st, owing to the large amount of casualties we had – about 350 in quite a short period.

Have had one draft of 100 since, also a few Officers. Smith-Cunningham (wounded in June) Mackinnon, Dundas (back from Brigade, to command L.F.), Holmes, Brodie (on Aug 1st)_

Roger has made me make out a Battn list for "New Year Honours" – a very difficult thing to do – there are so very many deserving people.

2nd Lieutenant Duncan Mackinnon †9.10.17 was the only completely new arrival

The 29th Divn have made a small advance over the STEENBEK, ready for the next push.

Frank Mann's brother, who commands a Batty of Guards Divl Artillery, has been wounded, not badly.

Major William Edgar Mann, Royal Field Artillery

13th

Wonderful to say, my baggage has at last arrived. Kit Cator is going on well.

Walked with Roger and Flossy in evening, & watched some French soldiers fishing.

In morning walked with Flossy to see the Battn bathing.

Heard I was to go on leave on 15th.

Officers v. Sergts football match – self unable to play owing to rib not yet being right._

14th

Anniversary of Battn coming out to France – so they were to have "dinners" – Officers, Sergts, Corpls, & men, also concert etc

Left with Trafford at 10 a.m. were picked up by a lorry & arrived DUNKERQUE 12 noon – luncheon with Mike on board his ship, also Sparrow – 20th Hussars_

During the afternoon a destroyer came in having been on fire – 1 killed 3 wndd – owing to rescuing a burning Airship.

Trained to CALAIS – where arrived 8 p.m., Hotel Sauvage, found Vanneck and Bethel also going on leave.

Heavy bombardment early, but never heard what it was all about.

Lieutenant Richard Wedgwood Sparrow, The 20th Hussars
Lieutenant The Honourable Andrew Nicholas Armstrong Vanneck, 2nd Scots Guards
Captain David Jardine Bethell, 2nd Scots Guards

15th

Left CALAIS at 8.45 a.m., on board the Arundel, very crowded. Was slightly seasick – likewise many others.

Just before leaving, a lady drove an Ambulance Car over the quay into the harbour, she was promptly rescued by a soldier who made a fine dive in after her.

Reached Dover 10 a.m. and left it in a Pullman Car at 11.15 – getting to Victoria 2 p.m.

While on leave Miles Barne received a telegram at Sotterley on 31 August.

Your attendance is requested at Buckingham Palace on Wednesday next the 5th Sept at ten thirty ock *[o'clock]* a.m. to receive your D.S.O. and also the M.C. awarded to your late Brother service dress regret that no one except those to be invested can be admitted to the palace please telegraph achnowledgement.

Lord Chamberlain London

Ten days later he set off again for France.

Saturday Sept. 15th 1917

After a months leave, left Victoria Sta. 8 a.m., had to wait at Dover till 4.30 p.m. to cross, on arrival at CALAIS, found Jack Stirling & Billy Wynne Finch on the quay, being down for 2 days fresh air – the latter recalled to join the Divl H.Q. to learn Staff work, cadging a lift in a motor car, got me one too._ Dined at ST. OMER where met Redmond Buxton, and reached our Divl H.Q. near International Corner at 11 p.m., slept in the French Interpreters bed.

The talk of the day seems to be concerning the multitude of bombs which have been falling about at nights all round in the back areas, doing a good deal of harm, & upsetting people's nerves, spoiling rest etc._ Some even say the men would rather be in the line than in a camp not far behind it._

The Battle of Langemarck began on 16 August, in which the Guards Division played no part. XIV Corps advanced a further fifteen hundred yards so that on their frontage the line was along the Broembeck, the next significant stream beyond Langemarck, itself captured in this attack. When Miles Barne rejoined from leave the 1st Scots Guards were up in the line at the Broembeck and Lieutenant Colonel Romer sent a note down telling him that he was not needed and so to stay with the Transport. The Transport Lines were at Michel Farm, northeast of Elverdinghe and west of Boesinghe, beside the minor road running roughly parallel to the north of the main Elverdinghe-Boesinghe road.

20

Epilogue

Lieutenant Trafford submitted an official report to his Commanding Officer on 19 September in which he stated:

> Sir, I have the honour to report that about 12.30 p.m. on Sept. 17th 1917, whilst at Emile Farm B.9.d.1.7. Sheet 28 N.W. I noticed a British aeroplane flying very low and approaching the Transport Lines of this Battalion.
>
> Shortly afterwards I saw the aeroplane directly over the lines, and a small object which proved to be a bomb, dropping from it. This bomb fell directly on the tent occupied by Major Barne D.S.O., who was then inside, and with him, at the time, was also No. 7538 Pte. Allen, S.
>
> As the result of the explosion, this Private was killed outright and Major Barne was so severely injured, that he subsequently died. Five other Privates who were standing near were also wounded.
>
> After dropping the bomb the aeroplane, still flying very low, proceeded and was seen to alight a short distance away.
>
> Medical assistance was at once obtained from 4th Battalion, Grenadier Guards. Subsequently I saw the Pilot in charge of the aeroplane, Lieut. H. Turner No. 9 Squadron R.F.C., who stated that he was unaware that he had dropped a bomb, as he had supposed that he had dropped all these over the German lines, and that he attributed the fact of this not having been done to a mechanical defect. He also stated that he was flying low and looking for a place to alight owing to shortage of petrol.
>
> I have the honour, to be Sir,
> Your obedient Servant,
> (Signed.) C.E. Trafford.
> Lieutenant.

Writing home afterwards Lieutenant Colonel Godman described hearing that Miles Barne had been writing a letter in his tent with the Battalion postman waiting for him to finish it. 7538 Private Samuel Allen, the postman, was killed instantly. The pilot may have been Captain Henry Turner, who died on 5 June 1918 when serving with No. 103 Squadron, Royal Air Force.

Miles Barne was quickly moved to No. 12 Casualty Clearing Station, but died later the same day. He is buried in Mendinghem Military Cemetery, northwest of Poperinghe, near the French border. Graves were marked by the Army with simple wooden markers and the more substantial and inscribed cross now in St Margaret's Church, Sotterley, which first replaced it on Miles Barne's grave, was probably made by the Pioneers of the 1st Battalion Scots Guards.

The War Office telegram informing Violet Barne of her husband's death was despatched on the afternoon of 23 September. The envelope has survived: the telegram has not. Miles Barne's wallet, his silver pencil, a blue patterned silk handkerchief, the Scots Guards buttons from his tunic and the two Royal Stewart tartan flashes sewn onto the sides of his Service Dress cap were sent home to Violet Barne.

The first paragraph of Scots Guards Regimental Orders published in London on 22 September 1917 read:

> Death of Major M. Barne, D.S.O.
> It is with the deepest regret that the Lieut. Colonel Commanding has to report the death on Sept.17th, from wounds accidentally received, of Major Miles Barne, D.S.O.
>   On behalf of the Regiment the Lieut. Colonel would further desire to place on record the most sincere appreciation of the services rendered to the Regiment by Major Barne, who has served as second in command of the 1st Battalion and has also at various times acted in Command of that Unit.

Captain Charles Green, Army Service Corps, with the British Salonika Force, erstwhile tenant of The Barne Arms, Dunwich, heard the news from his brother and wrote to Violet Barne:

> I cannot yet realise that I have lost my Best Friend. To you the loss is irreparable and thousands of others. I feel proud that I have served under his command and lived all my life as a Tenant. Never a better & more gallant soldier wore the King's uniform.

From the prison camp at Minden came an undated letter from Sergeant James Clarke, 7th Suffolk Regiment, formerly footman at Sotterley:

> May I write and express my great sympathy, and to say how grieved I was to learn the sad news.

A letter written at Sotterley on 22 September read:

> Honoured Madam
> I am very grieved indeed to hear of your great loss. I can assure you we all feel it very deeply, In fact I cannot find words to express my feelings of sympathy for you and the children And I feel his loss greatly as a good kind Master and friend to me. If I can be of any service to you I shall be more than pleased to be so. I am Madam
>   your obedient servant
>   Joseph Harper

He was the groom at Sotterley to begin with and later the chauffeur.

Captain Hugh Bayly, Royal Army Medical Corps, arrived in the 1st Scots Guards as Medical Officer towards the end of July 1916 when they were coming to the end of their time in the Ypres Salient. He wrote afterwards of his first assessment of Miles Barne as "a delightful man about forty, equally popular with officers and men".

Early in 1918, around the time of his twenty first birthday, Captain Henry Dundas began a chronicle of his wartime experiences, but did not get any further than the first few pages. He was highly intelligent, well educated, extremely alert, very witty and utterly intrepid. Much admired and respected by the men for his leadership, he had the intellectual confidence, as well as the instinct to judge everything in straight black or white, of someone of his achievements. These included having been Captain of the Oppidans at Eton, prizes there and an Open History Scholarship to Christ Church, Oxford. He described another unnamed officer saying that Miles Barne was "Probably the truest Christian one could possibly meet." He wrote himself that he "was far too kind to make a good commanding officer, far too diffident...to make an adequate second in command. An ideal platoon commander he would have made – as he was the bravest man I've ever seen, in the sense of being absolutely unconscious of danger, and cared only for the welfare of the men – but he was far too good – kind, and not nearly hard enough – with the result that anyone could get round him."

Henry Dundas showed no understanding of how often Miles Barne had been holding the Battalion together, which was apparent to others more senior. Were his total time as Acting Commanding Officer totted up it would exceed the periods of command of many others, while, particularly in the period after the Somme battles and up to his death, again and again he was propping up Sherard Godman and later Bertram Romilly. Had he survived it would have been only a matter of time before he was doing the same for Malcolm Romer, whose health also gave out.

A long time afterwards the former 13597 Private George Cumming remembered "the heroic Major Barne who carried up a sack of rations on his back on a memorable night in Sanctuary Wood when we were hard pressed."

Miles Barne was intelligent, observant, conscientious, humane, gently witty, completely honest, enthusiastic, very interested in his fellow men, and very brave. Rightly he was very well liked by all ranks. His flaws as an officer were being too self-effacing and unassertive. The Diary has a simplicity of style, because he himself had no guile, no calculation and no artifice to him and so his thinking was open and direct. His warmth, charm, devotion and kindness leave a memory touched with nobleness.

Many years later his grandson, Miles Barne, went to lunch with Fergus and Jean Matheson, neighbours in Suffolk. Also there was Fergus Matheson's mother, Lady Elizabeth Matheson, who was born Lady Elizabeth Keppel, by then elderly and rather forgetful, the widow of General Sir Torquhil Matheson of Matheson, Bt. Fergus Matheson told Miles Barne that she had nursed his Grandfather when he was dying.

Supporting Bibliography

Published Works

Dr Hugh Wansey Bayly, *Triple Challenge: Or, War, Whirligigs and Windmills* (London: Hutchinson & Co 1933)

Maj AF Becke, *History of the Great War Order of Battle of Divisions Parts 1, 2a, 2b, 3, 4 and Index* (London: HMSO 1945)

Maj CH Dudley Ward, *The Welsh Regiment of Foot Guards 1915-1918* (London: John Murray 1920)

Lt Col Rowland Feilding, *War Letters to a Wife 1915-1919* (London: The Medici Society Ltd 1929)

Cuthbert Headlam, *History of the Guards Division in the Great War 1915-1918* in two volumes (London: John Murray 1924)

John Jolliffe, *Raymond Asquith, Life and Letters* (London: Collins 1980)

Rudyard Kipling, *The Irish Guards in the Great War* in two volumes (London: Macmillan & Co Ltd 1923)

Randall Nicol, *Till The Trumpet Sounds Again: The Scots Guards 1914-1919 in Their Own Words* in two volumes (Solihull: Helion & Co Ltd 2016)

F Loraine Petre Wilfrid Ewart and Maj Gen Sir Cecil Lowther, *The Scots Guards in the Great War* (London: John Murray 1925)

Lt Col The Rt Hon Sir Frederick Ponsonby, *The Grenadier Guards in the Great War of 1914-1918* in three volumes (London: Macmillan & Co Ltd 1920)

Lt Col Sir John Ross of Bladensburg, *The Coldstream Guards 1914-1918* in two volumes (London: Oxford University Press, Humphrey Milford 1928)

Websites

Commonwealth War Graves Commission: www.cwgc.org

Infantry Battalion Commanding Officers of the British Armies in the First World War: www.ww1infantrycos.co.uk

Discovery The National Archives: www.discovery.nationalarchives.gov.uk

Unpublished: Private Collections

Miles Barne's Diary
Barne Family Papers
Dundas Papers

Unpublished: Scots Guards Archives

Enlistment Books
Officers Files
Soldiers Personal Records
War Diary 1st Battalion Scots Guards [Regimental Copy]
War Diary 2nd Battalion Scots Guards [Regimental Copy]

Unpublished: The National Archives

a. War Diary
2nd Guards Brigade Machine Gun Company – WO 95/1220/3

b. Officers' Files
Major Miles Barne – WO 374/5065
Captain George Nugent – WO 339/8664

c. First World War Medal Cards – WO 372

Index

INDIVIDUALS

LOCATIONS AND TOPOGRAPHY

OPERATIONAL FORMATIONS

GENERAL TERMS